Garden Way's
Joy of Gardening
COOKBOOK

Garden Way's
Joy of Gardening
COOKBOOK

By Janet Ballantyne

with Andrea Chesman and Dottie Rankin
Photographs by Didier Delmas

Garden Way, Inc. Troy, New York 12180

Garden Way's
Joy of Gardening
COOKBOOK

Editor: Andrea Chesman
Art Director: Ann Aspell
Production Manager: George Boilard
Photographer: Didier Delmas
Illustrator: Elayne Sears
Cover Designers: Ann Aspell and Leslie Welch
Production Assistant: Andrea Gray
Production Consultant: Irv Garfield
Editorial Consultant: Richard Alther
Second Cook and Propping: Dorothy Rankin
Assistant Cooks: Nancy Edwards and Kirk Trabant
With concept, design, and research assistance by Storey Communications, Inc.

Separations by Magna Graphic, Inc., Lexington, Kentucky
Printed in the U.S. by W. A. Krueger, New Berlin, Wisconsin

Dean Leith, Jr. Chairman of the Board, Garden Way, Inc., Troy, NY 12180

Cloth ISBN 0-88266-356-9
Paper ISBN 0-88266-355-0

Contents

At Garden Way Gardens, everyone lends a hand when the beans are ready for harvesting. Mark Hebert, general manager of the gardens, is helping me pick some beans to test a recipe.

I remember the first time I tasted Janet Ballantyne's cooking.

I was spending the morning at Garden Way's meeting house. At noon we broke for lunch prepared by Janet, who had recently been hired to manage the Garden Way Test Kitchen.

"What's cooking?" I asked Janet as she darted back and forth, bringing out a huge vegetable salad one minute, fresh warm rolls the next.

"Cream of Radish Soup," she responded with a grin.

"Cream of Radish Soup? Never heard of it!"

"Well," laughed Janet, "neither had I until this morning. But I figured I had to come up with some way to cook all those beautiful radishes that you had planted to mark rows and keep bugs away. I can't stand to see good food go to waste! Wait 'til you try this soup. It's delicious."

And so it was.

Janet Ballantyne's creative touch with vegetables is a product of long experience. From the age of 12, she spent many hours in the kitchen with her mother and Austrian-born grandmother who had studied cooking in Vienna. Then Janet worked in restaurants and cooked at a Vermont ski country inn while completing college.

She launched her professional career in England, working for a business called "A Moveable Feast," which specialized in catering executive lunches. She returned to the United States to cook at specialty restaurants in Burlington, Vermont, and eventually established her own business, "A Catered Affair."

Soon she was asked to give cooking demonstrations and appear on local television to share her innovative ideas.

The first year Janet worked for Garden Way, an early frost produced a bumper crop of green tomatoes. Janet rose to the challenge and created for us every delight from Chicken Dijon With Green Tomatoes to Green Tomato Chocolate Cake! That was the start of her first publication, *Garden Way's Red and Green Tomato Cookbook*. A year later, Janet was ready with *Desserts from the Garden*, a cookbook that offers recipes to transform healthful, vitamin-rich garden produce into delicious desserts.

Janet continually astounds me with her ability to cook imaginatively with vegetables. She hates to see good food wasted, so she has become just as skillful at transforming slightly gone-by vegetables into delicious dishes as she is in harvesting and preparing tender, young vegetables at the peak of their perfection. Janet really understands the need to produce tempting meals from the garden all season long; and as a working person, herself, she realizes that most cooks can't spend all day in the kitchen, either. This past year, Janet joined the gardening experts on Garden Way's nationally syndicated "Joy of Gardening" TV show to share with viewers great time-saving ways to celebrate that fresh vegetable bounty.

With Janet's new cookbook, it's going to be more fun than ever before to garden and to eat what we grow. I know you'll agree that this is the most exciting collection of vegetable cookery tips and recipes ever compiled in a single book! Here's wishing you the tastiest garden-produced eating ever, with Janet Ballantyne as your guide.

Sincerely,

Dean Leith, Jr.

Dean Leith, Jr.
Garden Way, Inc.

Enjoy Vegetables!

More than anything else, this is a book about enjoying good food and the bounty of summer. Raising my own fruits and vegetables brings a particular satisfaction that I find inspiring as a cook. Nothing beats the excitement of finding the first harvestable young vegetables in the garden. And nothing tops the pleasure of eating those tender vegetables, prepared sensitively, and served to good friends and family.

Roasted corn makes a picnic. To be sure the kernels cook without scorching, I like to soak the ears in ice water for about 30 minutes before cooking them. Because this corn was picked just before it was grilled, my guests are eating it plain—without butter!

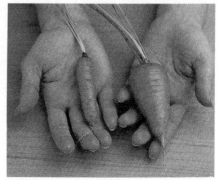

Carrots can be picked as soon as they are big enough to eat.

The smallest beans are the tenderest and most tasty.

Pick your zucchini young before the seeds are well developed.

These beets are the perfect size for harvesting—just the size of golf balls. The best thing about gardening is to be able to pick young.

Pick Young and Cook Early

The secret to enjoying vegetables at their best is to pick them young and to cook them as soon as possible.

Pick, pick, pick is the advice I've learned and passed on to gardening friends. By harvesting frequently, you will increase your yields and extend your harvest. More important, you guarantee your success as a cook when you prepare only fresh, young, tender vegetables.

Don't Spend Your Whole Day In the Kitchen

From garden to table in less than an hour is often my goal.

Young vegetables just don't require that much time to prepare and cook — a boon to working people. Sautés and stir fries are excellent for quick cooking, and so are vegetable-based sauces, delicious on broiled meat, fish, or chicken. Salads are quick and easy, too.

Even the Simplest Dishes Can Be Special Enough For Company

When I'm showing off my tender young vegetables, only the simplest preparations will do. So it makes no difference to me whether I'm cooking for 1 or for 20. I choose fast, easy-to-prepare dishes, and let the flavor of each vegetable come through.

In this Beet Stir Fry (p. 54), the beets have a slight crunch and a spicy flavor.

Waste Not, Want Not

But don't despair when your garden gets a little out of hand, and you find yourself with slightly overripe vegetables, or when your root cellar vegetables have lost their crisp summer texture. There's still plenty of good eating to be had.

When I have vegetables that are past their prime, I look for recipes that use grated or pureed vegetables or call for slow simmering, as in a soup or stew.

When you grow your own vegetables, you just hate to waste any of the harvest.

You can use slightly gone-by asparagus in this delicious Cream of Asparagus Soup (page 28). Smooth pureed soups disguise overgrown vegetables well.

Grate soft turnips for cooking.

Old winter squash makes great marmalade.

Chop tough beans for better results in many dishes.

Cook to Please Yourself

When following any recipe, the most important thing is to cook to please yourself. When I cook, I use plenty of spices and fresh herbs because I enjoy foods that have robust flavor. But if you are a timid taster, use the flavorings sparingly — the results will still please.

And feel free to substitute ingredients. Don't have fresh herbs? Fine, use dried. Don't have a certain vegetable? See if the recipe will work with a different one. Don't have red wine? Try white. The results won't be the same — who knows, they might be better!

As much as possible, these zesty flavors replace salt in my cooking.

When you cook to please yourself, you can use as much herbs and spices as you like. I like mine hot!

How does a person learn to cook these days? Some of us were lucky enough to learn from our mothers (and fathers) and grandmothers. Some of us went to school to learn. Some of us read books. Some of us learned by the necessity of getting food on the table.

I learned from all of the above. In this chapter, I want to share with you some of the tricks I've learned along the way.

Most important, I want to be sure that we are all speaking the same language. I hate to come across a term in a cookbook that I don't understand—especially when the foreign term turns out to refer to a common technique I've known how to do for years. So I'll explain the terms I'll be using throughout the book.

The recipes in this book don't require special skills. So experienced cooks can feel free to skip this chapter. I hope beginners will find it useful.

Cooking, to me, is both art and science, but you need to be neither artist nor scientist to be an accomplished cook. What you need is a healthy dose of common sense.

Common sense, for example, will teach you that using tools efficiently will save time, that having a repertoire of different slicing techniques will add a variety of textures and appearances to your dishes, that vegetables should be cooked quickly, that heavy sauces will mask the delicate flavor of fresh vegetables, while a generous complement of fresh herbs will enhance flavors. And that is what this chapter is all about.

Here Are My
Basic Techniques

Preparing vegetables begins with careful harvesting or discerning shopping. You'll find tips for buying individual vegetables on pages 316–318, and each chapter contains specific harvesting tips. But while the specifics may vary, the general rule stays the same for most vegetables: Pick tender, young vegetables for prime flavor.

Cooking with young vegetables has so many advantages! First, there is usually less preparation time involved. Overgrown cucumbers must be seeded; baby cucumbers can be just sliced; overgrown beans must be sliced to tenderize them, baby beans just require snapping on one end to remove the stems; baby carrots and potatoes just need scrubbing; older ones should be peeled. And so the list goes.

The older the vegetable, the more preparation, and probably the more involved the recipe to prepare the vegetables. For example, whereas I might lightly steam baby zucchini and serve with an herb butter, older zucchini get the "grate and disguise" treatment.

A further advantage of harvesting young vegetables is that continual harvesting usually increases the yield. Harvesting young vegetables, such as zucchini, before seeds have formed, forces the plant to produce more fruit, until the plant has had a chance to produce mature fruit, with fully developed seeds. The same is true for beans and peas. Most greens and lettuces will produce several cuttings, if you don't give the plants a chance to flower.

And don't forget taste! Nothing will guarantee your success like starting with tender, young vegetables.

This Sugar 'N Gold corn is one of my favorite varieties. Even though corn takes up quite a bit of space in the garden, I like to grow my own so I can take it from garden to kitchen within minutes. There's no trick to husking corn, but some vegetables do require extra work to prepare. This chapter covers all my basic techniques, from preparing vegetables to cooking them.

You Deserve the Proper Tools!

When You Invest in the Best Tool for the Job
No Preparation Task is Difficult or Time-Consuming

Although it would seem that the food processor can do everything a blender can, it can't. Blender-made sauces and purees are much, much smoother. You do have to add extra liquid when making purees in a blender, but you can always cook the purees down.

Some jobs are too heavy for a blender, particularly spreads and pâtés. That's when the food processor comes in handy.

lemon squeezer

Removing all the pits from a lemon can be tedious. That's why I am particularly fond of my lemon squeezer. It's a handy two-piece tool that is half squeezer/strainer and half measuring cup. I twist the lemon against the raised dome to extract the lemon juice, which is strained to remove pits as it drops into the handy measuring cup. Now that's convenience.

I don't use my Squeezo® Strainer year-round, but when it's needed to make tomato purees and applesauce for canning, no other piece of equipment will do. The Squeezo® removes the seeds and skin from raw tomatoes and berries, and from cooked apples, squash, and pumpkins. I wouldn't face the preserving season without one.

wide vegetable peeler

There's nothing particularly fun about peeling vegetables, so I use the largest tool I can easily handle. My favorite peeler has a 2-inch blade that makes fast work of most peels. My peeler has a grater on the handle which I use to grate the rinds of oranges and lemons. The pointed end of the grater can be used to remove bad spots from potatoes.

butter curler

Sometimes the unlikeliest tools turn out to be indispensible. I use my butter curler to remove seeds from winter squash and pumpkins. It works amazingly well, scraping up the fibers and seeds and leaving the flesh. The sharp edge of the butter curler works more effectively than a metal cooking spoon, which is my second choice for the job.

"My food processor saves me so much time, I wonder how I ever got along without one. I think every kitchen should have one."

The longer I've used my food processor, the more uses I've found for it. More than half of the recipes in this book can be made most efficiently using a food processor to slice, shred, puree, beat, mix, or knead.

When buying a new food processor, get one with a large enough bowl and feed tube to handle large quantities of vegetables and fruits.

Food processors come with several different blades. Inside the processor is a metal mixing blade that is perfect for making vegetable purees. The other blades shown are for grating and slicing.

Preparing Vegetables

I use a stiff vegetable brush for scrubbing potatoes and other root crops. These vegetables—carrots, beets, parsnips, and potatoes—should be brushed off outside to remove as much dirt as possible. Then scrub under running water.

The next step in preparing vegetables is washing. Loose dirt should be gently brushed off before the vegetables are brought into the house. Wash vegetables under running water or in a sink filled with water.

Lift the rinsed vegetables out of the water when you are through. Do not allow the water to run out of the sink and redeposit dirt on the vegetables. Wash dirty greens in several changes of water. You'll make less of a mess if you tear greens into manageable size pieces and discard tough stems before throwing them into the sink.

Don't leave vegetables soaking. Some vitamins are water soluble, and they will go down the drain with dirty water. An exception to this rule is with broccoli and cauliflower. A 30-minute soak in salted ice water will flush out camouflaged cabbage worms.

I use a sharp paring knife to peel beets and other tough-skinned vegetables. But the vegetable peeler peels with less waste, so I use it when I can. By the way, leaving a little green on the eggplant won't hurt a bit. The green flesh just under the skin indicates that the eggplant is still young.

The wide vegetable peeler is my tool of choice for peeling away the skins of carrots, cucumbers, eggplants, kohlrabi, parsnips, potatoes, salsify, butternut squash, turnips, and rutabagas.

I prefer to use a paring knife to peel tough-skinned beets and celeriac, irregularly shaped Jerusalem artichokes, and onions.

A chef's knife makes fast work of melon, squash, and pumpkin peels. Slice off the top and bottom of the vegetable so it stands flat. Then, following the contours of the vegetable, slice off the skin.

Deciding how much of a stem to leave isn't difficult — you only want to cook the tender parts.

I harvest only 3 inches of stem with broccoli and use all of that. Tough stems can be peeled to reveal the tender inner flesh. Cauliflower heads easily break into florets. Use a paring knife to trim off the stems.

Asparagus becomes tender where the pink color gives way to green. Snap off the tough stem ends.

With a Sharp Knife and a Little Practice
It's Easy to Produce
Uniform-Size Pieces That Will Cook Evenly

Top row: 1-inch asparagus roll-cuts.
Second row: Chopped sweet potatoes, chiffonade spinach, sliced carrots, sliced onions.
Third row: Julienne-sliced peppers, diagonally sliced celery, roll-cut asparagus.
Bottom row: Sliced onion, julienned sliced peppers.

It won't take long to slice this cabbage with a sharp knife.

A Chef's Knife Can Be an Efficient Machine

Although I do some of my slicing and chopping with a food processor, I rely on my chef's knife for a lot of work. If you use a *sharp* chef's knife efficiently, you can rapidly produce uniform-size pieces that will cook evenly.

Rule number 1 for efficient slicing is to give yourself enough space. I usually work on a Garden Way Kitchen Work Center, which gives me a full table-size chopping board. Don't crowd yourself into a corner with an undersize cutting board!

Rule number 2: Keep your knives sharp. I sharpen my knives frequently on a stone and hone with a steel.

Rule number 3: Hold your knife properly. Grip the vegetable to be sliced with the tips of your fingers. Grasp the knife firmly, using your index finger to steady the blade. The point of the knife is never lifted from the cutting board as you guide the rest of the blade up as high as your knuckle and down, along the length of the vegetable.

1. Slice the onion in half.

2. Slice every ¼ inch.

3. Rotate 90 degrees and slice every ¼ inch to dice.

Expect each vegetable to vary in texture when pureed.

The food processor is really great for processing quantities of food fast. I'll grate all those squash in just two minutes!

Food Processors Work Fast

Some people resist the idea of bringing "one more piece of equipment" into their kitchens, but I think their protests against food processors are silly. Food processors save time!

Food processors come with a number of different blades to slice — thin, thick, or french fry — shred, grate, and mince.

The food processor slices cucumbers, summer squash, and beets for pickles so fast, I'm sure my time in the kitchen is halved. The uniform slices result in a crisp pickle. To grind vegetables for relishes, I use the shredding blade or the steel mixing blade.

Grating, shredding, and mincing are chores I readily turn over to the food processor. Since grating and shredding tenderizes vegetables, I am likely to use this technique with woody or slightly overgrown vegetables. I have found plenty of uses for grated potatoes, beets, cabbage, turnips, and summer and winter squash — from stir fries to breads. I like the uniform shoestring pieces that the processor produces, and I am glad to have this technique to use up those less-than-perfect vegetables that escaped my attention when they were prime for harvest.

I do a lot of cooking with purees, and the food processor handles the job well (although blenders do make smoother purees). I also use my food processor for creaming, mixing, blending, and kneading — everything I cook with, not just vegetables.

There Are Some Things a Processor Can't Do . . . But You Can!

Here's a rundown on more of the slicing techniques you'll need for creating attractive foods.

Cubes. Slice vegetables horizontally and vertically to make squares that are uniformly 1 inch to a side.

Dices. Dices are cubes that are only ½ inch to a side.

Diagonal Slices. These are slices cut on a slant to expose the maximum surface area for quick cooking. When a recipe calls for diagonal slices, make the slices ½ inch thick, unless otherwise specified. I often slice celery, carrots, asparagus, snap beans, and broccoli stems on the diagonal for salads and stir fries.

Roll-cuts. The first slice of a roll-cut is on the diagonal. Then the vegetable is rotated a half turn and a second diagonal slice is made at the same angle as the first slice. Roll-cuts also expose surface area. Roll-cuts are especially attractive for asparagus, baby carrots, and snap beans. Make your pieces about ½ inch thick, unless otherwise specified.

Julienne Slices. These are thin slivers, usually made for salads and stir fries. I like to make my julienne slices ⅛ inch thick.

Chiffonade. This is a cutting term reserved for greens. Create a roll of greens and uniformly slice to make thin ribbons.

Cubed potatoes, a good size for salads and home fries.

Celery, sliced on the diagonal; good for salads and stir fries.

Diced red onions are perfect for salads.

Roll-cuts are a tenderizing cut. These beans will cook quickly.

Julienned slices are good for stir fries and salads.

Chiffonade sliced Swiss chard leaves can be stir fried.

Quick cooking on top of the stove brings out the flavor of fresh vegetables. Clockwise we have: Brussels Sprout Chicken Stir Fry (page 71), sautéed summer squash and herbs, and steamed carrots.

Oven and Stovetop Techniques
Here's a Summary of My Best Advice for
Perfectly-Cooked Vegetables Every Time

What's essential to know when it comes to cooking vegetables? Just one thing: Don't overcook! You'll lose vitamins and friends with overcooked vegetables. Nobody wants to eat tasteless, dull-colored, mushy vegetables when they could be enjoying flavorful, brightly colored, tender crisp ones.

Tender crisp is a term I use throughout this cookbook. It refers to vegetables that are perfectly cooked to pass the "bite test." If you bite into the vegetable, it will be tender, yet still have a pleasing crunch.

Color is another way to gauge whether a vegetable has been cooked to perfection. Greens are bright, not olive; oranges and yellows are bright, not dull.

Is it difficult to cook vegetables to perfection? Not at all. But there are a few steps that experienced cooks follow automatically, so that their vegetables are neither overcooked nor undercooked. Here are a few tricks experience has taught me.

• When steaming, set the vegetables in a steaming basket over the water. Be sure the vegetables are not under water.

• When steaming or blanching, begin counting your time as soon as you add your vegetables to the pot. Do not wait for the water to return to a boil.

• When timing any cooking procedure, follow your judgment more carefully than the clock. Sometimes vegetables will be done before the recipe says they will be.

• When stir frying or sautéing, make sure your oil temperature is hot, but not smoking, before adding the vegetables.

• When sautéing in butter, add the vegetables when the butter is melted, but not browned. Throw out browned butter; it will taste bitter and will discolor vegetables.

• Since a high cooking temperature seals in flavor best, I often sauté in butter *and* oil. The butter adds flavor, and the oil prevents the butter from burning.

• When stir frying, frying, and sautéing, be aware that the vegetables in the center of the pan may cook more quickly than the vegetables along the edges where the cooking temperature may be lower.

• Always cut your vegetables to uniform-size pieces so all pieces cook at the same rate. Obviously, large pieces take longer to cook than smaller ones.

• Regardless of size, older, stored vegetables take longer to cook than young, just-harvested ones.

• Know your pots and pans. Cooking times will vary depending on how heavy a pan you are using. Heavier pans distribute heat more evenly and assure more even cooking.

• When steaming or blanching, use a large pot and don't pack the vegetables too tightly in the pot. Leave space between pieces so steam or water can circulate. Use a sauté pan that is large enough so that the vegetables all have contact with the bottom of the pan.

Blanching cooks these green beans quickly and evenly so the texture is tender crisp and the color is bright green.

Blanching and Parboiling—

Same Technique, Different Timing

"I often add spices, herbs, or salt pork to blanching water for extra flavor. My favorite flavor combinations are the herb savory with dried or shell beans, salt pork with greens or beans, and onions and garlic with potatoes."

When you immerse vegetables in boiling water to partially cook them, you are parboiling. When you leave the vegetables in the water until they are tender crisp, you are blanching.

Blanching is also the term used when you briefly immerse vegetables in water to loosen their skins, as with tomatoes, or when you briefly cook before freezing. But let's not get tangled up in terminology; the method is simple.

Just bring enough water to a boil that will generously cover your vegetables. Drop in no more than 1 pound at a time (so you don't lower the water temperature too radically).

Start timing immediately because the vegetables start to cook immediately. How quickly they cook depends on the size of the pieces, so test frequently.

Save the blanching water, which is rich in vitamins, to use in soups, stews, and sauces.

"Shock" Your Vegetables To Stop the Cooking

As long as the vegetables hold heat, they continue to cook. To halt this process, plunge the vegetables into cold water to cool them rapidly. Then drain well. I do this to retain the bright color and crisp texture of vegetables I parboil for salads.

Steaming these brussels sprouts allows me to retain all the B and C vitamins this green vegetable has to offer. To be sure the vegetables cook evenly, check to make sure all of the vegetables are above, not in, the boiling water. Steam with the lid on.

Steaming Reduces Vitamin Loss

Vegetables cook a little slower when they are steamed than when they are blanched, but there are fewer water-soluble vitamins (B and C vitamins) left behind in the cooking water. (Save the steaming liquid for stock.)

Whether steaming takes more time overall than blanching is unlikely. Since you are bringing less water to a boil, your preparation time should be less with steaming.

Then the only way that steaming compares unfavorably to blanching is that there is a tendency for vegetables at the bottom of the steaming basket to overcook. This can be avoided by using a steaming basket big enough so the vegetables are not layered deeply and by steaming small quantities at a time. One pound, or less, is a good quantity to steam at one time. Make sure the vegetables are not under water.

Steaming is not recommended for vegetables that take a long time to cook for the simple reason that you are likely to run out of water and burn your pot before your vegetables are ready. For this reason, I blanch beets, potatoes, rutabagas, and winter squash.

When steaming, bring your water to a boil, add the vegetables to the steaming basket, cover, and begin counting time immediately. Test frequently for doneness.

No special sauce is needed to add flavor to this colorful sauté of okra, onions, peppers, and tomatoes.

Sautéing Seals in the Flavor of Garden Vegetables

You'll find me sautéing a lot. That's because sautéing seals in the flavor of vegetables—quickly.

The technique is simple. Heat a little butter or oil in a sauté pan, add the vegetables, and cook quickly over high heat, stirring or shaking the pan constantly.

What's a sauté pan? A sauté pan is a frying pan with high straight sides. The purpose of the design is to let you stir rapidly without sending vegetables flying all over the stove. Of course, you can sauté in a regular frying pan (which has shorter, curved sides that make slipping a spatula under the fried foods easy), or in a wok.

Here are the tricks for successful sautéing:

• Always slice your vegetables to uniform-size pieces for even cooking. The thinner the pieces, the faster the vegetables cook, which is usually desirable.

• When sautéing combinations of vegetables, start with the vegetable with the longest cooking time.

• Make sure your pan is hot when you add the vegetables. The hot butter or oil will sear the vegetables to seal in flavor and vitamins and prevent sticking.

• Your vegetables should be dry when you add them to the pan. You don't want any excess moisture in the pan to steam your vegetables, which will make them limp, not crisp.

• Use a pan big enough to easily hold all your vegetables in a single layer.

• To keep the vegetables from browning too quickly, keep stirring and shaking the pan.

• Onions are sautéed until they are limp and translucent, but not browned. Other vegetables are sautéed until they are tender crisp.

• To keep sautéed foods warm, hold them in the pan with the cover ajar. Do not hold the vegetables in a covered pan or steam will form to convert your crisp vegetables into limp ones.

1. Grate the squash.

2. Heat the butter and oil.

Winter squash cooks rapidly when you sauté and steam.

3. Sauté for 1–2 minutes.

4. Add liquid and cover.

Steam Sauté to Tenderize Vegetables

Some dense vegetables—such as carrots, beets, cauliflower, broccoli, and winter squash, —would become too browned if you simply sautéed them until they were tender. But, if you sauté briefly to seal in the flavor, then steam to finish off the cooking, you will end up with tender, brightly colored vegetables, cooked to perfection.

Again, there's nothing complicated about the method. Heat just enough butter or oil in a sauté pan to coat the bottom of the pan. Add the vegetables and sauté, uncovered, for a minute or two, until the vegetables are well coated with the oil. For extra flavor, sauté the vegetables with minced garlic, shallots, or ginger root.

Then for each 4–6 cups of vegetables, add about ¼ cup of liquid. That liquid could be water, stock, apple or orange juice, tamari or soy sauce, sherry, or a combination of liquids. Steam quickly, uncovered, until the vegetables are brightly colored and tender crisp and the water disappears.

As always, use a pan large enough to hold the vegetables in a single layer, so they can cook evenly.

Do not hold the vegetables in the pan once they are cooked, or they will continue to steam and become overcooked.

Don't Wait for a Chinese Meal To Stir Fry Your Way to Perfectly Cooked Vegetables

"When I stir fry, I cook each vegetable and any meat — a little shrimp, pork, chicken, or beef — separately. Then I combine them and heat through. It takes a little more time to stir fry this way than the traditional method, but each vegetable is guaranteed to be cooked to perfection."

The Chinese invented stir frying to quickly cook meats and vegetables. The method is quite similar to sautéing, with the main difference being that in a sauté, you occasionally shake the pan to keep the vegetables from burning; with a stir fry, you just keep stirring.

I prefer to use the rounded wok for stir frying, although you can use any large sauté pan. The main advantage of the wok is that its shape makes it easy to keep the vegetables moving. Also, if some vegetables are cooking too quickly, you can move them to the sides of the wok, leaving the center, where

1. Slow-cooking veggies go first.

2. Add the quick-cooking ones.

3. Cook the meat separately.

4. Combine the veggies and meat. Add the sauce.

the heat is most intense, for the vegetables that need further cooking.

Stir fries begin with the careful slicing of the vegetables to uniform-size pieces. The Chinese often slice their vegetables on the diagonal to expose the maximum amount of surface area for quick cooking.

Then you heat a few tablespoons of oil in a wok or sauté pan. I often use a combination of sesame oil (for flavor) and vegetable oil (for even cooking).

Then I cook the meat, which often has been marinated in a soy sauce mixture. When the meat is cooked, I remove it to a warmed bowl, and begin cooking the vegetables, usually one kind at a time.

I know that the traditional method of stir fries is to partially cook the longest cooking vegetables first, and to keep adding vegetables to the wok, in the order of their cooking times. Hopefully, during the last minute of cooking, all the vegetables reach the stage of tender crisp.

I find that I can't keep my wok hot enough to cook large quantities, so I cook everything separately, combining the meats and vegetables for a final minute of cooking to reheat.

Pan Frying

"Nothing beats a well-seasoned cast iron frying pan when it comes to even cooking without sticking or burning."

Pan frying is frying in just enough oil or butter to prevent foods from sticking and to help them brown. The finished dish will be crispy brown on the outside, soft and tender on the inside. With most foods, I like to pan fry in cast iron because the heat is so even. Stainless steel works well, too.

Cast iron is easy to care for—I don't understand why it has so much mystique. You must season cast iron by heating a coating of oil in the pan from time to time. Once heated, the oil is poured off and the pan is wiped clean. That's all there is to seasoning.

Since food doesn't stick in a well-seasoned skillet, a quick wipe with a soapy sponge and a rinse should be enough to clean the pan after each use. After I rinse, I like to check to see if the rinse water beads up on the surface. If it doesn't, I know it is time to reseason.

Some foods are notorious for absorbing oil—eggplant and fritters come to mind. Sometimes I pan fry in a non-stick coated frying pan so I can cut down on the amount of oil I need to use.

Regardless of the type of pan you fry in, make sure your oil or butter is hot before you add your vegetables. If your food is chilled, it will lower the temperature of the oil and make the final dish greasy. This is especially true with pancake and fritter batters. If you must make up your batters in advance, be sure to bring them to room temperature before frying.

It is difficult to pan fry in butter without burning the butter. A combination of butter and oil doesn't burn readily and has better flavor than oil alone. Butter and olive oil is my favorite pan frying combination.

Pan-fried fritters can be a standard in your house, too. Simply puree or grate your vegetables. Then combine them with eggs and some bread crumbs to hold the mixture together. Season with salt, pepper, and plenty of fresh herbs. In just a few minutes, you'll have an irresistible side dish.

Deep Frying

Your Fried Foods Won't Be Greasy If You Keep Your Oil Hot Enough

Deep fried foods have definitely become less popular as we have all become more health and diet conscious. I don't advocate a steady diet of fried foods, but every once in a while I enjoy crispy batter-coated vegetables, fritters, and vegetable chips.

The trick is to prevent the food from absorbing oil by keeping the temperature high enough. It isn't difficult.

Low frying temperatures are

Once the garden starts producing a variety of vegetables, I like to make Tempura Vegetables (see page 309). It's one of the few deep-fried vegetable dishes I make regularly. If your oil is hot enough, the vegetables won't be greasy. The batter coating will be crisp and golden, and inside is a barely cooked vegetable.

the enemy of fried foods. Your oil—a quality vegetable oil—should be hot before you add food to it. Usually the best frying temperature is 375° F. A frying thermometer is very helpful for monitoring the temperature.

My grandmother didn't have a thermometer. She used the "bread test." When she thought her oil was hot enough, she dropped a cube of bread into the oil. If the bread was browned by the count of sixty, the temperature was hot enough. I find the thermometer a little more reliable.

Don't add too much food at a time or you will lower the oil temperature. The food you are

about to fry should be at room temperature for the same reason.

Your food should be as dry as possible before coating it with batter or adding it to the oil. Moisture will cause the oil to bubble right over the edges of the pot—a dangerous situation.

Once fried, drain the food on racks or on paper towels. Keep on a warmed platter. Reheated fried foods will become soggy.

Now what do you do with all that expensive oil is the question. I usually strain the oil through a coffee filter and store in a glass jar. Usually I can fry with that oil one or two more times before it becomes dark and thick looking. Then the oil should be discarded.

Braising

It's Usually Done With Tough Cuts of Meat, But Tough Old Vegetables Can Be Improved by the Process, Too

First sauté the vegetable briefly to seal in the flavors. Then cover with sauce and cook or bake until the vegetables are tender. This cabbage will bake in a cream sauce.

Braising is done by first browning the meat or vegetable, then slowly simmering it on top of the stove or in the oven in a flavorful liquid.

That flavorful liquid could be leftover sauce, such as Italian Tomato Sauce (page 306), Tomato Fennel Sauce (page 306), or any of the other tomato-based or cream-based sauces on pages 305–306. Cream and soup stock are also tasty braising liquids.

Most garden vegetables are too tender to hold up to braising, but it is a good trick to have up your sleeve for tough old cabbages, carrots, turnips, rutabagas, and, even, broccoli.

Slice your vegetable into uniform-size pieces. Heat enough oil to cover the bottom of a large sauté pan. Add the vegetables and sauté until they are well coated with the oil and slightly tender. Then add the braising liquid. Cover and cook for about 20 minutes, or until the vegetables are tender.

To bake in the oven, preheat the oven to 350° F. while the vegetables sauté. Then transfer the vegetables to a baking dish and cover with the sauce. Cover the dish and bake for 20–30 minutes or until the vegetables are tender.

Although it is possible to overcook vegetables this way, I like to braise vegetables when I am concerned that a meal might not be served on time, or when stragglers might come seeking their dinner at all hours.

What's a Roux?

Just Butter and Flour That Thickens Sauces and Soups

Many of my cream soups and sauces are thickened by a paste of butter and flour, which is known as a roux (pronounced roo).

Simply melt some butter in a saucepan and whisk in an equal amount of white (unbleached all-purpose) flour. Then add your liquid slowly, stirring constantly to prevent lumps. The sauce thickens as it cooks. If you do find any lumps, press them out with the back of your wooden cooking spoon against the sides of the pan.

For a cream sauce, figure that 2 tablespoons of butter and 2 tablespoons of flour will thicken 1 cup of liquid.

Once the flour is added to the butter, and you have a smooth paste, cook for 3–5 minutes, to remove the flour taste. Keep your heat on low and make sure your roux is heated evenly. This helps the starch perform its thickening action.

There are white roux and brown roux. Brown rouxs are cooked for about 20 minutes and add a rich flavor to a sauce. Brown rouxs are used frequently in Creole cooking, as you will find in the gumbo recipes on pages 173 and 175. White rouxs, which are cooked for 3–5 minutes, are more commonly used in soups and sauces.

1. Combine the flour and butter.

2. Slowly add the liquid. Press out any lumps with your spoon.

3. The finished sauce is smooth.

Fennel Cheese Sauce (p. 306)

Fresh Cream of Tomato Soup (p. 276)

Blue Cheese and Scallion Sauce (p. 306)

Try Purees for a Kaleidoscope
Of Easy Soup and Sauce Ideas

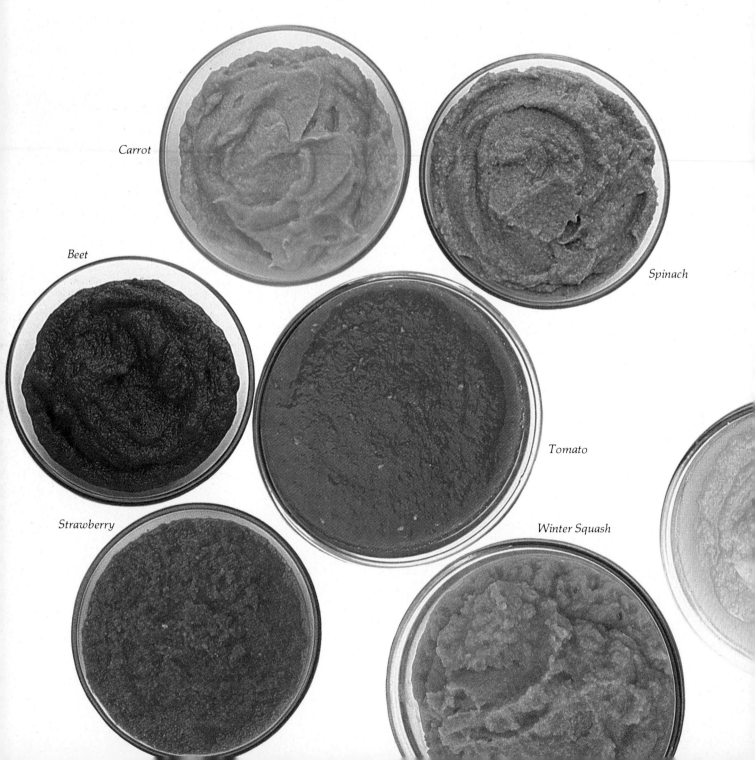

Carrot

Spinach

Beet

Tomato

Strawberry

Winter Squash

You know that you can thicken sauces with flour. Did you know that you can thicken them with vegetable purees just as easily?

A vegetable puree is usually made by cooking a vegetable, then pulverizing it in a blender or food processor or straining it through a metal sieve.

Then what do you do with the puree? Add a few cups of milk or cream and you have a cream soup. Or serve it piping hot with a pat of butter on top and you have an elegant side dish.

You can use vegetable purees as a stuffing for other vegetables. I like to make "carrot boats" with lightly steamed carrots. I fill the carrots with a vegetable puree piped out of a pastry bag. Vegetable purees can be used to fill beets, tomatoes, peppers, or turnips—colorful and tasty!

Some purees are too thin to hold their shape for a filling. No problem. I just slowly cook the puree over low heat, stirring constantly to prevent scorching, until the puree is thick enough to hold a spoon.

You can use vegetable purees to thicken soups and add punch to your sauces. Winter squash is a favorite of mine for this purpose. I simply puree extra winter squash in my food processor and add the sweet puree to a soup, sauce, or gravy. Potatoes thicken soups without adding much flavor; parsnips thicken with a sweet, almost nutlike flavor. Figure that 1 cup of puree will slightly thicken 3 cups of sauce or soup.

Whether to use a food processor, blender, or strainer for making purees depends on the vegetable.

A Squeezo® Strainer is great for tomatoes because it removes the seeds and peels as it strains raw tomatoes. It does a great job on cooked winter squash, but so does a food processor. Generally, I use the food processor when I have small quantities.

A blender makes a very smooth puree, when you add liquid as you puree. A food processor does a good job for most purees. Some vegetables, such as fresh shelled peas, should be strained after pureeing to remove the tough skins that don't break down when the peas are pureed.

Rutabaga

I am adding milk to broccoli puree to make an instant cream soup. A touch of nutmeg is great for seasoning.

Asparagus

The First Asparagus, For Me, Is the First Day of Spring!

Usually there is a single asparagus spear that pokes its way out of the ground before the others. I eat that stem raw, right out of the garden—and know that the harvest season has begun.

Soon there are many purple tips emerging from the soil to become tall green stems, 8–12 inches high. They should be harvested immediately. Asparagus grows quickly, and if you don't harvest every other day (or even daily toward the end of the season when the weather is warm), the asparagus will bolt and flower. The tall fernlike asparagus plants make a beautiful backdrop for the garden, but I like to harvest as much asparagus as possible, to keep the root producing.

I prefer to serve asparagus blanched until just tender crisp—with no sauce or flavoring—until everyone is tired of it. On the table there will be some butter for people who don't like to eat "just plain vegetables," but I eat mine plain, with nothing to mask the fresh spring flavor of this special vegetable.

The Stems Should Be As Thick As Your Index Finger

Any gardening book will tell you to harvest stems that are at least as thick as your index finger. Leave the smaller stems unharvested—it's better for the plants, and the thin stems tend to be woody.

I find that the diameter of the stems varies widely in a home garden. It's hard to cook vegetables that are different thicknesses without overcooking the thin stems or undercooking the thick ones. When I am harvesting asparagus stems that vary in thickness, I am more inclined to chop them up to prepare in soups or baked dishes. Because asparagus combines so well with eggs and cheese, it is a natural to bake in quiches, frittatas, soufflés, and the like. At the height of the harvest season, I make extra quiches and frittatas to freeze.

Harvesting every other day means serving asparagus every other day, which isn't always possible. When there is a surplus, I might store the stems standing up in water in the refrigerator for a day or so, although the fresh flavor is somewhat lost. What I most prefer to do with those few extra stems is to chop them raw and add them to green salads. Fresh, young asparagus is never too woody to be enjoyed raw.

I'm looking for uniform-size pieces so I can serve whole asparagus spears. I won't harvest the spears that are thinner than a pencil in diameter. They will grow bigger in the coming years.

ASPARAGUS AT A GLANCE

Yields

1 pound fresh equals about 20 large
  spears

or

  4 cups diagonal slivers

or

  3 cups chopped, sliced on the
  diagonal, or roll-cut

or

  1 cup cooked and pureed

Preparing Asparagus Is Easy

Snap off the woody ends of the
spears by holding in both hands and
snapping where the color changes
from light pink to light green.

Wash well. Asparagus is
sometimes quite sandy.

*Chose a pot tall enough to hold the
spears upright for steaming.*

Blanching Is Faster Than Steaming

Asparagus cooks more quickly
and evenly when blanched in boiling
water than when steamed over
boiling water.

To blanch, drop asparagus spears,
bundles of asparagus, or sliced
asparagus into boiling salted water
and boil until the asparagus is bright
green and tender crisp, 3–5 minutes,
depending on the size of the
asparagus. Serve immediately or
plunge into cold water to stop the
cooking.

Asparagus can be steamed over
boiling water for 5–7 minutes,
instead of blanching. Special
steamers aren't necessary. Just select
a pot tall enough to hold the
asparagus upright.

Stir frying is another method of
cooking asparagus. This takes 3–5
minutes. (See page 27.)

Take the bite test to see if the asparagus is cooked to the tender crisp stage.

No matter how you cook
asparagus, be sure all your pieces
are the same size so they cook
evenly. The asparagus should be
soft, not mushy; it should hold its
shape, but not be tough. You can
also test with a sharp knife—but
that isn't as much fun.

Cooking Times
  Blanch: 3–5 minutes
  Steam: 5–7 minutes
  Stir fry and *Sauté:* 3–5 minutes

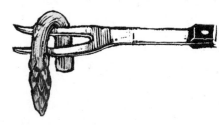

*Don't cook your asparagus until it is as
limp as this spear.*

Asparagus Purees

Cut the asparagus into 1-inch
pieces and blanch in boiling salt
water for 3–4 minutes until tender.
Drain and puree in a blender or
food processor. Asparagus purees
can be frozen for later use in soups,
soufflés, crêpes, and strudels.

13 Simple Ways To Serve Asparagus

Serve blanched asparagus with a
Hollandaise Sauce (page 307), or a
Cheese Sauce (page 305).

Toss blanched asparagus with
Mustard Butter (page 304), Herb
Butter (page 160), or Lemon Butter
(page 304).

Sprinkle blanched asparagus with
buttered bread crumbs, chopped
nuts, or hard-boiled egg yolks.

Cover blanched asparagus with
cheese and broil until the cheese is
melted and golden brown.

Briefly sauté blanched asparagus
in olive oil with minced garlic, or
stir fry in sesame oil and top with
sesame seeds.

Substitute asparagus for green
beans and blanch salad bundles tied
with chive blossoms as shown on
page 41.

Does Your Asparagus Grow In All Different Sizes? Make a Stir Fry!

Farmers who grow huge quantities of asparagus can grade the asparagus by size, and sell whole bunches that are all about the same diameter. We gardeners have to cook what grows— which is asparagus that can be as thick as a baby's wrist or as thin as your index finger. (Don't harvest asparagus that is thinner in diameter than your index finger.)

I like to stir fry asparagus when it varies in size because I can slice the stems to compensate for the varying widths. I slice the thin stems to about 1-inch lengths. The thicker stems are sliced smaller. I always slice on the diagonal for stir fries to expose the maximum amount of surface for quick cooking. Stir frying takes only 3–5 minutes.

If my asparagus harvest is spare, I'll stir fry the asparagus with other vegetables and meat, fish, or chicken and serve the stir fry as a main dish.

If I have enough asparagus to allow about ½–1 cup per person, then I stir fry the asparagus and serve it as a side dish. The rest of the meal doesn't have to be Oriental in origin. Stir fried asparagus goes well with everything from hamburgers to quiches to pasta dishes. And leftover asparagus is great as an omelet filler. But don't count on any leftovers!

1. Stir fry the vegetables.

2. Remove from the wok.

3. Stir fry the chicken.

4. Add vegetables and sauce.

My favorite way to stir fry asparagus

Heat a little sesame oil in a wok or large frying pan. Add minced garlic and nuts. Stir fry until well coated. Add the sliced asparagus, and stir fry until the asparagus is tender crisp, 3–5 minutes. Season to taste with a dash of tamari or soy sauce. Serve at once.

Asparagus Chicken Stir Fry

Slice 2 boneless chicken breasts into strips ½–1 inch long.

Heat 2 tablespoons peanut oil in a wok or large frying pan, and stir fry 1 cup sliced celery for 1 minute. Add ½ cup diced scallions and 4 cups diagonally sliced 1-inch asparagus pieces. Stir fry until the asparagus is bright green and tender crisp, 3–5 minutes. Transfer to a bowl.

Heat 1 tablespoon peanut oil with 1 tablespoon sesame oil. Add the chicken, 1 minced garlic clove, 1 tablespoon minced fresh ginger root, 2 teaspoons grated orange rind, and 3 tablespoons light soy sauce. Stir fry until the chicken is barely cooked, about 5 minutes.

In a small bowl, combine 1 tablespoon cornstarch, ½ cup water, ¼ cup orange juice, and 2 tablespoons frozen orange juice concentrate.

Return the vegetables to the wok. Add ½ cup roasted cashews and toss. Pour in the cornstarch mixture and stir fry to reheat and let the sauce thicken, about 3 minutes. Serve hot over rice. This recipe will serve 6.

If you can't cook right away, asparagus will stay fresh stored upright in water.

SOUP

Cream of Asparagus Soup

I use just the asparagus stems in this soup and save the tender tips for marinades or to serve as a vegetable. This soup is delicious!

2 tablespoons butter
2 cups sliced leeks
6 cups diced asparagus stems
1 quart chicken broth
1 cup light cream
2 tablespoons grated parmesan cheese
¼ teaspoon white pepper
salt
nutmeg

Melt the butter in a large soup pot, and sauté the leeks until they are limp, 3–5 minutes. Add the asparagus and chicken broth. Simmer until the asparagus is tender, 10–15 minutes. Cool the soup slightly, puree in a blender, and reheat. Add the cream, parmesan, pepper, salt and nutmeg to taste. Serve hot.

Preparation Time: 15 minutes
Cooking Time: 20 minutes
Yield: 6 servings

SALAD

Asparagus Pasta Salad

4 cups diced asparagus
1 pound spiral pasta
1 cup sliced pepperoni
1 cup diced scallions
1 cup diced ham
1 cup diced mozzarella cheese
1 cup diced carrots or quartered cherry tomatoes
⅔ cup olive or vegetable oil or half of each
2 tablespoons lemon juice
2 tablespoons wine vinegar
1 tablespoon minced fresh basil
2 teaspoons Dijon-style mustard
1 tablespoon grated parmesan cheese
salt and pepper

Blanch or steam the asparagus until bright green and tender crisp, 2–5 minutes. Plunge into cold water and drain.

Cook the pasta in boiling salted water until just tender. Plunge into cold water and drain.

In a large bowl, combine the asparagus, pasta, pepperoni, scallions, ham, mozzarella, and tomatoes or carrots.

Combine the remaining ingredients in a blender or food processor and blend until well mixed. Pour over the salad and toss to coat. Serve on a bed of lettuce.

Preparation Time: 30 minutes
Yield: 6–8 servings

MAIN DISHES

Each of these dishes, served with a salad made of tender new greens, makes an elegant meal. A dessert of Stewed Rhubarb (page 138) can complete a dinner that is straight out of the spring garden and fit for royalty.

Asparagus Soufflé

3 tablespoons butter
3 tablespoons all-purpose unbleached flour
1 cup milk
1 tablespoon minced fresh chives
½ teaspoon salt
¼ teaspoon white pepper
4 cups diced asparagus
6 eggs, separated

Preheat the oven to 350° F.

In a small saucepan, melt the butter, and stir in the flour to make a thick paste. Add the milk, a little at a time, stirring constantly to prevent lumps. Add the chives, salt, and pepper and set aside.

Blanch or steam the asparagus until just tender, 2–5 minutes. Remove 2 cups of asparagus and set aside. Puree the remaining 2 cups of asparagus in a food processor or blender. Mix the puree into the white sauce. Mix the egg yolks with 1 cup of the sauce to temper them, and blend this mixture into the sauce.

Beat the egg whites until stiff and fold them into the sauce.

Quick! Serve the Asparagus Gougère before the soufflé base falls and the Hollandaise Sauce grows cold.

Fold in the 2 cups of reserved asparagus. Pour the soufflé into an ungreased 2-quart soufflé dish. Bake for 30–35 minutes until golden brown and puffy. Serve immediately.

Preparation Time: 30 minutes
Baking Time: 30–35 minutes
Yield: 6 servings

Asparagus Gougère

A gougère (pronounced goo-jhair) is simply a cheese puff. This one is baked with a topping of ham, then smothered with asparagus and Hollandaise Sauce. It's sublime.

The trick is to have the Hollandaise almost ready in the blender, waiting for the addition of melted butter to complete it, just as you take the Gougère out of the oven.

1 cup water
½ cup butter
½ teaspoon salt
⅛ teaspoon white pepper
1 cup all-purpose unbleached flour
1 cup grated Gruyère or Swiss cheese
4 eggs
¼ pound sliced ham
½ pound asparagus, sliced into 4–5-inch spears
1 cup Hollandaise Sauce (page 307)

Preheat the oven to 375° F.

In a medium-size saucepan, combine the water, butter, salt, and pepper. Bring to a boil. Add the flour and cheese. Stir well to make a dough. Remove the pan from the heat and beat in the eggs, one at a time.

Grease a large au gratin pan or 10-inch pie pan. Smooth the dough over the bottom of the pan. Make a well in the center of the dough, building the dough up around the edges. Slice the ham into pieces ½ inch by 2 inches. Lay the ham in the center of the dough, overlapping each piece. Bake for 30 minutes. In the meantime, prepare the asparagus and Hollandaise Sauce.

Five minutes before the gougère comes out of the oven, blanch or steam the asparagus until tender, 3–5 minutes.

Take the gougère out of the oven and place the asparagus on top of the ham. Spoon the Hollandaise Sauce over the asparagus and serve immediately.

Preparation Time: 30 minutes
Baking Time: 30 minutes
Yield: 4–6 servings

Shell and Dried
Beans

There's Plenty of Protein-Packed Eating In These Easy-to-Grow Crops.

Take a snap bean and let the seeds mature in the pod, and you have shell beans. Let the seeds dry in the pod, and you have dried beans. That's the difference among snap, shell, and dried beans. And, of course, there are differences in how you cook these beans.

There are varieties of beans that taste best at each stage. For eating fresh shell beans, I prefer baby limas, butter beans (or large limas), fava beans, and horticultural beans. For eating dried, I'm not sure I have a preference. I like black beans in Black Bean Soup (page 34), chick peas in Hummus (page 34), and pinto and kidney beans in Mexican dishes. Each bean has a distinctive flavor.

Gardeners can grow bean varieties that just can't be found in the stores. Jacob's cattle beans are a beautiful maroon and white bean that is tasty in all sorts of baked dishes. The Vermont cranberry bean is good as a shell bean or a dried bean. It is pink-colored and can be substituted in any casserole that requires a red bean.

In recent years, more gardeners have been growing antique varieties of beans as well as the popular standards. It is fun to cook with new varieties of beans. There are literally dozens of varieties of beans to experiment with. I have found that it is very difficult to ruin a dried bean. I think you can safely experiment with substituting one bean variety for another in recipes. The flavors will vary, but the taste and texture will usually be very pleasing.

Serve Beans in Place of Meat

You don't have to worry about protein when you eat beans. Combined with grains or dairy products, cooked dried beans provide a complete protein. A serving of cooked dried beans provides as much protein as 2 eggs or ⅛ pound of hamburger. And beans are rich in B vitamins.

Shell beans are so hearty, I like to complement them with light dishes—salads and other vegetables.

When I cook with dried beans, I usually make them the main dish, slowly cooked on a woodstove, if possible—it's time-saving, and the flavors are always enhanced by slow cooking.

I keep my kitchen stocked with these tasty dried bean varieties. From left to right: (top row) Great Northern Beans, Kidneys, Pintos, Limas; (second row) Split Peas, Chick Peas, Black Turtle Beans, Soy Beans; (third row) Mung Beans, Split Yellow Peas, Jacob's Cattle Beans; (fourth row) Red Lentils, Lentils, Navy Beans.

SHELL BEANS AND DRIED BEANS AT A GLANCE

Harvesting Tips

Shell beans are ready for harvest when the beans inside the pod are well formed, but still tender. The pods look fat and lumpy. Harvest the pods and shell out the beans.

Dried beans are harvested late in the season when the plants are dead and brown, and the beans are beginning to be hard.

Fully dry the bean plants with the pods still attached by hanging the plants upside down in a dry area. When the beans are so hard you can't bite into them, thresh to separate the dry beans from the pods and stems. An easy way to do this is to bundle the beans in a burlap sack and beat the sack with a stick. To separate the chaff from the beans (winnowing), pour the beans from the bag onto a blanket several times on a windy day. The wind will blow away the chaff, leaving you with a blanket filled with beans.

Yields

1 pound fresh shell beans equals
    4 cups
1 pound dried beans equals
    2 cups uncooked
or
    4 cups cooked

Shell Beans Can Be Blanched or Steamed

To cook shell beans, cover with water and bring to a boil, then simmer for 5–20 minutes, depending on the size of the beans, until tender.

You can steam shell beans for the same amount of time you would blanch them. Some beans end up with wrinkled skins when steamed.

Cooked shell beans are delicious when served with butter, Italian Tomato Sauce (page 306), Pesto (page 161), or Tomato Fennel Sauce (page 306).

Presoaking Is Essential With Dried Beans

The first step in preparing dried beans is to rinse well in cold running water. Then soak overnight or use the quick soak method.

Overnight Soaking. Cover each cup of dried beans with about 3 cups of water. Let stand 12 hours or overnight. Then cook, according to the recipe directions. If the soaking water does not taste bitter, use that water in the recipe as it has some vitamins you do not want to lose.

Quick Soak Method. For each cup of beans, cover with 3 cups water. Bring to a boil. Boil for 2 minutes. Remove from the heat and let stand for 1 hour. Then cook, according to the recipe directions. Again, if the soaking water does not taste bitter, use that water in your recipe.

Fava beans

Limas

Horticulture beans

Fill a burlap bag with dried bean plants and beat it to separate beans from pod (above). Then spill the beans onto a blanket and shake lightly to let the wind blow away the chaff (right).

This combination of kidney and Vermont cranberry beans will be great in chili.

Times for Cooking Dried Beans

These cooking times are based on starting with presoaked beans (see page 32).

	Regular Pot	Pressure Cooker
Baby Limas and Butter Beans	30–60 minutes	
Black Beans	2½ hours	8–10 minutes
Black-Eyed Peas	20–50 minutes	
Chick Peas	4 hours	15–20 minutes
Great Northern and Marrow Beans	2½–3 hours	8 minutes
Kidney, Pink, Cranberry, and Pinto Beans	2–2½ hours	5–7 minutes
Lentils	30–40 minutes	
Navy, Pea, and Small White Beans	3–3½ hours	10 minutes
Small Red Beans	3–3½ hours	10 minutes
Split Peas	40–60 minutes	
Whole Dried Green Peas	60–70 minutes	

I like to mix and match dried beans in recipes. For example, when I make chili I use a combination of kidney, navy, Jacob's cattle and pinto beans. The flavor is much richer. Try mixing bean varieties in your favorite recipes; you can't really go wrong.

APPETIZERS

Hummus, a Mid-Eastern dip and sandwich spread, has become very popular in the last few years. Serve it with small triangles of pita bread.

Hummus

I've found that this basic recipe for Hummus is just as delicious made with lima beans as it is with the traditional chick peas.

2 cups cooked lima beans
   or chick peas
3 tablespoons lemon juice
¼ cup tahini
2 garlic cloves, minced
2 tablespoons water
salt

Combine all the ingredients, except the salt, in a food processor and process until smooth. Season to taste with salt. Serve with pita bread.

Preparation Time: 10 minutes
Yield: 4–6 servings

SOUPS

Black Bean Soup

A good smoky ham will produce the best soup.

1¼ cups dried black beans
4 cups water
3 tablespoons butter
1½ cups diced onion
2 garlic cloves, minced
1 cup finely diced carrots
2 cups chopped celery and leaves
⅛ teaspoon ground cloves
2 bay leaves
½ teaspoon mustard seeds
2–3 teaspoons salt
½ teaspoon pepper
1 ham bone, with meat on the bone
water
1½ cups light cream
3–4 tablespoons Marsala wine
salt and pepper

Soak the beans overnight in 4 cups water. Or combine the beans with the 4 cups water, bring to a boil, boil for 2 minutes, cover, and remove from heat. Let stand one hour.

In a large soup pot, melt the butter, and sauté the onion, garlic, carrots, and celery for 3–5 minutes, or until the onion is limp. Add the beans, soaking water, cloves, bay leaves, mustard seeds, salt, pepper, and ham bone. Simmer for about 3½ hours. Add more water as needed. Cool the soup slightly. Remove the ham bone and bay leaves and puree the soup in a food processor or blender with the cream and wine. Season to taste with salt and pepper. Reheat and serve hot.

Preparation Time: 30 minutes, plus soaking time
Cooking Time: 3½ hours
Yield: 6–8 servings

Dried Bean Soup With Pepperoni

2 cups dried lima beans, butter beans, or any other dried beans
2 tablespoons vegetable oil
1¼ cups diced onion
3 garlic cloves, minced
1 cup diced carrots
½ cup diced celery
6 cups water or stock
¼ teaspoon dried marjoram or ¾ teaspoon fresh
¼ teaspoon ground dried sage or ¾ teaspoon fresh
¼ teaspoon dried thyme or ¾ teaspoon fresh
2 bay leaves
1 cup diced pepperoni
salt and pepper

Soak the beans according to the directions on page 32.

In a large soup pot, heat the oil and sauté the onion, garlic, carrots, and celery until the onion is limp, 3–5 minutes. Add the water, herbs and beans. Simmer until the beans are very soft, about 2 hours. Add more water if necessary. Cool slightly.

In a blender or food processor, puree two-thirds of the soup. Return the puree to the pot. Stir in the pepperoni. Season to taste with salt and pepper. Serve hot.

Preparation Time: 25 minutes, plus soaking time
Cooking Time: 2 hours
Yield: 6–8 servings

SIDE DISHES
AND MAIN DISHES

Don't miss the recipe for Pumpkin and Baked Beans (page 230).

Succotash

Succotash is such a simple classic dish, I almost overlook it. But for those who have never tried this vegetable combination that the colonists enjoyed, here's an unadorned version.

Blanch fresh lima beans and corn kernels in boiling water until tender, 5–10 minutes. Drain and add melted butter. Season to taste with salt and pepper. Serve hot.

With the baby limas still sweet and tender, and the corn at its peak, too, this simple Succotash is easy to prepare and delicious.

Black-Eyed Peas With Bacon and Tomato

In a large sauté pan, brown ¼ pound diced bacon and pour off all but 2 tablespoons fat. Add ⅔ cup diced onion and ½ cup minced fresh parsley. Sauté until limp, 3–5 minutes. Add 4 cups cooked black-eyed peas, 2 cups tomato puree, and ½ teaspoon dried thyme. Season to taste with salt and pepper. Simmer for 10–15 minutes to let the flavors blend. Serve hot.

Preparation Time: 10 minutes
Cooking Time: 15–20 minutes
Yield: 6 servings

Brunswick Stew

This Southern stew has dozens of variations. I understand it is good made with rabbit.

¼ **pound bacon, diced**
6 **chicken pieces or 3–4 cups cooked chicken meat**
1½ **cups diced onion**
1 **tablespoon minced fresh basil or 1 teaspoon dried**
4 **cups diced tomatoes**
3 **cups fresh lima beans**
1 **cup corn kernels**
1 **cup water**
1 **tablespoon Worcestershire sauce**
salt and pepper

In a large stew pot, brown the bacon for 2–3 minutes and remove from the pan. Brown the chicken pieces on both sides in the bacon fat for 5–10 minutes and remove from the pan.

Sauté the onion in the remaining bacon fat until limp, 3–5 minutes. Return the bacon and chicken to the pot. Add the remaining ingredients. Simmer for 40 minutes or until the chicken is very tender when pierced with a fork. Serve hot.

Preparation Time: 35 minutes
Cooking Time: 1 hour
Yield: 6 servings

Refried Beans

Refried Beans can be served as a side dish with any Mexican meal or used as a filling for tacos, enchiladas, tostadas, even Chile Rellenos (see page 205). Pintos are the traditional bean to use, but you can substitute any brown or red bean—kidneys, Jacob's cattle beans, and Vermont cranberry beans are varieties I have used.

2 tablespoons vegetable oil
1½ cups diced onion
3 garlic cloves, minced
3 cups cooked pinto beans
1 cup chopped tomatoes
¼ teaspoon ground fennel
¼ teaspoon ground rosemary
1 teaspoon ground cumin
2 teaspoons chili powder
salt and cayenne

In a large sauté pan, heat the oil, and sauté the onion and garlic for 3 minutes. Add the remaining ingredients and cook for 15–20 minutes. As the beans cook, mash half with a spoon or a potato masher. If they do not break down easily, you can puree half the beans in a food processor or blender. Return to the pan to reheat. Serve hot.

Preparation Time: 10 minutes
Cooking Time: 20 minutes
Yield: 6–8 servings

Pork and Bean Bake

If you are cooking with dried beans, follow the instructions on page 32 for soaking the beans, but cook for 15 minutes only.

4 cups fresh limas or butter beans
    or partially cooked dried beans
1 cup chopped onion
1¾ cups chopped tomatoes
¼ cup thick tomato puree
1 cup sour cream
1 teaspoon paprika
1 teaspoon lemon juice
salt and pepper
1 pound pork (5–6 pork chops)
1 tablespoon vegetable oil or bacon fat
1½ tablespoons melted butter
⅓ cup bread crumbs
2 tablespoons grated parmesan cheese
½ teaspoon chili powder

Preheat the oven to 325° F.
In a 2-quart greased baking dish, combine the beans, onion, and tomatoes.
Mix the tomato puree, sour cream, paprika, and lemon juice. Add salt and pepper to taste. Pour this mixture over the vegetables.
Slice the pork into 2-inch pieces that are ½-inch thick.
Heat the oil and sear the pork pieces for about 2 minutes. Place the pork on the casserole.
Mix the butter, bread crumbs, parmesan, and chili powder. Sprinkle over the pork. Cover the casserole loosely with foil. Bake for 1 hour. Serve hot.

Preparation Time: 30 minutes
Baking Time: 1 hour
Yield: 6 servings

Cassoulet

Plan to use every pot and pan you own and to stay in the kitchen for hours. This classic French casserole is worth it!

3 pounds boned pork loin roast
salt and pepper
4 cups chicken broth
3 pounds dried white beans
    (Great Northern)
3 quarts water
2 pounds lamb (round bone steak or boned shoulder)
2 tablespoons vegetable oil
½ cup diced onion
2 garlic cloves, minced
4 cups drained, diced canned tomatoes
2 tablespoons tomato paste
1 bay leaf, crumbled
2½ teaspoons dried thyme
4 chicken legs with thighs (or 1 small roasting chicken, cut up)
1 medium-size onion, halved
1 pound garlic sausage (kielbasa)
1 cup dry red wine

Preheat the oven to 325° F.
Place the pork loin in a roasting pan. Sprinkle with salt and pepper. Add ½ cup of the chicken broth. Roast, covered, for ½ hour.
Meanwhile, rinse the beans. Combine in a large pot with 3 quarts of water. Bring to a boil, and boil for 2 minutes. Remove from the stove and let stand 1 hour.
Slice the lamb into 1-inch cubes. Heat the oil in a large sauté pan. Brown the lamb and remove the meat from the pan. Add the diced onion and garlic, and sauté for 2 minutes. Add the tomatoes, tomato paste, bay leaf, and thyme. Return the lamb to

the pan. Season to taste with salt and pepper. Simmer gently until tender, 20–30 minutes. Remove the lamb from the sauce and set aside.

After the pork loin has roasted for ½ hour, add the chicken pieces and roast, covered, for another ½ hour.

After the beans have soaked in water for 1 hour, drain off the water. Add 3½ cups chicken broth, the halved onion, and the sausage to the beans. Simmer, uncovered, for ½ hour. Then remove the sausage and set it aside. Continue to simmer until the beans are just tender, about ½ hour more.

By now the chicken should have roasted with the pork for ½ hour. Turn the chicken pieces over. Continue roasting, uncovered, until tender, about 1 hour. Then set aside to cool.

Check the beans for tenderness. Drain when barely done and reserve the cooking liquid.

Diagonally slice the sausage into ½-inch slices. Slice the pork loin into 2-inch cubes.

Combine the pork juices and lamb juices in a tall narrow container and set in the refrigerator or freezer to congeal the fat. Skim off the fat and discard.

Remove the onion from the beans and discard.

Combine the meat juices and cooking liquid from the beans.

Add the wine and season to taste with salt and pepper.

In a 10-quart ovenproof pottery or enamel casserole, place a layer of beans, then a layer of meat (pork, chicken, lamb, and sausage). Repeat the layers, ending up with beans on top. Add the remaining juices.

Bake, covered, at 350° F. for 2 hours, adding water if necessary. Serve hot.

Preparation Time: 3–4 hours
Baking Time: 2 hours
Yield: 10–12 servings

A loaf of bread, a jug of wine, and a light green salad together with the rich-tasting Cassoulet make a memorable meal. The Cassoulet serves twelve, so I serve it on special occasions. The extra time it takes to make this dish is worth it!

Green and Yellow
Snap Beans

The Biggest Garden Producer — and Fortunately the Most Popular . . .

Green and yellow snap beans are vegetables I count on. Everyone likes them, so they are perfect vegetables to serve to guests. And they are easy to prepare: just wash, snap off the tops, and steam over a little boiling water. Served with a delicate herb sauce, or tossed lightly with lemon juice and butter, nothing could be tastier.

The very best snap beans are picked when they are a bit thinner than a pencil in diameter, and the seeds inside are not yet visible. Length is not important. Yellow beans will have a greenish tinge; green beans will be pale green. As long as you harvest every 3 days, the plants will keep producing — which means that a surplus is inevitable. Fortunately, beans are a "snap" to preserve.

Beans Lead Novices Into Food Preservation

Many people blanch their beans before freezing. I prefer to freeze some of my green beans unblanched. Unblanched green beans will keep for at least 6 months in the freezer — *if* they are completely dry before they go in the freezer bags.

It's around the time that I've frozen most of the beans I'll need that I start losing my enthusiasm for freezing and eating beans. The beans take their revenge by *growing*. Then I am faced with large, over-grown, "muscular" beans. The pods are slightly tough, and the seeds begin to be visible in the pod.

Most cookbooks say, "Use only tender, young beans," but I like the challenge of making wonderful food from *all* that my garden produces. When cooking slightly overripe beans, I look for recipes that call for slow cooking, or simmering in a liquid or sauce, or blending in purees.

Snap beans can get too tough to harvest green. You can tell just by tasting. Are the pods tough? Bland tasting? Are the seeds large and mealy? These beans have gone by, but don't give up on them. Let the pods dry completely on the plant, then harvest and shell them out for cooking as dried beans or for next year's seeds. Of course, the bean plants will stop producing when you stop picking.

It's hot work blanching bushels of snap beans for the freezer. But I'll enjoy eating those beans all winter. Frozen snap beans can be used in most recipes that call for fresh beans.

Are All Beans the Same?

Pole beans have a slightly "nutty" flavor, produce a longer harvest, and require less growing space.

Bush beans tend to ripen all at once, which makes them good for preserving.

Dwarf or Pole Romano green snap beans hold their crispness longer than Tendercrop, Bountiful, and other standard green beans.

Yellow beans tend to taste blander than green ones.

Italian beans can be used in any recipe calling for green beans.

Purple beans turn green when cooked.

Yields

1 bushel beans equals
   30 pounds
1 pound fresh beans equals
   4 cups chopped, diagonally
   sliced in 1-inch pieces, or roll-cut
or
   3½ cups finely diced or
   diagonally sliced in ½-inch pieces
or
   3 cups grated (with a steel blade
   in a food processor using a
   pulsing action)
1 pound fresh steamed beans equals
   2½ cups coarsely ground puree
   for pâtés
1 pound fresh steamed beans plus ½
   cup water equals
   3 cups puree for soups

Sometimes You Have to Harvest and Store

When necessary, store unwashed beans in a sealed plastic bag in the refrigerator for up to 5 days.

Restore wilted beans by soaking in ice water for up to 30 minutes.

SNAP BEANS AT A GLANCE

Preparing Beans for the Table: Wash, Drain, Snap, Chop

Wash the beans in cold water, drain dry. Snap off or slice off the tops. Leave the tails. Stringing is not necessary.

Whole Beans. Leave young and mature beans whole for salads, appetizers, garnishes, and raw vegetable dips.

Halved Beans. Mature and older beans can be sliced along the seam to tenderize.

Diced. Good for mature and older beans in soups and casseroles.

Julienne. Exposes so much of the surface, the beans lose flavor.

Diagonal Roll-Cut. Tenderizes old beans by exposing the surface. Good for soups.

Diagonal Slivers. For garnishing, best with old beans.

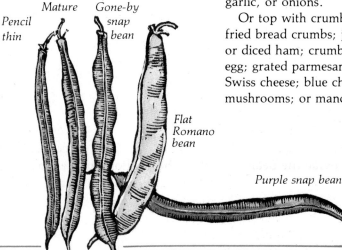

Pencil thin

Mature

Gone-by snap bean

Flat Romano bean

Purple snap bean

The best way to treat a young bean is to briefly steam it.

Bring about 1 inch of water to a boil in a saucepan. Place 1 pound of washed and trimmed beans in a colander or steam basket and set over the boiling water. Cover and steam for 3 minutes. The beans will be bright in color and slightly crunchy: *tender crisp.*

Unless you are going to serve the beans immediately, plunge them into cold water to stop the cooking, then drain.

Oh No! Not Just Beans Tonight!

Beans can be served with a variety of herbs, spices, flavorings, and sauces. Here are a few ideas.

Sauté the beans with butter and herbs. Some of my favorite herbs are summer savory, mint, basil, rosemary, parsley, dill, fennel, chives, and burnet.

Sauté the beans with sunflower seeds, pine nuts, slivered almonds, cashews, walnuts, sesame seeds, garlic, or onions.

Or top with crumbled bacon; fried bread crumbs; julienne-sliced or diced ham; crumbled hard-boiled egg; grated parmesan, cheddar, or Swiss cheese; blue cheese; sautéed mushrooms; or mandarin oranges.

Just before serving, I dress these Bean and Carrot Bundles with a vinaigrette dressing.

For the first beans of the season: Some very special dishes

The gardener in you is so proud of the tender young beans, the only way to serve beans tonight is plain. But the cook in you wants to make something special, something that will please all the senses. Try a bundle of beans, tied up with flowering chive stalks from your herb garden or scallions from your vegetable garden.

Salad Bundles

Trim a pound of beans so they are all the same length. Steam for 3 minutes and plunge in cold water; drain. Divide the beans into 4 equal portions. Wrap a chive stalk around each bundle so the blossom is on top. Dress with a vinaigrette dressing (page 300). Serves 4.

Scallion Bundles

Trim a pound of green or yellow beans so they are all the same length. Over boiling water, steam 4 scallions (green tops only) for 1–2 minutes. Divide the beans into 4 equal portions and tie each bundle with a scallion. Steam for 4 minutes, keeping the bundles separate so the steam circulates freely. Pour melted butter over the bundles. Serves 4.

Carrot and Bean Bundles

Follow the same procedure as with the scallion bundles, but divide a half pound of carrots cut to match the beans among the bundles.

Jonesy's Potatoes and Beans

Every cook knows that the best vegetables are the youngest ones taken straight from the garden and popped into the pot. Here's a recipe I learned from an old Vermont gardener.

Rob the potato patch of some tiny, new potatoes and harvest some tiny, new snap beans. Bring an inch of water to a boil in a saucepan. Add the potatoes, sliced in half, and the beans. Cook until the potatoes are fork tender. Flavor with salt, pepper, and butter. Wonderful!

APPETIZERS

It's funny how pâtés have become so popular in this country just over the last few years. I am including my favorite green bean pâté in this chapter. Whenever I serve it at parties, it seems to just disappear.

When I'm trimming beans, I want the job to go fast. I grab a handful of beans, with the tails all on one end. Then I tap the bundle to align the blossom ends. I don't bother to chop off the tails. It's amazing how quickly you can perform this task.

Green Bean Almond Pâté

Meatless pâtés, such as these green bean pâtés, can be served before a meal as cocktail food, with crackers, triangles of pita bread, or large carrot rounds used in place of crackers.

Nice looking, mature beans are needed for the garnish, but slightly overripe beans can be used in the puree.

¼ pound green beans, cut in 1-inch pieces
2 tablespoons butter
1 cup diced onion
1 teaspoon dried thyme
1½ cups green bean puree
1¼ cups toasted slivered almonds
1½ teaspoons tamari or soy sauce or salt or to taste
1 tablespoon lemon juice

Steam the green beans until tender crisp, about 3 minutes, and plunge into cold water. Drain and set aside.

Heat the butter, and sauté the onion until limp, 3–5 minutes. Add the thyme. Combine the bean puree in a processor with the sautéed onion, 1 cup of the almonds, the tamari or salt, and the lemon juice. Process until the almonds are ground and the pâté is well blended. Mound the pâté in the center of a plate and pat it into shape. Sprinkle the remaining ¼ cup almonds on top. Press the steamed green bean pieces around the sides of the pâté. Diagonally cut 6 thin slices of green beans for the center garnish and put in place. Chill the pâté until you are ready to serve.

Preparation Time: 20 minutes
Yield: 2 cups

Crispy Bean Sticks: Mexican-Style

These crispy vegetable appetizers take on many flavors—but use plenty of spices and herbs and a little more salt than you normally do—otherwise the flavor will be too bland.

2 cups wheat germ or whole wheat flour
1 tablespoon chili powder
1 teaspoon garlic powder
dash cayenne
salt
¾ pound green or yellow snap beans
2 eggs, beaten

Combine the wheat germ with the spices and salt.

Trim the beans.

Pour in just enough oil to coat the bottom of the frying pan and heat. Dip the beans into the eggs, then into the seasoned breading. Fry the beans until golden, 2–3 minutes. Keep rolling the beans as they fry to brown evenly. Drain and keep the cooked beans warm as you fry all the beans. Serve immediately.

Preparation Time: 30 minutes
Yield: 6 servings

Variations

Indian-Style. Season the breading with 1 tablespoon curry powder, a dash cayenne, and salt to taste. Fry in peanut oil or vegetable oil.

Italian-Style. Season the breading with 1 tablespoon dried basil, 1 teaspoon garlic powder, and salt and pepper to taste. Fry in olive oil.

SOUPS

When the bean harvest starts to overwhelm, I cook soup in a hurry. No one notices when the soup is made from slightly gone-by beans.

Wax Bean Cream Soup

Fennel gives this unique cream soup a very subtle flavor. I like to garnish each serving bowl with either a lavender chive blossom or a spray of fresh fennel leaf tips.

3 tablespoons butter
1½ cups diced onion
6 cups finely chopped or processor ground wax beans
2 teaspoons ground fennel
4 cups water or chicken or vegetable broth
1 cup heavy cream
1 cup milk
approximately 2 teaspoons salt or to taste
white pepper

In a large soup pot, melt the butter and sauté the onion until it is limp, 3–5 minutes.

Add the beans, fennel, and water to the pot and cook until the beans are tender, about 20 minutes.

Cool the soup slightly, pour into a blender, and blend until smooth. Return the soup to the pot and reheat. Stir in the cream and milk. Season to taste with salt and pepper. Serve hot.

Preparation Time: 30 minutes
Yield: 8 servings

Green beans in tomato soup? Delicious in this Mediterranean soup.

Mediterranean Fish And Bean Soup

The amount of water to add is directly proportional to the thickness of the tomato puree. Add enough to make a soup, not a stew.

2 tablespoons olive oil
1½ cups diced onion
2 garlic cloves, minced
4 cups thick tomato puree
½ cup dry white wine
approximately 2 cups water
2 teaspoons ground cumin
½ teaspoon dried thyme
1 tablespoon fresh basil or 1 teaspoon dried
2 cups green or yellow beans, cut in ½-inch diagonal roll-cuts or diced
1 pound cod or other firm white fish, cubed
½ cup halved, pitted black olives
salt and pepper
½ cup crumbled feta cheese

In a medium-sized soup pot, heat the oil, and sauté the onion and garlic until limp, 3–5 minutes. Add the tomato puree, wine, water, and spices and herbs. Simmer for 15 minutes. Add the beans, fish, and the olives. Continue cooking the soup for 5–10 minutes, just enough to cook the fish through. Season to taste with salt and pepper.

Ladle the soup into individual bowls and garnish each bowl with crumbled feta cheese.

Preparation Time: 25 minutes
Cooking Time: 25–30 minutes
Yield: 6 servings

SALADS

I don't like the taste or the texture of raw beans in salads. So I parboil them first. Try it my way: the color is so much brighter, too.

Green Bean, Celery, and Mushroom Salad

When tomatoes are in season, I garnish this light luncheon salad with them for color.

4 cups diagonally sliced green beans
¼ cup sliced scallions
1 cup diagonally sliced celery
1 cup sliced mushrooms
3 tablespoons tamari or soy sauce
1 teaspoon sesame oil
1 garlic clove, minced
2 teaspoons honey
1 teaspoon minced fresh ginger root
¼ cup wine vinegar
½ cup vegetable oil

Steam the beans until tender crisp, about 3 minutes, and plunge into cold water. Drain well. In a large salad bowl, toss the beans with the scallions, celery, and mushrooms.

Whisk together the tamari, sesame oil, garlic, honey, ginger root, vinegar, and vegetable oil. Pour over the salad. Toss and serve immediately.

Preparation Time: 30 minutes
Yield: 6 servings

I prefer blanched beans in salads. The color is brighter and the flavor and texture more pleasing.

Japanese Bean Salad

Trim 1½ pounds snap beans and slice into diagonal roll-cuts or leave whole. Steam until tender crisp, about 3 minutes. Plunge into cold water, then drain. Combine the snap beans with 1½ cups Tahini Dressing (page 303). Toss to coat. Serve cold.

Oriental Bean Salad

Trim 1 pound snap beans and slice into diagonal roll-cuts or leave whole. Steam until tender crisp, about 3 minutes. Plunge into cold water, then drain. Combine the beans with 1 cup Oriental Marinade and Dipping Sauce (page 303). Toss to coat. Refrigerate for several hours before serving.

Chicken Curry Salad

Trim ¾ pound beans and slice into diagonal roll-cuts. Steam until tender crisp, about 3 minutes. Plunge into cold water, then drain. Combine the green beans with 2 cups brown or white cooked rice, 3 cups grated Swiss cheese, 2 cups diced cooked chicken, 1 small diced red onion, 1 small diced sweet red or green pepper, and a drained 8-ounce can of water chestnuts. Pour 1¼ cups Honey Curry Dressing (page 303) over the salad. Toss to coat. Serve cold.

Chicken Chutney Salad

Served on a bed of curly leaf lettuce and garnished with mandarin oranges, this makes a glamorous company dish. Celery can replace the water chestnuts if necessary.

2 cups diagonally sliced green beans
3 cups shredded cooked chicken
½ cup toasted slivered almonds
½–⅔ cup diced water chestnuts
1½ cups drained mandarin oranges
1½ tablespoons minced fresh ginger root
2 tablespoons mango chutney
2 tablespoons ginger preserves
¾ cup Honey Curry Dressing (page 303)

Steam the beans until tender crisp, about 3 minutes. Plunge them into cold water and drain.

Combine the beans, chicken, almonds, water chestnuts, and mandarin oranges in a large bowl.

Combine the ginger, chutney, ginger preserves, and dressing in a food processor or blender. Process until the sauce is well mixed. Pour the dressing over the salad and toss to coat. Marinate the salad for at least 2 hours before serving.

Preparation Time: 20 minutes
Chilling Time: 2 hours
Yield: 6 servings

SIDE DISHES AND MAIN DISHES

The great thing about snap beans is that so many people like them. I never shy away from preparing a snap bean dish at a dinner party because I can be sure that most everyone will enjoy it.

Parmesan Beans Fettucine

4 quarts salted water
½ pound green beans, cut in 1-inch pieces
2 tablespoons butter
⅓ pound Canadian bacon, julienne-sliced
1 pound fettucine noodles
1½ cups grated parmesan cheese
⅓ cup heavy cream
salt and pepper

Bring 4 quarts of salted water to boil. While the water heats, steam the beans until they are tender crisp, about 3 minutes.

Melt the butter in a sauté pan, and sauté the Canadian bacon until browned, 2–3 minutes. Add the beans and toss to coat. Keep warm.

Cook the noodles in the boiling water until just tender. Drain the noodles well and toss them with the beans and bacon in a large bowl. Add the parmesan cheese and cream to the hot noodles and toss. Season to taste with salt and pepper. Serve immediately.

Preparation Time: 30 minutes
Yield: 6 servings

Blue Cheese and Green Bean Quiche

I like to serve quiches at room temperature to bring out the flavor.

1 single unbaked pastry crust (page 308)
½ pound whole trimmed green beans
2 tablespoons butter
1 cup diced onion
4 eggs, slightly beaten
2 cups light cream
dash nutmeg
½ teaspoon salt
¼ teaspoon pepper
1 cup crumbled blue cheese (⅓ pound)

Preheat the oven to 350° F.

Roll out a single pie crust and fit it into a 10-inch pie pan.

Steam the beans until they are tender crisp, about 3 minutes. Plunge into cold water, and drain.

Melt the butter in a sauté pan, and sauté the onion until limp, 3–5 minutes.

Beat together the eggs, cream, nutmeg, salt, and pepper. Pour the custard mixture into the pie crust. Sprinkle the onion evenly over the pie. Sprinkle the blue cheese evenly over the pie. Lay the green beans on top of the pie in a spoke pattern. Cut the beans to fit, if necessary. Fill in the center of the bean design with cut green beans.

Bake the quiche for 45 minutes or until golden brown. Remove it from the oven and allow it to sit for at least 15 minutes before serving.

Preparation Time: 30 minutes
Baking Time: 45 minutes
Yield: 8 servings

Pesto Turnovers

These turnovers make excellent use of slightly gone-by beans, or even canned beans, but they are good with young beans, too. You can use yellow or green beans with this recipe.

½ **pound yellow or green beans, diced**
¼ **cup olive oil**
1 **cup diced onion**
½ **pound mushrooms, sliced**
½ **cup chopped walnuts**
¼ **cup minced fresh basil**
1 **cup grated parmesan cheese**
⅓ **cup heavy cream**
¾ **pound filo dough**
½ **cup melted butter**

Preheat the oven to 350° F. Steam the beans until tender crisp, about 3 minutes.

Heat the oil in a sauté pan, and sauté the onion and mushrooms until browned, 3–5 minutes. Mix the onion, mushrooms, beans, walnuts, basil, cheese, and cream.

On a dry surface, lay out 2 sheets of filo dough on top of each other and brush the top sheet with melted butter. Fold the dough in half lengthwise. Place about ½ cup of the filling on one end of the dough. Fold the dough as you would a flag to make a triangle. Brush on butter between each fold. Continue folding to enclose the triangle. Place the turnover on a greased cookie sheet. Make 6 turnovers. Bake for 35 minutes or until golden brown.

Preparation Time: 40 minutes
Baking Time: 35 minutes
Yield: 6 servings

Pesto Turnovers are a favorite of mine for buffets because they hold their heat well. But watch it! They are liable to disappear before your very eyes.

1. Spoon about ½ cup of filling onto the filo dough.

2. Fold the dough over the filling to make a triangle.

Chicken and Green Bean Tarragon

Here's a dish that can be made in advance, if you keep the browned chicken, steamed beans, and sauce separate. Just before baking, assemble the chicken and beans and reheat the sauce. Pour the sauce over the chicken and bake in a preheated oven.

This dish is best with fresh young or mature beans, but you can use frozen beans. Defrost the beans and cut them to size before sprinkling over the browned chicken. Do not steam.

I like to serve the chicken over rice.

¼ cup vegetable oil

3 large boneless chicken breasts, split in half

¾ pound green beans, diagonally cut in 1-inch pieces

¼ cup water

¼ cup butter

1½ tablespoons fresh tarragon or 2 teaspoons dried

⅓ cup all-purpose unbleached flour

2 cups milk

½ cup dry white wine

approximately 2 tablespoons lemon juice

salt and white pepper

2 egg yolks

Preheat the oven to 350° F.

Heat the vegetable oil in a large sauté pan, and sauté the chicken breasts on both sides until golden brown. Do not try to cook the chicken all the way through—you are just browning for color.

In the meantime, steam the beans until tender crisp, about 3 minutes. Plunge into cold water. Drain.

3. Brush with melted butter each time you fold.

Place the chicken pieces in a baking dish and sprinkle the green beans over and around them. Pour ¼ cup water into the sauté pan to loosen the chicken juices. Pour out the enriched water and reserve it.

Melt the butter in the sauté pan. Sauté the tarragon in the butter to bring out its flavor. Stir in the flour, making sure you press out all the lumps. Slowly add the milk, wine, and reserved water a little at a time, stirring constantly to prevent lumps. Season the sauce with lemon juice, salt, and white pepper.

Spoon 1 cup of sauce into a small bowl and whisk in the egg yolks. Return the sauce to the pan and mix well. Pour the sauce over the chicken and green beans. Bake for 25 minutes. Serve hot.

Preparation Time: 30 minutes
Baking Time: 25 minutes
Yield: 6 servings

Beans Going By? Try Green Bean Potato Pancakes.

Combine ½ pound grated potatoes with ½ pound finely diced green beans, and a couple of diced scallions. Hold the batter together with 2–3 eggs. Fry the batter by the tablespoon in butter and oil. Top with freshly ground pepper. Delicious! The Swiss call this dish Green Bean Roësti.

Beets

Savor The Nutritious Greens and Flavorful Roots of This No-Fail Vegetable

My fondness for beets probably begins with the fact that I have never had a failure with them in the garden. They grow almost troublefree, providing a feast of greens early in the season; sweet, tender beets throughout the summer; and no-fuss storage beets in the fall. Even if I didn't enjoy eating them, I'd probably plant a wide row of beets just for their lush purple and green foliage.

Because each beet seed is actually a pod containing several seeds, beets require thinning. A few weeks after the first thinning with a rake, I thin to harvest the small greens, which are delicious briefly steamed or stir fried. I like to serve them with a pat of butter, a splash of lemon juice or tamari, or a dollop of sour cream.

Thinnings continue throughout the summer. Early thinnings yield baby beets that I peel and cook separately from the greens. Later thinnings yield beets that are a tender 1–2 inches in diameter. The greens stay tender throughout the season, although I have to spend more time finding nice-looking leaves to cook. The stems of the greens do get tough, so I remove them and just steam the leaves.

Have You Ever Eaten Raw Beets? They Are Delicious!

Beets lend themselves to both hot and cold dishes and can be eaten cooked or raw. I never tasted raw beets until I started growing my own, and looking for ways to bypass the comparatively long cooking times beets require. They are delicious! I like to slice large beets into finger-size sticks and serve them with dips.

A food processor makes fast, neat work of slicing raw beets to uniform, rounded shoestrings, which are terrific to add to a green salad or to combine with other grated vegetables. Grated raw beets are good steamed or stir fried.

Beets have one unfortunate characteristic: They bleed and stain. When I'm preparing beets, I cover my wooden chopping board with plastic film wrap to protect it. And I never serve beets in wooden bowls. When cooking beets, if you leave about an inch of stem, don't trim the tap root, and don't peel the root, the beets will bleed less, but they will still bleed. Golden beets bleed and stain less. I think the golden beets are fine as a novelty, but I love the color of red beets too much to grow any other kind.

In this Beet Stir Fry (page 55), the beets have a slightly crunchy texture and a distinctly spicy flavor. I'm so glad I discovered how easy it is to cook with grated raw beets!

Harvest Beets All Season Long

Harvest beet greens as soon as they are big enough to eat.

Continue to harvest the greens and small beets all summer.

My favorite size beet is about 2 inches in diameter—a 3-bite beet if served whole, yet large enough to handle easily for dicing and slicing.

Beets that are to be stored in a root cellar should be harvested as late as possible (before the ground freezes).

Beets can be stored in the refrigerator for 2–3 weeks.

Yields

1 pound fresh beets equals
   3 cups raw or cooked cubed beets
or
   4 cups raw or cooked diced or sliced beets
or
   4 cups raw grated beets
1 pound cooked beets plus ¼ cup water equals
   2 cups puree for dips and soups
1 pound beet greens equals
   1½–2 cups cooked greens

There are few tastes fresher than briefly cooked beet greens and baby beets.

I like to gather a handful of beet greens and marble-sized beets and sauté them in butter with a few scallions. If there are peas ready, too, I'll throw those in the pan, along with some sliced radishes. The secret is to cook these very tender young vegetables ever so quickly.

BEETS AT A GLANCE

Don't throw out woody, overgrown beets! They are excellent grated or pureed.

Grated beets can be sautéed in a little butter until well coated. Then add a little water, cover the pot, and cook the beets for 4–8 minutes, stirring occasionally. They will be tender crisp and simply delicious.

Overgrown beets can be pureed for use in soups and dips. To make a puree, cook the beets until tender. Peel and chop. Process in a food processor or blender with ¼ cup water for each pound of beets until the puree is smooth. You can freeze the puree or use it in your favorite recipe.

Leave 1 inch of stem. Do not trim off tap root.

Preparing Beets for the Table: Cook, Then Peel

Beets should be cooked before they are peeled to retain color and flavor.

One way I prepare beets is by baking them. This way there is less bleeding of color.

Wash the beets and trim off the greens and tap root. Pour about an inch of water in a baking dish and set the beets on a rack over the water. Cover the baking dish. Bake at 350° F. Two-inch beets will be tender in 1½ hours. Cool the beets in cold water and the skins will slip off easily.

You can also boil or steam beets. Boiling beets in water to cover takes less time than steaming takes, while steaming results in less flavor and color loss. But it is easy to run out of steaming water and burn the pot. I prefer baking, but I will boil beets when I don't want to heat up the kitchen. When boiling, baking, or steaming whole beets, be sure to wash the beets well, leave 1 inch of stem, and do not trim off the tap root.

Cooking Times

Steam(2–3-inch whole beets):
   15–20 minutes
   (½-inch cubes): 10–12 minutes
   (grated): 4–8 minutes
Blanch (2–3-inch whole beets):
   20–25 minutes
   (½-inch cubes): 8 minutes
Splash sauté or stir fry (grated):
   4–8 minutes
Beets are done when they are easily pierced by a fork.

Raw or cooked: beets belong in salads

Grated raw beets are absolutely wonderful added to green salads! I use even large, overgrown woody beets for this salad garnish—the woodiness is undetectable. I prefer to use young beets, however. If the leaves are in good shape, I will trim the stems and add the chopped greens to the salad, too. The greens are just a little tough so I chop them in small pieces. I add grated beets to salads at the last possible moment so they don't stain the greens.

There are dozens of beet salads you can make. Here are some of my favorites. These salads all use cooked beets, which makes them a convenient choice when I have leftovers or extras from pickling and canning.

Beet Vinaigrette

Combine cooked diced beets with a vinaigrette dressing (page 300). You can also add diagonally sliced celery, sliced radishes, sliced hard-boiled eggs, or chopped watercress.

Beets and Orange Salad

Slice cooked beets and combine with orange sections and minced scallions. Pour Honey Curry Dressing (page 303) over the salad.

Beets and Apple Salad

Dice cooked beets and combine with diced apples in a vinaigrette dressing (page 300) or Honey Curry Dressing (page 303).

You can sprinkle fresh, raw grated beets onto any green salad. Do it at the last minute because the beets stain the other vegetables. A particularly tasty salad is made by combining grated raw beets, grated carrots, nuts, grapes, and a vinaigrette dressing. There's lots you can do with grated raw beets!

Above: you have a choice of a sweet or tart dressing for this fall-inspired Beet and Apple Salad.

Beets 51

APPETIZERS

There are many recipes for pickled beets. The brine I developed for Pickled Beets and Purple Eggs could also be used as a basis for canning pickled beets.

Pickled Beets and Purple Eggs

You could also make this dish with your own favorite pickled beets. Simply open a jar of pickled beets and combine with the eggs. The egg whites turn purple in 3 days. Although they become a little rubbery in the process, the eggs are a delight served with the pickled beets as an appetizer, relish, or salad.

6 cups diced cooked beets
6–12 hard-boiled eggs, peeled
2 cups water
1½ cups white vinegar or wine vinegar
1½ cups sugar
1 cinnamon stick
20 whole cloves
5 allspice berries

Place the beets and eggs in a large glass or ceramic jar. Combine the remaining ingredients in a saucepan and heat. Pour the brine over the beets and eggs. Store in the refrigerator for 1 or 2 days before eating. The eggs will keep for 1 week, the beets for 2 weeks.

Preparation Time: 30 minutes
Yield: 8–10 servings

Variations
Marbled Eggs. Instead of peeling the hard-boiled eggs, tap the warm eggs with a teaspoon to crack the shells all over. Place the eggs in the jar. When you peel the eggs, the whites will be marbled pink.

Beet Cups

Boil whole small beets in their skins until tender, about 25 minutes. Slide off the skins, and hollow out part of the beet. Marinate the beet in a vinaigrette dressing (page 300) for about 1 hour. Then fill it with cream cheese flavored with horseradish.

Here's an appetizer that's sure to be a conversation starter. Aren't the colors of the Pickled Beets and Eggs beautiful!

SOUPS

Most beet soups are good served hot or cold.

Borscht

¾ pound hot Italian-style sausage, casing removed, or ¾ pound ground beef, or 6 slices bacon
1½ cups diced onion
2 garlic cloves, minced
3 cups diced raw beets
4 cups peeled and chopped plum tomatoes, or thick tomato puree
4 cups water or broth
½ cup red wine
3–4 tablespoons lemon juice (juice from 1 lemon)
1 tablespoon brown sugar
2 bay leaves, crumbled
¼ teaspoon ground cloves
¾ teaspoon dried thyme
salt and pepper
3 cups finely chopped cabbage

In a large soup pot, brown the sausage, breaking it up with a spoon. Drain off all but 3 tablespoons of fat, and sauté the onion and garlic in the fat until limp, 3–5 minutes. Add the beets, tomatoes, water, wine, lemon juice, brown sugar, and seasonings. Simmer the soup for about 1 hour. Add more water if needed. Season to taste with salt and pepper. During the last 10 minutes of cooking time, add the cabbage. This borscht is excellent reheated the next day.

Preparation Time: 30 minutes
Cooking Time: 1 hour
Yield: 6–8 servings

Pink Swirl Soup

This soup has no equal when it comes to appearance. It is a beautiful white potato soup with a beet puree marbled in.

3 tablespoons butter
4 large leeks, quartered and diced (4 cups)
5 cups finely diced potatoes
6 cups chicken broth
¾ cup heavy or light cream
¾ cup milk
salt and pepper
2 cups diced cooked beets

In a soup pot, melt the butter and sauté the leeks until they are wilted, about 3 minutes. Add the potatoes and the broth. Cook the soup until the potatoes are tender, 15–20 minutes. Cool the soup slightly and process it in a blender or food processor until smooth. Add the cream and milk. Season to taste with salt and pepper.

In a blender or food processor, puree the beets until smooth. Add 2 cups of the soup and process until smooth.

Ladle the hot soup into individual bowls or a clear glass serving bowl. Pour a little beet and potato puree into each bowl and swirl it with a spoon.

If you would like to serve this soup cold, chill the potato soup and the beet and potato puree separately and swirl together at the last minute. The beet and potato puree can be mixed completely with the potato soup for shocking pink soup.

Preparation Time: 30 minutes
Cooking Time: 15–20 minutes
Yield: 6–8 servings

A blender or a food processor is a must for this unusual soup. Basically, this is a vichysoisse mixed with a beet puree.

Leftover Beets Pose No Problem

Leftover cooked beets can be made into a wonderful dip for raw vegetables. Simply process the cooked beets in a food processor until you have a smooth puree. For every 1 cup of puree, combine with 8 ounces cream cheese, 1 tablespoon prepared horseradish, 1 teaspoon Dijon-style mustard, 2 tablespoons minced red onion, ¼ teaspoon salt, and 1 tablespoon grated orange rind. Mix it all together in a food processor and chill well before serving.

SIDE DISHES AND MAIN DISHES

"There must be something new I can make with beets," I said to myself one summer morning over a heaping basketful. It was a hot day, and I didn't want to heat the kitchen with baking. I decided to try a stir fry with beets and other vegetables that were ready in the garden. It was delicious! The next day, I experimented with baking grated beets, and the Blushin' Beet Pie was invented. If I do say so myself, it is one of the most colorful and satisfying vegetarian dishes I have ever had.

Mustard Honey Beets

Melt 2 tablespoons butter in a large sauté pan, and add 6 cups diced cooked beets. Toss to coat. Add 2 tablespoons Dijon-style mustard and 2 tablespoons honey. Continue cooking until the beets are heated through. Serves 6.

Beets in Orange Ginger Sauce

Melt 2 tablespoons butter in a large sauté pan, and add 6 cups diced cooked beets. Toss to coat. Add ¾ cup orange juice and 1½ teaspoons minced fresh ginger root. Continue cooking until the beets are heated through. Serves 6.

Minted Beets

Melt 2 tablespoons butter in a large sauté pan, and add 6 cups diced cooked beets. Toss to coat. Stir in 1 tablespoon fresh minced mint or 1 tablespoon mint jelly. Season to taste with salt and pepper. Sauté until heated through. Serves 6.

Breaded Fried Beets

Slice raw, peeled beets very thin. Dip the slices in a beaten egg, then in seasoned bread crumbs. Fry in oil on both sides over medium heat until browned. Serves 6.

1. Slice ¼ inch thick.

2. Dip in eggs, then in crumbs.

Ruby Red Sauce for Chicken or Pork

I find that vegetable-based sauces add a fresh, light taste to meat. This beet sauce, should be much lower in calories than a flour-thickened gravy.

2 cups grated raw beets
1½ cups peeled and grated apple
3 tablespoons dry red wine
2 tablespoons honey
2 tablespoons lemon juice
1 teaspoon grated lemon rind
3–4 tablespoons prepared horseradish
salt and pepper

In a medium-size saucepan, combine the beets, apple, wine, honey, lemon juice, and lemon rind. Add just enough water to cover. Cook for 15–20 minutes or until the beets are tender. Place this mixture in a food processor or blender and process until smooth. Add the horseradish, season to taste with salt and pepper, and reheat. Spoon the sauce over sautéed chicken breasts or pork chops.

Preparation Time: 20 minutes
Cooking Time: 20–30 minutes
Yield: 3 cups (6–8 servings)

Beet Stir Fry

6 tablespoons vegetable oil
1¼ cups scallions sliced in 2-inch pieces (8–10 scallions including green tops)
2 cups sliced red radishes
2 cups broccoli florets
⅓ cup water
6 cups grated raw beets
½ cup orange juice
2 teaspoons minced fresh ginger root
1½ cups grated white radish (daikon) or whole mung bean sprouts
2 teaspoons tamari or soy sauce

In a wok, heat 2 tablespoons of the vegetable oil. Stir fry the scallions and red radishes until the scallions are wilted. Transfer the scallions and radishes to a bowl.

Heat 2 more tablespoons of the oil. Add the broccoli. Stir fry for about 1 minute. Add ⅓ cup water and continue cooking and stirring until the broccoli is tender crisp. Add the broccoli to the radishes and scallions.

Add the remaining 2 tablespoons of oil to the wok. Stir fry the beets for 1 minute to coat them with oil. Add the orange juice and ginger. Continue to stir fry the beets until they are tender crisp, 5–10 minutes. Add the white radish to the wok, and toss to mix. Add the scallions, red radishes, and broccoli. Season with tamari or soy sauce. Stir fry just enough to heat. Serve at once.

Preparation Time: 20 minutes
Cooking Time: 15 minutes
Yield: 6–8 servings

Blushin' Beet Pie

1 cup all-purpose unbleached flour
¼ teaspoon salt
¼ cup sesame seeds
⅓ cup butter
2–4 tablespoons cold water
4 cups grated raw beets
2 cups grated raw carrots
2 tablespoons butter
1 cup diced onion
¾ cup chopped cashews
1¼ cups grated Swiss cheese

Preheat the oven to 425° F.

To make the pie dough, mix the flour, salt, and sesame seeds. Cut in ⅓ cup butter until the mixture resembles gravel and cornmeal. Add the water and mix to form a ball. Wrap the dough with plastic film wrap, and chill while you prepare the filling.

In a large bowl, combine the beets and carrots.

In a sauté pan, melt the butter and sauté the onion and cashews, until the onion is translucent and the cashews are browned. Add the onion mixture to the beets and carrots. Toss in the cheese and mix.

On a floured board, roll out the dough to a 12-inch circle. Transfer the dough to a 10-inch pie pan and ease the dough in to fit. Trim and crimp the edges.

Pour in the filling. Bake at 425° F. for 15 minutes, covered with foil. Then turn the oven down to 350° F., and bake uncovered for 30 minutes more. Serve hot.

Preparation Time: 30 minutes
Baking Time: 45 minutes
Yield: 8 servings

Pickled Beets and Radishes

The radishes take on the color of the beets, but they keep their distinctive crunch in this relish. An alternative to this recipe is to open up a quart of your favorite pickled beets and toss in 1½ cups of sliced radishes.

1 cup sugar
1 cup white vinegar
½ cup water
½ teaspoon salt
½ cup diced onion
3 cups sliced radishes
6 cups sliced cooked beets

In a small saucepan, heat the sugar, vinegar, water, and salt until the sugar is melted. Combine the remaining ingredients in a bowl and pour on the marinade. Set aside for at least 4 hours before serving. This will keep in the refrigerator for 5 days.

Preparation Time: 15 minutes
Marinating Time: at least 4 hours
Yield: 10–12 servings

Here I am trimming beets before I peel and grate them raw. If I were planning to cook these beets, I'd trim the stems to leave an inch of stem. That way they bleed less. I'd also leave an inch of stem if I were preparing these beets for the root cellar; they keep better that way.

Broccoli

Keep Harvesting Those Side Shoots— They're Just as Tender as the Main Head.

I'll never forget the first time I served my own homegrown broccoli. Being a novice gardener, I didn't know about cabbage worms. I didn't know that those bright green uninvited guests cling almost invisibly to the broccoli, not even letting go while the broccoli steams. Yes, you guessed it. I served "Broccoli a la Worm" that night.

No More Cabbage Worms

Since then I've learned that *most* of the cabbage worms will float up to the surface of the water if you soak broccoli in salted ice water for about 30 minutes before cooking. I've also learned to give each stalk a careful examination for worms—just in case! Even better, I've learned that I can spray broccoli (and the other plants in the cabbage family) with a safe, nonchemical worm killer, *Bacillus thuringiensis*. It's a spray made of naturally occurring bacteria and sold under various brand names, including BT, Dipel, and Thuricide. No more worms for me!

Broccoli is a delight for the cook. It can be prepared very simply—just steamed or blanched until tender crisp. Then served plain, with butter, or with a simple sauce. Or it can be combined with other vegetables in stir fries or casseroles. However broccoli is prepared, it always retains its distinctive taste and adds a pleasing texture to the dish or meal.

As a gardener, I really appreciate broccoli for the many pounds of side shoots I can cut after I have harvested the main head. These side shoots are just as tasty and tender as the main head, but they must be harvested every few days to prevent them from flowering.

In hot weather, broccoli tends to go to seed pretty quickly. You can still harvest when the buds just begin to open, but as soon as the yellow flowers appear, cut off the head or side shoot and compost— it is too tough and bitter to serve. Wait for new shoots to grow.

Broccoli is an excellent candidate for the freezer. I like to freeze whole stalks, which I steam for 3 minutes, cool in ice water, drain dry, and bag. In most of the recipes in this chapter, except the stir fries and salads, the dishes will be just as tasty with frozen or fresh broccoli.

With broccoli, everything works from complicated casseroles to simple salads. One of my favorite dishes is Broccoli Tempura. You'll find the batter recipe on page 309.

BROCCOLI AT A GLANCE

Ready for harvest:
full head with tight buds

Harvesting Tips

Harvest the main head before the tight blossoms begin to open, regardless of the size.

Slice off the head with about 3 inches of the stalk.

Continue to harvest the side shoots that form on the stem. Don't let these side shoots blossom or the plant will stop producing.

Yields

1 pound of fresh broccoli equals
  5–6 cups florets and sliced stems
or
  5 cups chopped broccoli
or
  4 cups finely chopped or diced broccoli
or
  4 cups pureed raw in a food processor
or
  3 cups cooked and pureed

Cooking Timetable

Broccoli should be cooked until it is bright green and tender crisp.
  Steam: 4–6 minutes
  Blanch: 3–6 minutes
  Stir Fry or Sauté: about 5 minutes
  Parboil for Salads: 2 minutes,
    then plunge into cold water

Different Ways to Slice Broccoli

Florets and Sliced Stems: My Favorite Way. First I cut off the florets so they are about 1½ inches long. I slice the florets so that they are no more than ½ inch in diameter—small enough to be eaten in one bite. Then I thinly slice the stems straight across or on the diagonal.

The stems can also be sliced in julienne matchsticks or into pieces the size of french fries.

Turned Stalks: The Fancy Way to Slice the Stems. Cut the stalks into 2-inch lengths. Using a knife, peel and shape the broccoli into football shapes. I serve parboiled turned stalks with other raw vegetables and dips, or I cook them in stir fries.

Chopped Broccoli. A chef's knife is all you need to roughly chop the broccoli, and a food processor with a pulsing action does a nice job of finely chopping broccoli.

When broccoli goes by, the head begins to flower

I Don't Believe in Peeling Broccoli Stalks—It's a Waste of Effort

My garden-fresh broccoli never gets a chance to grow woody. In hot weather, broccoli will flower before it becomes woody, so I rarely peel the stems. Broccoli that is woody enough to require peeling is best in soups and purees.

Making Broccoli Purees

Steam broccoli over boiling water for 4–6 minutes. In a food processor or blender, combine the broccoli with a small amount of water and process until smooth.

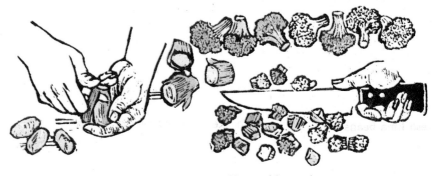

Turned stalks   *Chopped broccoli*

Broccoli is so tasty; most people prefer to eat it served simply. I like to top steamed broccoli with crumbled cheeses or bacon bits or toasted nuts or bread crumbs.

It's exciting to cook the first broccoli heads Of the season

I like to serve the first harvest of broccoli simply. Usually I slice the heads into serving-size spears and steam until tender crisp, 4–6 minutes. An extra large steaming basket can handle a large quantity at a time, without crowding the spears or overcooking. Plan to prepare the broccoli just before serving so the spears don't overcook.

Sauces

There are many sauces that are especially delicious on broccoli spears. Hollandaise Sauce (page 307) is my favorite. I also recommend Lemon Butter (page 304), Dijon Sauce (page 305), Caraway Mustard Sauce (page 305), any cheese sauce (pages 305–306), Hot Horseradish Cream Sauce (page 305), and any tomato sauce (page 306).

Sprinkled Toppings

My "sprinkled toppings" take less time to prepare than a sauce. Crumbled blue cheese, freshly grated parmesan cheese, toasted nuts, and crumbled bacon make tasty toppings for broccoli.

Buttered bread crumbs are another favorite. Just melt ¼ cup butter in a sauté pan. Add 1 cup dry bread crumbs and sauté until the crumbs are lightly browned. If you like, add 1 teaspoon dried herbs to the pan as you sauté. Sprinkle the bread crumbs on 4–6 servings of broccoli spears—simple and delicious.

Color is the best way to gauge whether or not broccoli is cooked to the tender crisp stage. The color is bright green, without a trace of olive. Whole spears should hold their shape well when lifted with a fork; they should not be limp.

If there are leftovers when I prepare these spreads to serve with raw vegetables or crackers, I use them in sandwiches.

Broccoli Feta Cheese Log

¾ pound broccoli
1 large garlic clove, minced
2 scallions, finely chopped
12 ounces cream cheese
¾ cup crumbled feta cheese
2 tablespoons minced fresh dill

Using a sharp knife, cut away the very tops of the broccoli flowers, so the pieces resemble green crumbs or tiny buds. Finely chop the remaining broccoli. The flower buds should equal ¾ cup, and the chopped broccoli should equal 2 cups. Set aside the buds.

Steam the chopped broccoli until bright green and tender crisp, 2–3 minutes. Plunge into cold water and drain well.

In a food processor or mixing bowl, combine the garlic, scallions, cream cheese, feta, and dill. Process until well blended. Mix in the chopped broccoli and chill the cheese until firm, about 2 hours.

Shape the cheese into a log, and press the broccoli buds into the surface. Garnish with carrot matchsticks. Serve with crackers or raw vegetables.

Preparation Time: 20 minutes
Chilling Time: 2 hours
Yield: 6–8 servings

The Broccoli Feta Cheese Log is a rich appetizer that I make for parties. It's a favorite of mine because I can make it up in advance and keep it chilled. Also, it is attractive served plain or garnished. The carrot matchsticks make a simple garnish, but you could use any of the radish garnishes from page 237 as well. Serve it with crackers and provide a knife for spreading. Leftovers are great in sandwiches.

1. With wet hands, shape the cheese mixture into a log.

2. Press the broccoli buds onto the surface.

If these soups don't tickle your fancy, try substituting broccoli in any of the soups in the cauliflower and spinach chapters.

Broccoli Tarragon Soup

2 tablespoons vegetable oil
1½ cups finely diced onion
3 tablespoons minced fresh tarragon
   or 1 tablespoon dried
6 cups finely chopped broccoli
2 cups chicken broth or water
1½ cups buttermilk
1 tablespoon lemon juice
salt and pepper

Heat the vegetable oil in a soup pot, and sauté the onion and tarragon until the onion is limp, 3–5 minutes. Add the broccoli and chicken broth. Simmer until the broccoli is tender, about 15 minutes. Cool the soup slightly. In a blender or food processor, combine the soup with the buttermilk and blend until smooth. Add the lemon juice and tarragon. Season to taste with salt and pepper. Serve the soup cold.

Preparation Time: 15 minutes
Cooking Time: 20 minutes
Chilling Time: 2 hours
Yield: 6 servings

Broccoli Soup With Blue Cheese

I prefer this soup hot, but it can be served cold if it is thinned with some extra milk.

6 cups finely chopped broccoli
¼ cup vegetable oil or butter
1½ cups chopped onion
1 tablespoon fresh thyme or
   1 teaspoon dried
2 cups chicken broth
salt and pepper
¾ cup crumbled blue cheese
3½ cups milk

Reserve ¼ cup of tiny broccoli florets for a garnish.

In a large soup pot, heat the oil, and sauté the onion and remaining broccoli for 3–5 minutes, until the onion is translucent, but not browned.

Add the thyme and chicken broth. Season to taste with salt and pepper. Simmer until the broccoli is very tender, about 15 minutes. Crumble in the blue cheese. Add milk until the soup reaches the desired consistency.

Cool the soup slightly and puree in a food processor or blender. Return the soup to the pot and reheat gently, but do not boil. Adjust salt and pepper, if necessary. Garnish with the broccoli florets.

Preparation Time: 20 minutes
Cooking Time: 20–25 minutes
Yield: 6–8 servings

I particularly like to use the small broccoli side shoots in salads because the florets are more attractive than sliced stems.

Broccoli, Summer Squash, and Bacon Salad

This salad must be served immediately after you pour the hot dressing on it, or the bacon grease will congeal.

¼ pound bacon, finely diced
4–5 cups broccoli florets and sliced
   stems
2 cups julienne-sliced summer
   squash
2 tablespoons lemon juice
1 teaspoon prepared horseradish

Fry the bacon until browned, and drain on a paper towel. Reserve 3 tablespoons of the bacon grease.

Steam the broccoli over boiling water until barely tender crisp, 3–4 minutes. Plunge into cold water, and drain. Steam the summer squash for about 2 minutes, and plunge into cold water. Drain.

In a small saucepan, combine the reserved bacon fat, lemon juice, and horseradish. Heat to simmering. Toss the vegetables and bacon together. Pour the hot dressing over the salad. Toss to coat. Serve immediately.

Preparation Time: 25 minutes
Cooking Time: 5 minutes
Yield: 6–8 servings

Broccoli and Barley Salad

This salad is a meal in itself on a hot summer night.

4 cups water
2 cups uncooked pearl barley
5 cups broccoli florets and
   sliced stems
1 cup diced carrots
½ cup diced scallions
½ cup julienne-sliced sweet red
   pepper
1 cup chopped nuts
½ cup vegetable or olive oil
¼ cup wine vinegar
½ cup lemon juice
2 teaspoons grated lemon rind
1 garlic clove, minced
1 tablespoon minced fresh mint
½ teaspoon salt
pepper

Bring the water to a boil and add the barley. Cover and cook for 30 minutes, until the barley is just barely tender. Drain and rinse with cold water until cooled. Drain well.

Steam the broccoli over boiling water until barely tender crisp, 3–4 minutes. Plunge into cold water. Drain.

In a large salad bowl, toss the broccoli, carrots, scallions, red pepper, and nuts with the barley.

In a food processor or blender, combine the remaining ingredients to make a dressing. Blend until well mixed. Pour the dressing over the salad and marinate for 1 hour before serving. Serve chilled.

Preparation Time: 1 hour
Cooling Time: 1 hour
Yield: 8 servings

SIDE DISHES AND MAIN DISHES

There is no end to the variety of dishes you can prepare with broccoli. This collection but skims the surface. Again, if you like, try substituting broccoli for spinach or cauliflower in your favorite recipes.

Broccoli-Pesto Stuffed Tomatoes

I use only broccoli stalks in this recipe, and save the more tender florets for stir fries and salads. This dish is delicious hot or cold.

3 cups finely diced broccoli stems
6 tablespoons Pesto (page 161)
salt and pepper
6 medium-size tomatoes

Steam the broccoli over boiling water for 4–6 minutes, until barely tender. Mix gently with the Pesto. Taste and adjust the seasoning.

Scoop out the centers of the tomatoes. Fill with the broccoli pesto. Serve chilled.

If you prefer to serve this dish hot, sprinkle with grated parmesan cheese and bake at 350° F. for 10–15 minutes until the tomatoes are soft but not mushy.

Preparation Time: 15 minutes
Chilling Time: 1 hour
  or Baking Time: 10–15 minutes
Yield: 6 servings

Broccoli and Fish With Lemon Sauce

Swordfish is a good fish for this dish, but at today's prices, I have sometimes substituted the relatively unacclaimed, but tasty, shark. Turbot, halibut, and haddock are excellent in this dish, too.

2 tablespoons butter
1 pound firm white fish, cut in
   cubes
1 cup sliced mushrooms
¾ cup sliced scallions with green
   tops
¾ cup water
½ cup dry white wine
1 tablespoon grated lemon rind
4 tablespoons lemon juice
4 cups broccoli florets and sliced
   stems
1½ cups quartered cherry tomatoes
1 tablespoon cornstarch
½ teaspoon ground fennel
salt and pepper

In a large frying pan or wok, melt the butter and add the fish, mushrooms, scallions, ¼ cup of the water, ¼ cup of the wine, the lemon rind, and 2 tablespoons of the lemon juice. Stir gently to mix. Cover. Let the vegetables and fish poach until the fish is cooked, 8–10 minutes.

Meanwhile, steam the broccoli until bright green and tender crisp, 4–6 minutes. Set aside.

When the fish is cooked and flakes easily with a fork, add the tomatoes to the pan.

Pour the poaching liquid into a separate pot. Mix 1 tablespoon of the liquid with the cornstarch. Add the remaining ½ cup water, ¼ cup wine, 2 tablespoons lemon juice, and the fennel to the cornstarch mixture, and add

The dressing is quickly absorbed in this Broccoli and Barley Salad. So serve it at once, or make extra dressing to pour over the salad just before you serve. You can use any nuts in this hearty salad; I recommend pecans.

this mixture to the poaching liquid. Season to taste with salt and pepper. Cook over high heat until the mixture thickens, about 2 minutes.

Add the broccoli to the fish and vegetables. Pour the sauce over the fish and vegetables. Reheat and toss to coat. Serve immediately.

Preparation Time: 30 minutes
Cooking Time: 15 minutes
Yield: 6 servings

Broccoli and Carrots With Curry Yogurt Sauce

In a large sauté pan, melt 3 tablespoons butter and add 2 tablespoons mustard seeds, 2 teaspoons curry powder, and ½ teaspoon ground cardamom. Add 4–6 cups broccoli florets and sliced stems and 2 cups sliced carrots. Pour in ¼ cup water, cover, and cook until the broccoli is bright green and tender crisp, about 5 minutes. Add ¼ cup yogurt and salt and pepper to taste. Stir to coat with sauce and serve immediately. Serves 6.

Broccoli, Garlic, And Ginger Stir Fry

Heat 2 tablespoons peanut or vegetable oil in a wok. Add 2 minced garlic cloves and 2 teaspoons minced fresh ginger root. Add 5–6 cups broccoli florets and julienne-sliced stems. Stir fry to coat with oil. Add 2 tablespoons water and 1 table-spoon tamari or soy sauce. Continue to stir fry until the broccoli is bright green and tender crisp, 3–4 minutes. Serve at once. Serves 6.

Broccoli Soufflé Roll

4 tablespoons butter
½ cup all-purpose unbleached flour
2 cups milk
1 cup grated cheddar cheese
¼ teaspoon salt
4 eggs
2 tablespoons vegetable oil
2 cups finely diced onions
4 cups finely chopped broccoli
¼ cup water
1½ cups finely diced ham (½ pound)
8 ounces cream cheese
2 teaspoons Dijon-style mustard

Preheat the oven to 325° F.

In medium-size saucepan, melt the butter and stir in the flour to make a smooth paste. Add the milk, a little at a time, stirring well after each addition to prevent lumps from forming. Stir in the cheddar cheese and salt. The mixture will be very thick.

Separate the eggs and beat the egg whites until stiff.

Mix a little of the cheese sauce in with the egg yolks to temper them. Add the remaining sauce and mix well. Carefully fold the beaten egg whites into the cheese sauce.

Grease a 15-inch by 1-inch jelly roll pan and line with waxed paper. Grease and flour the paper. Spoon in the soufflé mixture and spread it evenly. Bake for 35–40 minutes.

While the soufflé roll bakes, prepare the filling. In a saucepan, heat the oil, and sauté the onions until limp, 3–5 minutes. Add the broccoli and water. Cover and cook for 2 minutes, stirring occasionally. The broccoli should be bright green and tender crisp.

Add the ham. Cut the cream cheese into small chunks. Stir in the cream cheese and cook over low heat until it is melted and coats the vegetables. Stir in the mustard and set this filling mixture aside. Keep warm.

When the soufflé roll is golden brown on top, remove it from the oven and immediately turn it out onto another sheet of waxed paper. Peel off the waxed paper from the bottom. Spread the warm filling evenly over the roll. Roll the soufflé lengthwise, using the waxed paper to help you. Transfer the soufflé roll to a heated platter, slice into pieces and serve.

If you can't serve immediately, the soufflé roll can be kept cold until you are ready to serve it. Reheat the soufflé roll covered with foil in a 375° F. oven for 20 minutes.

Preparation Time: 45 minutes
Baking Time: 35–40 minutes
Yield: 6 servings

Broccoli and Oyster Sauce Stir Fry

Heat 2 tablespoons peanut or vegetable oil in a wok. Add 5–6 cups broccoli florets and julienne-sliced stems. Stir fry briefly to coat with oil. Add 2 tablespoons water and continue to stir fry until the broccoli is bright green and tender crisp, 3–4 minutes. Add 2 tablespoons oyster sauce and ½ teaspoon five spice powder. Stir fry to coat. Serve at once. Serves 6.

Broccoli-Filled Chicken Breasts

Leftovers from this recipe — if there ever are any — are delicious sliced in a sandwich.

2 cups finely chopped broccoli
4 tablespoons butter
¼ cup chopped scallions with some green tops
1 cup ricotta cheese
1 teaspoon grated lemon rind
4 teaspoons lemon juice
salt and white pepper
4 whole boneless chicken breasts with skins
approximately 1 cup chicken broth
2 tablespoons all-purpose unbleached flour

Preheat the oven to 350° F.

Steam the broccoli until it is barely bright green and tender crisp, 2–3 minutes.

1. Spoon filling under skin.

2. Fold skin over filling.

Melt 1 tablespoon of the butter, and sauté the scallions until limp. Combine the broccoli, scallions, ricotta, lemon rind, and 3 teaspoons of the lemon juice. Season to taste with salt and white pepper.

Divide the chicken breasts in half to make 8 portions. Peel back the skin and spoon in some filling. Cover the filling with the skin and curl the edges of the breast under to form a tight log-shaped roll. Place the chicken breasts in a buttered baking dish. Brush the top of the chicken with 1 tablespoon melted butter and bake for 50–55 minutes.

Drain and reserve the liquid from the chicken breasts and keep them warm. Add enough chicken broth to the liquid to equal 2 cups.

Melt the remaining 2 tablespoons of butter. Stir in the flour to form a smooth paste. Pour in the chicken broth, a little at a time, stirring well after each addition to prevent lumps from forming. Season the sauce with the remaining 1 teaspoon of lemon juice and salt and pepper to taste.

Slice the breasts and arrange on a serving platter to make neatly overlapping ½-inch slices or leave the breasts whole. Then pour the sauce over the chicken and serve.

Preparation Time: 30 minutes
Baking Time: 50–55 minutes
Yield: 8 servings

Broccoli and Beef Stir Fry

1 pound lean steak (flank, sirloin, or any other steak)
1 tablespoon dry sherry
1 tablespoon tamari or soy sauce
1 tablespoon minced fresh ginger root
3 tablespoons water
1 teaspoon cornstarch
4 tablespoons vegetable oil
6 cups broccoli florets and sliced stems
2 cups grated winter squash
1 cup sliced scallions
1 cup water chestnuts
½ cup oyster sauce

Slice the meat into very thin slices about 2 inches long, 1 inch wide, and ¼ inch thick. Place in a glass or ceramic bowl.

Mix the sherry, tamari, ginger root, water, and cornstarch. Pour this marinade over the meat, stir, and set aside while you prepare the vegetables.

Heat 2 tablespoons of the vegetable oil in the wok or large frying pan. Stir fry the broccoli and grated winter squash until the broccoli is bright green and tender crisp, about 5 minutes. Remove the broccoli and squash from the pan.

Heat the remaining oil in the wok. Stir fry the beef with the marinade until the beef is barely browned, about 5 minutes. Add the scallions and water chestnuts. Continue to stir fry until the steak is cooked. Add the broccoli, squash, and oyster sauce. Toss to coat. Serve immediately.

Preparation Time: 35 minutes
Cooking Time: 10–15 minutes
Yield: 6 servings

Broccoli-Filled Chicken Breasts: quick to make, great for company!

Brussels Sprouts

A Delicate Taste Treat When You Grow Your Own — And Don't Overcook

I think I know why brussels sprouts aren't half as popular as they should be. Too many people have eaten old, supermarket brussels sprouts or sprouts grown in the hot summer weather that have developed a strong cabbage flavor. Too bad, because freshly harvested brussels sprouts grown in the cooler temperatures of spring and fall don't taste at all like cabbage.

For all their delicate flavor, brussels sprouts are surprisingly rugged plants. You can harvest brussels sprouts well into the fall, when most of your garden plants have succumbed to frosts. They don't even mind snow. I love having a source of fresh garden vegetables so late in the season.

You don't have to wait for a frost to harvest brussels sprouts. You can begin to pick the sprouts as soon as they are about the size of marbles. Five to seven days before harvesting, strip the bottom 6–8 inches of leaves from the plant stalk to stimulate growth in the sprouts. As you harvest from the bottom of the stalk up, continue to strip leaves from higher up the stalk. This technique will give you bigger sprouts.

Brussels Sprouts Are Tasty Raw, Too!

The tiny, marble-size brussels sprouts you harvest early in the season are tender enough to be eaten raw, sliced in half, in green salads and coleslaws. Sometimes I cook them just as I do larger brussels sprouts, but I reduce the cooking time.

I think another reason people say they don't like brussels sprouts is because they have only eaten them overcooked. Overcooking is the worst thing you can do to brussels sprouts. It turns them olive green in color, soggy in texture, and makes them taste like yesterday's cabbage. Properly cooked brussels sprouts are bright green, tender crisp, sweet, and flavorful.

I am stripping away the leaves of the brussels sprout plant. This will encourage the plant to grow bigger sprouts — which means more good eating!

BRUSSELS SPROUTS AT A GLANCE

Yields

1 pound fresh brussels sprouts
 equals 4 cups quartered or halved
or
 3½ cups whole

Storage

Brussels sprouts keep best if left unharvested in the garden.

In the refrigerator, store for up to one week in a perforated plastic bag.

Preparing for Cooking

One of the best features of brussels sprouts is that they require very little in the way of trimming and chopping.

Trim off the outer leaves until you have a tight, firm head.

With the tip of your paring knife, mark an x on the stem end to help make the cooking more even.

Cut large brussels sprouts in half or quarters lengthwise to guarantee even cooking.

Cook Brussels Sprouts Until Just Tender Crisp

Take the bite test to decide if the sprouts are cooked. The color should be bright green and the texture just slightly crunchy.

Steam: 5 minutes
Blanch: 5 minutes
Sauté or Stir Fry: 3–6 minutes

The Brussels Sprouts Appeal: Herbs and Sauces Complement Its Sweet Taste

Brussels sprouts can be sautéed with butter and caraway seeds, cumin, cardamom, basil, dill, oregano, sage, or marjoram.

Or sauté the sprouts in butter with prepared horseradish, mustard, lemon juice, orange juice, tamari or soy sauce, or sautéed onions, nuts, or seeds. Or sprinkle grated cheese over cooked sprouts.

Over steamed or sautéed brussels sprouts, pour any of the cream sauces, cheese sauces, or tomato-based sauces presented on page 306. Or try Hollandaise Sauce (page 307) or the Oriental Marinade and Dipping Sauce (page 303).

Halved or quartered brussels sprouts can be added to soups, casseroles, and stir fries.

Don't forget to serve halved brussels sprouts along with raw vegetables with dips.

Brussels sprout leaves become lily pads in soups.

Great in Salads

Before I add brussels sprouts to salads, I like to wilt the sprouts by pouring boiling water over them, then draining. This brings out the flavor and brightens the color.

Tiny brussels sprouts are delicious in green salads and coleslaws. Or combine parboiled brussels sprouts, cherry tomatoes, and black olives in a vinaigrette dressing (page 300).

Children's favorite: Brussels sprouts Meatballs

You can follow my recipe or just use my idea, and make up your own favorite meatball mixture.

Here's how I make the Brussels Sprouts Meatballs.

First, preheat the oven to 350° F.

In a large bowl, mix 1 pound of lean ground beef, ½ cup finely chopped onion, 1 beaten egg, 2 tablespoons grated parmesan cheese, 1 minced garlic clove, 2 tablespoons Italian tomato sauce, ½ teaspoon salt, ⅛ teaspoon pepper, and ¼ teaspoon each of dried oregano, thyme, and basil.

In another bowl, soak ¼ cup bread crumbs in 2 tablespoons milk, until the crumbs are softened. Add the crumbs to the meat and mix until everything is well blended.

Steam 24–30 small brussels sprouts for 5 minutes, until the sprouts are bright green and tender crisp. Plunge into cold water to cool, then drain.

Wrap each sprout in the meat until it is completely covered. Bake the meatballs for 20 minutes or until browned.

Heat about 1 quart of your favorite Italian tomato sauce (see page 306 for my recipe). Add the cooked meatballs to the sauce and simmer until you are ready to serve. This recipe serves 6.

1. Steam the brussels sprouts.

2. Press the meat over the sprouts.

3. Add to your favorite sauce.

4. Don't simmer too long. Serve hot over pasta.

Brussels Sprouts Are Never Boring

These three special brussels sprout dishes take very little time to prepare.

Creamed Brussels Sprouts

Place 4 cups of whole brussels sprouts in a baking dish. Quarter or halve them first if they are particularly big. Pour enough cream over them to cover the bottom of the dish with ½ inch cream. Sprinkle with salt and pepper to taste. Cover and bake for 20–30 minutes at 350° F.

Brussels Sprouts Tossed With Pecans and Butter

Steam 4 cups of brussels sprouts for 5 minutes, until tender crisp. Sauté ¼ cup finely chopped pecans and ½ teaspoon ground rosemary in 2 tablespoons butter until the nuts are roasted, about 5 minutes. Pour the nuts over the sprouts, season to taste with salt and pepper, and toss to coat. Serve immediately. Serves 4–6.

Brussels Sprouts With Orange Sauce

Steam 4 cups of brussels sprouts for 5 minutes, until tender crisp. Sauté ½ teaspoon grated orange rind, ½ cup orange juice, 1 cup chopped water chestnuts, and the brussels sprouts in 2 tablespoons butter for 2 minutes. Serve immediately. Serves 4–6.

SOUPS

Brussels sprouts can be added to many of your favorite soups. Toss halved sprouts into the soup during the last 5 minutes of cooking. Or toss individual leaves into the soup. The leaves will float on top of a clear broth and look like lily pads.

Carve a small X on the bottom of whole brussels sprouts to ensure even cooking.

Sweet and Sour Brussels Sprout Soup

2 cups beef broth
1½ cups water
2 tablespoons tamari or soy sauce
1½ cups peeled, diced tomatoes
1 cup tomato puree
1½ teaspoons fresh thyme or ½ teaspoon dried
1 teaspoon fresh basil or ½ teaspoon dried
salt and plenty of pepper
4 cups quartered brussels sprouts
2 teaspoons wine vinegar
½ teaspoon sugar
1 cup grated carrots

In a large soup pot, combine the broth, water, tamari, tomatoes, tomato puree, thyme, basil, and salt and pepper.
Simmer for 15 minutes to blend the flavors. Add the brussels sprouts and simmer for 5 minutes. Add the remaining ingredients and simmer for 5 minutes more. Serve hot.

Preparation Time: 20 minutes
Cooking Time: 25 minutes
Yield: 4–6 servings

SALADS

For serving brussels sprouts in salads, nothing beats a marinade.

Marinated Brussels Sprouts

4 cups whole or halved brussels sprouts
2 tablespoons tarragon vinegar
6 tablespoons vegetable oil
1 heaping tablespoon minced fresh dill
1 heaping tablespoon minced fresh chives
1 tablespoon lemon juice
¼ teaspoon salt
pepper

Steam the brussels sprouts for 3–5 minutes, until bright green and just tender crisp. Plunge into cold water to stop the cooking. Drain.
Mix the remaining ingredients and pour the mixture over the brussels sprouts. Marinate the sprouts at least 6–8 hours.

Preparation Time: 15 minutes
Marinating Time: at least 6–8 hours
Yield: 6 servings

SIDE DISHES AND MAIN DISHES

If you try only one dish in this section, let it be the Brussels Sprouts and Chicken Stir Fry. I don't know why brussels sprouts are neglected in stir fries. The flavor is delicate, and the color is bright green and beautiful.

Tomato Sauce on Brussels Sprouts

Place 4 cups whole brussels sprouts in a buttered baking dish. Quarter or halve them first if the sprouts are big. Pour over the sprouts 1½ cups Italian Tomato Sauce (page 306). (You can use tomato puree seasoned with 1 teaspoon of either thyme, basil, or oregano.) Sprinkle with 3 tablespoons of grated parmesan cheese, if desired.
Cover and bake whole sprouts for 30 minutes at 350° F. Bake quartered or halved sprouts for 20 minutes. Serves 4–6.

A Little Frost Helps the Flavor
If you can bear to wait until the first frost, you will find that your sprouts are sweeter and more flavorful than those you harvest before the frost.

Brussels sprouts are terrific in stir fries. Slice them into quarters for quick and even cooking.

Brussels Sprout Frittata

2 tablespoons butter
1 cup thinly sliced onion
1 cup grated carrots
1½ cups grated Swiss cheese
¾ cup cooked brown rice
1½ tablespoons all-purpose
  unbleached flour
1 teaspoon fresh basil or ¼
  teaspoon dried
⅛ teaspoon ground rosemary
salt and pepper
2–3 cups halved brussels sprouts
½ cup milk
½ cup light cream
2 eggs
½ cup grated parmesan cheese

Preheat the oven to 350° F.

Melt the butter, and sauté the onion until limp and slightly browned, about 5 minutes. Transfer the onion to a greased 10-inch pie pan.

Mix the carrots, cheese, rice, flour, basil, rosemary, and salt and pepper. Spoon this mixture into the pie pan. Press the brussels sprouts into this mixture until the sprouts are partially covered.

Mix the milk, cream, and eggs. Pour this custard over the brussels sprouts. Sprinkle the top with the grated parmesan cheese. Loosely cover the frittata with foil and bake for 30 minutes. Then uncover and continue baking for 25 minutes. Remove the frittata from the oven and allow it to cool for 5–10 minutes before serving.

Preparation Time: 30 minutes
Baking Time: 55 minutes
Yield: 8 servings

Brussels Sprouts And Chicken Stir Fry

2 tablespoons peanut oil
2 garlic cloves, minced
4 cups quartered brussels sprouts
½ cup chicken broth
1½ cups julienne-sliced sweet red
  peppers
2 boneless chicken breasts, diced
½ cup sliced scallions
2 teaspoons minced fresh ginger root

Heat 1 tablespoon of the oil in a wok until very hot. Add the garlic and brussels sprouts and stir fry to coat. Add the chicken broth and red peppers and stir fry for 2 minutes. Cover and steam for 1 minute. Remove the vegetables to a warmed bowl and set aside.

Heat the remaining 1 tablespoon of oil in the wok and stir fry the chicken until it is almost cooked. Add the scallions and ginger and continue to stir fry until the chicken is just done. Return the vegetables to the wok and stir fry long enough to heat through. Serve immediately over rice.

Preparation Time: 25 minutes
Cooking Time: 8–10 minutes
Yield: 4–6 servings

Cabbage

Green, Red, Savoy, Chinese, Bok Choy: Discover the Cabbage Family!

When I was a child, my favorite cabbage dish was red cabbage steamed in a little bit of water, then sautéed with butter and brown sugar. When it was brought to the table, we'd each sprinkle vinegar over our servings and watch delightedly as the cabbage, reacting with acid, turned from purple to magenta.

I don't even have a name for the cabbage dish that is currently my favorite — another very simple dish. I steam chopped green cabbage with a little bit of water in a covered pan until the water disappears. Then I add butter and sauté until the cabbage is browned, almost burnt. The cabbage tastes very, very sweet. It's delicious!

As a child, I was only familiar with green, red, and Savoy cabbages. A course in Chinese cooking introduced me to Chinese cabbages — and my cooking style has never been the same!

Chinese Cabbages Are Easy to Grow From Seed

Adventurous gardeners will raise cool-weather Chinese cabbages along with their regular cabbages. Between the different names in the seed catalogs and the different ways I've seen Chinese cabbages labeled on supermarket produce shelves, I know there is a lot of confusion about which Chinese cabbage is which.

The Chinese cabbages grown most frequently in this country are *Brassica pekinesis*. These have loose heads and a very mild, sweet flavor. Of the several varieties you can grow, my favorite is Napa, or Wong Bok, which has a short, dense head. Another popular variety is Michihli, which looks somewhat like pale Romaine lettuce. These two cabbages are pretty similar in taste.

Bok Choy, or Pak Choy, is known botanically as *Brassica chinesis*. It is really a Chinese mustard, which is how you will see it listed in some seed catalogs. I think of Bok Choy as two vegetables in one: the stalks make a tender, sweet celery substitute, and the leaves are very much like spinach.

In many countries, green and red cabbage dishes are served with meat and potatoes: peasant food, some people call it. The more delicate Chinese cabbage is best briefly cooked with other vegetables and small quantities of meat. Either way, there is usually a cabbage dish that is just perfect for every occasion.

Some of my cabbage harvest is always made into sauerkraut. It's easy to make, as long as you measure the cabbage and pickling salt accurately.

A Garden of Many Shapes And Flavors

Green cabbage is the best all-round cabbage—good for slow braising, quick stir fries and sautés, sauerkraut, and coleslaws.

Red cabbage has a coarser texture and sharper flavor. It is good for slow braising and sauerkraut. Cooking times must be increased with red cabbage.

Savoy cabbage, with its tender, crimped leaves, is more delicately flavored than either green or red cabbage. Savoy cabbage is the most easily handled for stuffing and rolling. The bright green color is retained during cooking. Its only disadvantage is that it does not hold up well under a heavy salad dressing.

Chinese cabbages and bok choy are best for quick stir fries. They are very sweet and delicately flavored.

Green cabbage

Red cabbage *Savoy cabbage* *Napa* *Michili* *Bok Choy*

CABBAGES AT A GLANCE

Yields

1 pound fresh red, green, Savoy, Chinese cabbage, or Bok Choy equals

4½ cups finely chopped

or

5 cups, chopped

or

4 serving wedges cut 1½ inches thick

Firm Heads Keep Best

Cabbages can be harvested all summer long, at any size, but the best ones for storage are firm heads, harvested late.

Green and red cabbages will keep 1–2 months in the coldest section of your root cellar.

Green, red, and Savoy cabbages will keep for about 2 months in the refrigerator. Chinese cabbage and Bok Choy will keep for about 2 weeks in the refrigerator.

Wilted Chinese cabbage and Bok Choy can be restored by soaking in ice water for up to 30 minutes.

There's No Reason For Leftovers

Green, red, and Savoy cabbages can be harvested before they are fully grown. By harvesting a small head, you give the plant the chance to grow additional heads.

Small heads mean no leftovers. Cabbage, like most garden vegetables, is rarely as tasty reheated in a leftover dish as it is freshly prepared.

Boiling Cabbage Is Old-Fashioned

Boiling robs cabbage of its vitamins and sweet flavor. The best way to prepare cabbage for a simple meal is to steam it or sauté it in butter or sesame oil.

Steam: 5–8 minutes

Blanch: 4–8 minutes

Splash sauté or stir fry (in oil, not butter): 3–5 minutes

Don't Be Afraid To Use Strong Flavors

Steamed cabbage is delicious with any tomato-based, cream, or cheese sauce found on pages 305–306.

Cabbage can be sautéed with herbs and spices such as caraway, fennel, cilantro, tarragon, basil, dill, thyme, marjoram, curry, cloves, allspice, ginger, or juniper berries.

Whole stuffed cabbage — classic and easy.

Here's a dish that really shows off your beautiful homegrown cabbage — Whole Stuffed Cabbage With Lebanese Vegetarian Filling. The cabbage bakes for 45 minutes; but it should take you only 40 minutes to put together.

Start by preheating your oven to 350° F.

In a large soup pot, cover a whole, medium-size Savoy cabbage with boiling water and boil for 10 minutes.

While the cabbage cooks, combine 3 cups cooked brown rice, 1 cup diced onion, ½ cup minced fresh parsley, ¾ cup grated carrot, 1 cup diced tomato, ¼ cup currants or raisins, ¼ cup chopped walnuts, ½ cup crumbled feta cheese, 1½ teaspoons cinnamon, 2 tablespoons lemon juice, ¼ teaspoon salt, and 2 eggs.

Remove the cabbage from the water and run cold water over it. Drain well. Trim the stem just enough to allow the cabbage to sit flat in a baking dish. Choose a baking dish or ovenproof bowl that will just fit the cabbage. Set the cabbage in the dish, stem side down.

Carefully peel back the leaves, leaving them attached to the stem, until you reach the small center leaves. Remove the center

1. Pack a third of the filling.

2. Fold leaves over the filling.

3. Pack in more filling.

4. Fold final leaves over all.

core and leaves. Pack one-third of the filling into the center. Fold up some leaves to cover the filling. Pack another third of the filling and fold up another layer of leaves. Pack in the last of the filling, and fold up the remaining leaves to completely cover the filling.

Heat 1 tablespoon vegetable oil in a small saucepan, and sauté 1 cup diced onion. Add 1½ cups tomato puree, ¼ teaspoon cinnamon, 1 teaspoon honey, and salt and pepper to taste. Pour this sauce over the cabbage. With a piece of aluminum foil, make a "tent" over the cabbage. Keep the foil from touching the cabbage. Bake for 45 minutes.

Remove the cabbage from the oven and let it sit for 10 minutes.

Transfer the cabbage to a large serving platter. Remove wedge-shaped pieces for serving. A medium-size cabbage should yield 6–8 servings.

Variations

Stuffed Cabbage With German Filling. Use the filling from the recipe for Cabbage Rolls (page 81) in place of the Vegetarian filling. Pour a cream sauce over the cabbage in place of the tomato sauce before baking.

Lamb Stuffed Cabbage. Add ½ pound sautéed ground lamb to the Lebanese Vegetarian filling.

For appetizers, I occasionally substitute cabbage slices for crackers.

Egg Rolls

4 tablespoons peanut oil
3 tablespoons minced fresh ginger root
3 garlic cloves, minced
1½ cups finely diced onion
2 cups thinly sliced celery
2 cups sliced mushrooms
1 eight-ounce can water chestnuts, coarsely chopped
6 cups finely chopped Chinese cabbage
¼ cup tamari or soy sauce
¼ cup Chinese rice wine or sherry
2 cups chopped spinach
2 cups mung bean sprouts
salt and pepper
oil for deep frying
15–16 egg roll wrappers
1 egg white
approximately 1 cup cornstarch or all-purpose unbleached flour

Heat 2 tablespoons of the peanut oil in a large wok. Stir fry the ginger, garlic, onion, and celery until barely tender crisp, about 2 minutes. Add the mushrooms and water chestnuts, and stir fry for 1 more minute. Remove the vegetables from the wok.

Heat 2 more tablespoons of peanut oil. Stir fry the cabbage with the tamari and wine until the cabbage is slightly wilted.

Add the spinach and sprouts and stir fry until the spinach is wilted. Remove these vegetables from the wok and toss all the vegetables together. Adjust the seasonings; it should taste somewhat salty.

Drain the vegetables for 30 minutes. The liquid can be reserved for soup stock.

Preheat the frying oil to 375° F.

On a lightly floured board, lay out one egg roll wrapper with a corner facing toward you. Into the center of the wrapper, spoon out about ½ cup of filling. Bring the two side corners of the wrapper in toward the middle. Hold them in place with your finger while bringing the corner nearest you up over the filling. Begin rolling the egg roll. Keep tucking in the extra dough along the sides as you roll. You are aiming for a tight roll, not a loose envelope. With a pastry brush or your fingers, moisten the flap with a little egg white. Seal. Set the rolled egg roll on a heavily floured baking sheet. Continue making rolls until all the filling is used. Do not allow the egg rolls to touch each other on the baking sheet. If you have drained the filling sufficiently, and if there is enough cornstarch or flour on the baking sheet, the egg rolls can be held for up to an hour before frying.

If you prefer, you can lightly fry the egg rolls once, drain, and refrigerate. Just before you are ready to serve them, refry the egg rolls until they are golden brown. Fry a few at a time. Drain and serve with a mustard sauce or a sweet and sour sauce.

1. Fold bottom, then sides.

2. Roll to keep the round shape.

3. Seal with egg white.

4. Make a mustard sauce with dry mustard and vinegar.

SOUPS

I've used different types of cabbage in each of the soups that follow. My favorite is the Purple Passion Soup. The color is wonderful.

Tex-Mex Soup With Sausage

1 pound spicy sausage links
   (Chorizo is recommended)
4 cups finely chopped green cabbage
1½ cups diced onion
1 large green pepper, diced
1 cup corn kernels
1½ cups cooked kidney beans
2 quarts tomato puree
1½–2 tablespoons chili powder
2 teaspoons ground cumin
salt and pepper

Cut the sausage into ½-inch pieces. Brown the sausage in a large soup pot. Drain and set aside, reserving 2 tablespoons of fat in the soup pot. Sauté the cabbage in the soup pot until wilted. Add the onion and pepper, and continue cooking, stirring often. Add the corn, beans, tomato puree, and sausage. You may need to add some water to thin the soup. Add the remaining ingredients. Simmer for 45 minutes. Serve hot.

Preparation Time: 30 minutes
Cooking Time: 1 hour
Yield: 8–12 servings

Purple Passion Soup

This red cabbage soup takes on the color of raspberry sherbet—a little shocking perhaps, but beautiful garnished with a yellow nasturtium or blue borage flowers. One of the many nice features of this soup is that it freezes well, so it can be cooked ahead of time.

2 tablespoons vegetable oil
2 tablespoons butter
1½ cups diced onion
6 cups finely chopped red cabbage
2 cups apple cider
2 cups water
1 teaspoon salt
1 tablespoon lemon juice
3 tablespoons honey or brown sugar
1 cup milk
½ cup heavy cream

In a large soup pot, heat the oil and butter, and lightly sauté the onion; do not let it brown. Add the cabbage and continue to sauté for 5 minutes, stirring constantly. Add the cider, water, salt, and lemon juice. Cover the pot and simmer for 45–60 minutes until the cabbage is very tender. Cool slightly.

Pour two-thirds of the soup into the blender or food processor and blend until smooth. Return the blended soup to the pot with the rest of the soup. Reheat and serve, or chill and serve.

Preparation Time: 20 minutes
Cooking Time: 45–60 minutes
Yield: 6 servings

Chinese Vegetable Soup

Although the recipe calls for Chinese cabbage, spinach, and celery, I have substituted Bok Choy for any and all of the vegetables with great success. The tops replace the spinach and the succulent stalks are excellent substitutes for either the celery or the Chinese cabbage.

1 tablespoon vegetable oil
1 tablespoon sesame oil
½ pound ground pork or 1 boneless
   skinned chicken breast, finely
   sliced
½ cup finely diced scallions
½ cup finely diced celery
¼ cup bamboo shoots (optional)
1½ cups thinly sliced Chinese
   cabbage
1 garlic clove, minced
2 teaspoons minced fresh ginger root
2 tablespoons tamari or soy sauce
2 tablespoons dry sherry
½ teaspoon salt
2 quarts chicken broth
1 cup finely sliced fresh spinach
½ cup thinly sliced mushrooms

In a large soup pot, heat the vegetable oil and the sesame oil. Brown the pork or sauté the chicken, and remove from the pot, about 5 minutes. Briefly sauté the scallions, celery, bamboo shoots, cabbage, and garlic, about 2 minutes. Add the ginger, tamari, sherry, salt, and chicken broth. Return the meat to the soup and simmer for 5 minutes. Add the spinach and mushrooms and simmer for 2 minutes more. Serve hot.

Preparation Time: 30 minutes
Cooking Time: 15–20 minutes
Yield: 6–8 servings

SALADS

When it comes to deciding what to combine with the cabbage and dressing, I let what I have on hand be my guide. Grated carrots, diced green and red peppers, diced red or green tomatoes, red onions, and scallions are great with cabbage. Sometimes I add a combination of chopped apples, pineapple, grapes, walnuts, sesame seeds, sunflower seeds, and cashews. I vary the herbs and flavorings, too. The ways to alter basic coleslaw are infinite.

Delight picnickers with coleslaws made from garden vegetables.

My Favorite Coleslaw Dressing

This dressing is for people with a sweet tooth like mine. The dressing should be combined with 6–8 cups of finely chopped green or red cabbage, and other vegetables, fruits, and nuts as desired.

1½ cups mayonnaise
¼ cup pure maple syrup
¼ cup lemon juice
¾ teaspoon nutmeg

Whisk together all the ingredients. Combine the dressing with the cabbage and allow the salad to sit for at least 1 hour before serving.

Preparation Time: 10 minutes
Chilling Time: at least 1 hour
Yield: 2 cups (enough for 6–8 cups chopped cabbage)

Red Ruby Slaw

The absence of mayonnaise in the dressing makes this salad an excellent addition to picnics and large summer buffets. The recipe can be easily doubled or tripled for a crowd.

I like to garnish the salad with minced green scallion tops for a vivid color contrast.

¾ cup wine vinegar
⅓ cup pure maple syrup or brown sugar
¼ cup water
2 tablespoons fresh tarragon or 1 tablespoon dried
1 teaspoon caraway seeds
½ teaspoon salt
6 cups finely chopped red cabbage
1 medium-size onion, finely diced

In a saucepan, combine the vinegar, maple syrup, water, tarragon, caraway seeds, and salt. Heat until simmering. Add the cabbage and onion, and stir. Cook, stirring often, for 5 minutes, or until the cabbage is bright magenta and slightly tender but still crunchy. Transfer the cabbage to a ceramic or glass (not wooden) salad bowl and chill before serving.

Preparation Time: 20 minutes
Cooking Time: 5 minutes
Chilling Time: at least 1 hour
Yield: 6 servings

Spikey Coleslaw Dressing

1 egg
1 egg yolk
½ teaspoon ground mustard
2 teaspoons sugar
1 teaspoon salt
1 teaspoon prepared horseradish
¼ teaspoon caraway seeds
¼ teaspoon white pepper
¼ cup white vinegar
¼ cup olive oil
½ cup vegetable oil
½ cup sour cream

In a blender or a food processor, mix all the ingredients except the oils and sour cream. Slowly pour in the oils in a thin stream. Stir in sour cream.

Combine the dressing with the cabbage and allow the salad to set for at least 1 hour before serving.

Preparation Time: 10 minutes
Chilling Time: at least 1 hour
Yield: 2 cups (enough for 6–8 cups chopped cabbage)

The food processor takes all the work out of making coleslaws.

Savoy Cabbage Salad

Most coleslaw dressings are best with regular green cabbage because the tender texture of savoy cabbage wilts under the weight of creamy dressings. This rather tart dressing was created especially for savoy cabbage, but it is equally good with green cabbage.

¾ cup vinegar
2 tablespoons pure maple syrup or brown sugar
1 teaspoon paprika
1 teaspoon salt
1 teaspoon ground mustard
1 teaspoon dill seeds
1 garlic clove, minced
1 cup vegetable oil
¼ cup tomato catsup
1 savoy cabbage, finely chopped (8 cups)
1–1½ cups diced green pepper
1–1½ cups diced tomato
1 small red onion, cut in half and thinly sliced

In a small bowl, combine the vinegar, maple syrup, paprika, salt, mustard, dill seeds, and garlic. Whisk the mixture as you pour in the oil in a thin stream. Add the catsup and mix.

Combine the cabbage, green pepper, tomato, and red onion. Pour the dressing over the vegetables and toss. Set the salad aside for at least 1 hour to allow the cabbage to wilt before serving.

Preparation Time: 20 minutes
Chilling Time: at least 1 hour
Yield: 6–8 servings

Shrimp Salad In Edible Salad Bowls

1 large carrot
1 Chinese cabbage, chopped
3 scallions, sliced
½ pound cooked baby shrimp
¼ cup peanut oil
1 tablespoon sesame oil
2 tablespoons tamari or soy sauce
4 tablespoons rice vinegar
1 teaspoon minced fresh ginger root
2 garlic cloves, minced
oil for deep frying
2 tablespoons toasted sesame seeds
6 egg roll wrappers

Slice the carrot on the diagonal or cut out stars using a small food press (similar to a cookie press). Mix the carrots, cabbage, scallions, and shrimp in a large bowl.

Whisk together the peanut oil, sesame oil, tamari, vinegar, ginger, and garlic. Pour the dressing over the salad, toss, and set aside.

In a large pot, heat the oil for deep frying to 375° F. Take a clean, empty, metal soup can and make 3 or 4 openings in the bottom with a can opener. Place an egg roll wrapper on top of the oil. With a pair of tongs, press the bottom of the can into the egg roll wrapper, which will curl the wrapper into a bowl shape. Remove the can when the wrapper will hold its curved shape. Continue frying until the wrapper is golden brown. Drain the wrappers and fill with the salad. Sprinkle sesame seeds on top.

Preparation Time: 40 minutes
Yield: 6 servings

SIDE DISHES
AND MAIN DISHES

If you look over the recipes here, you'll see that cabbage lends itself to both rich and light meals.

Most of the recipes can be made with whichever cabbage you have on hand, with one exception. I recommend only Savoy cabbage for the stuffed cabbage dishes. It is so much easier to handle than the other cabbages. Don't forget to remove the rib for easier rolling.

Cabbage Au Gratin

Prepare 2 cups of Cheese Sauce, according to the directions on page 305.

Sauté 3 cups of finely chopped cabbage with 3 chopped scallions or 1 small diced onion. Place half the cabbage in a buttered casserole dish and pour over it ¾ cup Cheese Sauce. Briefly sauté 1½ cups grated carrots. Sprinkle half the carrots over the casserole. Top with ¾ cup Cheese Sauce. Add the remaining cabbage and ½ cup sauce. Mix ½ cup of grated Swiss or cheddar cheese with the remaining carrots and sprinkle on top. Bake uncovered for 40 minutes at 350° F.

Spicy Beef Roulade

I like to serve this beef dish with buttered noodles.

2 tablespoons vegetable oil
1 cup diced onion
3 garlic cloves, minced
4 cups finely chopped green or Savoy cabbage
1¾ cups tomato puree
7 teaspoons honey
¼ cup dry red wine
1 tablespoon wine vinegar
1 tablespoon fresh basil or 1 teaspoon dried
1½ teaspoons fresh thyme or ½ teaspoon dried
4½ teaspoons curry powder
1½ pounds flank steak
salt and pepper

Preheat the oven to 325° F.

In a large sauté pan, heat the oil and sauté the onion and garlic until limp, 3–5 minutes. Add the cabbage and continue to sauté for 5 minutes, stirring often. Add 1 cup of the tomato puree, 6 teaspoons of the honey, the wine, vinegar, basil, thyme, and 1 teaspoon of the curry powder. Continue cooking the mixture until it's quite thick, stirring occasionally.

In the meantime, cut the flank steak into pieces that are about ½ inch thick and 3 inches wide by 4 inches long. Rub one side of the meat lightly with 3 teaspoons of the curry powder.

When the cabbage mixture is thick, adjust the salt and pepper to taste. Spoon some cabbage filling onto each piece of meat and roll the meat to enclose the filling. Use a toothpick to hold the meat closed. The curry powder should be on the outside.

Sauté the meat rolls on all sides until browned. Some of the stuffing may fall out, which is fine; leave it in the pan.

Transfer the rolls to a baking dish. To the filling left in the pan, add the remaining ¾ cup tomato puree, 1 teaspoon honey, and ½ teaspoon curry powder. Heat this sauce and pour it over the rolls. Bake for 1 hour or until the meat is tender. Serve hot.

Preparation Time: 40 minutes
Baking Time: 1 hour
Yield: 6 servings

Variations

Chicken Roulade. Instead of the flank steak, use 3 boneless skinned chicken breasts cut in half and pounded thin. Stuff in the same manner as the flank steaks, and sauté to brown. Bake for 35 minutes.

Beef and Orange Braised Cabbage

Cut 1½-inch-wide wedges of green or red cabbage (1 wedge per person), and brown each wedge in vegetable oil on both sides, about 5 minutes. Transfer the wedges to a covered casserole dish, crowding the pieces in. Heat 1 cup beef broth with ¼ cup dry red wine and the rind of 1 orange cut in slivers (orange part only, the white part is bitter). Pour the broth over the cabbage. Cover and bake for 30 minutes at 350° F. or until the cabbage is tender.

Two-in-One Cabbage Kielbasa Pie

I call this recipe "Two-in-One" because I found that I can take the cabbage mixture that is pressed into the bottom of the pie pan, mix it with a diced onion, and transform the crust into a pancake batter.

4 cups boiling water
4 cups finely chopped green cabbage
4 eggs, slightly beaten
½ cup milk
1 cup all-purpose unbleached flour
1 teaspoon fennel seeds
1 teaspoon salt
¼ teaspoon pepper
1 tablespoon vegetable oil
2 cups thinly sliced leeks
¾ pound kielbasa, thinly sliced on the diagonal

Preheat the oven to 375° F.

Pour the boiling water over the cabbage and set the cabbage aside to wilt for 10 minutes. Drain the cabbage and stir in the eggs, milk, flour, fennel, salt, and pepper. Grease a 10-inch pie pan. Pour in the cabbage mixture, and press onto the sides and bottom of the pan to form a crust.

Heat the vegetable oil in a sauté pan, and sauté the leeks until they are limp, but not brown. Sprinkle the leeks over the pie. Lay the kielbasa in an overlapping circle around the pie. Fill in the center of the pie with slices of kielbasa laid in a floral pattern.

Bake the pie for 40 minutes. Then let it sit for 10 minutes before serving.

Preparation Time: 30 minutes
Baking Time: 40 minutes
Yield: 8 servings

German-Style Cabbage Rolls

1 pound ham (4 cups cubed)
½ cup minced fresh parsley
½ cup finely diced scallions
½ cup finely diced dill pickles
2 eggs, slightly beaten
2 tablespoons Dijon-style mustard
1 teaspoon prepared horseradish
16–18 Savoy cabbage leaves, steamed until tender crisp
1¼ cups Caraway Mustard Sauce (page 305), or Hot Horseradish Cream Sauce (page 305)
¼ cup milk

Preheat the oven to 350° F.

Cube the ham and grind it in a food mill or process it in a food processor until it is finely crumbled. In a large bowl, combine the ham with the parsley, scallions, pickles, eggs, mustard, and horseradish. Mix well.

Remove the rib from each cabbage leaf. Put a small amount of filling (¼ cup) on each leaf and fold in the sides. Roll the cabbage to completely enclose the filling. Place the cabbage roll seam side down in a greased baking dish. Prepare the sauce and thin it with the milk to make it the consistency of whipping cream. Pour the sauce over the cabbage rolls and bake for 35 minutes.

Preparation Time: 30 minutes
Baking Time: 35 minutes
Yield: 6 servings

Dark beer, dark bread, and Cabbage Kielbasa Pie—a hearty meal.

Carrots

Begin the Harvest With "Fingerlings"— Carrots at Their Tender Best

My favorite carrots are sweet baby carrots, as big as my little finger and just pulled from the soil. After baby carrots come satisfying mature carrots, then overgrown woody carrots, then limp, old carrots stored too long in the root cellar.

I like to begin to harvest carrots as soon as there is something big enough to eat. With succession plantings I can have a summer-long harvest of carrots. By the time the root cellar has cooled from the chilly fall nights, I usually have enough mature carrots to store in the root cellar.

Harvesting the fingerling-size carrots is a good way to thin carrots. I do find, though, that once my carrot patch is well thinned, I have a tendency to forget about carrots, especially when other vegetables demand my attention. I know I can safely leave a carrot in the ground, but it's impossible to ignore summer squash or beans once they start coming along. Of course, carrots left in the ground too long sometimes become woody, but I just remove the woody core and enjoy the rest of the carrot.

Even Limp, Old Carrots Can Be Used!

Carrots do keep well in a root cellar. But toward the end of the winter, they often become limp. Soaking in ice water for about 30 minutes often restores a limp carrot; otherwise, limp carrots are acceptable in most soups, purees, and juices.

Climate and soil conditions are important factors to consider when deciding which carrot variety to plant. From a cook's perspective, the long thin carrots are preferable to the short stubby ones. In my opinion, the fatter the carrot, the less attractive are the slices. Of course, stubby carrots are fine diced, grated, pureed, or juiced—and there are no taste differences involved.

No part of the carrot need be wasted. Although too bitter to be tasty in salads, carrot tops make an excellent addition to a soup stock. Likewise, I save the peels from older carrots for soup stock. In hot weather, carrot tops hold up better than parsley as a garnish, or lettuce as a bed for salad platters. I have even heard that some people add carrot tops to boiled New England dinners—maybe I'll try that this year.

I like to pick carrots when they are young. The small ones are just perfect for steaming and serving with a flavored butter. The larger ones are delicious sliced or grated in salads.

CARROTS AT A GLANCE

Yields

1 pound carrots equals
   3 cups sliced or diced
or
   4 cups grated or processor ground
or
   3 cups cooked and pureed

Carrots Can Be Stored Easily

You can store carrots in the coldest part of your root cellar for 3–4 months. Remove the tops, and store the carrots in food-safe, perforated plastic bags, or pack them in boxes of moist peat moss or sawdust.

Carrots will also keep in perforated plastic bags for several months in a refrigerator.

Limp carrots usually can be restored by soaking in ice water for 30 minutes.

Carrots can be pickled or frozen.

Carrots Cook Quickly

New carrots should be scrubbed but not peeled. Older carrots should be peeled.

Once sliced, diced, julienned, or grated, carrots can be cooked until they are bright orange and tender crisp.

Cooking Times

Steam (sliced or diced): 5–7 minutes
Blanch (sliced or diced): 4–6 minutes
Splash sauté or stir fried (sliced or diced): 5–8 minutes
Steam sauté or stir fried (grated): 4–6 minutes
Parboil for salads (sliced, diced, or julienned): 2–3 minutes

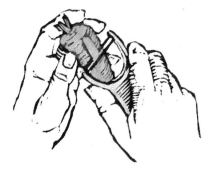

I always peel older carrots.

Restore limp carrots in ice water.

What Do You Do With Overgrown Carrots? Make A Puree!

To make a puree, slice the carrot into quarters and chop into 2–4-inch pieces or grate. (If the carrot has a woody core, discard the core and use the still tender parts.) Blanch for 5–7 minutes. Puree in a food processor or blender until smooth. Add water if necessary. Purees can be frozen or used immediately.

Carrot purees make nice additions to gravies and sauces as thickeners. Or they can be combined with mashed potatoes for a little variety.

Baby carrots should be pampered! Steam them briefly and treat them to a light dressing of butter and herbs.

Steamed baby carrots can be sautéed with a Mustard Butter, Herb Butter, or maple syrup or honey sweetened Lemon Butter (pages 160 and 304).

Or sauté steamed baby carrots with orange juice, ginger, and butter; apple slices, cinnamon, and butter; or raisins, nuts, and apple cider.

Other fruits and nuts that can be sautéed with carrots are oranges, pineapple, grapes, peaches, apricots, raisins, coconut, walnuts, cashews, pecans, pine nuts, and sesame seeds.

Or sauté in butter with a splash of Pernod, Galliano, Madeira, or sherry.

A scant helping of a cream sauce or Hollandaise Sauce (page 307) is delicious on steamed carrots.

Herbs Complement Carrot Dishes

Many carrot dishes are enhanced by the addition of herbs and spices. Flavors that go particularly well with carrots are anise, caraway, cinnamon, nutmeg, ginger, allspice, mint, curry, cilantro, thyme, basil, rosemary, and mustard.

Carrot garnishes decorate my dishes all year long

Because carrots are available all year, I rely on them for garnishing. Here's how, and a tip: Hold the carrot garnishes in ice water if you can't serve immediately.

Carrot Curls. From a large carrot, peel off a wide strip, using a wide vegetable peeler. Wrap the strip around your finger. Set a pitted or stuffed olive into the center of the curl.

Carrot Flowers. Trim off the ends of a fat carrot so the carrot can stand flat on your work surface. Carve the sides of the carrot to form a 5-sided carrot. Using a paring knife, remove a small triangle of carrot, from the center of each side. Lay the carrot on its side and slice off pieces that are about ¼ inch thick. Each piece will be shaped like a flower.

Julienne Carrots. Julienne-sliced carrots can be arranged on top of a dish. I often arrange the carrots in a spoke pattern on top of a round dish, such as a molded salad, or in a crisscross pattern.

Sprinkled Carrot Garnishes. Processor ground carrots, which have the consistency of bread crumbs, can be sprinkled on top of any dish, as can finely diced carrots.

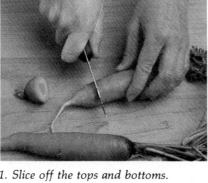

1. Slice off the tops and bottoms.

2. Carve out each side.

3. Carve to make 5 sides.

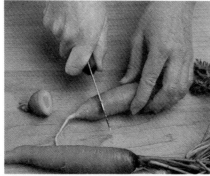

4. Slice into carrot flowers.

Carrot garnishes: the carrot flowers in both salads are the same; only the angle of the cuts is different.

SOUPS

Although I have included only one soup here, I recommend using carrots freely in soups. In fact, throughout this book, you will notice that I frequently add carrots to soups.

Carrot Orange Ginger Soup

2 tablespoons butter
1½ cups diced onion
6 cups sliced carrots
3 cups orange juice
2 cups chicken broth
2 tablespoons minced fresh ginger root
1 whole orange with rind, quartered
¾ cup heavy cream
2 tablespoons orange juice concentrate
salt and pepper

In a soup pot, melt the butter, and sauté the onion on medium heat until limp, 3–5 minutes. Add the carrots, orange juice, chicken broth, ginger root, and orange. Simmer for 20–30 minutes or until the carrots are very tender. Let the soup cool a little.

Remove the orange pieces and discard. In a blender or food processor, blend the soup until smooth. Return the soup to the heat, add the cream, orange juice concentrate, and salt and pepper to taste. Serve hot.

Preparation Time: 15 minutes
Cooking Time: 30 minutes
Yield: 6 servings

SALADS

Don't forget to add sliced or grated carrots to green salads and coleslaws. Here are a few more recipes.

California Carrot Salad

4 cups diced carrots
2 cups diced potatoes
1½ cups sliced black olives
½ cup chopped scallions, including green tops
2 tablespoons minced fresh dill
2 cups flaked tuna (13-ounce can)
¾ cup olive oil
¼ cup wine vinegar
2 tablespoons lemon juice
1 teaspoon paprika
¼ cup tomato puree or catsup
1 teaspoon honey or sugar
salt and pepper
lettuce leaves
1 cup cherry tomatoes, quartered

Parboil the carrots until just tender, 2–3 minutes. Plunge into cold water. Drain.

Parboil the potatoes until tender, 5–10 minutes. Plunge into cold water. Drain.

Combine the carrots, potatoes, olives, scallions, dill, and tuna in a large salad bowl. Toss to mix.

In a blender or food processor, combine all the remaining ingredients except the lettuce leaves and cherry tomatoes, and blend until smooth. Pour the dressing over the salad and toss to coat. Pack the salad into a 5-cup ring mold. Chill for at least 2 hours. Invert the mold onto a serving plate lined with lettuce leaves. Fill the center with quartered cherry tomatoes and serve.

Preparation Time: 35 minutes
Chilling Time: 2 hours
Yield: 6–8 servings

Carrot Slaw

Combine 6 cups grated carrots with a handful of raisins and nuts. Sprinkle with fresh minced parsley. Combine 1 cup pineapple or orange juice, 2 tablespoons lemon juice, and 2 tablespoons honey. Pour over carrots. Toss to coat. Serves 6.

Carrot-Stuffed Avocados

Parboil 1½ cups diced carrots until barely tender crisp, 2–3 minutes. Split 3 avocados in half remove the pits, scoop out the flesh, and dice.

Combine 2 cups diced cooked chicken; 1 cup mayonnaise; 3 tablespoons lemon juice, and 1–2 tablespoons curry powder with the carrots and diced avocado. Season to taste with salt and pepper. Mix well.

Spoon the salad into the avocado shells. Decorate with carrot curls and serve. Serves 6.

SIDE DISHES AND MAIN DISHES

Most of these dishes were especially developed for older carrots that may have lost some flavor in storage.

Baked Carrots

For grilled dinners or picnics, try carrots baked in foil.

Take whole or chunked carrots and dot with butter and fresh herbs, such as dill. Wrap in foil. Place on a rack over water and bake 20–30 minutes. Serve hot.

Garden Chicken Rolls

4 large boneless, skinned chicken breasts
½ large lemon, quartered
2 garlic cloves, minced
1 cup ricotta or cottage cheese
8 baby carrots, quartered lengthwise
1 baby zucchini
¼ cup melted butter
½ cup wheat germ
3 cups grated carrots
3 tablespoons butter
3 tablespoons all-purpose unbleached flour
½ cup milk
½ cup heavy cream
2 tablespoons lemon juice
salt and pepper

Preheat the oven to 350° F.

Cut each chicken breast in half to make 8 portions. Place the breasts between waxed paper and pound the meat ¼ inch thick.

Remove all the seeds from the lemon and combine the lemon —

A tangy carrot sauce tops this delicate chicken and vegetable dish.

rind and all — with the garlic in a food processor. Process until finely ground. Add the ricotta and mix. Spoon the cheese mixture into the center of each piece of chicken.

Parboil the carrots for 2–3 minutes until just barely tender crisp. Place 4 pieces of carrot on each chicken breast.

Slice the zucchini into sticks 2 inches long and ½ inch wide. Place 2–4 pieces of zucchini on each piece of chicken.

Roll the breast to enclose the filling and vegetables. Place each breast seam side down in a greased baking dish. Brush the breasts with ¼ cup melted butter. Sprinkle with wheat germ. Cover the dish with aluminum foil and bake for 30 minutes; uncover, and continue baking for 15 minutes more.

While the chicken bakes, steam the grated carrots until very soft, 6–8 minutes. Blend to make a puree.

Melt 3 tablespoons butter in a saucepan. Add the flour, and stir to form a paste. Add the milk and cream a little at a time, stirring constantly to prevent lumps. When the sauce is smooth, add it to the puree and blend together in a blender or food processor. Return the sauce to a saucepan to warm and season with lemon juice and salt and pepper.

When the chicken is done, serve a half breast to each person and spoon a small amount of sauce over each breast.

Preparation Time: 45 minutes
Baking Time: 1 hour
Yield: 8 servings

Carrot Eggplant Pastry

Carrot and eggplant is an unusual combination—but good!

4 tablespoons vegetable or olive oil
1½ cups diced onion
1 garlic clove, minced
4½ cups peeled, finely diced
    eggplant
2 cups sliced mushrooms
3 cups finely grated carrots
2 tablespoons fresh thyme or
    2 teaspoons dried
¼ cup chopped fresh parsley
1½ cups crumbled feta cheese
salt and pepper
½ cup butter
10 sheets filo dough

Preheat the oven to 375° F.

In a sauté pan, heat the oil and sauté the onion, garlic, and eggplant for 5 minutes. Add the mushrooms, and continue to sauté for another 5 minutes. Add the carrots, thyme, parsley, cheese, and salt and pepper to taste.

Melt the butter and brush a 9-inch by 13-inch baking dish with some of it. Fold 1 sheet of filo dough in half and place it in the dish. Brush with butter. Continue to layer on 4 more sheets of dough, buttering between each sheet. Spoon in the filling. Place a folded sheet of filo dough on top, and brush with butter. Continue to layer the remaining dough, again buttering between each layer. Brush the top with butter. Bake for 35–40 minutes or until golden brown. Cut into squares and serve.

Preparation Time: 30 minutes
Baking Time: 35–40 minutes
Yield: 6–8 servings

Curried Carrot and Bean Tart

If you'd like to make this an "all garden" tart, substitute 1½ cups grated radishes or turnips for the mushrooms.

1 cup plus 2 tablespoons all-purpose
    unbleached flour
¾ teaspoon salt
¼ cup toasted sesame seeds
⅓ cup butter or shortening
2–4 tablespoons water
3 cups raw grated carrots
1 cup green beans, cut in 1-inch
    pieces
2 tablespoons vegetable oil
1 cup diced onion
1 teaspoon curry powder
1 teaspoon ground cumin
1 teaspoon cardamom
4 tablespoons butter
1½ cups sliced mushrooms
¾ cup light cream
¼ cup milk
2 egg yolks
¼ teaspoon white pepper
1 teaspoon lemon juice
½ cup grated Swiss cheese

Combine 1 cup of the flour, ¼ teaspoon of the salt, and ¼ cup sesame seeds. Cut ⅓ cup butter or shortening into the flour until

After a few months in the root cellar, my carrots tend to go limp and lose flavor. That's when I start looking for dishes, such as the Curried Carrot and Bean Tart, which is strongly flavored and uses grated carrots.

the mixture resembles gravel and sand. Add the water and mix until the dough forms a ball.

Preheat the oven to 425° F. Roll out the pie crust on a lightly floured board and fit it into a 9-inch or 10-inch pie pan. Prick with a fork all over and bake for 10 minutes in a 425° oven. When crust is removed from the oven, reduce the oven temperature to 350° F.

Parboil the carrots and beans for 2–3 minutes until slightly limp. Drain and set aside.

In a sauté pan, heat the oil, and sauté the onion and spices over medium heat until limp, 3–5 minutes. Add the butter and mushrooms, and sauté for 2 minutes. Sprinkle the remaining 2 tablespoons flour over the onion-mushroom mixture and slowly add ¾ cup light cream, stirring constantly. Cook until the sauce thickens. Remove from the heat.

Whisk ¼ cup milk into the 2 egg yolks and add the onion mixture. Season with the remaining ½ teaspoon of salt, pepper, and lemon juice. Fold the parboiled carrots and beans into the onion-mushroom mixture. Taste and adjust the seasoning.

Fill the baked pie shell with the vegetables. Sprinkle ½ cup grated Swiss cheese over the top. Bake for 30 minutes at 350° F. Let set for 5–10 minutes before serving.

Preparation Time: 40 minutes
Baking Time: 30 minutes
Yield: 8 servings

Carrot Fritter Puffs

These puffs taste very much like potato knishes, but are much easier to make.

4 cups diced carrots (or 2 cups puree)
4 cups diced potatoes (or 2 cups mashed)
3 eggs, slightly beaten
1 cup all-purpose unbleached flour
1 cup bread crumbs
2 cups grated sharp cheddar cheese
2 cups diced onion
2 tablespoons butter or vegetable oil
1 teaspoon salt
1 teaspoon pepper
oil for deep frying

Cook the carrots and potatoes together in water to cover until soft, about 20 minutes. Drain and mash together. Add the eggs, flour, bread crumbs, and cheese.

Sauté the onion in the butter until browned and add to the batter with the salt and pepper.

Heat the oil to 375° F. Drop the batter into the oil by the teaspoon and fry for 1 minute or until golden brown, tuning once to brown the other side. Drain on a paper towel and serve warm.

Preparation Time: 30 minutes
Cooking Time: 15 minutes
Yield: 6–8 servings

BAKED GOODS

Carrot cake. Who can resist this garden-produced dessert?

Roger's Carrot Cake

This cake will taste best if kept in a cool place for a day before frosting.

½ cup currants
4–5 carrots
1¼ cups vegetable oil
1 cup brown sugar
1 cup white sugar
4 eggs
1¼ cups all-purpose unbleached flour
¾ cup whole wheat flour
2 teaspoons baking powder
2 teaspoons baking soda
1 tablespoon cinnamon
1 teaspoon nutmeg
1 teaspoon ground cloves
1 cup walnuts
1 teaspoon vanilla extract
¾ cup butter at room temperature
8 ounces cream cheese at room temperature
4 cups confectioner's sugar

Preheat the oven to 350° F.

Cover currants with hot water and let stand. Peel 4 or 5 large carrots. Cut into chunks. In a food processor fitted with a steel blade, process the carrots to a finely ground consistency. Measure out 3 cups carrots.

Beat the oil, brown sugar, and white sugar. Add the eggs and continue beating until well blended.

Carrot Cake. Who can resist it?

In another bowl, sift together both flours, the baking powder, baking soda, cinnamon, nutmeg, and cloves.

Drain the currants and process with the walnuts in a food processor fitted with a steel blade until they are roughly chopped. Add the 3 cups ground carrots, the currants and walnuts, and the dry ingredients to the oil and sugar mixture, beating the mixture and scraping the sides of the bowl. Add the vanilla and mix well.

Pour the batter into 2 or 3 greased and floured 9-inch cake pans. Bake 2 layers for 50–60 minutes, 3 layers for 45 minutes.

Cool the cake and frost with a cream cheese frosting.

To make the frosting, cream together the butter and cream cheese until the mixture is light and fluffy. Slowly add the confectioners' sugar until well-blended, using more sugar if necessary to get a spreading consistency.

Cauliflower

Freeze It, Pickle It, or Eat It
While It's Still Snow White and Fresh.

When cauliflower is ready to be harvested, we eat it in quantity because cauliflower will bolt if left unharvested. The tight curds unfurl, opening up into sprigs of unappetizing, leggy flowers that go straight from the garden into the compost heap. There is absolutely nothing you can do with a bolted cauliflower head.

Cauliflower doesn't hold all that well in the refrigerator, either. It takes on a cabbage odor, and will often develop brown spots within 5 or 6 days. So when there is a generous cauliflower harvest, there are three choices: freeze it, pickle it, or eat it.

Frozen cauliflower is excellent in soups and purees. To my mind, these are the best uses for it. When I freeze cauliflower, I find flavor is fine and the color is nice and white, but the texture is mushy.

Cauliflower pickles are delicious in a variety of brines. I blanch the cauliflower for 1 minute, pack it into jars, cover with just about any hot brine that suits green bean pickles, and process for 15 minutes. Three small heads will make an average of 6 pints of crispy cauliflower pickles. I serve the pickles plain or add them to salads throughout the winter, when store-bought cauliflower is expensive or unappealing after a long cross-country haul.

I Love Fresh Cauliflower!

I would prefer to eat fresh cauliflower all year long. There are so many different ways to prepare it! One of my favorite ways is to trim the cauliflower, break it up into florets, and serve it with vegetable dip. Sometimes I blanch the cauliflower for a minute to remove the sharp bite raw cauliflower often has. When cauliflower is in season, so are broccoli, carrots, green peppers, snap beans, radishes, beets, and cherry tomatoes. Instead of a green salad, I make a "summer garden platter" of vegetables. In the center of the platter, I set a whole cauliflower head that has been briefly blanched. Into the head, I stick bamboo skewers or toothpicks loaded with cubes of vegetables and cherry tomatoes.

An interesting aspect of cauliflower is that it lends itself to a variety of ethnic cuisines. In this chapter, you will find recipes that are based on Mediterranean, Mideastern, Indian, Italian, French, and British styles of cooking. Enjoy!

I like to blanch my cauliflower before adding it to salads to remove that sharp "bite." Warm cauliflower absorbs the marinade best.

CAULIFLOWER AT A GLANCE

Harvesting Hints

Sunlight will turn the white heads of cauliflower brown, unless you shade them. When cauliflower gets to be 4–5 inches across, begin "blanching" by partially breaking an outside leaf at the stem, laying it over the top of the cauliflower, and tucking it in on the other side of the plant.

When the cauliflower head is anywhere from 6 to 12 inches in diameter, depending on the variety, it is ready to be harvested. Harvest by slicing the stem about 3 inches below the head.

Be sure to harvest before the tight flower buds begin to open (bolt).

If cabbage worms are a problem in your garden, soak the cauliflower in salted water for 30 minutes before preparing.

Yields

1 large head equals
  6 cups florets
1 medium-size head equals
  4 cups florets
1 small head equals
  2½–3 cups florets
1 pound trimmed cauliflower equals
  4 cups florets or chopped
  cauliflower
1 pound cooked cauliflower plus a few tablespoons of water equals
  2 cups puree

Storing Cauliflower

You can keep cauliflower in a perforated plastic bag in the refrigerator for about 5 days. Watch for brown spots and a strong cabbage odor. For best results, use right out of the garden.

Extra cauliflower can be frozen or pickled.

Preparing for the Table: Trim and Break into Florets

Cut the cauliflower head in half, remove the core. Compost the core and leaves.

Then cut or break apart the stem of the cauliflower for florets.

Or cut the head into quarters and slice thinly.

I like to wilt cauliflower florets for salads to soften the texture and the sharp, biting flavor.

To wilt cauliflower for salads, pour boiling water over the florets and let them stand in the water for 10 minutes. Then drain.

For all other dishes, I prefer to steam, blanch, or steam sauté florets.

Cooking Times

Steam: 3–6 minutes
Blanch: 3–6 minutes
Steam Sauté: 3–5 minutes

For an absolutely white cauliflower, blanch with a tablespoon of lemon juice in the water. Blanching is also preferred with an old head that has a heavy cabbage odor.

To make a cauliflower puree, steam the cauliflower for 5–8 minutes until very tender, and process in a food processor or blender with a little water. For every 2 cups of florets, add about ¼ cup of water.

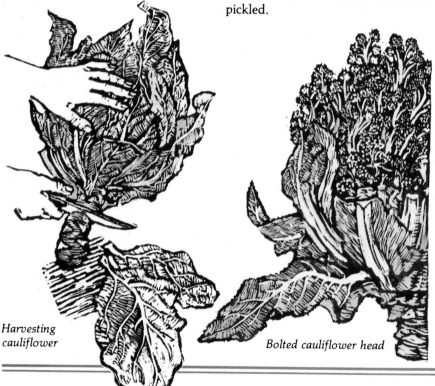

Harvesting cauliflower

Bolted cauliflower head

1. *Remove the center core.*

2. *Steam until tender crisp.*

3. *Smother in sauce.*

4. *Serve the cauliflower whole.*

I really enjoy serving a whole baked cauliflower: The dish is showy and simple at the same time.

To make a whole "frosted" baked cauliflower, trim a perfect head of cauliflower and remove the leaves. Place the whole head in a steamer and steam for 15 minutes, or until tender crisp.

Place the cauliflower in a baking dish or on a serving platter. Pour over it 1¼ cups hot Blue Cheese and Scallion Sauce (page 306), Dijon Sauce (page 305), Hot Horseradish Cream Sauce (page 305), Caraway Mustard Sauce (page 305), or Cheese Sauce (page 305). Serve immediately, or broil for 5 minutes to brown the top.

Simple Dishes Are Favorites

When I am harvesting cauliflower at its peak, I like to make simple dishes that show off the vegetable. My favorite way is to steam the florets, and then lightly sauté them with a flavored butter (page 304), or sprinkle with buttered bread crumbs or grated parmesan cheese.

Flavorings that go well with cauliflower are basil, dill, oregano, fennel, thyme, mint, cilantro, garlic, chili powder, caraway seeds, horseradish, and mustard.

Does Your Cauliflower Turn Pink?

Sometimes when I blanch cauliflower, or when I preserve it as a pickle, the cauliflower turns pink. This is a normal chemical reaction and doesn't affect the flavor or texture at all.

Cauliflower Adds Crunch And Flavor to Salads

After I have wilted the cauliflower to tenderize it, I like to combine it with a variety of vegetables and dressings.

A salad like this makes a whole meal: Combine cauliflower, sliced pepperoni, red and green peppers, and a vinaigrette dressing (page 300).

Another favorite combination is cauliflower, diced apples, walnuts, scallions, and Curry Yogurt Dressing (page 302).

Oriental Marinade and Dipping Sauce (page 303) is delicious with cauliflower and scallions.

Another seasonal favorite starts with a bed of sliced tomatoes and raw sliced zucchini. Mound wilted cauliflower florets on top and smother with a Tahini Dressing (page 303).

This Cauliflower Broccoli Pâté is surprisingly easy to make. Its rich and creamy flavor comes from using plenty of cream and cheese in the recipe. Because it is so rich, a little goes a long way.

APPETIZERS

Both of these appetizers can be made with fresh or frozen cauliflower.

Cauliflower Broccoli Pâté

I try to make this appetizer in advance because it improves with age. This pâté has a smooth spreading consistency and should be served with crackers or thin pieces of homemade bread.

4 cups cauliflower florets
¼ cup butter
1 cup chopped onion
½ cup ricotta cheese
¼ cup sour cream
¼ teaspoon white pepper
1 teaspoon salt
1 tablespoon fresh minced chives
2⅔ tablespoons minced fresh dill
1 teaspoon lemon juice
1 tablespoon gelatin
2 tablespoons water
4 cups chopped broccoli
1 cup heavy cream
⅓ cup pine nuts
⅛ teaspoon pepper
dash nutmeg
salt and pepper

Steam the cauliflower over boiling water until very tender, 6–8 minutes.

Melt the butter, and sauté the onion until limp, 3–5 minutes.

Combine the cauliflower, onion, ricotta cheese, sour cream, white pepper, salt, chives, 2 tablespoons of the dill, and the lemon juice in a food processor and process until smooth.

Sprinkle the gelatin over the 2 tablespoons of water and set aside for 5 minutes. Then gently heat until the gelatin melts. Blend the gelatin into the cauliflower mixture. Line a small (8-inch by 5-inch) loaf pan with plastic film wrap. Spoon in the cauliflower. Smooth the top.

Steam the broccoli over boiling water until very tender, 6–8 minutes. Combine the remaining ingredients with the broccoli in the food processor and process until smooth. Season to taste with salt and pepper. Spoon the mixture over the cauliflower and smooth the top. Cover and chill for 2–3 hours. Unmold and serve with crackers.

Preparation Time: 40 minutes
Chilling Time: 2–3 hours
Yield: 8–10 servings

Cauliflower Cashew Balls

I serve these appetizers hot with the Oriental Marinade and Dipping Sauce (page 303) or with the Tahini Sauce (page 303).

4 cups cauliflower florets
3 tablespoons vegetable oil
½ cup chopped onion
1 large garlic clove, minced
1½ cups chopped cashews
1½ teaspoons ground cumin
1 teaspoon curry powder
½ teaspoon ground fennel
½ teaspoon turmeric
salt and pepper
½ cup minced fresh parsley
1 cup grated parmesan cheese
1 egg, beaten
1 cup bread crumbs
oil for deep frying

Steam the cauliflower over boiling water for 3–6 minutes or until tender. Finely chop the cauliflower. A pastry cutter works well for this task.

Heat the oil, and sauté the onion, garlic, and cashews, with the cumin, curry, fennel, and tumeric until lightly browned. Combine with the cauliflower. Season to taste with salt and pepper. Add the parsley, parmesan, egg, and 2 tablespoons of the bread crumbs.

Preheat the oil for deep frying to 375° F.

Form the mixture into walnut-size balls and roll in the remaining bread crumbs. Deep fry for approximately 1 minute or until browned. Drain and serve hot.

Preparation Time: 20 minutes
Cooking Time: 20 minutes
Yield: 6–8 servings

Cauliflower and cream seem to be meant for each other. I have included four special creamed cauliflower soups—but the number of possibilities is infinite.

Cauliflower Pesto Soup

Feel free to use frozen cauliflower and pesto in this recipe instead of fresh. If you're using frozen cauliflower, convert it to soup by pureeing it and then combining 4 cups of puree with 4 cups of chicken broth and the sautéed onion. Swirl in the pesto mixture as the recipe directs.

2 tablespoons butter
1½ cups diced onion
6 cups finely chopped cauliflower
4 cups chicken broth
½ cup heavy cream
1 cup milk
salt and pepper
2 tablespoons Pesto (page 161)

In a large soup pot, melt the butter and sauté the onion until limp, 3–5 minutes. Add the cauliflower and the chicken broth. Simmer until the cauliflower is very tender, about 20 minutes. Cool the soup a little and puree in a blender or a food processor. Return the soup to the pot and stir in the cream and milk. Season to taste with salt and pepper. Spoon 3 tablespoons of soup into a small bowl. Add the pesto and stir to blend.

Transfer the soup from the soup pot to individual soup bowls or a soup tureen. Drizzle in the pesto in a spiral pattern and stir briefly to swirl. Serve hot.

Preparation Time: 30 minutes
Cooking Time: 20 minutes
Yield: 6 servings

Variations

Curry Cauliflower Soup. Sauté 2 teaspoons curry powder with the onions. Omit the pesto.

Cauliflower Cheese Soup. Stir in 2 cups grated sharp cheddar cheese or 1½ cups crumbled blue cheese with the milk. Reheat to melt the cheese. Omit the pesto.

Cauliflower Carrot Soup. Add 2 cups grated carrots to the cauliflower and increase the broth by 1 cup. Omit the pesto and season with a dash of nutmeg.

Just before serving, swirl the pesto sauce into the creamed cauliflower soup.

Cauliflower salads have a heartiness that complements green salads. I sometimes serve a cauliflower salad as a second "side" salad.

Spiced Cauliflower Salad

The combination of spices gives this salad a hint of the Middle East.

4–6 cups cauliflower florets
¼ cup lime juice
1 teaspoon grated lime rind
¼ cup vegetable oil
½ teaspoon paprika
¼ teaspoon cinnamon
½ teaspoon ground cumin
½ teaspoon crushed hot red pepper
½ teaspoon salt
¼ teaspoon sugar
1 cup julienne-sliced sweet red peppers
½ cup minced fresh parsley

Pour boiling water over the cauliflower, and let it stand while you prepare the dressing.

Combine the lime juice, rind, oil, spices, hot pepper, salt, and sugar. Whisk to blend.

Drain the cauliflower. Plunge into cold water and drain well. Combine the cauliflower in a salad bowl with the sweet peppers and parsley. Pour the dressing over the salad and toss to coat. Serve immediately or chill first.

Preparation Time: 20 minutes
Yield: 6 servings

Cauliflower a la Grecque

Blanching takes away the "bite" of cauliflower.

¾ cup olive oil
6 tablespoons lemon juice
½ teaspoon dried oregano
½ teaspoon dried basil
1 garlic clove, minced
6 cups cauliflower florets
¼ cup fresh minced parsley
⅓ cup sliced red onion
1 cup whole baby red radishes
¼ cup crumbled feta cheese
¾ cup Greek olives
8 cups spinach, torn into bite-size
   pieces

In a saucepan, whisk together the olive oil, lemon juice, oregano, basil, and garlic. Simmer while you prepare the cauliflower.

Parboil the cauliflower in boiling water for 5 minutes. Drain.

Add the cauliflower to the dressing in the saucepan. Toss to coat. Set aside to marinate for 1 hour. Then chill.

Just before serving, add the parsley, onion, radishes, feta cheese, and olives. Toss well.

To serve, cover a large platter with the spinach. With a slotted spoon, spoon the salad onto the center of the platter. Pour the remaining dressing over the spinach. Serve immediately.

Preparation Time: 30 minutes
Marinating and Chilling Time: 3
   hours
Yield: 6 servings

SIDE DISHES AND MAIN DISHES

Cauliflower Pasta Rolls

4 quarts salted water
16–18 spinach lasagna noodles
   (page 245)
2 tablespoons olive oil
1 cup minced fresh parsley
1 cup chopped scallions with green
   tops
3 garlic cloves, minced
6 cups finely chopped cauliflower
¼ cup water
1 cup grated mozzarella cheese
¾ cup grated parmesan cheese
1 cup ricotta cheese
1½ tablespoons fresh basil or 1½
   teaspoons dried
salt and pepper
4 cups Italian Tomato Sauce
   (page 306)

Preheat the oven to 350° F.
Bring 4 quarts of salted water to a boil. Add the noodles and cook until just tender. Drain and rinse in cold water.

In a large sauté pan, heat the olive oil, and sauté the parsley, scallions, and garlic for 5 minutes. Add the cauliflower and water, cover, and cook for 5 minutes, or until the cauliflower is tender crisp. Transfer the vegetables to a bowl and add ½ cup of the mozzarella, the parmesan, ricotta, basil, and salt and pepper to taste.

In a deep baking dish, spoon in enough tomato sauce to cover the bottom of the dish. Lay 1

piece of pasta on a clean work surface. Spread some cauliflower filling over the pasta and roll the pasta to make a roll. Set the roll on end in the baking dish. Continue making rolls and place them closely together in the pan. Pour the remaining sauce over the rolls and sprinkle on the remaining ½ cup of cheese. Cover and bake for 1 hour. Serve immediately.

Preparation Time: 40 minutes
Baking Time: 1 hour
Yield: 8 servings (2 rolls each)

Braised Cauliflower In Indian Spices

3 tablespoons vegetable oil
¾ cup diced onion
1 large garlic clove, minced
½ teaspoon cardamom
½ teaspoon turmeric
½ teaspoon curry powder
½ teaspoon salt
2 tablespoons currants
4 cups cauliflower florets
1 cup chopped, peeled tomatoes
2 teaspoons minced fresh ginger root
2 tablespoons dry red wine

In a sauté pan, heat the oil and sauté the onion and garlic until the onion is soft. Add the spices, salt, and currants. Add the cauliflower, chopped tomatoes, and ginger root. Simmer, covered, over low heat until the cauliflower is almost tender, about 3 minutes.

Uncover, add the wine, and simmer until the cauliflower is tender.

Preparation Time: 20 minutes
Yield: 4–6 servings

Cauliflower Dill Sauce With Salmon

The colors of the sauce and salmon are lovely, but it is also delicious served on sautéed chicken breasts or spinach pasta.

2 tablespoons butter
1 cup diced onion
1¾ cups cauliflower puree
2 tablespoons lemon juice
¼ cup heavy cream
½ cup plus 2 tablespoons dry white wine
4 teaspoons minced fresh dill
salt and pepper
1½ cups water
½ teaspoon salt
2 sprigs fresh dill
6 salmon steaks
2 egg yolks

In a small saucepan, melt the butter and sauté ½ cup of the onion until limp, 3–5 minutes.

In a food processor or blender, combine the puree, lemon juice, cream, 2 tablespoons of the wine, the minced dill, and the sautéed onions. Process until smooth. Return to the saucepan. Season to taste with salt and pepper. Simmer gently while you prepare the fish.

To prepare the salmon, combine the water, the remaining ½ cup of wine, the remaining ½ cup of onion, ½ teaspoon salt, and 2 sprigs dill in a frying pan. Place the steaks in the pan and simmer gently until the fish is tender, 8–10 minutes.

Spoon out ½ cup of the cauliflower sauce and add 2 egg yolks to it; mix well. Pour this mixture back into the sauce and mix to incorporate. Heat very gently to prevent the sauce from splitting (curdling). Place the salmon on individual serving plates or a serving platter and smother with the cauliflower sauce. Serve immediately.

Preparation Time: 30 minutes
Cooking Time: 10 minutes
Yield: 6 servings

Cauliflower Curry In Winter Squash

This recipe makes 6 cups of stuffing, which can be used to stuff any winter squash—Butternut, Buttercup, Hubbard, and Acorn are my favorites. Extra squash halves can be stuffed, cooked, and frozen for later use. You can use frozen cauliflower with this recipe.

2 tablespoons vegetable oil
4 cups cauliflower florets
1 cup sliced carrots
1 cup diced green pepper
½ cup diced sweet red pepper
½ cup sliced scallions
½ cup water
1 cup diced unpeeled apple
½ cup yogurt
½ cup cider
2 teaspoons curry powder
3 tablespoons tomato paste
1 tablespoon lemon juice
½ teaspoon salt
3 Acorn squash, halved and seeded

Preheat the oven to 350° F.

In a large sauté pan, heat the oil, and sauté the cauliflower, carrots, peppers, and scallions for 5 minutes. Add ½ cup of water, cover, and cook for 5 minutes. Then add the apple.

Mix together the yogurt, cider, curry powder, tomato paste, lemon juice, and salt. When the vegetables are just tender crisp, pour this sauce over the vegetables and toss to coat.

Spoon the vegetables into squash halves. Place the squash in a baking dish. Cover the dish with foil. Bake for 1 hour, or until the squash is tender.

Preparation Time: 30 minutes
Baking Time: 1 hour
Yield: 6 servings

Fresh dill makes this Cauliflower Dill Sauce very flavorful. Dill is one of the easiest herbs you can grow.

Celery

Extra Effort for the Gardener — Extra Flavor for the Cook

When was the last time you ate at a restaurant and were served celery as a cooked vegetable? Can't remember when? Now that I know how fussy a garden plant it is, I treat celery as a special vegetable. But I think many people don't cook celery because they take it for granted! Or they think of it as a diet snack.

Celery is a very delicious cooked vegetable. But if overcooked, it becomes limp and tasteless. Undercooked, it can be tough. You have to treat celery with as much respect in the kitchen as you do in the garden.

Flood Your Celery Patch Once A Week

In the garden, you have to see that your celery is getting enough water. If not, it will become tough and bitter. Tough celery can be used to flavor soup stocks, but sometimes it gets too bitter to even use that way and should be composted.

Most gardeners blanch the celery stalks about 4 weeks before harvest. This prevents sunlight from reaching the stalks. Mark Hebert recommends that you hill the celery plants by bringing loose soil 4 or 5 inches up the stalks. I know some people claim this method of blanching makes the celery dirty, but celery is pretty easy to wash, so I don't see it as a problem. I think blanching is worthwhile because it produces a milder-flavored celery.

You don't have to wait until the end of the long growing season to enjoy your celery. You can harvest the dark, young outer stalks as soon as there is something big enough to eat. That's why I freely use celery as a flavoring agent throughout this book; I can harvest small stalks of celery as I need them throughout a good part of the summer.

It is unfortunate that celery does not preserve or keep well. The only way to can celery is to pressure can it, which results in a limp, overcooked product. You can freeze it, but I think frozen celery is best in prepared dishes, such as soups and stews. I have dried celery successfully; it makes an excellent addition to soups. All in all, I think it is easiest to harvest celery throughout the summer, and to plan your garden so that you won't have a large surplus at the end of the season.

Whether I'm fixing a celery soup, a glass of tomato juice with a celery stirrer, or a snack of stuffed celery, I know I am enjoying the most refreshing, low-calorie vegetable in the garden.

CELERY AT A GLANCE

rib

bunch

What Midwesterners call a stalk, Easterners call a bunch—the whole plant.

Yields

1 pound fresh celery equals
  4 cups chopped, diced, sliced, diagonally sliced, or julienne-sliced
1 pound fresh celery leaves equals
  6 cups chopped

Cooking Tips

Here are some cooking times for celery:
  Stir Fry: 2 minutes
  Oven Braise: 1 hour
  Sauté: 5–7 minutes
Celery is particularly tasty when sautéed in Mustard Butter (page 304) or Herb Butter (page 160). Herbs that go well with celery are burnet, lovage, caraway, curry, garlic, dill, tarragon, chives, and basil.

For efficiency, stack the ribs, then slice.

Preparation Tips

Celery is often dirty and should be washed well. It is easiest to do this by separating the ribs and gently scrubbing with a vegetable brush under running water.

Wilted celery can be restored by soaking in ice water for up to 30 minutes. It should be used immediately or it will wilt again rapidly.

If woody, cut away the white ends of each stalk.

Outside ribs frequently have tough strings. To remove the strings, slice under the surface of the stalk at the base. Pull away along the stalk and the strings will pull off.

A food processor slices, chops, and minces celery very efficiently.

To hand slice celery efficiently, stack several ribs on top of each other and slice through all the ribs at once.

You'll often find celery on hors d'oeuvre platters. Raw celery is very versatile: you can use it for garnish, offer it with dips, or serve it stuffed.

Here are some of my favorite celery stuffings.

- Spinach Boursin (page 246)
- Radish Butter (page 238)
- Egg salad
- Cream cheese and anchovies or olives
- Cream cheese, blue cheese, and sesame seeds
- Cream cheese, watercress, lemon rind, and lemon juice
- Cream cheese and chopped chives

Or you can make Celery Fans and Ferns to garnish raw vegetable platters.

To make a Celery Fan, slice the celery rib into 3-inch pieces. From the top of the piece, make a series of very close parallel cuts, 1-inch deep. From the bottom, make a second series of parallel cuts 1 inch deep. Chill the fans in ice water, and the thin strips attached to the ½-inch center will curl into fans.

To make a Celery Fern, take a whole rib and make a series of diagonal slices three quarters of the way into the rib at ⅛-inch intervals. Continue along the whole rib. Place the rib in ice water, and the pieces will feather away from the intact rib.

Braised or Sautéed Celery Keeps Its Crisp Texture and Subtle Flavor

I especially like to serve celery as a side dish with roasts and other meats as a light side dish.

Be careful not to overcook. The color of the celery should be an attractive pale green.

Braised Celery With Mint

In a sauté pan, melt ¼ cup butter, and sauté 6 cups diagonally sliced celery, ¼ cup minced fresh chives, and ¼ cup minced fresh mint (or 2 tablespoons dried mint) for 5 minutes. Add 1 cup chicken broth and 2 teaspoons lemon juice. Season to taste with salt and pepper. Cook until the celery is just tender, 3–5 minutes. Makes 6–8 servings.

Celery Sauté With Almonds

In a large sauté pan, heat 2 tablespoons each of butter and vegetable oil, and sauté 6 cups of sliced celery, ½ cup sliced scallions, ¾ cup sliced almonds, 2 teaspoons minced fresh basil, and 1 tablespoon minced fresh fennel leaves, until the celery is just tender, 5–10 minutes. Season to taste with salt and pepper. Makes 6–8 servings.

You can vary the recipe by replacing 1 tablespoon of the vegetable oil with sesame oil, the almonds with other nuts, or selecting different herbs for flavoring.

Waste not, want not with this delicious Celery Leaf Stuffing.

Don't Waste the Leaves— An Extra Helping of Flavor

What do you do with the celery leaves you chop off the top of the ribs? You can dry them or use them fresh in pot herbs or soup stocks. Or you can make the two recipes that follow.

Before you begin, taste the leaves to be sure they aren't too bitter to use.

Celery Leaf Salad Dressing

In a food processor, blender, or mixing bowl, combine 1½ cups minced fresh celery leaves with 1 tablespoon minced fresh chives, ½ cup yogurt, 6 tablespoons vegetable oil, and 1 teaspoon Dijon-style mustard. Blend until the dressing is well mixed and creamy. Season to taste with salt and pepper. Serve over green salads, parboiled vegetable salads, coleslaws, or potato salad. This recipe yields 1½ cups.

Celery Leaf Stuffing

In a large sauté pan, brown 1 pound of bulk sausage, breaking it up with a spoon. Remove the meat and drain off all but 2 tablespoons of fat. Sauté 4 cups chopped celery leaves, 1 teaspoon ground sage, and 1 teaspoon ground rosemary in the fat, until the celery leaves are wilted. Add 4 cups of small bread cubes, ¼ cup chicken broth or water, and 2 beaten eggs. Mix well. Season to taste with salt and pepper.

This recipe yields 6 cups of stuffing, which is enough to stuff a 5–6 pound roasting chicken. Or if you prefer, you can bake the stuffing separately. Spoon the stuffing into a buttered casserole dish and bake in a 350° F. oven for 30 minutes. Keep the dish covered for the first 20 minutes of baking.

SOUPS

Celery and celery leaves are frequently added to soups for flavor. In these two soups, the celery flavor dominates, but is never boring (as I think some cream of celery soups can be).

Celery Tomato Clam Soup

Heat 2 tablespoons olive oil in a soup pot; and in it, sauté 1½ cups diced onion, 3 cups diced celery, ¾ teaspoon ground rosemary, ½ teaspoon ground fennel, and 1 bay leaf, until the onion is limp, about 5 minutes. Add 3–4 cups tomato puree, 1–2 cups water, and 2 cups shelled clams. Simmer for 20 minutes. Season to taste with hot pepper sauce, salt, and pepper. Remove the bay leaf and serve hot. Serves 6.

Double celery fans make a lovely garnish for cold platters. Single fans, on just one end of the celery stick, makes a tasty garnish for tomato juices.

Celery Bacon Soup

2 slices bacon, diced
4 tablespoons butter
1½ cups diced leeks
6 cups diced celery
1 tablespoon minced fresh basil
4 cups chicken broth
2 tablespoons all-purpose unbleached flour
1 cup milk
salt and pepper

Sauté the bacon in a medium-size soup pot until browned. Remove the bacon. Add 2 tablespoons of the butter to the bacon fat and sauté the leeks, celery, and basil for 5–8 minutes, until the vegetables are limp. Add the chicken broth, and simmer until the vegetables are tender, 10–15 minutes.

In a separate saucepan, melt the remaining 2 tablespoons of butter and stir in the flour to make a thick paste. Add the milk a little at a time, stirring well after each addition to prevent lumps. Cook for a few minutes, until the sauce thickens. Add the sauce to the soup and stir well to blend.

To make a smooth soup, cool the soup slightly, puree two-thirds of the soup in a blender, and return it to the pot. Add the bacon slices and reheat.

Season to taste with salt and pepper.

Preparation Time: 20 minutes
Cooking Time: 20–30 minutes
Yield: 6 servings

SALADS

Add celery ribs and leaves to your green salads, egg salads, meat and fish salads, and potato and pasta salads—just about every salad benefits from the crunchy texture of celery.

Celery Anchovy Vinaigrette

Parboiling the walnuts brings out the flavor and changes the texture in an interesting way.

2 cups water
⅔ cup roughly chopped walnuts
4 cups thinly sliced celery
½ cup crumbled feta cheese
2 tablespoons lemon juice
1 tablespoon vinegar
1 heaping tablespoon anchovy paste
¼ cup olive oil
½ teaspoon dried thyme
½ teaspoon dried oregano

Bring the water to a boil. Add the walnuts and simmer for 2 minutes. Drain. Plunge the walnuts into cold water. Drain again.

In a large bowl, combine the walnuts, celery, and feta cheese.

In a small bowl, whisk together the remaining ingredients. Pour over the salad. Toss to coat. Let the salad marinate for 30 minutes before serving.

Preparation Time: 20 minutes
Marinating Time: 30 minutes
Yield: 6–8 servings

Creamy Celery Salad

4 cups diagonally sliced celery
2 cups julienne-sliced boiled ham
   (⅔ pound)
3 cups diced apples (2 whole)
½ cup minced fresh parsley
½ cup sour cream
½ cup buttermilk
1 tablespoon vinegar
1½ teaspoons prepared horseradish
1 tablespoon pure maple syrup
salt and pepper
lettuce

Combine the celery, ham, apples, and parsley in a large bowl.

Combine the remaining ingredients, except the lettuce, in a food processor or blender and blend until smooth. Pour the dressing over the salad and toss to coat. Serve on a bed of lettuce.

Preparation Time: 30 minutes
Yield: 6 servings

SIDE DISHES AND MAIN DISHES

Celery Cheese Tart

2 cups all-purpose unbleached
   flour
1 teaspoon salt
2 tablespoons minced fresh
   chives
10 tablespoons butter or
   vegetable shortening
5 tablespoons cold water
5 cups ½-inch by 2-inch celery
   pieces
1 cup cottage cheese
8 ounces cream cheese
¾ cup grated parmesan cheese
2 eggs
1 teaspoon celery seeds
2 tablespoons melted butter

Preheat the oven to 400° F.

In a large bowl, combine the flour, salt, and chives. Cut in the butter or vegetable shortening until the mixture resembles gravel and sand. Add the cold water and mix just enough to form a ball. Wrap the dough in plastic film wrap and chill while you prepare the filling.

Parboil the celery in water to cover for 2 minutes. Drain.

In a food processor or mixing bowl, blend together the cottage cheese, cream cheese, ½ cup of the parmesan cheese, the eggs, and celery seeds to make a smooth, soupy mixture.

Roll out the dough to fit a 9-inch by 15-inch cookie sheet and form a ½-inch rim to edge the crust. Prick the crust all over and bake for 10 minutes.

Pour the cheese mixture into the baked tart shell and spread it evenly. Place the celery pieces in even rows to completely cover the top of the tart. Brush the celery with the melted butter and sprinkle with the remaining parmesan cheese. Bake for 30 minutes or until the cheese on top is golden brown. Cut into squares and serve hot.

Preparation Time: 30 minutes
Baking Time: 30 minutes
Yield: 8 servings

Celery Dill Sauce

This creamy sauce is delicious on fish or chicken.

4 tablespoons butter
1½ cups diced onion
4 cups diced celery
2 tablespoons minced fresh dill or
   2 teaspoons dried
1 cup water
½ cup dry white wine
½ cup sour cream
salt and pepper

In a large sauté pan, melt the butter and sauté the onion, celery, and dill for 3–5 minutes, until the onion is limp.

Add the water and wine. Simmer until the vegetables are tender, 5–10 minutes. Transfer the sauce to a processor or blender and blend until smooth. Reheat the sauce and add the sour cream. Season to taste with salt and pepper. Serve immediately.

Preparation Time: 10 minutes
Cooking Time: 15 minutes
Yield: 4 cups

Swiss and Ruby
Chard

I Can't Think of a Green That's More Dependable. It's Tasty, Too!

Swiss and Ruby chard thrive in both cool and hot weather. You can begin harvesting the leaves and stems as soon as the plants are a few inches tall—and keep harvesting. You can enjoy a long harvest season with this vegetable.

The best way to harvest Swiss and Ruby chard is to use a long bread knife and slice through the whole plant, harvesting both the larger outer leaves and the smaller inner leaves. Leave about one inch of stem. Then wait and watch the plant grow some more. You can get several cuttings from each plant.

I like to raise both Swiss and Ruby, or Rhubarb (red-stemmed), chard. The two varieties can be used interchangeably in recipes, but there is a difference in flavor. The Ruby variety has a pretty distinctive beet flavor, particularly in the stems. This is no surprise since chard belongs to the beet family. The white stems of Swiss chard are somewhat blander.

You Get Two Plants in One . . .

Chard has a long succulent stem like celery and a large tangy leaf like spinach. It's like getting two plants in one. When the plant is young and tender, I sauté the small leaves and stems in butter and top with buttered bread crumbs or grated parmesan. Tender chard is also delicious sautéed in sesame oil with garlic, or steamed and topped with a cheese sauce (pages 305–306). Sometimes I substitute chard in recipes for greens or spinach. When it is still young and tender, chard can be cooked and the surplus frozen, just like any other green.

But once the plant is older, the stems tend to become tough and require longer cooking times than the leaves. So I cook the stems first and add the leaves later, or chop the whole vegetable to use in fillings. Several of the recipes in this chapter use finely chopped chard—meat loaf, calzone, cannelloni. It's a good way to use up quantities of chard.

Sometimes I'll make a dish using just the leaves, because the stems are tough. Then I use the stems for flavoring soup stock. It's nice to know that there isn't any waste to this dependable garden crop.

Chard is a hardy plant, supplying fresh greens late into the fall. These plants still have time to grow new leaves to replace those I'm harvesting here.

SWISS AND RUBY CHARD
AT A GLANCE

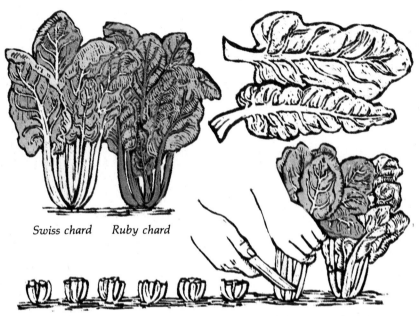

Swiss chard   Ruby chard

I am harvesting the chard by giving the plants a "haircut harvest." The plants will produce more cuttings of this dependable green. With chard, the more you harvest, the more you'll get.

Yields

1 pound fresh chard equals
   17 cups roughly chopped
or
   12 cups finely chopped
or
   4 cups blanched or steamed
1 pound fresh stems equals
   5 cups sliced

Harvest As You Need It

Chard doesn't bolt or flower like other greens. It just gets larger and tougher. Try to harvest regularly so the leaves don't grow too large.

You can store these greens for a few days in a perforated plastic bag in the refrigerator—but they don't hold up that well. I prefer to harvest chard as I need it.

It's Easier to Wash
When You Separate the Stems
From the Leaves

Swiss and Ruby chard leaves can be enormous. When wet, they drip water all over. I like to separate the stems from the leaves and wash them separately. Since I often cook the leaves and stems separately, washing separately is convenient. First, I wash the stems under running water, like celery. Then I wash the leaves by dunking in lukewarm water, just as I do spinach. Then I pat dry, and drain well or use a salad spinner. The leaves are rather crinkled, so they hold water easily—which is okay if you plan to blanch or steam them.

String Tough Stems
Just Like Celery

The stems of older chard can be as stringy as celery. Remove the strings by slipping a paring knife under the outside of the stalk and pull the strings away.

Remove the center rib from the large leaves if they are tough.

Young leaves can be cooked with their center rib, and they don't require stringing.

Cooking Times

Cooking times vary according to the size and age of the chard, as well as the quantity being cooked and the size of the pot.

I prefer to steam chard when I am cooking large quantities. Cooking will be more even in a large pot where the leaves are not tightly packed. I use a 4-gallon soup pot for steaming.

Steam (leaves): 2–5 minutes
        (stalks): 4–6 minutes
I prefer to blanch or sauté small amounts. Sautéed chard has more flavor *and* more calories from the butter or oil in which it was sautéed.

Parboil (leaves): 2 minutes
         (stalks): 3 minutes
Sauté (leaves): 1–2 minutes
        (stalks): 3–4 minutes
When I sauté chard, I use 3 tablespoons butter or oil for 4–6 cups chopped chard.

To be sure not to overcook chard, I add the stalks to the pot first. After a minute or so of cooking, I add the leaves.

Kids Love Cheesy Pocket Pizzas Filled with Swiss Chard and Summer Squash

Here's a combination that can't be beat: calzones made with Swiss chard, summer squash, and plenty of cheese. I serve the calzones with a large bowl of Italian Tomato Sauce (page 306) for dipping or spooning over the top.

To make the calzones, make a yeast dough first. In a large bowl, sprinkle 1 tablespoon dried baker's yeast over 1½ cups warm water. Stir in a pinch of sugar and set aside until the yeast foams, about 5 minutes.

Then add 2 tablespoons olive oil, 1 teaspoon salt, and 2 cups all-purpose unbleached flour. Stir well. Stir in 2 cups whole wheat flour. Cover the dough and let rise in a warm, draft-free place for 1 hour.

While the dough rises, prepare the filling. In a large sauté pan, heat 2 tablespoons olive oil, and sauté 1½ cups diced onion and 1 minced garlic clove for 2 minutes. Add 3 cups grated summer squash. Sauté for 3 minutes, or until the vegetables are limp. Remove the vegetables to a bowl and stir in 2½ cups grated mozzarella cheese and ¾ cup grated parmesan cheese.

Steam 12 cups of roughly chopped Swiss or Ruby chard until limp, 3–5 minutes. Drain well.

In the sauté pan, heat 1 tablespoon butter, and sauté 1 tablespoon minced fresh basil, 1 tablespoon minced fresh parsley, 2 cups chopped mushrooms, and ½ teaspoon ground fennel until the mushrooms are limp, about 3 minutes. Combine the chard and mushroom mixtures.

Punch down the dough and divide it into 8 pieces. Roll each piece of dough out on a floured board to make an 8-inch circle. Onto each dough circle, spoon an eighth of the squash mixture and an eighth of the chard mixture. Brush the edges of the dough with water and fold the dough circles in half. Crimp the edges. Use a fork to pierce the tops in several places to allow steam to escape. Place the calzones on a greased baking sheet.

Preheat the oven to 375° F. Let the calzones rise for 20 minutes. Brush with a beaten egg. Bake for 30 minutes. Serve hot.

Whenever you steam greens, such as Ruby chard, try to squeeze out as much moisture as possible before using.

1. Roll out to an 8-inch circle.

2. Spoon on the filling.

3. Fold dough over the filling.

4. Crimp the edges, then prick holes to allow steam to escape.

APPETIZERS

Sometimes I line appetizer trays with the beautiful leaves of Ruby chard.

Swiss Chard Cheese Balls

I love to serve these Swiss Chard Cheese Balls with the Fennel Cheese Sauce (page 306) over pasta. As an appetizer, I serve them with the Dijon Sauce (page 305).

4 tablespoons butter
1 large garlic clove, minced
1 cup chopped onion
1½ cups finely chopped fresh fennel root
24 cups roughly chopped Swiss or Ruby chard
4 eggs, beaten
1 cup grated Swiss cheese
½ cup grated parmesan cheese
2–3 cups bread crumbs

Preheat the oven to 400° F.

Melt the butter in a sauté pan, and sauté the garlic, onion, and fennel until the onion is limp, 3–5 minutes.

Steam the Swiss chard until limp, 3–5 minutes.

In a large bowl, combine the Swiss chard, garlic, onion, fennel, eggs, cheeses, and enough bread crumbs to bind. Shape the mixture into walnut-sized balls and place on a greased baking sheet. Bake for 20 minutes. Serve warm.

Preparation Time: 25 minutes
Baking Time: 20 minutes
Yield: 4–6 servings as a main course,
    8–12 servings as an appetizer

Here's a tangy Red and White Salad using just the stems of Swiss and Ruby chard. The stems alone have a nice crunch.

SOUPS

The recipes in the Spinach chapter (pages 242–249) are also delicious when made with Swiss or Ruby chard.

Chard, Beef, and Lemon Soup

6–8 cups finely chopped Swiss or Ruby chard
1 lemon
2 tablespoons olive oil
2 cups diced onions
2 garlic cloves, minced
½ teaspoon ground rosemary
5 cups beef broth
salt and pepper

As you prepare the chard, separate the stems from the leaves.

Using a vegetable peeler, strip off 6 thin slivers of lemon peel, making sure you do not get any white pith. Squeeze the lemon to extract the juice. You should have 6 tablespoons. Set both juice and peel aside.

Heat the oil in a large soup pot, and sauté the onions and garlic until limp, 3–5 minutes. Add the rosemary, beef broth, lemon juice, and lemon peels. Simmer for about 10 minutes and remove the lemon peels. Add the Swiss chard stems to the soup and simmer for 3 minutes. Then add the chard leaves and simmer for 5 minutes more, or until the chard is wilted.

Season to taste with salt and pepper. Serve hot.

Preparation Time: 20 minutes
Cooking Time: 15 minutes
Yield: 6–8 servings

Swiss and ruby chard stems are similar to celery. Sometimes you must remove the tough, stringy fibers before slicing. Just slip a paring knife under the skin and pull the fibers away. Then you can use the stems in salads or in place of celery in cooked dishes.

SALADS

Tender, young Swiss and Ruby chard can be chopped and added to green salads. The leaves are never bitter.

Tangy Chard Salad

24 cups roughly chopped Swiss or
    Ruby chard
½ cup thinly sliced celery
½ cup thinly sliced radishes
¼ cup sliced scallions
2 tablespoons minced fresh parsley
¼ cup olive oil
¼ cup lemon juice
1 teaspoon prepared horseradish
1 teaspoon Dijon-style mustard
¼ teaspoon celery seed
1 garlic clove, minced
salt and pepper

Steam the Swiss chard until limp, 3–5 minutes; drain. Rinse under cold water to cool and drain well.

In a large bowl, combine the chard, celery, radishes, scallions, and parsley. Toss.

In a blender or food processor, combine the oil, lemon juice, horseradish, mustard, celery seed, and garlic. Blend until mixed. Pour over the salad and toss to coat. Season to taste with salt and pepper. Serve immediately.

Preparation Time: 15 minutes
Cooking Time: 3–5 minutes
Yield: 6–8 servings

Red and White Salad

4 cups sliced Ruby chard stems
4 cups sliced Swiss chard stems
2 tablespoons wine vinegar
2 tablespoons white rice vinegar
1 garlic clove, minced
1 teaspoon sesame oil
1 teaspoon tamari or soy sauce
3 tablespoons vegetable oil
¼ teaspoon minced fresh ginger
    root
½ cup minced fresh parsley
salt and pepper

Steam the stems until barely tender, 3–5 minutes. Plunge into cold water to stop the cooking and drain.

Whisk together the remaining ingredients. Pour over the stems and toss to coat. Serve at once.

Preparation Time: 15 minutes
Cooking Time: 3–5 minutes
Yield: 6–8 servings

SIDE DISHES AND MAIN DISHES

Don't forget that Swiss or Ruby chard can be substituted for most of the greens in the Greens chapter (pages 148–153), too.

Sesame Chard With Currants

The flavor of this dish is inspired by Middle Eastern cuisine. Sesame Chard goes especially well with roast chicken or lamb.

2 tablespoons olive oil
1 cup diced onion
⅓ cup currants or raisins
1 tablespoon sesame seeds
4 teaspoons lemon juice
18 cups roughly chopped Swiss or
    Ruby chard
salt and pepper

Heat the olive oil in a large sauté pan, and sauté the onion until limp, 3–5 minutes. Add the currants, sesame seeds, lemon juice, and chard. Stir to coat. Cover and steam for 2 minutes.

Remove the cover and sauté until the chard is wilted and well coated with sesame seeds and currants. Season to taste with salt and pepper. Serve hot.

Preparation Time: 10 minutes
Cooking Time: 10 minutes
Yield: 4–6 servings

Cannelloni

Cannelloni are tube-shaped pasta, similar to manicotti. I buy cannelloni shells at the supermarket. If you have trouble finding cannelloni, substitute manicotti or large shells. Or better still, make Spinach Pasta (page 245). Cut the dough into 4-inch squares to fill and roll.

12 cups roughly chopped Swiss or
   Ruby chard
12–16 cannelloni shells
2 tablespoons olive oil
¾ cup diced onion
2 garlic cloves, minced
2 cups sliced mushrooms
¼ cup minced fresh parsley
1½ cups ricotta cheese
1½ cups grated parmesan cheese
1 tablespoon lemon juice
salt and pepper
3–4 cups Italian Tomato Sauce
   (page 306)

Preheat the oven to 350° F.

Steam the chard until limp, 3–5 minutes. Drain well. When the chard is cool enough to handle, wring out the excess moisture with your hands.

Cook the cannelloni shells in 4–5 quarts of boiling salted water until barely tender; drain, and set aside.

Heat the oil in a sauté pan, and sauté the onion and garlic for 2 minutes. Add the mushrooms and parsley, and sauté until the vegetables are limp.

In a large bowl, combine the Swiss chard, onion and mushrooms, ricotta, 1 cup of the parmesan cheese, and the lemon juice. Season to taste with salt

1. Stuff with the chard mixture.

2. Smother with sauce; bake.

and pepper. Fill the cannelloni shells with the chard mixture.

Spoon a small amount of sauce in the bottom of a 9-inch by 13-inch baking dish. Lay the stuffed shells on top and spoon on the remaining sauce. Sprinkle with the remaining ½ cup of parmesan cheese.

Bake for 30–40 minutes or until heated through.

Preparation Time: 30 minutes
Baking Time: 30–40 minutes
Yield: 6–8 servings

Chard-Stuffed Meat Loaf

¾ cup bread crumbs
¼ cup milk
1 pound ground beef
1 teaspoon minced fresh oregano or
   ¼ teaspoon dried
¼ teaspoon fresh thyme or a pinch
   of dried
1 teaspoon minced fresh marjoram
   or ¼ teaspoon dried
2 teaspoons minced fresh basil or
   ½ teaspoon dried
1 tablespoon vegetable oil
½ cup minced onion
1 cup finely diced Swiss or Ruby
   chard stems (approximately)
1¾ cups Italian Tomato Sauce
   (page 306)
2 eggs
½ teaspoon salt
12 cups roughly chopped Swiss or
   Ruby chard leaves
2 cups grated provolone cheese

Preheat the oven to 350° F.

In a large bowl, combine ½ cup of the bread crumbs and the milk. Add the ground beef and herbs.

Heat the oil in a small sauté pan, and sauté the onion and chard stems for 5 minutes. Add the onion and stems to the meat with ¼ cup of the tomato sauce, 1 egg, and the salt. Mix well and set aside.

Steam the 12 cups of chard leaves until limp, 3–5 minutes; drain well. Squeeze out as much liquid as possible.

In a separate bowl, combine the chard leaves, ½ cup of the tomato sauce, the remaining ¼ cup bread crumbs, 1 egg, and 1 cup of the cheese.

Grease a 9-inch loaf pan and press three-quarters of the meat onto the bottom and along the sides of the pan. Spoon the Swiss chard mixture over the meat. Cover with the remaining meat mixture. Spoon the remaining 1 cup sauce over the loaf and sprinkle on the remaining 1 cup cheese.

Place the loaf in the oven and bake for 50 minutes. Leave the loaf in the pan for 5 minutes before unmolding. Then slice and serve.

Preparation Time: 35 minutes
Baking Time: 50 minutes
Yield: 6 servings

Green Rice

If you cook the rice in salted chicken broth, reduce the amount of salt.

¼ cup butter
½ cup sliced leeks
½ cup sliced scallions
½ cup minced fresh parsley
2 large garlic cloves, minced
¼ cup finely minced green peppers
2 cups finely minced Swiss chard
½ teaspoon salt
2 cups uncooked brown rice
4 cups water or chicken broth

In a large saucepan, melt the butter and sauté the leeks, scallions, parsley, garlic, and green pepper until the vegetables are limp, about 5 minutes. Add the Swiss chard, salt, rice, and water. Stir and cover the pot. Reduce the heat. Cook the rice without stirring for 45 minutes, or until all the water is absorbed. Toss with a fork and serve.

Preparation Time: 15 minutes
Cooking Time: 50 minutes
Yield: 6–8 servings

Swiss Chard Carrot Terrine

6 tablespoons butter
3 cups grated carrots
¼ cup sliced scallions
½ teaspoon ground rosemary
¼ teaspoon pepper
3 tablespoons all-purpose unbleached flour
2 cups milk
6 tablespoons grated parmesan cheese
4 eggs
salt and pepper
24 cups chiffonade Swiss chard
1 tablespoon minced fresh basil or 1 teaspoon dried
5 tablespoons bread crumbs

Preheat the oven to 350° F.

In a large sauté pan, melt 4 tablespoons of the butter, and sauté the carrots, scallions, and rosemary for 2–3 minutes, or until the carrots are wilted. Remove from the pan and combine with the pepper, 1 tablespoon of the flour, 1 cup of the milk, 4 tablespoons of the cheese, 2 eggs, and salt to taste.

Grease a 9-inch loaf pan and place the carrot mixture in the pan.

Steam the Swiss chard until limp, 2–5 minutes.

In a small saucepan, melt the remaining 2 tablespoons butter, and stir in 2 tablespoons of the flour to make a thick paste. Stir in the remaining cup of milk a little at a time, stirring well after each addition to prevent lumps. Add the remaining 2 tablespoons cheese.

Squeeze the Swiss chard to remove as much moisture as possible. Combine the Swiss chard, cheese sauce, the

remaining 2 eggs, the basil, and 4 tablespoons of the bread crumbs. Season to taste with salt and pepper.

Sprinkle the remaining 1 tablespoon bread crumbs over the carrot mixture and spoon the Swiss chard mixture on top. Bake the loaf for 1 hour. Let sit for 10 minutes after removing from the oven. Then unmold and slice.

Preparation Time: 40 minutes
Baking Time: 1 hour
Yield: 6–8 servings

When the leaves are large, the stems tend to be tough. I like to remove the tough center rib before cooking or adding to salads. To do this I fold the leaf in half, then slice off the rib. This same technique can be used on collard leaves, mustard greens, and spinach. I also remove the center rib from cabbage leaves before stuffing and rolling.

Thinly sliced, Swiss chard stems make a tasty addition to tossed salads—as long as the stems are tender and without "strings." Or finely diced, the stems can be added to tuna or chicken salads in place of celery. Sliced on the diagonal, chard stems are perfect for mixed vegetable stir fries.

Corn

Please Save Some Ears For These Exciting "Off-the-Cob" Recipes

Gardeners have a huge advantage over nongardeners when it comes to sweet corn: they can bring their corn from plant to pot and have it cooked in minutes—the sweetest, freshest tasting corn imaginable. And nothing compares to it, especially when the corn is picked at the peak of its perfection.

It's easy to determine if sweet corn is ready for harvest. Find the top of the ear and press down. If the ear is pointed, the corn is not ready to pick. But if the top of the ear is fairly flat and almost rounded, the ear is ripe. This is a no-fail method if you feel the *top*, not the *sides*, of the ear. It sure beats having to pull the husk to test for readiness—which is an invitation for insects and birds to ruin your harvest.

The Fresher the Better

Fresh corn does not keep well. As soon as the corn is picked, the natural sugars begin converting to starch. That's why it's important to cook corn as soon as possible to halt this reaction.

I've learned by experience that you must stagger your planting dates or else plan to do some marathon corn preservation. By starting the planting season early, I can grow early-season varieties and enjoy plenty of fresh eating. I plant late season varieties which have the best flavor, to extend the season and provide corn for the freezer. I like to have some frozen corn kernels in the freezer, but I prefer to eat most of my harvest fresh.

Fresh corn-on-the-cob is so delicious most people can eat it for days on end without tiring of it. But corn blends so well with other vegetables and meats that I have enjoyed cooking with it off the cob, and I hope you will too.

Corn is one of the few truly American foods, and my recipes reflect that fact. The continent of North America includes Mexico, of course, and many of the recipes I have developed have been influenced by the wonderful foods I have enjoyed while traveling in that country.

Many of my recipes use just a few cups of corn kernels. That's because over the years most of my experiments have been made with those pesky, small quantities of leftover corn or extra ears.

It's early September and the corn harvest is at its peak. This corn—an early yellow and white kernel variety—is going straight from the garden into a pot filled with boiling water just waiting in the kitchen.

Yields

1 pound fresh corn equals 5–6 ears
5–6 ears equals 3 cups kernels

Eat Corn Fresh!

If you must store harvested ears, keep them refrigerated. With the husks intact, corn will keep for 3–4 days. Or you can husk and store in perforated plastic bags for 3–4 days. The flavor loss will be noticeable.

To test for ripeness, pinch the top of the ear to see if it is well rounded.

Keep the Crunch In Your Corn-on-the-Cob

Whether you are boiling, steaming, or roasting corn-on-the-cob, do not overcook. Here are some guidelines: the times vary depending on the size of the ears.

Cooking Times
Boil: 3–7 minutes
Steam: 5–10 minutes
Roast (in husk): 25 minutes
Roast (in foil): 15 minutes
Soak your corn in water before roasting in husk. This prevents scorching.

CORN AT A GLANCE

Corn Kernels Cook Quickly

If you are cooking corn in a recipe, you will need to remove the kernels from the ears. I hold the cob upright in a bowl and run my sharp paring knife straight down the rows; the kernels fall into the bowl.

Cooking Times
Blanch: 3–5 minutes
Steam: 4 minutes
Sauté: 3–10 minutes

Cooking With Frozen Corn Kernels

You can add frozen corn kernels (undefrosted) to any recipe that calls for corn kernels. You can add undefrosted frozen kernels to salads, or you can quickly blanch first.

Canned corn is acceptable in most corn recipes, but I don't particularly like the taste of it myself.

Sautéed Corn Kernels Shouldn't Be Missed

Corn kernels are delicious sautéed in butter with herbs. Herbs and spices that go well with corn include dill, mint, cilantro, basil, oregano savory, marjoram, tarragon, chili powder, and curry powder.

Sauté 4 cups corn kernels with 2 tablespoons Pesto (page 161) for an unusual side dish.

Grated cheese, peppers, onions, celery, tomatoes, and cooked dried or shell beans go well with sautéed corn.

There is a lot you can do with leftover corn!

First off, slice the kernels off the ears to save space in the refrigerator.

Add leftover corn kernels to yo' favorite quiches and frittatas.

Add up to 1½ cups corn kernels to your favorite cornbread recipe.

Add up to 1 cup of corn kernels to your favorite pancake or fritter batter.

Add corn kernels to chili.

Use overripe corn in chowders.

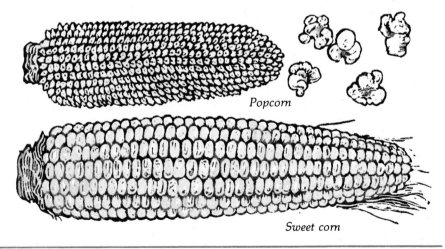

Popcorn

Sweet corn

1. Spoon filling onto husks.

2. Wrap husks over filling.

The foil wrapping keeps these Corn Tamales piping hot.

Bring the flavors of Mexico into your kitchen
With fresh corn tamales

Tamales, steaming corn-husk packets of meat and vegetables are popular evening snacks in Mexico. After my first visit, I created this recipe to bring back the pleasure of eating foreign foods, while still using my own homegrown vegetables.

Tamales are fun to make and to eat. I like to serve them as a side dish with meat at informal suppers and barbecues. You can eat them with your hands, which makes them very popular with kids. This recipe makes 24 tamales, enough for 6–8 servings.

To make tamales, remove the husks from 8 ears of corn and save all the tender inside leaves to wrap the filling.

Using a sharp paring knife, remove the kernels from the ears. You should have 4 cups of kernels.

Combine the kernels, ¾ cup diced onion, ½ cup butter, 1 cup cornmeal, 2 teaspoons chili powder, 1 teaspoon salt, and 2 tablespoons milk in a food processor. Blend until well mixed. Remove the mixture to a bowl and stir in 2 cups grated Monterey jack cheese.

Heat 1 tablespoon vegetable oil in a small frying pan, and sauté 1½ cups diced green pepper until tender crisp, 3–5 minutes. Mix the pepper into the corn mixture. The filling is now ready.

To wrap the tamales, place 2 corn leaves along the length of your hand, overlapping them slightly. Spoon ¼ cup or less filling into the middle of the leaves. Place 2 more corn leaves on top of the filling at right angles to the first set. Overlap these leaves slightly. Fold the husks around the filling to completely enclose it.

Place each tamale on a 7-inch square of aluminum foil and fold the foil to enclose the tamale completely.

When all the tamales are wrapped, arrange the packets on a steaming basket over boiling water. Steam for 1 hour. Remove the foil before serving. Fold back the husks to eat.

The Corn Cheese Puffs make great "finger food" at a party.

Corn Cheese Puffs

¼ cup butter
1 cup milk
½ teaspoon salt
1 cup all-purpose unbleached flour
4 eggs
1 cup grated Swiss cheese
½ teaspoon chili powder
1 teaspoon minced fresh basil or
  ¼ teaspoon dried
⅛ teaspoon cayenne
2 cups corn kernels

Preheat the oven to 375° F.

In a small saucepan, combine the butter, milk, and salt. Bring to a boil and remove the pan from the heat. Add the flour and stir well. The dough will form a ball, rolling off the sides of the pan. Return the pan to the heat and cook for about 1 minute to dry out the dough, stirring constantly.

Remove the pan from the heat and stir in the eggs, one at a time. Add the remaining ingredients and stir well.

Grease a cookie sheet and drop teaspoons of dough onto it, leaving at least 2 inches between each puff. Bake for 25 minutes or until puffy and browned.

Serve hot.

Preparation Time: 25 minutes
Baking Time: 25 minutes
Yield: 20–24 puffs (6–8 servings)

Tomato Corn Soup combines tomatoes and corn just when they are at their peak—a great harvest dish.

SOUPS

Corn Chowder With Variations

Corn Chowder should be enjoyed year-round. When fresh corn isn't in season, substitute frozen or canned corn.

3 tablespoons butter
2 cups diced onions
2 cups diced potatoes
4 cups corn kernels
4 cups milk
2 bay leaves
salt and pepper

In a large soup pot, melt the butter, and sauté the onions until limp, 3–5 minutes. Add the potatoes, corn, milk, and bay leaves. Simmer for 15–20 minutes, or until the potatoes are tender.

Cool the soup slightly. Remove the bay leaves. Puree two-thirds of the soup in a food processor or blender. Return the puree to the pot and reheat. Season to taste with salt and pepper.

Preparation Time: 20 minutes
Cooking Time: 20 minutes
Yield: 6–8 servings

Variations

Curry Corn Chowder. Add 2–3 teaspoons curry powder to the onions when sautéing. Then proceed with the recipe.

1. Slice open all the kernels.

2. Scrape out the pulp for creamed corn.

Bacon Corn Chowder. Brown ¼ pound diced bacon in the soup pot and remove from the pan. Drain off all but 2 tablespoons bacon fat, and sauté the onions in bacon fat instead of butter. Return the diced bacon to the soup as a garnish.

Cheese Corn Chowder. Add 2 cups grated Swiss or cheddar cheese to the soup after you have returned the puree to the pot.

Garden Corn Chowder. Add 1½–2 cups cooked diced vegetables to the soup after you have returned the puree to the pot. Recommended vegetables are snap beans, lima beans, carrots, sautéed peppers, and peeled and seeded cucumbers.

Chicken Corn Chowder. Add 1–1½ cups shredded cooked chicken to the soup after you have returned the puree to the pot.

Creamy Chicken Corn Chowder. Use 3 cups chicken stock and 1 cup heavy cream in place of the milk.

Tomato Corn Soup

When fresh corn and tomatoes are in season, I make this soup from fresh ingredients. It's delicious made with canned tomatoes and frozen corn, too. Try the Cheesy Corn Dumplings (page 119) with this soup.

1 tablespoon vegetable oil
1 pound ground beef
3 cups corn kernels
3 cups diced tomatoes
2 cups water or beef broth
1 cup diced onion
1 garlic clove, minced
2 tablespoons minced fresh basil or 2 teaspoons dried
1½ tablespoons fresh thyme or 1½ teaspoons dried
1½ teaspoons crumbled fresh rosemary or ½ teaspoon dried
3–4 tablespoons minced fresh parsley
salt and pepper

In a large soup pot, heat the vegetable oil, and brown the ground beef, breaking it up with a spoon. Drain off all the fat. Add the remaining ingredients and simmer for 30 minutes. Season to taste with salt and pepper. Serve hot.

Preparation Time: 20 minutes
Cooking Time: 40 minutes
Yield: 6–8 servings

SALADS

I think corn salads should be as popular as potato salads. Try one of these and you will find yourself agreeing.

Corn, Radish, and Parsley Salad

This salad is so beautiful that I try to find special ways to serve it. Sometimes I hollow out tomatoes and serve the salad in the tomatoes. Other times I serve it on a bed of lettuce, garnished with tomato wedges or radish roses.

4 cups corn kernels
1 cup sliced radishes
¼ cup minced fresh parsley
¼ cup olive oil
2 tablespoons lemon juice
2 tablespoons minced fresh basil
2 tablespoons grated parmesan cheese
1 garlic clove, minced
salt and pepper

Blanch the corn in boiling water for 3–4 minutes and drain. Run under cold water to cool, and drain again.

In a salad bowl, combine the corn, radishes, and parsley.

Whisk together the oil, lemon juice, basil, cheese, and garlic. Pour over the corn. Toss to coat. Season to taste with salt and pepper. Serve at once or chill first.

Preparation Time: 20 minutes
Yield: 6 servings

Corn and Tomato Salad

4 cups corn kernels
2 cups diced tomatoes
¼ cup minced fresh parsley
½ cup diced red onion
2 tablespoons lime juice
2 tablespoons vegetable oil
2 teaspoons minced fresh cilantro
salt and pepper

Blanch the corn in boiling water for 3–4 minutes and drain. Run under cold water to cool, and drain again.

In a salad bowl, combine the corn, tomatoes, parsley, and onion.

Whisk together the lime juice, oil, and cilantro. Pour over the salad. Toss to coat. Season to taste with salt and pepper. Chill the salad for at least 1 hour before serving.

Preparation Time: 1 hour
Chilling Time: 1 hour
Yield: 4–6 servings

Corn and Mint Salad

The oil-free dressing makes this salad a good one for dieters.

4 cups corn kernels
2 cups finely diced carrots
5 tablespoons minced fresh mint
¼ cup roasted sunflower seeds
½ cup orange juice
4 tablespoons lemon juice
1 teaspoon Dijon-style mustard

Blanch the corn in boiling water for 3–4 minutes and drain. Rinse under cold water to cool, and drain again.

In a salad bowl, combine the corn, carrots, mint, and sunflower seeds. Whisk together the remaining ingredients and pour over the salad. Toss to coat. Chill for at least 1 hour before serving.

Preparation Time: 20 minutes
Chilling Time: 1 hour
Yield: 6 servings

Blue Cheese, Corn, And Chicken Salad

This salad can be served on a bed of lettuce or stuffed into pita bread pockets.

3 cups corn kernels
1½ cups diced cooked chicken
1 cup sliced celery
½ cup diced green pepper
¼ cup sliced scallion
2 tablespoons white vinegar
6 tablespoons vegetable oil
½ cup crumbled blue cheese
½ cup sour cream
½ cup mayonnaise
1 tablespoon lemon juice
½ teaspoon salt

Blanch the corn in boiling water until just cooked, 3–4 minutes. Drain immediately and run under cold water to cool. Drain again.

Combine the corn, chicken, celery, peppers, and scallions in a salad bowl.

Combine the remaining ingredients in a food processor or blender and process until smooth. Pour over the salad and toss to coat. Chill for at least 1 hour before serving.

Preparation Time: 25 minutes
Chilling Time: 1 hour
Yield: 4–6 servings

Corn salads are an excellent way to use up a few extra ears of corn. These hearty salads make excellent side dishes with meat.

SIDE DISHES AND MAIN DISHES

On the cob in season, off the cob out of season. Most of these recipes can be made with frozen corn—out of season, of course.

Cheesy Corn Dumplings

I particularly like to eat these dumplings in the Tomato Corn Soup (page 117), but they are great in any tomato-based soup.

1 cup all-purpose unbleached flour
½ cup cornmeal
2½ teaspoons baking powder
½ teaspoon salt
1 egg
½ cup milk
½ cup grated cheddar cheese
1 tablespoon minced fresh parsley
1 cup corn kernels

Sift together the flour, cornmeal, baking powder, and salt.

Beat together the egg and milk.

Stir the wet ingredients into the dry ingredients until just blended. Add the remaining ingredients and stir to mix.

Drop the dumpling dough by the tablespoon on top of a simmering soup or stew or into boiling water. Cover the pot and steam the dumplings undisturbed for 15 minutes. Serve hot.

Preparation Time: 15 minutes
Cooking Time: 15 minutes
Yield: 6 servings.

Last night's corn-on-the-cob becomes this morning's tender sweet waffles, packed with extra protein.

Corn Waffles

Here's a Sunday brunch favorite, made with leftover, frozen, or fresh corn.

2 cups sifted all-purpose unbleached flour
1½ teaspoons baking powder
½ teaspoon baking soda
½ teaspoon salt
1 tablespoon sugar
3 eggs, separated
1½ cups buttermilk
6 tablespoons melted butter
1½ cups corn kernels

Preheat the waffle iron.

Sift together the flour, baking powder, baking soda, salt, and sugar.

Whisk together the egg yolks, buttermilk, and butter.

Beat the egg whites until stiff.

Add the egg yolk and buttermilk mixture to the dry ingredients. Mix until just blended. Fold in the corn kernels, then the egg whites.

Make the waffles according to the waffle iron manufacturer's instructions. Serve hot with butter and pure maple syrup.

Preparation Time: 20 minutes
Cooking Time: 25 minutes
Yield: 6 servings

Cucumbers

Continual Harvesting Means Crisp, Low-Calorie Cucumbers All Summer!

My choice for the best all-round cucumber is a "burpless" hybrid cucumber. This thin-skinned, dark green cucumber is good for slicing into salads, cooking, and pickling. I also like to grow some "lemon" cucumbers on a trellis. They are attractive in the garden and sweet to eat.

I have a friend, though, who swears by pickling cucumbers. She says that pickling cucumbers have smaller seeds, that they tend to be more flavorful, and that they are delicious prepared any way you might prepare a slicing cucumber. She likes never having a half-consumed cucumber in the refrigerator because pickling cucumbers are much smaller than slicing cucumbers. The skins are tender, too, and don't require peeling.

I suspect that her preference begins with her interest in pickling. It does make sense to me to grow pickling cucumbers if you are planning to pickle your extra—unless you have the space to grow both the small pale pickling cucumbers and the large slicing cucumbers.

Pickle the Extras

Pickling is an excellent way to preserve excess cucumbers. I have not included any pickle recipes here, as pickling is an art in itself, and there are other books that cover the subject thoroughly. Garden Way has a book I recommend called *Pickles and Relishes, 150 Recipes from Apples to Zucchini*. Once you get started on pickling, you will realize that just about any garden vegetable can be pickled or made into relish with delicious results. Sweet bread and butter pickles and sour dills are especially popular cucumber pickles.

One way to avoid having excess cucumbers is to stagger your plantings. Also, if you keep harvesting your cucumbers as soon as they are 2–3 inches long, the plants will keep producing, and you will be harvesting cucumbers all summer long.

Harvest your cucumbers in the early morning if possible. The cucumbers will be crisper then, because the heat of the sun hasn't had a chance to wilt them. Chill them quickly—in the refrigerator or on ice. Then remember to serve them as soon as possible for the freshest flavor.

Cucumbers galore! I'll put up quarts of pickles and still have more cucumbers to make into tasty soups and salads.

CUCUMBERS AT A GLANCE

Yields

1 pound fresh cucumbers equals
　4 cups sliced or cubed
or
　3 cups diced
or
　2 cups pureed raw

To Peel, Or Not to Peel?

Unless a recipe specifically calls for peeling, the choice is yours.

I prefer to peel the cucumbers in most dishes, unless I want the dark green skins to contribute color to the dish. (I *always* peel storebought cucumbers that have been waxed.)

To peel in a decorative style, peel alternate strips from the cucumber. The sliced cucumbers will appear striped. Or score the cucumber along its length with the tines of a fork. Then slice.

Why Are Cucumbers Sometimes Bitter?

Since most of the bitterness has been bred out of new cucumber varieties, bitterness is usually the result of poor growing conditions.

To rid cucumbers of bitterness, remove the stem and blossom ends, peel, and slice the cucumbers. Sprinkle with salt and let drain in a colander for about 1 hour. The salt will draw off the bitterness.

Cucumbers won't water down salad dressings if salted and drained first.

Regular cucumber

Pickling cucumbers

Lemon cucumbers

Armenian cucumber

Food Processors Save Time

The thin cucumber slices that a food processor can produce are particularly nice for pickles and some salads. The food processor is also handy for grating and pureeing.

I use a chef's knife to make thick slices of cucumbers.

To peel cucumbers, I prefer to use my 2-inch-wide vegetable peeler.

To seed cucumbers, I slice the cucumber in half, then run the tip of a teaspoon down the center, scooping away the seeds. Overgrown cucumbers can be seeded, then sliced, and used as you would a younger cucumber. The resulting slices are an attractive crescent shape.

Storing Cucumbers

Keep cucumbers chilled in the refrigerator in perforated bags for 3–5 days.

Store large quantities of cucumbers over ice in a clean bucket or garbage can.

To restore wilted cucumbers, soak in salted ice water for 1–2 hours.

Cooking and Preparation Ideas

Slice or dice cucumbers and sauté in butter with herbs for about 5 minutes. Do not brown. Add ¼ cup heavy cream or chicken broth, if desired. Herbs that go well with cucumbers include dill, mint, basil, thyme, cilantro, rosemary, tarragon, fennel, borage, and lovage.

Other flavorings you can add to the butter include mustard, caraway seeds, curry powder, horseradish, chives, onions, garlic, currants, and bread crumbs.

Add sliced or grated cucumbers to green salads and other mixed vegetable salads.

Large cucumbers can be peeled, halved, and seeded to make cucumber "boats" to hold salads.

Sliced cucumbers can be added to stir fries during the last 1–2 minutes of cooking.

Chilled cucumber soups make refreshing fare for summer— And so easy to prepare for a crowd!

Cucumber Buttermilk Soup

I consider this soup a summer standard. If it begins to taste too familiar, I vary the herbs and the soup tastes new. The recipe can be doubled or tripled easily for a crowd—a good way to keep up with the harvest.

Combine 6 cups peeled, seeded and chopped cucumbers, 2 cups buttermilk, 1 cup sour cream, ½ cup diced scallions, 3 tablespoons lemon juice, 1 teaspoon salt, and 2 tablespoons minced fresh cilantro, mint, or dill in a food processor or blender. Process until smooth. Chill well and serve. Garnish with grated cucumber if desired. This recipe serves 6–8.

Syrian Cucumber Soup

Combine 4 cups finely chopped or grated peeled cucumbers with 2 cups yogurt, 2 cups water, 2 minced garlic cloves, ½ teaspoon ground cumin, and 1 teaspoon salt. Ladle the soup into individual bowls and place 2 ice cubes in each bowl. Serve immediately.

Iranian Cucumber Soup

Combine 4 cups finely chopped or grated peeled cucumbers with 2 cups yogurt, 2 cups water, 2–3 tablespoons minced fresh mint, ¼ teaspoon nutmeg, ¼ cup currants, and 1 teaspoon salt. Ladle the soup into individual bowls and place 2 ice cubes in each bowl. Serve immediately.

Syrian Cucumber Soup seems doubly refreshing when garnished with parsley frozen in ice.

SOUPS

Cucumber soups use up quantities of cucumbers, fast. While the cold soups on page 123 are very popular, I've also included a recipe for a hot soup for variety.

Cucumber Lemon Soup

Here's a hot cucumber soup for a change. The larger the diameter of your sauté pan, the faster the soup cooks.

¼ **cup butter**
1 teaspoon grated lemon rind
3 tablespoons lemon juice
¼ **cup chopped scallion**
4 cups chicken broth
4 cups peeled, seeded, sliced
    cucumbers
salt and white pepper

In a large sauté pan, melt the butter, and sauté the lemon rind, juice, and scallion for 1–2 minutes. Add 2 cups of the chicken broth and simmer until the mixture is reduced by half, 4–5 minutes.

Add the remaining 2 cups chicken broth and the cucumbers. Simmer until the cucumbers are tender, about 15 minutes. Cool the soup slightly. Process the soup in a blender or food processor, in batches, until smooth. Season to taste with salt and white pepper. Serve hot.

Preparation Time: 10 minutes
Cooking Time: 25 minutes
Yield: 6 servings

Inundated with cucumbers? Make low-calorie salad dressings flavored with tarragon (front) or Oriental seasonings.

SALADS

If you are inundated with cucumbers, try a wilted cucumber salad. You start with 8 cups of cucumbers and end up with 5 cups. Or try a cucumber-based salad dressing to use up several cucumbers in an unusual, low-calorie way.

Tarragon Cucumber Salad Dressing

2 cups unpeeled diced cucumbers
2 tablespoons tarragon vinegar or
    white vinegar
1 tablespoon minced fresh tarragon
    or 1½ teaspoons dried
¼ **teaspoon salt**
1 scallion, minced
1 egg
½ **cup vegetable or olive oil**

Puree the cucumbers in a food processor or blender. Add the vinegar, tarragon, salt, scallion, and egg. Process until smooth. With the processor going, pour in the oil in a thin stream. Serve over a green salad, spinach salad, or parboiled vegetables.

Preparation Time: 10 minutes
Yield: 2 cups

You can vary the way you prepare your cucumbers. Try scoring the cucumbers with a fork, peeled or unpeeled, then slice. Or peel strips, then slice for a striped effect.

Oriental Cucumber Dressing

The cucumber gives the dressing an interesting texture. The oil content is so low, this becomes a dieter's favorite.

2 cups unpeeled diced cucumbers
1 large garlic clove, minced
1 tablespoon tamari or soy sauce
1 teaspoon sesame oil
1 tablespoon white vinegar
1 scallion, diced
1 tablespoon tahini

Combine all the ingredients in a food processor or blender and process until smooth. Pour over a green salad, parboiled chilled carrots, or other vegetables.

Preparation Time: 10 minutes
Yield: 1 cup

Cucumber With Feta Dressing

5–6 cups thinly sliced cucumbers
1 teaspoon salt
½ cup cider vinegar
1 garlic clove, minced
¼ cup crumbled feta cheese
¼ cup yogurt
¼ cup sour cream
1 teaspoon Dijon-style mustard

Place the cucumbers in a colander and sprinkle with salt. Weight the cucumbers with a heavy plate and let them drain for 1 hour. Then transfer to a large bowl.

Combine the remaining ingredients. Pour over the cucumbers. Toss well. Serve chilled.

Preparation Time: 20 minutes
Draining Time: 1 hour
Chilling Time: at least 1 hour
Yield: 6–8 servings

Mexican Cucumber Salad

4 cups grated cucumbers
2 cups finely chopped tomatoes
¾ cup minced scallions
½ cup minced green pepper
⅓ cup lime juice
¼ cup vegetable oil
2 tablespoons minced fresh cilantro
¼ teaspoon salt
2–3 teaspoons minced fresh hot pepper or ½ teaspoon red pepper flakes

Combine all the ingredients in a bowl and toss to coat. Chill and serve as a salad or cold side dish.

Preparation Time: 15 minutes
Yield: 6–8 servings

Cucumber Orange Salad

2¼ cups orange juice
2 cups water
½ teaspoon salt
2 cups uncooked brown rice
2 cups diced cucumbers
½ cup chopped scallions
2 oranges, peeled and diced
½ cup chopped roasted peanuts
2 tablespoons lemon juice
1 teaspoon Worcestershire sauce
¼ cup vegetable or peanut oil

Combine 2 cups of the orange juice with the water and salt in a large saucepan. Bring to a boil. Add the rice, cover, and cook until the liquid is evaporated and the rice is tender, about 45 minutes. Transfer the rice to a bowl and cool to room temperature. Add the cucumbers, scallions, oranges, and peanuts.

In a small bowl, combine the remaining ¼ cup orange juice, lemon juice, Worcestershire sauce, and oil. Whisk to blend. Pour over the salad. Toss to coat and chill.

Preparation Time: 20 minutes
Cooking Time: 45 minutes
Chilling Time: 1–2 hours
Yield: 4–6 servings

Shrimp and Cucumber Salad

2 cups water
3 lemon slices
3 peppercorns
2 cups peeled deveined shrimp
4 cups quartered and sliced
  cucumbers
⅓ cup lime juice (3 limes)
¼ cup vegetable oil
2 tablespoons minced fresh mint
¼ cup minced fresh parsley
¼ cup minced scallions
salt and pepper

Bring the water, lemon, and peppercorns to a boil, and add the shrimp. Simmer the shrimp gently for 2 minutes, or until they are just barely done. Plunge into cold water and drain.

Combine the shrimp and cucumbers in a bowl. Mix the remaining ingredients and toss with the cucumbers. Chill the salad for 30–60 minutes to let the flavors mingle. Serve on a bed of lettuce or spinach with sprouts to decorate.

Preparation Time: 20 minutes
Chilling Time: 30–60 minutes
Yield: 4–6 servings

Swedish Dill Cucumbers

6–8 cups thinly sliced cucumbers
1 teaspoon salt
1 cup sour cream
2 tablespoons white vinegar
1 tablespoon superfine sugar
1 tablespoon minced fresh dill or
  1 teaspoon dried
3 tablespoons minced fresh chives
⅛ teaspoon white pepper

Place the cucumbers in a colander and sprinkle with salt. Weight the cucumbers with a heavy plate and let them drain for 1 hour. Transfer to a large bowl.

Combine the remaining ingredients. Pour over the cucumbers. Toss well. Serve chilled.

Preparation Time: 20 minutes
Draining Time: 1 hour
Chilling Time: at least 1 hour
Yield: 6–8 servings

Scandinavian Cucumber Salad

8 cups thinly sliced cucumbers
1 teaspoon salt
½ cup white vinegar
1 tablespoon sugar
2 teaspoons honey
¼ cup vegetable oil
¼ cup minced fresh dill, fennel,
  parsley, or chives
½ cup sliced red onion or scallions

Place the cucumbers in a colander and sprinkle with the salt. Weight the cucumbers with a heavy plate and let them drain for 1 hour. Transfer to a large bowl.

Mix the vinegar, sugar, honey, and oil. Pour over the cucumbers. Toss in the herbs and onion or scallions. Serve chilled.

Preparation Time: 20 minutes
Draining Time: 1 hour
Chilling Time: at least 1 hour
Yield: 6–8 servings

SIDE DISHES AND MAIN DISHES

Cucumbers may star in chilled soups and salads, but they should not be neglected as a cooked vegetable. When you think about it, cucumbers are rather similar to zucchini.

Hoisin Cucumber Chicken

Hoisin sauce is a Chinese barbecue sauce, available wherever Oriental foods are sold.

2 tablespoons vegetable oil
2 boneless chicken breasts, diced
4 cups sliced seeded cucumbers
1 cup diced scallions
2 tablespoons hoisin sauce
1 tablespoon tamari or soy sauce
2 teaspoons minced fresh ginger root
½–1 cup fresh or frozen peas

Heat the oil in a wok or large frying pan, and add the chicken. Stir fry until the chicken is barely cooked, about 5 minutes. Add the cucumbers and scallions and continue to stir fry for 2–5 minutes.

Mix the hoisin sauce, tamari, and ginger root and add to the wok. Add the peas. Stir fry long enough to coat the chicken and vegetables with the sauce. The cucumbers should be tender crisp and the peas barely cooked.

Preparation Time: 15 minutes
Cooking Time: 10 minutes
Yield: 4–6 servings

Once cucumbers mature, the seeds get quite large. Whether I'm making a cooked dish, such as the Cucumber Curry, or a salad, I like to remove the seeds. First I split the cucumbers in half. Then I scoop out the seeds with a spoon.

This Cucumber Curry is pretty mild. If you like your curries hot, add extra curry powder and hot sauce—and serve plenty of rice!

Cucumber Curry

This dish looks best with unpeeled cucumbers.

2 tablespoons butter
1 cup diced onion
½ teaspoon turmeric
1–3 teaspoons curry powder
4 cups diced cucumbers
1 tablespoon all-purpose unbleached flour
¼ cup chicken broth
1 tablespoon lemon juice
1 teaspoon tamari or soy sauce
½ cup yogurt
salt and pepper
dash hot sauce

In a large sauté pan, heat the butter and sauté the onion, turmeric, and curry powder until the onion is limp, 3–5 minutes. Add the cucumbers, and sauté for 2 minutes. Sprinkle with flour and stir well. Add the chicken broth, lemon juice, and tamari. Cook until the cucumbers are just tender, 2–5 minutes. Stir in the yogurt and season to taste with salt, pepper, and hot sauce.

Preparation Time: 10 minutes
Cooking Time: 10–15 minutes
Yield: 6–8 servings

Cucumbers Sautéed With Herbs

2 tablespoons butter
1 teaspoon minced fresh basil
1½ teaspoons fresh thyme or ½ teaspoon dried
1 tablespoon minced fresh chives
4 cups quartered, sliced cucumbers
salt and pepper

Melt the butter in a large sauté pan, and sauté the herbs and cucumbers until the cucumbers are tender crisp and somewhat translucent, 2–5 minutes. Season to taste with salt and pepper. Serve hot.

Preparation Time: 10 minutes
Cooking Time: 3–6 minutes
Yield: 4–6 servings

Eggplant

What Can You Do With All That Eggplant? I Have Never Run Out of Ideas

When friends see my garden for the first time, they usually comment on my "eggplant orchard." A corner of my garden is always set aside for those beautiful purple-blossomed plants. They get plenty of attention, because I love an abundant harvest from those heat-loving plants. When it comes to cooking with eggplant, I have never run out of ideas.

Eggplant is a fairly neutral vegetable. By that I mean it absorbs flavors easily and doesn't fight against strong spices. So when I have eggplant on hand, I raid the herb garden and the spice rack and do some exotic cooking from other cuisines. It also absorbs cooking oil easily, a tendency you can circumvent if you follow my tips on page 130.

Eggplant is often used as a meat substitute. Nutritionally, that isn't a good idea, since eggplant is low in protein and isn't particularly vitamin rich. However, eggplant does add "heartiness" to a dish. When cooked in combination with cheese, or served along with other high protein grains or vegetables, eggplant can form the basis for a very satisfying vegetarian meal.

Frozen Eggplant Dinners Save Time

My favorite eggplant recipes are ones that can be cooked in quantities and frozen. When eggplants are in season, I prepare double quantities of Eggplant Rolls (page 134), and Eggplant Parmesan. Half goes into the freezer and half is eaten right away. Sometimes I make Eggplant Lasagna, substituting breaded fried eggplant slices for ground beef. The Eggplant Pasta Sauce (page 132) and the Moussaka (page 133) all freeze well, too. These frozen dinners come in handy all year long. It's a good thing that many eggplant dishes do freeze well, because eggplant doesn't keep for very long in the refrigerator.

Beneath that glossy, dark purple skin is a vegetable that is a little hard to gauge for ripeness. You can't use size as a guide. Try pressing the eggplant flesh with a finger. If it feels very hard, the eggplant is underripe. If it feels soft, the eggplant is overripe; the seeds will be brown and perhaps bitter. If the flesh yields somewhat, but then springs back, you have a ripe eggplant to enjoy.

I think eggplants are beautiful with their lavender blossoms and glossy fruits. This medium-size eggplant is good for about 4 servings.

Yields

1 pound fresh eggplant equals
   12–16 slices
or
   5–6 cups sliced
or
   6 cups cubed
or
   5 cups diced
or
   2 cups, baked and pureed

To Peel or Not to Peel: Your Choice

Some people hate eggplant skins, others don't see what all the fuss is about. I peel if the eggplant is tough-skinned, but most young eggplants, fresh out of the garden, don't need peeling.

Don't peel more eggplant than you are planning to cook; the flesh turns brown when exposed to air.

Peeling eggplant

EGGPLANT AT A GLANCE

To Salt or Not to Salt

If the eggplant is bitter (more likely with storebought than with homegrown eggplant), salting can help to draw the bitter juices from the vegetable.

Also, eggplant has a notorious capacity for absorbing oil. Salting reduces that tendency somewhat.

To salt, sprinkle the sliced or cubed eggplant with salt in a colander, weight, and set aside for 30 minutes to drain. Rinse with water and pat dry.

The Blanching Alternative

Instead of salting, you can blanch eggplant to rid it of bitterness and reduce its tendency to absorb oil. I don't like to blanch because it destroys some of the eggplant flavor. If you do want to try this method, blanch the sliced or cubed eggplant in boiling water for 2 minutes. Then proceed with your recipe.

Cooking Timetable

Steam sauté (cubes): 5–10 minutes
Pan fry (slices): 10–14 minutes
Broil (slices): 8–10 minutes
   (whole): 15–20 minutes
Bake (whole): 10 minutes at 350° F.
   (halves): 15 minutes at 350° F.
   for stuffing

When Cooking Eggplant, Don't Be Tricked Into Using Too Much Oil!

The oil is hot, you add the cubed or sliced eggplant to the sauté pan or frying pan, and what happens? The eggplant absorbs all the oil in the pan! *Don't add more oil* or you will end up with a very greasy dish.

Here are some tricks for keeping your oil use to a minimum.
• Use a coated, non-stick frying pan if you have one.
• Be sure your pan is very hot before you add the eggplant.
• Keep tossing and turning the eggplant so the oil evenly coats each piece.
• If the pan appears too dry, stir more frequently. Or add 2–3 tablespoons water to the pan, cover, and let the (unbreaded) eggplant steam for a few minutes.
• If the eggplant seems greasy, drain on paper towels before proceeding with the recipe.

Dressing Up Eggplant Dishes

The subtle flavor of eggplant is enhanced by many different herbs and spices. When you sauté eggplant, try adding one of these: basil, oregano, marjoram, thyme, fennel, dill, tarragon, mint, parsley, garlic, cayenne, cumin, curry, or cardamom.

This huge eggplant sandwich is great for a casual picnic.

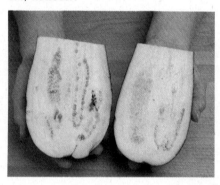

An overripe eggplant will have dark, well-developed seeds. It is still good to eat, however.

Simple Eggplant Dishes: Too Tasty to Pass By

Eggplant can be broiled, pan fried, or sautéed and the results are always satisfying. Here are some easy preparations.

Breaded Fried Slices: The Start Of Eggplant Parmesan And Great Sandwiches

Slice the eggplant into slices about ½ inch thick. Dip the slices in flour, then in egg beaten with a little milk, then in bread crumbs seasoned with dried basil, thyme, oregano, marjoram, garlic powder, parmesan cheese, wheat germ, or any combination.

Heat enough olive oil (or half olive and half vegetable oil) to coat the bottom of a heavy frying pan. Pan fry the slices until they are golden on each side. Drain well.

Broiled Slices: Good Results, Less Oil

You can slice eggplant, brush the slices with a little oil, and then broil for 2 minutes on each side. The slices won't be crispy like the breaded pan-fried slices are, but they will be tasty.

Herbed Sautéed Eggplant

Coat the bottom of a heavy sauté pan with oil; heat, and add diced eggplant with minced fresh herbs, onions, or garlic. Sauté for 6–8 minutes, until the eggplant is browned and tender. Season with salt and pepper.

Deep-Fried Eggplant Sticks: Finger-Licking Good

Slice the eggplant into sticks 2 inches long, ¼ inch wide, and ¼ inch thick.

Prepare a Tempura Batter as directed on page 309.

Heat oil for deep frying to 350° F. Carefully pat the eggplant dry. Coat each eggplant piece in flour, then in batter. Fry a few pieces at a time for 4–5 minutes, or until the eggplant is golden. Drain well. Once all the pieces are fried, serve immediately with a dipping sauce, such as the Oriental Marinade and Dipping Sauce (page 303) or Tomato Fennel Sauce (page 306).

APPETIZERS AND SALADS

If you are looking for a "classic," try the Baba Ganouj (pronounced ba ba ga noosh'). It is a wonderful Middle Eastern spread served on small triangles of pita bread.

Baba Ganouj

Here's my basic recipe for Baba Ganouj. You can vary the flavor by adding ½ cup yogurt, ¼ cup finely diced onion, or 1 cup finely diced tomato.

1 medium-size eggplant
2 garlic cloves, minced
1½ cups minced fresh parsley
6 tablespoons tahini
4 tablespoons lemon juice
salt and pepper

Pierce the eggplant all over with a fork. Place the eggplant under a broiler and broil it, turning frequently, until the skin is blackened and charred all over. This takes 15–20 minutes. Set the eggplant aside until it's cool enough to handle. Peel off the charred skin. Chop the eggplant *finely*, or process the pulp in a food processor. Add the remaining ingredients and blend until smooth.

Preparation Time: 10 minutes
Broiling Time: 15–20 minutes
Yield: 6 servings

Tuna Eggplant Salad

2 tablespoons plus ½ cup olive oil
6 cups unpeeled diced eggplant
½ cup water
2 tablespoons wine vinegar
2 large sweet red peppers
2 large green peppers
2 cups flaked tuna (one 13-ounce can)
⅔ cup diced red onion
½ cup sliced green olives
¼ cup white vinegar
1 garlic clove, minced
1 teaspoon Dijon-style mustard
2 tablespoons minced fresh basil or
    2 teaspoons dried
2 tablespoons lemon juice
salt and pepper

In a large sauté pan, heat 2 tablespoons of the olive oil, add the eggplant and toss to coat. Add the water and wine vinegar. Simmer gently until the eggplant is tender, 5–7 minutes. Remove the eggplant to a large bowl.

Place the red and green peppers under the broiler and broil, turning frequently, until the skins are well charred all over. Remove the peppers from the oven and place them in a paper bag for 10 minutes to steam. Then peel off the charred skin and slice them into strips. Add the peppers, tuna, onion, and olives to the eggplant.

Combine the remaining ½ cup oil, ¼ cup white vinegar, garlic, mustard, basil, and lemon juice in a blender or food processor and mix well. Pour the dressing over the salad and toss to coat. Season to taste with salt and pepper. Marinate for 30 minutes.

Preparation Time: 30 minutes
Marinating Time: 30 minutes
Yield: 6–8 servings

SIDE DISHES AND MAIN DISHES

Eggplant Pasta Sauce

3 hot Italian sausages
½ pound ground beef
½ cup diced onion
2 garlic cloves, minced
3 cups peeled diced eggplant
½ cup finely diced carrots
3 tablespoons minced fresh basil or
    1 tablespoon dried
1 tablespoon fresh oregano or
    1 teaspoon dried
2 teaspoons flour
½ cup heavy cream
½ cup milk
salt and white pepper

Remove the casings from the sausage, and brown the sausage meat and hamburger together, breaking the meat up with a spoon. Remove the meat from the pan and drain off all but 2 tablespoons of the fat. Sauté the onion, garlic, eggplant, carrots, basil, and oregano in the fat until the eggplant is tender, 10–15 minutes.

Sprinkle the flour over the vegetables and stir. Pour in the cream and milk. Cook until the sauce thickens slightly, 5–10 minutes. Season to taste with salt and pepper. Spoon over hot pasta and serve.

Preparation Time: 15 minutes
Cooking Time: 20–30 minutes
Yield: 4–6 servings

Moussaka

3 medium-size eggplants
5 tablespoons olive oil
½ cup water
5 tablespoons lemon juice
1½ cups diced onion
1 garlic clove, minced
1 pound ground lamb
½ cup tomato paste
¼ cup red wine
1½ teaspoons dried thyme
1 teaspoon dried oregano
salt and pepper
2 eggs, slightly beaten

Preheat the oven to 350° F.

Slice the eggplants in half lengthwise. Score the flesh of the eggplant in a crisscross pattern, making 1½-inch squares.

In a large frying pan, heat 2 tablespoons of the olive oil. Brown 3 halves of the eggplant on their cut side. When the eggplants are browned, add ¼ cup water and 2 tablespoons lemon juice. Cover the pan and cook the eggplants until soft, about 10 minutes. Remove the eggplants from the pan and set aside to cool. Heat 2 more tablespoons oil and brown the other halves of the eggplants.

When the eggplants are browned, add the remaining ¼ cup water and 2 tablespoons lemon juice. Cover and cook until the eggplants are soft, about 10 minutes.

When the eggplants are cool enough to handle, scoop out the flesh, being careful not to pierce the skin. Chop the eggplant flesh.

Grease a 2-quart baking dish (oval-shaped is nice). Line the casserole dish with the eggplant skins, with the purple sides on the outside. The skins can extend over the sides of the dish so they can be folded over the filling.

In the large frying pan, heat the remaining tablespoon of oil, and sauté the onion and garlic until limp, 3–5 minutes. Add the lamb and brown it, breaking the meat up with the spoon. If the

lamb is very fatty, drain off all but about 2 tablespoons of the fat. Add the tomato paste, wine, thyme, oregano, remaining 1 tablespoon lemon juice, and chopped eggplant to the fat. Cook for 10 minutes or until the mixture becomes quite thick. Season to taste with salt and pepper.

Remove the eggplant and meat mixture from the heat and stir in the eggs. Spoon the mixture into the casserole dish and fold the skins over the filling to cover it completely. Cover the casserole and bake for 1 hour. Remove from the oven and let the moussaka sit for 10 minutes, then unmold it onto a serving platter, and serve.

Preparation Time: 40 minutes
Baking Time: 1 hour
Yield: 6 servings

Moussaka served in the eggplant skins becomes a very fancy dish.

Italian Eggplant Rolls

This is a variation of Eggplant Parmesan. If you want, omit the ham, and you will still have a hearty dish.

2 large eggplants
¼–½ cup olive oil
16 slices boiled ham
2 cups ricotta cheese
3 garlic cloves, minced
½ cup minced fresh parsley
½–¾ pound mozzarella cheese, grated or thinly sliced
½ cup grated parmesan cheese

Preheat the oven to 350° F.
Peel the eggplants and slice each one lengthwise into eight ¼-inch-thick slices.

In a large frying pan, heat ¼ cup oil, and brown the slices on both sides. Add more oil as needed.

To make the eggplant rolls, fold the slices of ham in half lengthwise and place one on each slice of eggplant.

In a small bowl, combine the ricotta, garlic, and parsley. Spoon the cheese mixture on top of the ham. Spread the cheese evenly to the edges. Top with mozzarella. Roll the eggplant and place seam side down in a baking dish. Make 16 rolls in this fashion. Spoon the tomato sauce over the rolls and sprinkle with parmesan cheese. Bake for 30 minutes. Serve at once.

Preparation Time: 35 minutes
Baking Time: 30 minutes
Yield: 8 servings

1. Slice eggplant lengthwise.

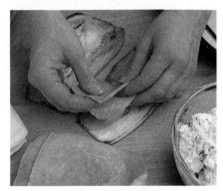
2. Place ham on the eggplant.

3. Spread ricotta over the ham.

4. Roll the filled slice.

Szechuan-Style Eggplant

¼ cup peanut oil
2 cups cubed onions
½ cup julienne-sliced sweet red pepper
½ cup julienne-sliced green pepper
3 teaspoons sesame oil
3 cups peeled cubed eggplant
2 tablespoons tamari or soy sauce
¾ pound julienne-sliced pork roast
2 garlic cloves, minced
2 teaspoons minced fresh ginger root
1 tablespoon hoisin sauce
1 tablespoon dry sherry
2 teaspoons to 2 tablespoons chili paste with garlic

Heat 1 tablespoon of the peanut oil in a wok or large frying pan, and stir fry the onions and peppers until tender crisp, 2–3 minutes. Remove the vegetables from the wok to a heated bowl. Add 1 more tablespoon of the peanut oil and 1 teaspoon of the sesame oil to the wok. Add the eggplant and tamari, and stir fry until the eggplant is tender, about 5 minutes. Remove the eggplant from the wok. Heat the remaining 2 tablespoons peanut oil and 2 teaspoons sesame oil. Add the pork, garlic, and ginger, and stir fry the pork until cooked, about 5 minutes. Return the vegetables to the wok and add the remaining ingredients. The chili paste is hot, so add to taste. Stir to mix and heat. Serve immediately over rice.

Preparation Time: 20 minutes
Cooking Time: 15 minutes
Yield: 4 servings

Creamy Eggplant Tomato Pie

Here's a luscious vegetable pie that can be made with all garden vegetables. I like to serve this pie with a salad.

1 single unbaked pie crust
   (page 308)
4 tablespoons butter
3 tablespoons diced onion
2 garlic cloves, minced
1 cup diced sweet red peppers
1 cup diced green peppers
5 cups peeled diced eggplant
¼ cup water
8 ounces cream cheese
5 tablespoons grated parmesan
   cheese
1 tablespoon lemon juice
2 tablespoons minced fresh basil
   or ¾ teaspoon dried
salt and pepper
2 large tomatoes, sliced
½ cup wheat germ
¼ cup bread crumbs

Prepare the pie dough and set aside to chill while you prepare the filling.

Preheat the oven to 350° F.

In a large sauté pan, melt 2 tablespoons of the butter and sauté the onion, garlic, and peppers until the onion is limp, about 5 minutes. Add the eggplant and the water. Cover the pan and cook the eggplant for 5 minutes, stirring occasionally. Slice the cream cheese into cubes and add to the eggplant. Cook until the cream cheese melts. Stir in all but 3 tablespoons of the cheese, the lemon juice, and the basil. Season to taste with salt and pepper.

Roll out the pie dough and fit it into a 10-inch pie pan. Crimp the edges. Spoon half of the eggplant mixture into the pan. Cover with the tomato slices. Spoon in the remaining eggplant mixture.

Mix the wheat germ, bread crumbs, the remaining 2 tablespoons of the butter, and the remaining 2 tablespoons cheese. Sprinkle the topping over the pie. Bake for 40 minutes. Serve hot.

Preparation Time: 30 minutes
Baking Time: 40 minutes
Yield: 8 servings

Lamb and Eggplant Casserole

I use dried herbs in the breading because they mix better than fresh herbs. Incidentally, the breading presented here is the one I use for Eggplant Parmesan. Just layer the eggplant slices with tomato sauce and sliced mozzarella cheese and bake for 1 hour at 350° F.

1 large, peeled eggplant, sliced thin
about 1⅓ cups all-purpose
   unbleached flour
2 eggs, beaten
2¼ cups milk
1 cup bread crumbs
¼ teaspoon dried oregano
¼ teaspoon dried thyme
¼ teaspoon dried basil
½ cup olive or vegetable oil
1 cup diced onion
2 garlic cloves, minced
⅔ cup minced fresh parsley
1 pound ground lamb or beef
½ cup crumbled feta cheese
6 tablespoons butter
2 tablespoons grated lemon rind
4 tablespoons lemon juice
salt and pepper

To bread the eggplant, set up 3 bowls. Place about ¾ cup flour in the first bowl, the eggs and ¼ cup milk in the second bowl, and the bread crumbs and herbs in the last bowl.

In a large skillet or frying pan, heat 3 tablespoons of the oil.

Dip the eggplant first in the flour, then in the egg, then in the crumbs. Fry the eggplant in the oil until browned and drain on paper towels or a paper bag.

Preheat the oven to 350° F.

Grease a 9-inch by 13-inch baking dish. Lay half the eggplant in the pan, covering the bottom.

Heat the remaining 1 tablespoon oil in a sauté pan, and sauté the onion, garlic, and parsley until limp, 3–5 minutes. Remove the vegetables from the pan, and brown the meat in the same pan, breaking it up with a spoon. Drain off the fat. Return the vegetables to the pan with the meat. Add the feta cheese.

In a small saucepan, melt the butter and stir in 6 tablespoons flour to make a thick paste. Add the remaining 2 cups milk a little at a time, stirring well after each addition to prevent lumps. Add the lemon rind and juice. Season to taste with salt and pepper. Add ¼ cup of this sauce to the meat mixture in the pan.

Spoon the meat mixture over the eggplant and layer on the remaining eggplant. Pour the remaining sauce over the eggplant. Bake for 30 minutes.

Cut the casserole in squares to serve.

Preparation Time: 45 minutes
Baking Time: 30 minutes
Yield: 8 servings

Fruits

Don't Miss the Refreshing Sweetness of Homegrown Rhubarb, Berries, and Melons

Mouthwatering, tart rhubarb, juicy strawberries, and honey-sweet melons—these are the fruits I grow in my garden and serve with pleasure in the kitchen.

Rhubarb starts the fruit harvest for me. As soon as the soil warms up in the spring, the perennial rhubarb begins to send up stems and those large elephant-ear leaves. Then, as the weather becomes warm, the plants send up white flower stalks. As long as you keep cutting off the flower heads, you can continue to harvest rhubarb.

My grandmother tells me that when she was a child, she used to go out into the garden with a salt shaker and eat raw, salted rhubarb stems as a treat. The very idea makes my mouth pucker! When I prepare rhubarb, I'm inclined to use plenty of sugar, honey, or maple syrup, because rhubarb is *so* tart.

Strawberries and Melons Are Naturally Sweet

Strawberries, on the other hand, are naturally sweet, so I can go easy on the sweetener when I serve them. Strawberries lose sweetness the minute they are picked. Growing your own strawberries enables you to pick and eat—that's the way to enjoy strawberries at their best. I raise a few varieties which ripen at different times so I can extend my harvest season.

Melons *should* be sweet, but sometimes my homegrown melons disappoint me. Some cantaloupes and muskmelons I've grown have been bland tasting. I don't like to serve a flavorless melon, but combined in a Smoothie (page 142) or made into a Creamy Cantaloupe Mousse (page 145), I don't notice the lack of flavor so much.

Watermelons, on the other hand, I like to serve plain or in fruit salads. The flesh is so watery and tender, it really doesn't hold up well when combined with other ingredients in a dessert or salad. No matter, the kids just love Watermelon Popsicles (page 145), and there isn't a grown-up I know who's above a watermelon seed-spitting contest every once in a while.

My idea of a perfect summer meal is fresh roasted corn, grilled vegetable and meat kabobs (page 224), sliced tomatoes and cucumbers, and for dessert: chilled, juicy, refreshing watermelon.

All the children in the neighborhood stop by when it's time to pick strawberries. I'm not sure which they prefer most—harvesting or eating!

The Fruit Harvest Begins With Tart-Flavored Rhubarb And Can Last All Summer Long

As long as you fool a rhubarb plant by preventing the flower stalks from setting seeds, you can keep the plant producing tender young stems for many extra weeks.

And that's just about all you have to do for an established rhubarb plant. Give the plants a good start with rich soil, and divide them every 4 or 5 years.

Figure that a single rhubarb plant will provide enough fruit for 6–8 pies. For most families that means that 4 plants will provide plenty of pies, sauces, compotes, and conserves.

Don't Eat the Leaves, Please!

Rhubarb leaves are toxic! Only the stems can be eaten.

When the rhubarb stems are about as thick as your thumb, they are ready for harvest. There are both red-stemmed and white-stemmed varieties, so ignore the color.

Harvest by twisting the stems off near the base of the plant. Harvest the outer stems first to prevent them from becoming woody.

The stems are easy to prepare. If they are particularly stringy, remove the strings just as you would the strings on Swiss chard (page 109) or celery. Slip the edge of your paring knife just under the skin at the base of the stem and pull away the strings.

Then slice into 1-inch pieces and cook.

Yields

1 pound fresh rhubarb equals 4 cups sliced or 2 cups cooked and pureed.

When You Can't Keep Up With the Harvest . . .

Because rhubarb is mostly water, it doesn't store well. You can keep rhubarb stems in the refrigerator in perforated plastic bags for a few days only. I prefer to make Stewed Rhubarb with any extra rhubarb I have.

Freezing is another good way to keep rhubarb. I simply wash the stems and dry well. Then, if necessary, I string the stems, slice into 1-inch pieces, pack into bags, and freeze. It couldn't be simpler. I freeze the rhubarb in 4-cup batches, which is handy for pies and other dishes.

Stewed Rhubarb Is Simple

I like to serve Stewed Rhubarb topped with a little fresh cream or whipped cream. It is also delicious as a topping for ice cream, and makes a tasty pudding when combined with a custard sauce.

In a heavy-bottomed saucepan, combine 4 cups of sliced rhubarb stems with ½ cup sugar, honey, or maple syrup, and ½ cup water. Simmer over medium heat until the rhubarb is tender, about 15 minutes. Season to taste with more sweetener, and cinnamon, ginger, or nutmeg. Serves 4.

Tomato Rhubarb Sauce

3 tablespoons butter
2 cups diced tomatoes
4 cups diced rhubarb
1 cup orange juice
4 tablespoons brown sugar
½ teaspoon ground rosemary

Melt the butter in a large sauté pan. Add all the ingredients and simmer until the rhubarb is soft, 10–15 minutes. Spoon the sauce over cooked chicken or fish.

Preparation Time: 20 minutes
Cooking Time: 10–15 minutes
Yield: 6 servings (5 cups)

Strawberry Rhubarb Pie Should Win a Prize For Being the American Gardener's Classic Dessert

Strawberry Rhubarb Pie is the "American Gardener's Classic Dessert." Over the years, I have experimented to perfect the recipe. Strawberry rhubarb pies have a tendency to be runny, which makes the bottom crust soggy. I found that using tapioca as a thickener works better than flour or cornstarch.

You'll need 7 cups of prepared fruit—you can make it half rhubarb and half strawberries, or you can vary the proportions depending on what's on hand or in the freezer. Yes, you can make this pie out of frozen fruit, and it will be as fresh-tasting as the one you made fresh last June.

The first Strawberry Rhubarb Pie of the season makes a great occasion for an impromptu picnic.

Strawberry Rhubarb Pie

1 double pie crust (page 308)
4 cups diced rhubarb
3 cups sliced strawberries
1½ cups sugar
6 tablespoons quick-cooking tapioca
1 teaspoon grated orange rind
milk or beaten egg

Preheat the oven to 400° F. Make the pie dough, roll out the bottom crust, and fit into a 10-inch pie pan.

Toss together the rhubarb, strawberries, sugar, tapioca, and orange rind. Spoon the fruit onto the bottom crust.

Roll out the top crust to a circle slightly larger than the pie. Place the crust over the fruit. Trim the crust to hang ½ inch over the edge of the pie pan and fold the extra pastry under. Crimp the edges. Brush the top crust with milk or a beaten egg and pierce in several places.

Bake the pie for 10 minutes at 400° F. Then turn the oven down to 350° F. and bake for another 35 minutes. Cool for 10 minutes before slicing.

Preparation Time: 40 minutes
Baking Time: 45 minutes
Yield: 8 servings

Variation

Strawberry Rhubarb Pie With Crumb Topping. Prepare the crumb topping by combining 1 cup all-purpose unbleached flour, 1 cup sugar, and 1 teaspoon salt. Using a pastry cutter, cut in ½ cup butter until the mixture resembles gravel and sand. Spoon the fruit filling onto the bottom crust. Top with the crumb topping, and bake as directed above.

Hot Rhubarb Pudding

2 eggs, beaten
1 cup sugar
1 teaspoon vanilla extract
¼ cup all-purpose unbleached flour
4 cups diced rhubarb
whipped cream

Preheat the oven to 350° F.

Whisk together the eggs, sugar, vanilla, and flour. Stir in the rhubarb.

Grease a 1½-quart baking dish and pour in the rhubarb mixture. Bake for 40 minutes or until the pudding is firm. Serve warm with whipped cream.

Preparation Time: 15 minutes
Baking Time: 40 minutes
Yield: 4 servings

To string the rhubarb stems, slip your paring knife under the skin and pull away the strings.

There's Nothing Complicated About Strawberries

Strawberries are ripe when the fruit is evenly red. There should be no soft spots, which indicate an overripe berry.

Strawberries should be eaten as soon as they are picked for full flavor. You can store strawberries, lightly covered, in the refrigerator for 1–2 days, but the flavor loss is noticeable.

When the harvest gets beyond what we can eat fresh, I make jam or freeze whole berries without any sugar. I think this method gives the best results.

1 pound fresh strawberries equals 3½ cups sliced berries.

Pureed Strawberries Make An Instant Sauce

You can make an instant sauce for fresh fruit (particularly melons), ice cream, yogurt, or pound cake by making a strawberry puree.

Simply pour 3 cups strawberries into a blender or food processor and blend until smooth. Makes 2 cups of puree. Add honey, sugar, or maple syrup, if desired.

You can make a chunky strawberry sauce by sprinkling sugar over strawberries and letting the fruit sit for about 30 minutes. The sugar will draw juices from the berries. Mash with a spoon or a potato masher.

Strawberry Spice Cake

¼ cup butter at room temperature
1 cup sugar
3 eggs
½ cup yogurt
1 cup pureed strawberries
2 cups all-purpose unbleached flour
1 teaspoon cinnamon
¼ teaspoon ground cloves
¼ teaspoon ground mace
2 cups sliced strawberries

Preheat the oven to 350° F.

Cream the butter until light and fluffy. Add the sugar and continue beating for 1 minute. Add the eggs, one at a time, then the yogurt. Beat until smooth. Mix in the strawberry puree.

Sift together the flour, cinnamon, cloves, and mace. Combine a third of the flour and a third of the butter and strawberry mixture and blend well. Continue to combine the dry and wet ingredients, blending well after each addition. Gently stir in the strawberries at the end.

Grease a 9-inch springform pan. Pour in the batter. Bake the cake for 45 minutes, or until a toothpick inserted in the center comes out clean. Cool the cake slightly before serving. Serve with a dollop of whipped cream or ice cream.

Preparation Time: 30 minutes
Baking Time: 45 minutes
Yield: 8 servings

Chocolate and Strawberry Cream Roll

Chocolate and strawberries seem meant for each other in this very special cake roll.

3 eggs
1½ cups sugar
1 teaspoon vanilla extract
¾ cup all-purpose unbleached flour
¼ cup cocoa
½ teaspoon baking powder
½ teaspoon baking soda
2½ cups diced strawberries
1 cup milk
1 cup heavy cream
¼ cup cornstarch
pinch salt
5 egg yolks
1 teaspoon almond extract
confectioners' sugar

Preheat the oven to 375° F.

Beat the eggs until light and frothy. Add ¾ cup of the sugar and the vanilla, and beat for 1 minute.

Sift together the flour, cocoa, baking powder, and baking soda. Add the dry ingredients to the eggs and sugar. Beat until smooth. Fold in 1 cup of the strawberries.

Grease a 9-inch by 15-inch jelly roll pan or cookie sheet. Line the bottom of the pan with waxed paper. Grease and flour the waxed paper. Pour in the cake batter and spread it evenly over the bottom of the pan. The batter will be quite thin. Bake the cake for 20 minutes or until it bounces back when pressed lightly with your finger.

While the cake bakes, prepare the filling. Combine the milk, cream, the remaining ¾ cup sugar, cornstarch, and salt in the top of a double boiler that is over, but not in, boiling water. Heat this mixture, stirring constantly, until it thickens slightly.

Beat the egg yolks and spoon a small amount of the warm milk mixture into the egg yolks. Blend. Pour the egg yolks into the warmed milk and cook for 1 minute. Remove the custard from the heat and stir in the almond extract. Cool to room temperature, stirring often.

Just before the cake is done, place a tea towel on a flat surface and dust with confectioners' sugar. As soon as the cake comes out of the oven, invert it onto the towel. Carefully peel off the waxed paper. Roll the cake lengthwise inside the tea towel and set aside to cool.

When the custard is cool, unroll the cake roll and spread with the custard. Roll the cake with the filling and transfer to a serving plate. Dust with confectioners' sugar and chill for at least 1 hour. Spoon the remaining 1½ cups diced strawberries over the cake just before serving.

Preparation Time: 35 minutes
Baking Time: 20 minutes
Cooling Time: at least 1 hour
Yield: 8 servings

1. Spread the batter in the pan.

2. Roll the cake in a towel.

3. Spread the filling.

4. Reroll the filled cake. Chill well before serving.

Fruit Smoothies Make a Healthful Breakfast
Or a Creamy, Refreshing Snack or Dessert

Powdered milk, or sometimes yogurt, plus fruit and fruit juice make up a Smoothie.

You can use any combination of fruit you like—berries, melons, peaches, pears, or bananas. Fruit juices you can use are orange, pineapple, pear, apple, white or purple grape juice, or cider.

The basic recipe is to pour 2–3 cups of fresh or frozen fruit into a blender. Cover with fruit juice. Add ¼ cup powdered milk (or ¼–½ cup yogurt), and ½ teaspoon vanilla or almond extract (optional). Blend until smooth. If you use frozen fruit, the drink will be extra chilled and refreshing.

Strawberry Banana Smoothie

In a blender, combine 1 cup sliced strawberries with ½ cup sliced banana, 1 cup orange juice, and ¼ cup powdered milk. Process until smooth. Serves 2.

You could substitute 1 cup blueberries for the strawberries. The resulting blue color is a real treat.

Cantaloupe Peach Smoothie

In a blender, combine 1½ cups diced cantaloupe with 1¼ cups sliced peeled peaches, 1¼ cups orange juice, ¼ cup powdered milk, and ½ teaspoon vanilla extract. Process until smooth. Serves 4.

Aren't these Smoothies scrumptious looking? Make your own with the fruit you have on hand.

Strawberry Cheese Strudels

12 ounces cream cheese at room temperature
⅓ cup sugar
1 tablespoon grated orange rind
½ teaspoon vanilla extract
4 cups sliced strawberries
16 sheets filo dough
½ cup melted butter

Preheat the oven to 400° F.

Cream the cream cheese in a mixing bowl or food processor. Add the sugar, orange rind, and vanilla. Beat until smooth, scraping the sides of the bowl as necessary. Fold in the strawberries.

Grease a cookie sheet and place 2 sheets of filo dough on it. Brush the filo dough with butter. Continue layering filo dough and butter until you have used 8 sheets of dough.

Spoon half of the strawberry mixture onto the middle of the dough. Fold up the ends and roll the strudel lengthwise to enclose the filling. Turn the strudel over so the seam is on the bottom and place on a greased baking sheet. Brush the top of the strudel with melted butter.

Prepare the second strudel in the same manner. Bake both strudels at once, or freeze one until another time.

Bake the strudel for 30 minutes. Cool slightly before serving. To bake a frozen strudel, add 10 minutes to the baking time. Do not defrost before baking.

Preparation Time: 40 minutes
Baking Time: 30 minutes
Yield: 10–12 servings

Did Someone Mention Breakfast? Strawberries Brighten up the Dullest Mornings . . .

It is my pleasure to pick a few ripe strawberries for my cereal during strawberry season. If I'm feeling ambitious enough to make pancakes, I'll fold a cup of sliced strawberries into the batter, and spoon sliced strawberries on top. Strawberries and whipped cream turn ordinary waffles into Belgian waffles, which I enjoy as a dessert.

Strawberry crêpes are a welcome breakfast. Blintzes are a Russian variation on crêpes. Usually they are filled with just cheese, but the combination of cheese and strawberries is unforgettable. I like to serve blintzes for Sunday brunch.

Fresh strawberries were the occasion for this impromptu champagne brunch. I keep a supply of crêpes in the freezer; they can double as wrappers for blintzes. The combination of cheese and strawberries in the filling of these blintzes makes a rich, satisfying dish.

Strawberry Blintzes

12 crêpes (page 309)
2 ounces cream cheese
1 egg yolk
⅛ teaspoon salt
1 teaspoon vanilla extract
1 tablespoon lemon juice
1 teaspoon grated lemon rind
¼ cup sugar
1½ cups cottage cheese
¼ cup ricotta cheese
4 cups sliced strawberries

Preheat the oven to 350° F.
Prepare the crêpes according to the recipe directions and set aside.

Combine the cream cheese, egg yolk, salt, vanilla, lemon juice, lemon rind, and sugar in a food processor or mixing bowl and process until well blended. Add the cottage cheese and ricotta. Using the pulsing action on the processor, process for 3 short pulses; in a mixing bowl, mix gently until the cheese is just blended but not soupy. Remove the cheese mixture from the processor and stir in 2 cups of the strawberries.

Spoon ¼ cup of the cheese mixture onto each crêpe. Fold in the sides of the crêpe to make an envelope that completely encloses the filling. Place seam side down in a greased baking dish big enough to hold all the blintzes in a single layer. Cover the dish with foil and bake for 20 minutes or until the blintzes are hot. Remove the blintzes from the oven and sprinkle with the remaining strawberries. Serve at once.

Preparation Time: 20 minutes
Baking Time: 20 minutes
Yield: 6 servings

Fresh Melons From the Garden Are Always Terrific — For Breakfast, Lunch, or Dinner

As you will see from the recipes here, fresh melons are great any time of the day, including snack time.

Melons don't require much in the way of preparation — just peel and slice. I like to chill mine for a few hours in the refrigerator before serving. Melons will keep for a few days in the refrigerator, if unopened. Opened melons should be wrapped in plastic film wrap and stored for no more than 2 days.

Serving Melon

You can use the natural shape of melon to make it into a serving dish. I like to fill cantaloupes with cottage cheese, blueberries, yogurt, fruit salad, or ice cream, depending on whether I'm serving the melon as an appetizer, light lunch, or dessert. Watermelons can be hollowed out and filled with fruit salad or melon balls for parties.

As a dessert, a melon can be made into a "spirited" dish. Try filling a cantaloupe half with port wine and serving. Or remove a small piece from a whole watermelon, pour in rum or vodka, and replace the melon piece. Refrigerate for at least 4 hours before slicing and serving.

Frozen Melon Is Great In Fruit Salads

I like to freeze melon balls to put in fruit salads year-round.

It's easy enough to do: simply seed the melon, scoop out melon balls with a melon baller, pack into bags, and freeze.

Frozen Melon Sherbet: Another Sweet Treat

I love Honeydew Sherbet. It's refreshing, light, and has no added sugar. In fact, I like homemade sherbet made with any melon or berry. Here's how to make it.

Break apart 4 cups of frozen melon or strawberries so you have pieces that are 1–1½ inches in diameter. With the processor running, drop the fruit into the processor, a little at a time. Pour in ¼–¾ cup fruit juice. (Orange juice or cider is what I usually use. You can also use a liquor.) A sweetener is not necessary, but you can replace some of the liquid with honey, maple syrup, or sugar. Process until smooth and thick. Serve at once. Serves 4.

1. Peel along the contours.

3. Dice each melon half.

2. Scoop out seeds with a spoon or butter curler.

Creamy Cantaloupe Mousse

4⅓ cups diced cantaloupe
8 ounces cream cheese, diced
1 cup cottage cheese
1 cup yogurt
1 tablespoon grated lemon rind
1 tablespoon lemon juice
½ cup sugar
2½ packages (¼-ounce) gelatin
¼ cup cold water

Place the diced cantaloupe in a food processor fitted with a steel blade, and process until smooth. Remove the cantaloupe from the processor and set aside. Don't wash the processor.

With the processor running, add the cream cheese a little at a time until it is creamed in the bowl. Add the cottage cheese, yogurt, lemon rind, lemon juice, and sugar. Process until smooth, scraping down the sides of the bowl occasionally. Add the pureed cantaloupe and process until blended.

In a small saucepan, sprinkle the gelatin over the cold water and set aside until the water is absorbed, about 5 minutes. Heat the gelatin on very low heat, stirring gently until the liquid is clear. Add the gelatin to the cantaloupe and cheese mixture and process until well blended.

Pour the mixture into a decorative 6-cup mold and chill until set, at least 2 hours. Unmold the gelatin and garnish with mint sprigs and strawberries. Serve immediately.

Preparation Time: 30 minutes
Chilling Time: at least 2 hours
Yield: 6–8 servings

When warm weather approaches, I keep a supply of watermelon popsicles for visiting children. It's a great snack—to be eaten outdoors if possible!

Watermelon Popsicles

100 percent natural goodness kids can't resist! I know when I serve kids Watermelon Popsicles that I am giving them a healthful, naturally sweet snack.

Seed the watermelon and puree it in a food processor or blender. Pour into plastic popsicle molds or paper cups and freeze for several hours. If you are using paper cups, wait until the popsicle is partially frozen, then insert a popsicle stick.

The new plastic popsicle molds are very convenient—and they catch some of the drips. This is a messy treat! P.S. Grown-ups love these popsicles, too.

Melon Salads

Melon salads are refreshing and sweet. The combination of sweet melon, crunchy vegetables, and tart dressing is surprisingly pleasant.

You can substitute melon varieties in these recipes. Keep in mind colors as well as flavors when you make your substitutions.

Honeydew Walnut Salad

If you've misjudged the ripeness of a honeydew and open an underripe one, this is the recipe to prepare. The firm texture of the honeydew is what makes this salad special.

4 cups slightly underripe honeydew, cubed
1 cup roasted walnuts
4 tablespoons minced parsley
1 cup diced celery
1 cup finely diced sweet red pepper
4 tablespoons lime juice
2 teaspoons honey
2 tablespoons white vinegar
½ cup vegetable oil
1 teaspoon salt
⅛ teaspoon pepper

In a large salad bowl, toss together the honeydew, walnuts, parsley, celery, and red pepper. Whisk together the remaining ingredients and pour over the salad. Toss to coat. Serve at once or chill and serve.

Preparation Time: 20 minutes
Yield: 6 servings

Curried Cantaloupe Turkey Salad

I like to serve this salad on a bed of lettuce or with a rice salad such as the Pepper Rice Salad (page 204). Garnishes of cherry tomatoes, radish roses, or carrot curls are especially pretty on this salad.

2 cups diced cooked turkey (or chicken)
2 cups diced cantaloupe
1 cup finely diced celery
¼ cup slivered toasted almonds
⅓ cup diced red onion
½ cup chopped apple (unpeeled)
2 tablespoons minced fresh parsley
½ cup yogurt
2 tablespoons lemon juice
½ teaspoon grated orange rind
2 tablespoons orange juice
2 tablespoons mayonnaise
2¼ teaspoons curry powder
salt and pepper

In a large salad bowl, toss together the turkey, cantaloupe, celery, almonds, onion, apple, and parsley.

Whisk together the yogurt, lemon juice, orange rind, orange juice, mayonnaise, and curry powder. Pour over the salad and toss to coat. Season to taste with salt and pepper. Chill for at least 1 hour before serving.

Preparation Time: 25 minutes
Chilling Time: at least 1 hour
Yield: 4 servings

Honeydew Ham Salad

The colors of this beautiful salad look best with honeydew — but cantaloupe also tastes wonderful here.

2 cups diced honeydew (or cantaloupe)
2 cups diced ham
1 cup diced Swiss cheese
½ cup julienne-sliced green pepper
⅔ cup diced cucumber
¼ cup minced dill pickle
⅓ cup chopped scallion
2 tablespoons minced fresh parsley
⅓ cup chopped toasted pecans
¼ cup olive oil
2 tablespoons lemon juice
2 tablespoons wine vinegar
1½ teaspoons Dijon-style mustard
½ teaspoon salt
⅛ teaspoon pepper
dash Worcestershire sauce

Toss together the honeydew, ham, cheese, green pepper, cucumber, pickle, scallion, parsley, and pecans.

Whisk together the remaining ingredients and pour over the salad. Toss to coat. Chill for 1 hour. Serve on a bed of lettuce.

Preparation Time: 20 minutes
Chilling Time: 1 hour
Yield: 6 servings

I can't think of a side dish more refreshing than a cool melon salad on a hot summer night. Going clockwise, these salads are: Cantaloupe Radish Salad, Curried Cantaloupe Turkey Salad, Honeydew Ham Salad, Oriental Cantaloupe Shrimp Salad, and Honeydew Walnut Salad. These salads should be served well chilled.

Cantaloupe Radish Salad

The radishes add an extra zip.

4 cups diced cantaloupe
1 cup sliced radishes
1 tablespoon minced fresh mint
3 tablespoons lime juice
1 teaspoon grated lime rind
1 teaspoon sugar

Place the cantaloupe and radishes in a bowl. Whisk together the remaining ingredients and pour over the salad. Toss to coat. Serve at once.

Preparation Time: 15 minutes
Yield: 4–6 servings

Oriental Cantaloupe Shrimp Salad

3 cups diagonally sliced carrots
4 cups diced cantaloupe
  (or honeydew)
3 cups diced cooked shrimp
⅔ cup diced scallions, including green tops
2 cups diagonally sliced celery
⅔ cup julienne-sliced water chestnuts
4 tablespoons minced fresh parsley
2 tablespoons orange juice
4 tablespoons lemon juice
½ cup vegetable oil
1 teaspoon minced fresh ginger root
2 garlic cloves, minced
2 teaspoons tamari or soy sauce
salt and pepper

Parboil the carrots until just tender, 2–3 minutes. Drain. Plunge into cold water to stop the cooking, and drain again.

In a large salad bowl, toss together the cantaloupe, shrimp, scallions, celery, water chestnuts, parsley, and carrots.

Whisk together the orange juice, lemon juice, oil, ginger, garlic, and tamari. Pour over the salad and toss to coat. Season to taste with salt and pepper. Chill the salad for at least 1 hour before serving.

Preparation Time: 25 minutes
Chilling Time: at least 1 hour
Yield: 6 servings

Cantaloupe Chicken Salad

Instead of the usual tossed salad, try your hand at a "composed" salad. It makes a beautiful dish.

4 cups salad greens
2 cups diced cantaloupe (or honeydew)
1½ cups diced cooked chicken
½ cup sliced celery
1 cup sliced radishes
½ cup julienne-sliced green pepper
1 cup diced cucumber
2 tablespoons minced red onion
2 tablespoons minced fresh parsley
⅓ cup crumbled blue cheese
2 tablespoons lemon juice
1 tablespoon wine vinegar
3 tablespoons buttermilk
1 garlic clove, minced
½ teaspoon salt
½ teaspoon sugar
pepper

Place the salad greens in a serving bowl. Arrange the cantaloupe, chicken, celery, radishes, green pepper, cucumber, onion, and parsley in concentric circles on top.

Combine the remaining ingredients in a food processor or blender and process until smooth. Just before serving, pour the dressing over the salad.

Preparation Time: 25 minutes
Yield: 6 servings

Greens

There's No Excuse for Overcooking These Vitamin-Packed Vegetables

I have a theory to explain why greens aren't more popular than they are. You need so much of them for cooking! Most adventuresome cooks are willing to cook small quantities of new vegetables to see if they like them. But with greens, you have to cook a whole armful! It seems like an enormous amount of food to grow and prepare. But small quantities of greens cook down to almost nothing, so you have to think big.

I remember asking my mother to cook collard greens one time, because I had read about them but never eaten them. My mother told me that collards were grown only in the South. In our Vermont garden, we grew spinach and Swiss chard. Those are popular vegetables, and I have devoted a chapter to each. But I had to wait until I was grown to taste the lesser appreciated cooking greens this chapter is dedicated to: collards, kale, mustard, beet, and turnip greens, and broccoli de rabe. (See Lettuce and Salad Greens, pages 162–169, for more greens recipes.)

Easy to Grow in Most Climates

The South has a long tradition of cooking greens, but that doesn't mean that greens can't be raised in abundance in northern climates, even in a small garden. Greens are easy to grow, particularly in wide rows. They thrive on cool temperatures, rich soils, and plenty of water. From a cook's perspective, providing lots of water is very important: without sufficient water the greens sometimes become quite bitter.

Spring greens have a fairly short growing season. If you sow them early, the greens will be ready for harvest before other vegetables demand your attention. Often a second crop is possible in the fall. This is a real bonus for those of us who like to eat from our gardens for as much of the year as possible.

Greens do have similarities, but you have to cook each green as a unique vegetable. Not only do the flavors vary, but cooking times are different. On the next page you'll find a "Cook's Tour" of various greens. Please notice the different cooking times. There's nothing worse than gray, mushy, overcooked greens—and no excuse for it either!

My "greens season" begins with beet greens and concludes with the kale you see here. Kale gets high marks for dependability in cold weather. It stays firm even under snow!

A Cook's Tour of Greens

Each green has its own unique flavor and cooking times when steamed, parboiled, or blanched. Use the greens interchangeably in recipes, but be prepared for the flavor changes and adjust cooking times accordingly.

Beet Greens. Very mild flavored, a little sweet. Plant spring and fall crops. Harvest to thin your rows when the beets are no bigger than a marble. Just trim off the end of the hairy root.
Steam, blanch, sauté, or stir fry; 3–4 minutes

Turnip Greens. Mild flavored; greens that are bitter are too old. Plant spring and fall crops. Harvest to thin rows when turnips are no bigger than a marble. Just trim off the end of the hairy root.
Steam or blanch: 4 minutes
Sauté or stir fry: 2–3 minutes

Broccoli de Rabe. You'll recognize it by its resemblance to broccoli. Distinctive, but mild flavor.
Sauté: 2 minutes
Blanch: 3 minutes
Steam: 5 minutes

GREENS AT A GLANCE

Mustard Greens. I've found the flavor of mustard greens to vary from mild to bitter. If you have a bitter crop, blanch the greens in bouillon. Remove the tough stems before cooking.
Steam or blanch: 2–5 minutes
Sauté or stir fry: 2–5 minutes

Kale. Harvest to thin rows. Withstands frost. Pot a few kale plants for your window sill and snip leaves for soups and garnishes. Chop finely as the texture is a little tough. It holds its shape well.
Steam or blanch: 5–10 minutes

Collards. Harvest outer leaves leaving inner growing tip intact. Remove the stems and tough center rib. Best blanched in a smoky, ham bouillon.
Blanch: 10–20 minutes
Steam sauté: 8–15 minutes

Many of my recipes call for just "greens." Use what you grow, and trust the cooking times.

Yields

The yields of greens vary depending on how much water they hold. Generally,
1 pound fresh greens equals 1½–2 cups cooked greens
1 pound fresh greens approximately equals 12 cups chiffonade, sliced, or diced greens

Try Some of My Favorite Spinach Recipes With Greens

Spinach Onion Soup (page 246). Good for all greens except collards.
Creamed Spinach With Garlic (page 247). Good for all greens except collards and kale.
Spinach Pizza (page 248). Use any finely chopped green.
Chicken and Spinach Pastry (page 248). Use any finely chopped green.
Greek Spinach Casserole (page 248). Especially good with broccoli de rabe, mustard greens, and beet and turnip greens.

Mustard greens

Kale

Collards

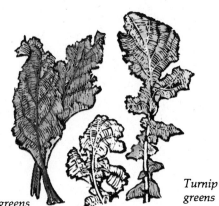

Beet greens

Turnip greens

1. Start with 16 cups collards.

2. The greens will cook down considerably. Don't overcook or the greens will be mushy.

The Canadian bacon will give the collards plenty of flavor.

Greens Really Do Have a Lot of Flavor Cooked Simply and Quickly

When those tender greens start to come up, I like to serve my three favorite "basics."

Greens Sautéed With Bacon and Lemon

Greens have a natural affinity for the flavor of bacon. Even salad greens are tasty prepared this way. Use whatever greens you have growing.

In a large sauté pan, heat 2 tablespoons olive oil, and sauté ½ cup diced Canadian bacon and 1 large minced garlic clove for 5 minutes. Add 16 cups roughly chopped greens and toss to coat. Add 2 tablespoons lemon juice and cover. Cook, stirring occasionally, until the greens are limp, 3–7 minutes (more for collards). Season to taste with salt and pepper. Serves 6.

Oriental Sauté of Greens

Collards may require more than 10 minutes of cooking. Adjust your cooking times so that the vegetables are limp, but not mushy.

Heat 1 tablespoon peanut oil in a large sauté pan, and sauté 1 minced garlic clove until golden. Add ½ cup julienne-sliced water chestnuts, 16 cups roughly chopped greens, and 1 tablespoon tamari or soy sauce. Cover and steam the greens, stirring occasionally, until they are limp, 3–7 minutes. Serves 4–6.

Greens Sautéed With Apples

Here's a dish for that late fall crop of greens.

In a large sauté pan, heat 2 tablespoons vegetable oil and 2 tablespoons butter. Briefly sauté ¼ cup sunflower seeds and ½ teaspoon ground coriander. Add 12 cups roughly chopped greens and toss to coat. Cover and steam until limp, 5–10 minutes. Add 2 cups peeled chopped apples and sauté for 2 minutes. Season to taste with salt and pepper. Serve immediately. Serves 4–6.

Snip kale into soups at the last minute—green and delicious!

SOUPS

Cream of Greens Soup

Enjoy this delicious soup fresh; the greens turn a nasty olive overnight.

1 tablespoon butter
1 tablespoon vegetable oil
1½ cups diced onion
2 garlic cloves, minced
1½ teaspoons fresh thyme or
    ½ teaspoon dried
1½ teaspoons fresh marjoram or
    ½ teaspoon dried
4 cups peeled diced potatoes
12 cups roughly chopped greens
6 cups water
1 cup cream, yogurt, or milk
salt and pepper

In a large soup pot, heat the butter and oil, and sauté the onion, garlic, thyme, and marjoram until the onion is limp, about 5 minutes. Add the potatoes, greens, and water, and simmer for 15 minutes. Let the soup cool slightly, then puree in a blender or food processor. Return the soup to the pot and reheat. Add the cream, and heat through. Season to taste with salt and pepper. Serve at once.

Preparation Time: 20 minutes
Cooking Time: 20 minutes
Yield: 6 servings

Smoky Mustard Greens Soup

High-quality (home-smoked or storebought) Canadian bacon has the strong smoke flavor that is desirable here.

½ pound sweet Italian sausage
¼ pound smoky Canadian bacon,
    diced
2 cups diced onions
2 garlic cloves, minced
2 cups thick tomato puree
4 cups chicken broth
8 cups finely chopped mustard
    greens
salt and pepper

Remove the casings and brown the sausage, breaking it up with a spoon. Remove the sausage from the pan and drain off all but 1 tablespoon of the fat. Sauté the bacon, onions, and garlic in the fat until the onions are limp, about 5 minutes. Add the tomato puree, chicken broth, and sausage. Simmer the soup for 10 minutes. Add the mustard greens and simmer the soup long enough to wilt the greens; they should be bright green and tender in 3–5 minutes. Season to taste with salt and pepper. Serve hot.

Preparation Time: 15 minutes
Cooking Time: 25 minutes
Yield: 6 servings

SIDE AND MAIN DISHES

I can't say it often enough: Don't overcook your greens.

Wrapped Vegetable Terrine

This dish takes some time to prepare but it's a very glamorous way to show off your garden produce. I serve this dish along with a salad and fresh homemade bread.

10–15 whole collard leaves
4 cups grated summer squash
1 teaspoon salt
4 tablespoons butter
2 cups diced onions
1 garlic clove, minced
2 cups diced carrots
⅓ cup water
1 tablespoon minced fresh dill
1 cup grated Swiss cheese
3 cups sliced mushrooms
1 cup grated parmesan cheese
2 teaspoons minced fresh tarragon
    or ¾ teaspoon dried
3 eggs, beaten
1 cup milk
¼ teaspoon pepper

Preheat the oven to 350° F.
Remove the tough, large stems from the collard leaves. Steam the leaves until bright green and limp, 3–5 minutes. Remove from the heat and cool slightly. Grease a 9-inch loaf pan and line the pan with leaves, letting them drape over the edges of the pan.
Layer the summer squash and ½ teaspoon salt in a colander. Weight with a heavy plate and

drain while you prepare the remaining ingredients.

Melt 2 tablespoons of the butter in a large sauté pan, and sauté the onions and garlic until limp, 3–5 minutes. Remove from the pan. Add the carrots and water and cook the carrots uncovered until they are just tender and the water has evaporated. Remove the carrots from the pan to a bowl and stir in ½ cup of the onions, the dill, and the Swiss cheese. Place the mixture in the loaf pan as a bottom layer.

Melt 1 tablespoon butter in the same sauté pan, and sauté the mushrooms until limp, about 5 minutes. Mix in 1 cup of the onion mixture. Spoon this mixture into the loaf pan on top

of the carrots. Sprinkle half the parmesan cheese on top.

Heat the remaining 1 tablespoon of butter in the pan, and sauté the summer squash for 2 minutes. Add the remaining onion, parmesan cheese, and tarragon. Stir to mix. Spoon this mixture on top of the mushrooms.

Mix the eggs, milk, ½ teaspoon salt, and the pepper. Pour the custard mixture into the loaf pan and let it slowly seep down to the bottom. Fold the collard greens over the loaf and place a few remaining leaves on top to cover the dish. Cover with aluminum foil. Place the loaf pan in a larger baking dish and fill the dish with boiling water halfway up the sides of the loaf pan. Bake for 1 hour. Let the loaf sit for 10 minutes before unmolding. Cut into slices with a serrated knife.

Preparation Time: 45 minutes
Baking Time: 1 hour
Yield: 8 servings

1. Spoon over the leaves.

2. Slowly pour in the custard mixture.

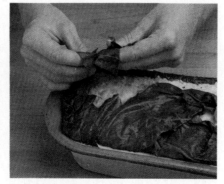

3. Fold the greens over the top to cover the filling.

Stuffed Pork Chops

1 tablespoon butter
1 tablespoon vegetable oil
2 garlic cloves, minced
1 cup chopped onion
1½–2 cups chopped mushrooms
½ teaspoon ground rosemary or thyme
6 cups chopped mustard greens
¼ cup fresh bread crumbs
1 cup grated Swiss cheese
salt and pepper
4–6 centercut pork chops, 1½ inches thick
approximately ¼ cup water or broth

Preheat the oven to 325° F.

In a large sauté pan, heat the butter and oil, and sauté the garlic, onion, mushrooms, and herbs until the onion is limp, 3–5 minutes. Add the mustard greens and cover. Cook, stirring occasionally, until the greens are limp, 3–5 minutes. Remove the pan from the heat and stir in the bread crumbs and cheese. Season to taste with salt and pepper.

Sear the pork chops by rubbing the fatty ends of the chops around a hot frying pan, then laying the chops in the pan, and browning quickly on both sides over high heat. Split the pork chops to make a pocket. Divide the filling among the chops and stuff the pockets. Place the chops in a baking dish, and add water or broth to cover the bottom with ¼ inch of liquid. Loosely cover the dish. Bake for 2 hours. Add more liquid if needed. Serve at once.

Preparation Time: 20 minutes
Baking Time: 2 hours
Yield: 4–6 servings

Herbs

I Hope You Grow Your Own — What a World of Difference!

I don't think people can truly know the joys of gardening and cooking until they begin to raise their own herbs.

Herbs are rewarding for the gardener because they are beautiful and easy to grow. For the cook, nothing tops the flavor of fresh, fresh herbs. It's a pleasure to step outside one's kitchen and snip a sprig of fresh herbs to throw into a pot.

And step outside my kitchen is just what I do when I am seeking fresh herbs. I grow most of my herbs near my house in a border bed that contains both herbs and flowers. That way, I enjoy the beautiful plants whenever I look outside my kitchen window, and I don't have far to go when I need a sprig of this or that for a recipe. My repertoire of cooking herbs—which includes plenty of basil, tarragon, and cilantro—has increased as my garden has grown.

Fresh Herbs Impart a Lot of Flavor

I prefer to use fresh herbs for cooking, so I grow plenty to see me through the summer. Throughout the rest of the year I rely on dried and frozen herbs.

Dill weed are herbs I have frozen with great success. You simply mince the herbs and freeze in small amounts in plastic bags. You can use frozen herbs just as you would fresh herbs.

Parsley and chives also freeze well, but I like to transplant a few garden plants and keep them growing in pots all winter long. So my recipes always call for these herbs fresh.

I get the most consistent results when I dry herbs in a dehydrator. But for convenience, I dry some herbs by bundling stems together and hanging them upside down in perforated paper bags.

Let your taste buds be your guide when deciding how much fresh herbs to use in place of dried. The general formula is to use about 3 times as much fresh herbs as dried for the same flavor. Tarragon is an important exception; it becomes more powerful when dried, so use only twice as much of the fresh herb as the dried.

The flavor of dried herbs will vary depending on how old the herbs are, how protected they have been from sunlight, how quickly they dried, and whether or not they were harvested at their peak—just before the flower buds open.

I use plenty of herbs in my cooking, so I'll bundle up most of the basil, dill, sage, and thyme that you see here and hang the bundles to dry. Some of the herbs will wind up in herb vinegars, some are made into fresh bouquets, and still others are dried to make potpourris.

A Cook's Tour of Herbs

Basil. Group this annual in large quantities for use in Pesto (page 161), herb vinegars, and flavoring. Good with most vegetables and an important seasoning for Italian dishes. The opal variety has rich maroon-colored leaves that look beautiful in bouquets.

Chives. A perennial that goes well with all vegetables. The blossoms make lovely garnishes. Keep a pot of chives growing all year to supply fresh herbs.

Borage. A self-seeding annual. The blossoms make lovely garnishes.

Chervil. An annual that has a delicate anise flavor.

Cilantro, or fresh Coriander. Also known as Chinese parsley, cilantro has a flavor that is both smoky and flowery. I prefer to use the fresh herb. An important seasoning for Mexican and Oriental dishes.

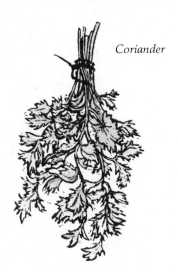

Coriander

HERBS AT A GLANCE

Dill. An annual that can be grown in large quantities for pickling. Harvest both the ferny leaves and the seed heads.

Dill

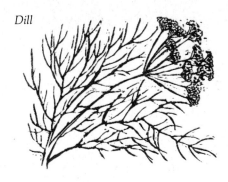

Fennel. Not to be confused with "fennel root" (pages 294–295), this perennial is grown mainly for its seeds, which are used whole or crushed. The leaves may be used for flavoring. It also has a delicate anise flavor.

Lemon Balm. A lemon-scented perennial whose leaves are used in salads, teas, soups, and stuffings.

Marjoram. A perennial that will not tolerate frosts. Delicious fresh or dried with all vegetables.

Mint. A perennial that spreads easily in the garden. Use as a flavoring or garnish.

Oregano. A perennial used extensively in Italian cooking.

Parsley. A biennial that can be brought in from the garden and kept growing in a pot all winter. Delicious with all vegetables.

Rosemary. A perennial that will grow into a good-size bush. I prefer to grind dried rosemary; otherwise, the dried leaves can be quite woody.

Sage. A perennial that is good fresh or dried.

Savory. Summer savory is an annual, and winter savory is a perennial. Particularly good in bean dishes.

Tarragon

Tarragon. Grow only French tarragon, a hardy perennial. Strongly flavored, it goes well with most vegetables. A favorite for herb vinegars.

Thyme. A perennial that comes in many different varieties. Lemon thyme has a pleasant lemon scent.

Herb Vinegars Make Salads Taste Better

If making homemade Christmas presents is something you like to do — or wish you had more time for — try making herb vinegars. The process takes less than 10 minutes, but the pleasure of cooking with herb vinegars lasts and lasts.

When do you use herb vinegars? I use most of my herb vinegars in salad dressings. But you can use them in almost any recipe that calls for vinegar — even pickle recipes.

Harvest Herbs at Their Peak

For best flavor, herbs should be harvested at their peak. This is after the flower buds appear and before the flowers have opened, when the aromatic oils of the herbs are strongest. Try to harvest early in the day before the sun has dried the dew from the leaves.

My favorite herbs to use in vinegars are basil (regular or opal), burnet, chives, dill, marjoram, mint, oregano, rosemary, sage, tarragon, and thyme. I use both single herbs and herb blends.

Use Wine Vinegar For a Superior Base

I like to use red or white wine vinegar for my herbed vinegars. The taste is smooth and goes well with herbs. You will save money by making herb vinegars with white vinegar, or even cider

Old wine bottles are great to use for the initial stage of mixing herb vinegars. After 10 days, I'll bottle them in sterilized jars.

vinegar, but I don't recommend them. (See page 315.)

Here's a recipe for 1 quart of herbed vinegar. Make as many quarts as you desire.

Place 1½–2 cups of minced herbs in a glass jar. I use clean recycled wine bottles. In a stainless steel or enamel pot (don't use aluminum), heat 4 cups of wine vinegar to just below the boiling point. Pour the hot vinegar over the herbs. Cork with a nonmetallic cork. Place the bottle in the sun or in a warm place. Shake or stir daily for 10 days.

After 10 days, strain the vinegar through a fine cheesecloth. Pour the strained vinegar into sterilized jars and add a fresh sprig of herbs for a garnish. Cork and store in a dark cupboard.

1. Stuff with 1½–2 cups herbs.

2. Then fill with very hot wine vinegar.

APPETIZERS AND SOUPS

Nothing whets the appetite like a dish made with plenty of fresh herbs.

These dips are flavored with herbs. They are great with raw veggies.

Boursin Cheese

Great with crackers or bread or as a stuffing for cherry tomatoes, celery sticks, new potatoes, or baby beets. Thin the Boursin with sour cream, milk, or yogurt for an herb dip with vegetables. The only thing you can't do with Boursin Cheese is make it with dried herbs. It just won't do.

8 ounces cream cheese at room
    temperature
1 tablespoon lemon juice
1 garlic clove, minced
½ teaspoon Worcestershire sauce
½ teaspoon dry mustard
1 tablespoon minced fresh parsley
1 tablespoon minced fresh chives
    or scallion
¼ cup minced fresh herbs
    (rosemary, summer savory,
    sage, thyme, dill, basil,
    marjoram, or oregano)

Combine all the ingredients in a food processor and process until well mixed. Serve at room temperature or chilled.

Preparation Time: 15 minutes
Yield: 1¼ cups

Cottage Cheese Herb Spread

1 cup cottage cheese
¼ teaspoon salt
1 teaspoon fresh thyme or
    ¼ teaspoon dried
1 teaspoon fresh marjoram or
    ¼ teaspoon dried
1 teaspoon fresh sage or
    ¼ teaspoon dried
1 teaspoon minced fresh chives
1 tablespoon minced fresh parsley
2 hard-boiled eggs
pepper

Combine the cottage cheese, salt, herbs, and 1 of the eggs in a food processor and process until smooth. Remove the mixture from the processor. Finely chop the remaining egg and stir into the cheese mixture. Season to taste with pepper. Serve chilled.

Preparation Time: 10 minutes
Chilling Time: 1 hour
Yield: 1½ cups

Sour Cream Dill Dip

A very popular dip for vegetables and chips.

2 ounces cream cheese at room
    temperature
2 tablespoons minced fresh parsley
¼ cup minced fresh dill
¼ cup mayonnaise
2 garlic cloves, minced
1 teaspoon lemon juice
½ teaspoon salt
3 tablespoons Worcestershire sauce
dash hot sauce
1½ cups sour cream

Combine all the ingredients, except the sour cream, in a food processor and process until well blended. Remove this mixture from the processor and stir in the sour cream. Chill the dip for at least 30 minutes to allow the flavors to mingle. Serve chilled.

Preparation Time: 15 minutes
Chilling Time: 30 minutes
Yield: 2 cups

Herb Cheese Soup

3 tablespoons butter
1½ cups finely diced onion
1½ cups finely diced green peppers
1 cup finely diced carrots
2 tablespoons minced fresh parsley
1 tablespoon minced fresh chives
1 teaspoon fresh marjoram or
   ¼ teaspoon dried
2 teaspoons fresh thyme or
   ¾ teaspoon dried
2 teaspoons fresh savory or
   ¾ teaspoon dried
¼ teaspoon Worcestershire sauce
¼ cup all-purpose unbleached flour
1 cup chicken broth
3 cups milk
3 cups grated cheddar cheese
   (packed)
salt and pepper

In a large soup pot, melt the butter, and sauté the onion, peppers, carrots, parsley, chives, marjoram, thyme, and savory for 5–8 minutes, or until the onion is limp and the peppers and carrots are tender crisp. Add the Worcestershire sauce. Sprinkle the flour over the vegetables and stir well. Add the chicken broth, stirring constantly to prevent lumps. Add the milk a little at a time, stirring well after each addition to prevent lumps. Add the cheese and heat to melt the cheese. Season to taste with salt and pepper. Serve the soup hot.

Preparation Time: 20 minutes
Cooking Time: 20 minutes
Yield: 6–8 servings

DRESSINGS, SAUCES, AND SEASONINGS

These are recipes that really show off the flavor of fresh herbs. Yes, you can substitute dried herbs (using the formula of 1 part dried herbs to 3 parts fresh), but I think the dressings and sauces are best with fresh herbs.

Creamy Herb Salad Dressing

This salad dressing is great with green salads and raw or blanched vegetable salads.

⅔ cup sour cream
½ cup buttermilk
2 tablespoons minced capers
2 tablespoons minced fresh parsley
1 teaspoon minced fresh dill
1 teaspoon minced fresh basil
1 garlic clove, minced
1 teaspoon dry mustard
1 tablespoon lemon juice
¼ teaspoon celery seeds
salt and pepper

Whisk together all the ingredients. Let sit for at least 30 minutes before serving.

Preparation Time: 10 minutes
Sitting Time: 30 minutes
Yield: 1½ cups

Dill and parsley are two herbs that freeze quite well. Simply bundle the herbs and place in a plastic freezer bag. Try to remove as much air as possible from the bags before sealing. You can use frozen herbs in the same proportions you would use fresh herbs. Don't try the freezer method with basil, though. The basil will turn black.

Creamy Tarragon Dressing

This is a great dressing for sliced tomatoes. It's also good on green salads and other raw or parboiled vegetable salads.

2 shallots, minced
2 tablespoons minced fresh tarragon
1 teaspoon Dijon-style mustard
3 tablespoons lemon juice
½ cup plus 2 tablespoons vegetable
   or olive oil
⅛ teaspoon white pepper
salt and white pepper

Combine all the ingredients in a food processor or blender and process until smooth. Season to taste with salt and additional white pepper.

Preparation Time: 10 minutes
Yield: ¾ cup

Yogurt Mint Salad Dressing

I particularly like this dressing on green salads and tomato and cucumber salads. It can also be used with fruit if you replace the salt and pepper with honey to taste and omit the scallions.

2 cups yogurt
½ cup minced scallions
⅓ cup minced fresh mint leaves
1 tablespoon lemon juice
salt and pepper

Whisk together all the ingredients and serve.

Preparation Time: 10 minutes
Yield: 2⅓ cups

Basil Salad Dressing

Serve with sliced tomatoes, green salads, and other raw vegetables.

2–3 garlic cloves, minced
¼ cup minced fresh basil
¼ cup minced fresh parsley
4 teaspoons Dijon-style mustard
2 tablespoons wine vinegar
½ teaspoon sugar
¾ cup olive oil

Combine all the ingredients, except the oil, in a food processor or blender and process until smooth. With the processor running, pour in the oil in a thin stream. Process until well blended. This sauce will not be as thick as mayonnaise.

Preparation Time: 10 minutes
Yield: 1¼ cups

Herbed Mayonnaise

Serve with fish, instead of tartar sauce, or as a dip for vegetables.

3 egg yolks
¼ cup lemon juice
1 teaspoon Dijon-style mustard
2 tablespoons minced fresh parsley
2 tablespoons minced scallion
½ teaspoon salt
⅛ teaspoon black pepper
¼ cup olive oil
1¼ cups vegetable oil
2 tablespoons minced fresh dill
2 tablespoons minced fresh basil

Combine the egg yolks, lemon juice, mustard, parsley, scallion, salt, and pepper in a blender or food processor and blend until smooth. With the blender going, add the oils in a thin stream. The mayonnaise will thicken as the oil is poured in. Stir in the minced herbs and serve.

Preparation Time: 15 minutes
Yield: 2 cups

Herb Butter

It's delicious on cooked vegetables.

4 tablespoons butter
1–2 tablespoons minced fresh herbs (tarragon, summer savory, sage, marjoram, oregano, thyme, basil, parsley)

Melt the butter in a sauté pan and add the herbs. Sauté for 1–2 minutes. Toss with 4–6 cups cooked vegetables and serve.

Preparation Time: 10 minutes
Yield: 6 servings

Béarnaise Sauce

Béarnaise sauces are variations on hollandaise—just as tricky and delicate. This sauce is best made in a blender and served immediately. Don't try to reheat.

¼ cup white wine
2 tablespoons tarragon vinegar
1 tablespoon minced fresh tarragon
1 tablespoon finely chopped shallot
½ teaspoon white pepper
¾ cup butter
3 egg yolks
2–3 tablespoons lemon juice
½ teaspoon salt
dash cayenne

In a small saucepan, combine the wine, vinegar, tarragon, shallot, and pepper. Simmer until reduced by half, about 5 minutes. Remove this mixture from the heat.

Melt the butter and keep it warm.

Combine the egg yolks, lemon juice, salt, and cayenne in a blender and blend until smooth. With the blender going, slowly pour in the melted butter in a thin stream. Remove the sauce from the blender and stir in the vinegar and herb mixture. Serve the sauce immediately with cooked vegetables, steak, or seafood.

Preparation Time: 10 minutes
Yield: 1 cup (6 servings)

Variation

Tomato Béarnaise. Stir 2 tablespoons tomato paste into the wine and vinegar solution after you have removed it from the heat. Then proceed with the recipe.

1. Chop the fresh basil.

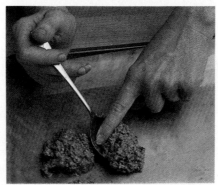

3. Cover with oil, refrigerate.

2. Process the basil, cheese, oil, pine nuts, and seasonings.

4. Or freeze by the tablespoon. Then store in plastic bags.

Pesto

Pesto is just about the best use of fresh basil I know. It is easy to make in a food processor and will keep in the refrigerator for 2 months or in the freezer for 1 year. Replace the coating of olive oil after each use. The best time to harvest basil for quality Pesto is before the plant blossoms.

⅓ cup plus 1 tablespoon olive oil
1 cup chopped fresh basil leaves
½ cup pine nuts
3 garlic cloves, minced
⅔ cup grated parmesan cheese
salt and pepper

Combine ⅓ cup olive oil with the remaining ingredients in a food processor and process to make a thick paste. Transfer the Pesto to a container and smooth out the top. Cover with a thin coating of olive oil, approximately 1 tablespoon.

Preparation Time: 15 minutes
Yield: 1½ cups

Italian Seasoning Mix

Mix 2 tablespoons dried oregano, 3 tablespoons dried marjoram, 2 tablespoons dried thyme, 3 tablespoons dried basil, and 2 teaspoons ground rosemary. Use as a seasoning for Italian tomato sauces, meat loaves, or combine a tablespoon of the herb mix with butter and toss with cooked vegetables.

Parsley Sauce for Chicken or Fish

Since I always have fresh parsley growing — in the garden or on a windowsill -- I can make this sauce year-round. I like to serve it over baked or sautéed fish or chicken.

6 tablespoons butter
⅓ cup minced shallots
½ cup minced fresh parsley
⅓ cup all-purpose unbleached flour
1¾ cups chicken broth
¼ cup dry white wine
⅛ teaspoon grated lemon rind
2 tablespoons lemon juice
salt and pepper

In a large sauté pan, melt the butter, and sauté the shallots and parsley until the shallots are limp, about 3 minutes. Sprinkle the flour over the shallots and blend well. Add the chicken broth and wine a little at a time, stirring well after each addition to prevent lumps. Add the lemon rind and lemon juice. Season to taste with salt and pepper.

Preparation Time: 10 minutes
Cooking Time: 10 minutes
Yield: 2½ cups (6 servings)

Herb Salt

Here's a flavor enhancer for meats and vegetables that you can keep on hand in a salt shaker. Combine 1 tablespoon crumbled dried herbs with ½ cup salt. Use as needed.

Salad Greens and
Lettuce

For the Gardener, It's a Smorgasbord From Mild Head Lettuce to Pungent Arugula

My grandmother taught me to serve green salads European style—after the main course. Now that I grow my own salad greens, bringing out my old wooden salad bowl filled with lettuce and greens and decorated with freshly picked nasturtium blossoms brings me special pleasure. Ending a summer meal with a salad is an especially appreciated light touch.

Wide Rows Mean an Abundance of Lettuce

Planting in wide rows brings nonstop supplies of lettuce and greens. I harvest as I need, and I keep planting. Whenever a space opens up in the garden, I throw in a new patch of greens. That way, I grow more than I need and allow the extra to go to seed, but I never do without. And I never eat wilted lettuce from the refrigerator because there is always fresh from the garden.

I like to grow a wide variety of lettuce for the different flavors the varieties contribute. I grow some head lettuce, though I find it rather bland tasting. Ruby lettuce adds color to both my garden and my salads. Romaine has a rich flavor that is especially nice in Caesar salads. Black Seeded Simpson is a very dependable leaf lettuce that comes back well after the first harvest. Oak Leaf has an attractive shape. Boston lettuce and Buttercrunch are my favorites for their tender texture and buttery flavor.

Of the greens I grow for salads, Arugula is my favorite. Also known as Rugula, Rocket, and Roquette, it is a rather peppery tasting green that gets bitter in hot weather. I find it is so flavorful I can serve it without any dressing.

I like to add watercress to salads, even though I don't grow any myself. Dandelion greens, wild or cultivated, are a nice change of pace as well.

In the winter, it gives me a real thrill to harvest Belgium or French endive (Witloof Chicory), which I force from roots grown the previous summer. The endive ends my harvest, but it isn't long before I'm harvesting fresh greens again.

Create your own salad bar with homegrown lettuce and greens. Starting clockwise at the top, we have Romaine, Ruby, Boston, Escarole, Oak leaf, Escarole, and Curly leaf lettuces.

LETTUCE AND SALAD GREENS AT A GLANCE

Yield

1 pound fresh lettuce or greens equals 24 cups chopped

or

12 cups chiffonade (shredded)

Don't Store—Harvest As You Need It

If you do find yourself with extra lettuce or greens, wrap them unwashed in a damp paper towel and place in a perforated plastic bag in the refrigerator. They should keep for 3–4 days.

Washing Tips

Wash dirty lettuce and greens by dunking in lukewarm water and lifting out of the water. I usually inspect each leaf to be sure it's dirt-free before tearing it into the salad.

Salad Spinners Do Great Job

I want my lettuce and greens bone dry when I add them to a salad, so I use my salad spinner to spin off the water clinging to the leaves. The spinner works!

In the old days, folks used to stuff a pillow case with wet lettuce and greens and spin the pillow case in the air until all the water had spun off the leaves. Same principle, but more work.

Seven Salad Tips

• Lettuce and greens should be torn into bite-size pieces. Cutting lettuce at the table with a fork and knife should not be necessary.

• To prevent soggy salads, dress the salad at the table. Toss and serve.

• The proportion of oil to vinegar in a salad dressing is a matter of taste. Everything from an equal proportion of oil to vinegar or lemon juice, to 4 parts oil to 1 part vinegar is acceptable. For more salad dressing recipes, see pages 300–303.

• I like to make my dressings ahead of time for the sake of convenience and to insure a good blending of flavors.

• Edible flowers are delightful in salads. Try them. My favorites are calendula, nasturtium, opal basil, rose petals, borage blossoms, day lilies, squash blossoms, chive blossoms, thyme blossoms, pansies, mint blossoms, chamomile, and marigolds.

• Fresh herbs are excellent in salads—everything from the familiar basil and dill, to salad burnet and borage. See the Herb chapter (pages 154–161) for more ideas.

• Young Swiss and Ruby chard (pages 104–111) are good in salads, too.

Salads Don't Have To Be Tossed

You can make a "composed" salad by arranging vegetables on a bed of greens on a platter or in a bowl. Try several different patterns—rows of vegetables, concentric circles, V-shaped rows, alternating half circles. The vegetables should be chopped or sliced in fairly uniform-size pieces for the most visual harmony.

Opal basil   *Rose*

Dandelion   *Arugula*

Daylily   *Calendula*

Nasturtium   *Borage*

Ever Wonder How To Toss Together the Classic Salads? Here's How . . .

If you're like me, most of your tossed salads are snatched from the garden at the last moment. Here are some salads that are just as easily tossed together, but have become classics because they are so popular.

Chef Salad

Make a bed of greens and top with julienne-sliced ham, turkey, roast beef, and Swiss cheese. Garnish with wedges of hard-boiled eggs and dress with your favorite dressing.

Greek Salad

Buy the best Greek olives for this one. Combine diced tomatoes, diced cucumbers, diced red onion, minced garlic, cubed feta cheese, and Greek olives. Dress with an herb vinaigrette (page 300) and serve on a bed of greens.

Caesar Salad

To make the dressing, combine 1 raw egg, 2 anchovies, 2 garlic cloves, 4 tablespoons lemon juice, and ½ cup grated parmesan cheese in a blender or food processor. With the blender running, slowly pour in ½ cup olive oil. Season to taste with salt and freshly ground black pepper. Pour the dressing over torn romaine lettuce and toasted unseasoned croutons. Anchovy fillets are optional.

1. Harvest a variety of greens.

2. Dry the greens carefully.

A garnish of edible flowers is an attractive and tasty finish for salads. Here I'm adding nasturtium blossoms from the garden.

Frosted Lettuce Wedges

Combine 1 cup crumbled blue cheese, 2 tablespoons lemon juice, 2 tablespoons wine vinegar, 3 tablespoons minced scallion, and 2 tablespoons minced fresh parsley in a blender or food processor. Process until well mixed. With the blender running, slowly pour in ½ cup vegetable oil. Transfer to a bowl and fold in ½ cup whipping cream that has been whipped stiff.

Using a spatula, spread the dressing over 8 wedges of head lettuce. Chill for 1 hour before serving.

Tricks for Avoiding Leftover Salad

While the Leftover Salad Soup page 166 is really tasty, I prefer to prepare just enough to avoid leftovers. With green salads, I figure that 1 cup of salad per person is adequate—if there are other dishes. Big salad eaters may consume up to 2 cups of salad, especially on hot summer days when heartier foods seem unappealing.

If you don't dress your salad before serving, you can store leftovers in a sealed plastic bag for about a day. The tomatoes don't hold up—unless they are whole cherry tomatoes. I remove sliced or diced tomatoes before storing.

Of course, if you do dress your salad before serving, you will use far less dressing.

You'll be surprised how much flavor lettuce can impart to a soup. The first soup is a very delicate cream soup that is delicious made with any green. The second soup, Leftover Salad Soup, is much more robust in flavor—an old-fashioned, hearty, chilled vegetable chowder.

Creamy Lettuce Soup

2 tablespoons butter
½ cup chopped scallions
16 cups chopped mild-flavored
 lettuce or greens
3 cups chicken broth
⅛ teaspoon white pepper
salt
6 ounces cream cheese

In a large soup pot, melt the butter, and sauté the scallions and lettuce until the lettuce is limp, 2–4 minutes. Add the chicken broth and pepper. Simmer for 5 minutes. Season to taste with salt.

Cool the soup slightly and puree in a food processor or blender. Return the soup to the pot to reheat. Dice the cream cheese and add to the soup. Heat until melted. Serve the soup hot, with minced herbs or a flower as a garnish.

Preparation Time: 15 minutes
Cooking Time: 15 minutes
Yield: 6–8 servings

Leftover Salad Soup—it started as a joke and became a favorite.

Leftover Salad Soup

Vary the amount of liquid according to the amount of leftover salad you have. Add more lemon juice if your salad wasn't dressed with a vinaigrette dressing.

Puree about 4 cups of leftover dressed salad in a food processor or blender. Add 1 cup buttermilk, ½ cup yogurt, ¼ cup sour cream, 1 tablespoon lemon juice, 1 minced garlic clove, 1 tablespoon minced fresh dill, and 6 tablespoons water. Puree until smooth. Season to taste with salt and pepper. Pour into a serving bowl and stir in ¾ cup diced tomatoes. Serve chilled. This recipe serves 3–4.

SALADS

Arugula and dandelion greens are early spring greens. To celebrate their harvest, I make these salads, which don't require other greens.

Arugula Salad

½ cup olive oil
2 tablespoons lemon juice
2 tablespoons wine vinegar
2 teaspoons Dijon-style mustard
3 large garlic cloves, minced
1 tablespoon capers
5–6 cups torn Arugula leaves
2 hard-boiled eggs, chopped
½ cup walnuts
1 cup grated carrots

Whisk together the oil, lemon juice, vinegar, mustard, garlic, and capers in a small bowl.

Place the Arugula on individual salad plates and garnish with the eggs, walnuts, and grated carrots. Drizzle the dressing over the salad and serve.

Preparation Time: 15 minutes
Yield: 6 servings

Dandelion Salad With Horseradish Dressing

8 cups dandelion greens
½ cup peeled julienne-sliced Jerusalem artichokes
½ cup grated carrots
2 tablespoons currants
2 teaspoons finely minced onion
¾ teaspoon prepared horseradish
½ teaspoon Dijon-style mustard
4 teaspoons lemon juice
½ teaspoon sugar
¼ cup vegetable oil
¼ cup olive oil
¼ teaspoon salt
¼ teaspoon white pepper

Combine the dandelion greens, Jerusalem artichokes, carrots, and currants in a salad bowl. Whisk together the remaining ingredients and pour over the salad. Toss to coat. Serve at once.

Preparation Time: 20 minutes
Yield: 4–6 servings

SIDE DISHES AND MAIN DISHES

Endive With Seafood Sauce

1 pound shrimp, peeled and deveined
3–4 Belgium or French endives, sliced in half lengthwise
2 tablespoons butter
1 garlic clove, minced
½ cup chopped onion
1 cup chopped tomato
¼ teaspoon ground rosemary
1 tablespoon minced fresh basil or 1 teaspoon dried
¼ teaspoon white pepper
1 teaspoon lemon juice
3–4 tablespoons dry white wine
⅔ cup crumbled feta cheese

Steam or boil the shrimp until just cooked, 3–5 minutes, and remove from the heat.

Steam the endives for 10–12 minutes or until tender.

In the meantime, melt the butter in a sauté pan, and sauté the garlic and onion until limp, 3–5 minutes. Add the tomato, rosemary, basil, pepper, lemon juice, and wine. Cook for 5 minutes more. Add the feta and shrimp and heat through.

Place a half endive on each plate and spoon the shrimp mixture over it. Serve immediately.

Preparation Time: 25 minutes
Cooking Time: 20 minutes
Yield: 6–8 servings

Baked Sole On a Bed of Lettuce

3 tablespoons butter
½ cup chopped leeks
4 cups sliced mushrooms
22 cups chopped lettuce (Romaine is recommended)
1 tablespoon minced shallot
⅓ cup minced fresh dill
½ cup heavy cream
1 teaspoon lemon juice
salt and pepper
6 sole fillets

Preheat the oven to 350° F.

In a large sauté pan, melt 2 tablespoons of the butter, and sauté the leeks and mushrooms until they are limp, 3–5 minutes. Add the lettuce and continue to sauté until the lettuce is limp, about 2 minutes. Reserve ¾ cup of lettuce and spoon the remainder into a greased baking dish. The dish should be large enough to arrange the fish in a single layer on top of the lettuce.

In a small saucepan, melt the remaining 1 tablespoon butter and sauté the shallot and dill for 2 minutes. Combine with ¾ cup of the sautéed lettuce, the cream, and lemon juice in a food processor or blender. Process until smooth. Season to taste with salt and pepper.

Lay the fillets on top of the sautéed lettuce. Pour the sauce over the fillets.

Bake uncovered for 30 minutes. Serve immediately.

Preparation Time: 25 minutes
Baking Time: 30 minutes
Yield: 6 servings

1. Remove center rib.

2. Steam briefly.

3. Roll carefully.

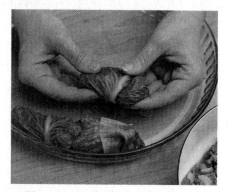

4. Place seam side down. Handle with care; the rolls are fragile.

Stuffed Lettuce Rolls

Stuffed lettuce rolls are a more delicate version of stuffed cabbage rolls. The fillings can be used interchangeably. (See page 81.)

I use the large outer Romaine leaves for rolling, and the smaller inner leaves for the filling.

8–10 dried black Chinese
 mushrooms
boiling water
3 tablespoons peanut oil
1 garlic clove, minced
2 teaspoons minced fresh ginger
 root
½ cup minced celery
⅓ cup chopped scallions
⅓ cup minced water chestnuts
3 cups finely chopped Romaine
 lettuce
1 cup chicken broth
2 teaspoons sesame oil
½ pound ground pork
3 tablespoons dry red wine
2 tablespoons tamari or soy sauce
¾ cup chopped mung bean sprouts
2 tablespoons cornstarch
16–18 large Romaine leaves

Place the mushrooms in a bowl and pour boiling water over them. Let them sit for 20 minutes.

Preheat the oven to 350° F.

In a wok or large sauté pan, heat 2 tablespoons of the peanut oil, and stir fry the garlic, ginger, celery, scallions, and water chestnuts for 2 minutes. Add the chopped lettuce and ¼ cup of the chicken broth. Cover and simmer for 2 minutes. Transfer the vegetables to a bowl.

Heat the remaining tablespoon of peanut oil with the sesame oil. Stir fry the pork, wine, and 1 tablespoon of the tamari until the pork is no longer pink. Add the bean sprouts and stir fry for 1 minute.

Mix 1 tablespoon of the cornstarch and ¼ cup chicken broth. Return the vegetables to the wok. Add the cornstarch mixture. Stir fry until the sauce thickens slightly, 1–2 minutes.

Remove the large ribs of the Romaine leaves. Steam the leaves over boiling water until just limp, about 2 minutes. Place a few tablespoons filling on each leaf. Fold the sides of the leaf in to enclose the filling and roll the leaf to make a small roll. Place the rolls seam side down in a baking dish.

Mix the remaining tablespoon of cornstarch with ¼ cup of the chicken broth until smooth. Add the remaining ¼ cup chicken broth. Season with 1 tablespoon tamari. Cook over medium heat and stir until the mixture becomes clear and thickened. Pour over the lettuce rolls. Bake the rolls for 20 minutes. Serve hot.

Preparation Time: 40 minutes
Cooking Time: 20 minutes
Yield: 4–6 servings

Thai Chicken in Lettuce Leaves

This recipe is a classic. I prefer to use Boston lettuce because of its buttery flavor and ability to hold its cup shape. Use your fingers to eat this dish. Wrap the lettuce leaves around the chicken and take a bite.

2 large boneless chicken breasts
2 egg whites
½ teaspoon salt
3 tablespoons plus 1 teaspoon lime juice
1 tablespoon cornstarch
2–3 teaspoons chili paste with garlic
3 tablespoons peanut oil
⅔ cup chopped scallions
¼ cup diced sweet red pepper
1 cup diced celery
½ cup diced water chestnuts
2 teaspoons minced fresh ginger root
2 tablespoons plus 1 teaspoon tamari or soy sauce
16 Boston lettuce leaves

Slice the chicken breasts into thin strips 1½ inches long and ¼ inch thick.

Whisk together the egg whites, salt, lime juice, cornstarch, and chili paste. Add the chicken and marinate for 30 minutes.

Then heat 1 tablespoon of the peanut oil in a wok or large frying pan, and stir fry the scallions, pepper, celery, water chestnuts, and ginger until the vegetables are tender crisp, 2–3 minutes. Remove the vegetables from the wok.

Heat the remaining 2 tablespoons peanut oil and stir fry the chicken with the marinade until the chicken is just cooked, about 5 minutes. Return the vegetables to the wok, add the tamari, and stir fry to reheat.

Arrange the whole Boston lettuce leaves on a serving plate, with the stems toward the center of the plate. Spoon some of the chicken mixture onto each leaf. Serve immediately.

Preparation Time: 15 minutes
Marinating Time: 30 minutes
Cooking Time: 10–15 minutes
Yield: 6–8 servings

Thai Chicken in Lettuce Leaves is an exotic, spicy dish. You serve the chicken on fresh lettuce and use the lettuce to carry the food to your mouth. No forks, please!

Okra

Exotic Eating for Yankees—
Prolific Staple in the South

I love to eat okra. To me, a Northerner, eating okra is an adventure in exotic eating. Southern friends laugh when they hear me say that—okra can be very prolific in the South.

Most of my experience with cooking fresh okra comes from cooking vegetables grown at Garden Way Gardens. By starting the okra seeds under grow tunnels, the plants get a good start, so we have a good harvest—at least a few cupfuls a day, which is enough for gumbos and often enough for a tasty okra sauté.

In the South, people make some very fine pickles with their surplus okra. I've sat in on a few pickling sessions, and I am impressed with the ease of the process. All you do is wash and trim the raw okra and pack it in jars. Then you pour in a hot pickling brine, usually the same brine that is used for snap beans. The jars are processed in a boiling water bath for 10 minutes. Now that's a fast and easy pickle! And okra pickles don't have the "slippery" texture many people object to in freshly cooked okra.

Turn Okra's Texture to Your Advantage

Okay, so okra is a little on the ropy side. That is to say, okra secretes a gummy liquid, which is unpleasant to some people. That's no reason to ban it from your kitchen.

There are several ways to get around this problem. One way is to take advantage of the gummy liquid by using okra as a thickener in soups and stews. Another way is to add a tablespoon or so of lemon juice or vinegar to the pan when you are sautéing okra. The acid seems to cut the "roping" tendency of the okra liquid. Keep sautéing until the liquids disappear.

Cooking the okra whole keeps the juices inside the pod, which improves the texture of the finished dish. When trimming the stems, you have to be careful not to cut into the pod, or the juices will leak. Finally, you can give okra a good coating of bread crumbs or cornmeal, as I do with the Crusty Okra Circles on page 175. The coating helps to absorb the gummy liquids.

Once you've learned to compensate for okra's texture, you will want to cook it regularly—whether you look on it as an exotic taste treat or an overabundant surplus vegetable.

This okra is a spineless variety, which means you don't have to wear gloves when you are harvesting. Do the flowers remind you of hibiscus? They are from the same family.

Harvesting Tips

Harvest a few days after the flowers fall, while the pods are young.

Pods should be 2–4 inches long, still soft, with undeveloped seeds.

The older the pod, the tougher and stringier they become.

The more you pick, the more the plants produce. Harvest every 2–3 days.

Wear gloves and a long-sleeved shirt to protect you from the spiny leaves.

Yields

1 pound fresh okra equals
   8 cups whole
or
   4 cups sliced

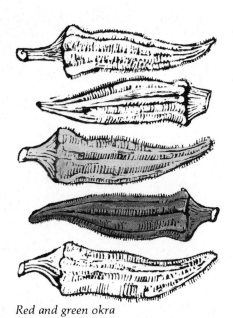

Red and green okra

OKRA AT A GLANCE

Okra slices

Pick and Cook

Okra should be cooked as soon as it is picked. The pods lose color and toughen in the refrigerator. Brown spots develop. If you find yourself with extra, you can store okra in a perforated plastic bag in the refrigerator for up to 2 days.

Extras can be blanched and frozen, or pickled.

There's Little to Do But Wash and Trim

Okra pods should be washed well. The sticky surface fuzz is easily removed with a stiff vegetable brush.

Trim off the stem end of the pod with a paring knife. If you plan to cook the okra whole, be sure you do not trim so deeply that you expose the inside of the pod. This will allow the sticky juices to escape, making your dish gummy in texture.

Breaded and Fried Okra: Crispy and Satisfying

My favorite way to prepare okra is breaded and deep fried. But sautés, particularly with onions, peppers, tomatoes, and corn, are wonderful, too. Here are some time guides.

Cooking Timetable
Blanch (whole): 3–5 minutes
Steam (whole): 3–8 minutes
Parboil (whole): 3 minutes
Sauté (slices): 5–10 minutes
Good spices and herbs to complement okra's flavor are curry, coriander, cumin, rosemary, thyme, garlic, and chives.

When the Crop Gets Really Out of Hand . . .

Okra pods are easily dried and look lovely in dried floral arrangements. Simply harvest the pods still attached to their stems and hang them upside down in a cool, dark place to dry.

Dried okra pods

From Louisiana's Creole kitchens
Gumbo is a unique American classic

A gumbo is a hearty soup, often served as a stew over rice. The key ingredient is okra.

Traditional gumbo recipes call for filé powder, which is made from sassafras leaves. Filé would be added as a thickener during the last few minutes of cooking. But the FDA has banned filé as a carcinogen, so I have dropped it from my recipes.

Instead, this gumbo is thickened with okra and a slowly cooked brown roux, another tradition of Creole cooking.

Fish Gumbo for a Crowd

In a small saucepan, heat ¼ cup vegetable oil and stir in ½ cup all-purpose unbleached flour to make a roux, or thick paste. Cook over medium heat, stirring often, until the roux turns dark brown, about 20 minutes.

In a large pot, melt 2 tablespoons butter, and sauté 2 cups diced onions, ½ cup minced fresh parsley, 1½ cups diced green pepper, ½ cup sliced celery, and 3 cups sliced okra for 10 minutes. Add 6 cups canned whole tomatoes or peeled, chopped fresh tomatoes. Add 5 cups water, ¼ teaspoon dried summer savory, ⅛ teaspoon ground rosemary, and 3 tablespoons lemon juice. Mix in the roux. Simmer for 30 minutes.

Then add 1½–2 pounds boned, cubed firm white fish and ½ pound peeled and deveined raw shrimp. Cook for 5–10 minutes. Season to taste with salt, pepper, and hot sauce. Serve hot over rice. This recipe will serve 12.

The rich flavor of this hearty Fish Gumbo is owed, in part, to cooking the roux until it is dark brown in color (above). The roux, together with the okra, thickens this soup until it is almost a stew. I like to serve it over plenty of rice. With a green salad on the side, Gumbo becomes a complete meal.

SOUPS

Is gumbo a soup or a stew? I usually serve it over rice, and call it a stew. If you're looking for gumbo, see pages 173 and 175.

Tomato Okra Soup

2 tablespoons vegetable oil
2 tablespoons butter
1½ cups diced onion
1 cup diced green pepper
2 cups sliced okra
4 cups canned whole tomatoes or peeled, diced fresh tomatoes
1½ cups sliced kielbasa
3 cups chicken stock
1 tablespoon wine vinegar
1 tablespoon minced fresh basil or 1 teaspoon dried
¾ teaspoon fresh thyme or ¼ teaspoon dried
2 tablespoons minced fresh parsley
salt and pepper

In a large soup pot, heat the oil and butter, and sauté the onion, pepper, and okra for 10 minutes. Break up the tomatoes and add to the vegetables with the remaining ingredients. Simmer for 15 minutes. Season to taste with salt and pepper. Serve hot.

Preparation Time: 20 minutes
Cooking Time: 30 minutes
Yield: 6 servings

SIDE DISHES AND MAIN DISHES

These recipes have converted many people to the joys of okra . . .

Deep-Fried Okra

A word of caution: When you bite into these, bite into the skinny end first so that you don't pull the whole okra out of its coating.

oil for deep frying
3 eggs, beaten
⅓ cup milk
1 tablespoon plus ⅓ cup all-purpose unbleached flour
1 teaspoon salt
1 tablespoon cornmeal
½ cup bread crumbs
½ cup grated parmesan cheese
¼ teaspoon cayenne
4 cups whole trimmed okra

Preheat the oil to 375° F. for deep frying.

In a small bowl, combine the eggs, milk, 1 tablespoon of the flour, and ½ teaspoon of the salt. In a separate bowl, combine the remaining ⅓ cup flour, the cornmeal, bread crumbs, cheese, cayenne, and remaining ½ teaspoon salt.

Dip the okra first in the egg wash and then the crumbs to coat. Deep fry until golden brown. Drain on paper bags or paper towels and serve hot.

Preparation Time: 10 minutes
Cooking Time: 20 minutes
Yield: 4–6 servings

Lamb and Okra Tart

1 pound ground lamb
1 tablespoon olive oil
1 cup diced onion
2 garlic cloves, minced
2 tablespoons minced fresh dill
½ teaspoon ground rosemary
1 cup grated carrots
4 cups cooked brown rice
2 eggs, beaten
½ cup grated parmesan cheese
salt and pepper
4 cups whole okra

Preheat the oven to 400° F.

In a large sauté pan, brown the lamb, breaking it up with a spoon. Drain off the fat and set the meat aside.

Heat the olive oil, and sauté the onion, garlic, dill, rosemary, and carrots until the onion is limp, 3–5 minutes. Remove from the heat and combine the lamb, vegetables, brown rice, eggs, and cheese. Season to taste with salt and pepper.

Trim the okra and steam or parboil for 3–5 minutes, or until bright green.

Grease a 9-inch springform pan and press half of the rice and meat mixture into the pan. Arrange the okra over the rice with the trimmed ends touching the outside edge of the pan.

Press the remaining rice and meat mixture on top of the okra. Cover and bake the tart for 35 minutes. Remove the sides of the pan and serve pie-shaped wedges.

Preparation Time: 30 minutes
Baking Time: 35 minutes
Yield: 6 servings

Chicken Gumbo

Spicy, hearty, and delicious!

¼ cup vegetable oil
½ cup all-purpose unbleached flour
5 bacon slices, diced
2 garlic cloves, minced
2 cups diced onions
½ cup minced fresh parsley
1½ cups diced green peppers
½ cup sliced celery
3 cups sliced okra
4 cups chicken broth
2 cups water
¼ teaspoon pepper
¼ teaspoon cayenne
2 cups diced or shredded cooked
   chicken
1 cup diced ham
salt and pepper

In a small saucepan, heat the oil and blend in the flour to make a roux, or thick paste. Cook over medium heat, stirring often, until the roux is a rich dark brown. This will take about 20 minutes.

In a large sauté pan, brown the bacon, and remove it from the pan. Pour off all but 2 tablespoons of the fat. Sauté the garlic, onions, parsley, peppers, celery, and okra for 10 minutes. Add the chicken broth, water, spices, chicken, ham, and the roux. Cook for 30–45 minutes over medium heat. Season to taste with salt and pepper. Serve hot over rice.

Preparation Time: 30 minutes
Cooking Time: 1–1½ hours
Yield: 6 servings

The breading keeps these Crusty Okra Circles crispy.

Okra With Bacon

3 bacon slices, diced
4 cups sliced okra
1 cup sliced onion
1 garlic clove, minced
¼ cup minced celery
¼ cup sliced scallion tops
salt and pepper

Brown the bacon in a large sauté pan. Remove the bacon and reserve the fat. Sauté the okra in 2 tablespoons of the bacon fat for 5–10 minutes or until most of the roping has disappeared. Remove the okra from the pan and set aside.

Heat 1 more tablespoon of bacon fat, and sauté the onion, garlic, celery, and scallions until the onion is limp, 3–5 minutes. Return the okra and bacon to the pan to reheat. Season to taste with salt and pepper. Serve hot.

Preparation Time: 10 minutes
Cooking Time: 15 minutes
Yield: 6 servings

Crusty Okra Circles

Most of the ropiness of the okra is absorbed by the bread crumbs, making this dish a favorite to serve as an introduction to this less common vegetable.

2 tablespoons bread crumbs
3 tablespoons grated parmesan
   cheese
1 tablespoon cornmeal
⅛ teaspoon cayenne
¼ teaspoon salt
3 cups sliced okra
¼ cup olive oil
2 garlic cloves, minced

Mix the bread crumbs, cheese, cornmeal, cayenne, and salt. Add the okra and stir to coat. Heat the olive oil, and sauté the okra and garlic for 5–10 minutes or until most of the roping has disappeared, and the okra is tender. Serve immediately.

Preparation Time: 10 minutes
Cooking Time: 10 minutes
Yield: 4–6 servings

Onions

Break the Yellow Onion Habit!
Add Welcomed Variety to Your Cooking

I think of onions as a companion vegetable for cooks, the way a gardener thinks of radishes as a companion plant for the garden. There's hardly a recipe in this book that doesn't call for some member of the onion family for flavor enhancement.

Even before the soil in the garden can be worked in early spring, I begin my onion harvest. First come the chives, then the perennial Egyptian onions—both of these are planted in a bed near the kitchen that has in it flowers and herbs. In the woods, wild leeks grow in profusion—just perfect for Potato Leek Soup (page 212). All this before the garden is even planted!

Of course, the old standard is the yellow cooking onion, which stores very well in the root cellar. I count on having this onion year-round. Closely related to the yellow onion is the mild red onion, which I use raw in salads and sandwiches only. Red onions bleed and become watery when cooked.

Leeks are a special onion—mild, yet distinctive. They are more delicate than yellow onions in both flavor and texture, so I use them in soups and vegetable sautés that are cooked briefly.

Garlic is another standard. I use its sharp pungent flavor in many dishes. Garlic is used as a flavoring all over the world.

The Rose of the Onion Family

I think shallots must be the rose of the onion family. I can't quite find the words to describe their delicate flavor. But I do know that once you get hooked on cooking with them you will never want to be without them.

Shallots are so expensive in the supermarket! It may be worth it to buy a couple of bulbs (a small shallot bulb goes far in flavoring a dish) to see if you agree with my appreciation of this delicacy. Then you will probably decide to grow some for yourself. Shallot bulbs multiply as garlic bulbs do.

The list of onion family members continues with scallions (my favorite for stir fries), white pearl onions (excellent for pickling and for cooking in creamed onion dishes), and several perennial varieties. Why settle for plain old yellow cooking onions, when so much variety is available?

I use onions liberally in my cooking. The Onion Soup is made with spinach and can be found on page 246. You'll find all the members of the onion family in recipes throughout this book.

ONIONS AT A GLANCE

Harvesting Tips

Harvest spring onions—chives, white bunching onions, scallions, self-seeding leeks—as soon as there is something big enough to eat.

Harvest bulbs—yellow onions, sweet red and white onions, shallots, garlic—7–10 days after the tops die back.

Onions should be thoroughly dried before storing. Pull the onions from the ground and allow them to dry for 2–3 days in the garden or on the porch. Brush off extra soil and "cure" for up to 2 weeks in a warm airy place. Once the onions are dry, hang them in bags or braid them and hang them where they will get good air circulation.

Yields

1 pound fresh onions equals
   6½ cups cubed or sliced
or
   4 cups diced
1 pound fresh leeks equals
   6 cups sliced
1 pound fresh garlic, shallots, or
   scallions equals
   4 cups chopped

Preparing Onions: Can Tears Be Avoided?

My grandmother wore ski goggles and a scarf around her mouth when chopping onions in quantity. Other people chew gum or hold bread in their mouths. I suffer tears. If I had room in my refrigerator, I would keep my onions chilled—this does help prevent tears.

Washing Leeks

Leeks tend to hold dirt in between their layers and must be washed carefully. First remove the root hairs and tough outer leaves. Wash under running water. Slice and wash again. If you want to cook whole leeks, partially slice the leeks into quarters, keeping the bottoms connected. Wash under running water.

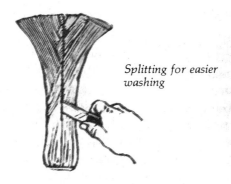

Splitting for easier washing

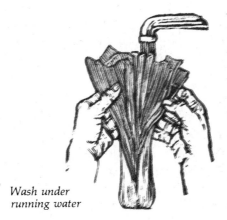

Wash under running water

It's Easy to Mince Garlic

My garlic press does a great job of pressing through all the garlic and leaving behind the skin. I use it all the time.

If you don't have a garlic press, you can crush and mince garlic with a chef's knife or food processor.

Cooking Times

Blanch (whole 1–3 inch onions):
   10–20 minutes
Stir Fry or Sauté (sliced, diced, or minced onions, garlic, leeks, scallions): 3–5 minutes
Sauté (minced shallots):
   2–3 minutes
Bake (whole): 30–40 minutes at 350° F.

Usually Onions Are Sautéed Until Limp

To bring out the most flavor, I sauté onions until limp and translucent, but not browned. This takes 3–5 minutes, depending on how well the pan conducts heat.

If you sauté onions until well-browned, 10–15 minutes, the onions become very sweet.

Low-Fat Onion Sauté

You don't need oil to bring out the onion flavor. Try this method instead of sautéing. Heat a tablespoon of water to boiling in a sauté pan. Add 1 cup diced or sliced onion. Stir until the water disappears and onions are soft and slightly browned. Season to taste with tamari or soy sauce, if desired.

For Very Special Occasions: A Swedish-Style Roast Leg of Lamb Flavored With Shallots, Garlic, Coffee, and Currant Jelly

Preheat the oven to 450° F.

Mix 1 teaspoon salt, ½ teaspoon ground rosemary, and ¼ teaspoon white pepper. Rub into a small leg of lamb. Pierce the top of the roast to a depth of ½ inch at regular intervals and partially insert thin slivers of garlic. Use about 2 cloves.

Place the roast in the oven and immediately lower the temperature to 325° F. Roast for 25 minutes per pound.

One hour before the roast is done, scatter ½ cup coarsely chopped shallots over the bottom of the roasting pan around the roast. Baste with ¼ cup coffee. Fifteen minutes later, baste again with the pan juices and ½ cup water.

Half an hour before the roast is done, baste with ½ cup whipping cream, pan juices, and ½ cup water. Fifteen minutes later, baste again with pan juices and ½ cup water.

When the roast has reached an internal temperature of 165° F. (medium rare) or 175–180° F. (well done), remove the roast to a platter and keep it warm.

Remove excess fat from the pan, stir in 1–2 tablespoons flour. The amount of flour depends on the size of the roast. Over low heat, stir and scrape brown bits up from the edges and bottom of the pan. Stirring constantly, add more water to the pan juices, if necessary. Add 2 tablespoons currant jelly and salt and pepper to taste. Serve the gravy with the sliced lamb.

This scrumptious leg of lamb is flavored with shallots, garlic, coffee, and currant jelly.

SOUPS

The Spinach chapter has an Onion Soup (page 246) which I highly recommend. And don't forget the Potato Leek Soup (page 212).

Spring Onion Soup

The success of this soup depends on the bright color and crisp texture of the vegetables. It must be served immediately and should not be reheated.

2 tablespoons butter
2 cups sliced scallions, including some green tops
2 teaspoons minced fresh ginger root
3 tablespoons light soy sauce or tamari
½ cup dry white wine
6 cups chicken broth
salt
1 cup pea pods, sliced diagonally in thirds

Melt the butter in a soup pot, and sauté the scallions and ginger for 2 minutes. Add the soy sauce, wine, chicken broth, and salt to taste. Cook just long enough to soften the scallions, 1–2 minutes. Add the pea pods and simmer 1 minute more. Serve immediately.

Preparation Time: 20 minutes
Cooking Time: 3–5 minutes
Yield: 6 servings

A Spring Onion Soup is the lightest, most delicate onion soup you will ever serve. It makes a delightful first course.

French Onion Soup

Some people think that you can't make a good onion soup without beef stock. But I find this soup equally delicious with or without the beef broth—which makes it nice for my vegetarian friends.

2 tablespoons vegetable oil
2 tablespoons butter
7 cups sliced onions
¼ cup all-purpose unbleached flour
6 cups water and 5 tablespoons tamari or 6 cups beef stock
2 bay leaves
½ cup dry white wine
6 slices toasted French bread
2–3 cups grated Gruyère or Swiss cheese

In a large sauté pan, heat the oil and the butter and sauté the sliced onions until golden brown, 10–15 minutes. Sprinkle the flour over the onions and blend well. Add the water and tamari or beef stock. Add the bay leaves and wine. Simmer for 1 hour.

Just before serving, place 1 slice of toasted bread in each soup bowl or crock. Ladle in the soup and sprinkle the top with the cheese. Broil just long enough to melt the cheese and brown it slightly, about 5 minutes. Serve hot.

Preparation Time: 25 minutes
Cooking Time: 1 hour, 20 minutes
Yield: 6 servings

Onion Apple Soup

The onion is sweet and not overpowering in this adaptation of Indian mulligatawny soup.

2 tablespoons butter
6 cups diced onions
1 tablespoon curry powder
3 cups grated unpeeled apples
2 cups chicken broth
1 cup cider
2 cups milk or cream
salt and pepper

Melt the butter in a large soup pot, and sauté the onions, curry, and apples over medium-low heat, until the onions are limp but not browned, 3–5 minutes. Add the chicken broth and cider. Cook the soup for 20 minutes more, until the onions are very soft. Cool the soup a little and puree in a blender or food processor. Stir in the milk and season to taste with salt and pepper. Reheat and serve hot.

Preparation Time: 20 minutes
Cooking Time: 30 minutes
Yield: 6–8 servings

Yellow Onions Are Best for Cooking

I don't like to substitute other onions for yellow cooking (Spanish) onions. Red onions lose their flavor and color when cooked. White onions are okay in a pinch, but they don't have the sweetness of the yellow ones.

SAUCES

Shallot and Dill Cream Sauce

This very delicate sauce is delicious on fish, chicken, and vegetables.

2 tablespoons butter
⅔ cup minced shallots (6–10 bulbs)
1½ tablespoons minced fresh dill
2 teaspoons all-purpose unbleached flour
2 tablespoons white wine
¾ cup heavy cream

Melt the butter in a sauté pan, and sauté the shallots and dill until the shallots are limp, 3–5 minutes. Sprinkle the flour over the shallots, and stir in the wine and cream. Simmer until the sauce is reduced by half and has thickened, about 10 minutes. Serve hot.

Preparation Time: 5 minutes
Cooking Time: 15 minutes
Yield: 1 cup

Red Garlic Sauce For Pasta

3 tablespoons olive oil
8 large garlic cloves, minced
1 cup chopped scallions
4 cups thick tomato puree
2 tablespoons minced fresh basil
2 teaspoons fresh thyme or ½ teaspoon dried
¼ cup dry white wine
salt and pepper

In a large sauté pan, heat the oil, and sauté the garlic and scallions until the scallions are wilted, about 3 minutes. Add the tomato, herbs, and wine. Simmer the sauce for 10–15 minutes. Season to taste with salt and pepper. Spoon the sauce over cooked pasta (spaghetti is best) and garnish with grated parmesan cheese.

Preparation Time: 10 minutes
Cooking Time: 20–25 minutes
Yield: 6–8 servings

Garlic Cream Sauce For Pasta

This sauce is wonderful on Spinach Pasta (page 245). Pass grated parmesan cheese with the sauce.

½ cup butter
¼ cup chopped garlic
2 tablespoons minced fresh basil
¼ teaspoon ground rosemary
¼ teaspoon white pepper
2 cups light cream
salt
¼ cup minced fresh parsley

In a large sauté pan, melt the butter, and sauté the chopped garlic for 2 minutes. Add the basil, rosemary, pepper, and cream. Simmer slowly until the cream is reduced and the sauce is thickened, about 5 minutes.
Salt to taste and stir in the parsley. Serve immediately.

Preparation Time: 10 minutes
Cooking Time: 7–10 minutes
Yield: 6 servings (sauce for 1½ pounds pasta)

Creamed Onions and Chestnuts

Chestnuts are most available in the fall.

2 cups water
4 cups pearl onions
¾ cup peeled and quartered chestnuts
2 tablespoons butter
2 tablespoons all-purpose unbleached flour
1⅓ cups milk
salt and pepper

In a medium-size saucepan, bring the water to a boil and add the onions. Boil for 10 minutes. Add the chestnuts and continue boiling until the onions are tender, 5–10 minutes more. Remove the onions and chestnuts from the heat, drain off the liquid, and save it. Cover the onions and chestnuts and keep them warm.

Melt the butter in a small saucepan, and stir in the flour to form a thick paste. Slowly add the cooking water and the milk a little at a time, stirring well after each addition to prevent lumps. Season to taste with salt and pepper. Add the onions and chestnuts to the sauce and stir gently to coat. Serve immediately.

Preparation Time: 30 minutes
Cooking Time: 15–20 minutes
Yield: 6 servings

Sole Wrapped Leeks

This delicate dish needs a light hand or the sauce will split (curdle).

6 tablespoons butter
6 medium-size leeks, sliced
¼ cup minced fresh chives
2 tablespoons chopped shallots
¼ cup dry white wine
¾ cup cream
4 egg yolks
¼ teaspoon white pepper
2 teaspoons lemon juice
salt
6 sole fillets

Preheat the oven to 325° F.

Melt 2 tablespoons of the butter in a sauté pan, and sauté the leeks until they are limp, 3–5 minutes. Transfer the leeks to a bowl and set aside.

Melt the remaining 4 tablespoons butter, and sauté the chives and shallots for 2 minutes. Add the wine and cream. Simmer the sauce briefly.

Beat the egg yolks and spoon a small amount of the sauce into the yolks to temper them. Add the egg yolks to the sauce and heat gently. Add the pepper and lemon juice. Heat until the sauce thickens slightly. Season to taste with salt. Mix a quarter of the sauce with the leeks. Divide the mixture among the sole fillets and roll the fillets to enclose the leeks. Place the fillets seam side down in a baking dish. Pour the remaining sauce over the fish. Cover with foil. Bake for 30 minutes. Serve immediately.

Preparation Time: 30 minutes
Baking Time: 30 minutes
Yield: 6 servings

Sauté 3–5 minutes until limp.

Sauté about 15 minutes until golden. This mellows the flavor.

Reuben Pie

2 cups all-purpose unbleached flour
½ teaspoon salt
2 teaspoons caraway seeds
⅔ cup vegetable shortening or butter
4 tablespoons water
2 tablespoons butter
6 cups diced onions
2 cups grated carrots
⅔ cup light cream or milk
2 eggs
2 teaspoons Dijon-style mustard
2 teaspoons prepared horseradish
2 cups chopped corned beef

Preheat the oven to 425° F.

In a large bowl, combine the flour, salt, and caraway seeds. Cut in the shortening until the mixture resembles gravel and sand. Add the water and form into a ball. Wrap the dough in plastic film wrap, and refrigerate while you prepare the filling.

Melt the butter in a sauté pan, and sauté the onions until golden brown, 10–15 minutes. Add the carrots and sauté for 2 minutes more.

Beat together the cream, eggs, mustard, and horseradish.

Roll out half of the pie dough and fit into a 10-inch pie pan. Spread half of the onion mixture onto the crust. Spread the corned beef on top, then the remaining onion mixture. Pour the egg and cream mixture over the onions.

Roll out the remaining dough and place the crust on the pie. Trim and crimp the edges. Bake for 10 minutes. Then reduce the oven temperature to 350° F. and bake for 30 minutes more. Serve warm.

Preparation Time: 35 minutes
Baking Time: 40 minutes
Yield: 6–8 servings

Mussels With Garlic And Shallots

Mussels should be cooked as soon as they are bought or harvested.

3 pounds fresh mussels (with shell)
2 cups dry white wine
4 garlic cloves, chopped
3 large shallots, chopped
4 tablespoons minced fresh basil
2¼ teaspoons fresh thyme or
  ¾ teaspoon dried
½ cup minced fresh parsley
pepper
3 tablespoons butter
1½ tablespoons flour
1 teaspoon lemon juice
salt

It's the combination of garlic, shallots, herbs, and wine that makes these mussels tasty. Serve as an appetizer or main course.

Scrub the mussels, removing beards. Discard any mussels with open shells.

Bring the wine to a boil in a large pot with a tight-fitting lid. Add the mussels, garlic, 1 shallot, 2 tablespoons of the basil, 2 teaspoons of the thyme, ¼ cup of the parsley, and pepper to taste. Steam for 3 or 4 minutes, just until the mussels open. Remove the mussels with a slotted spoon and keep them warm.

Strain the mussel broth twice through 2 thicknesses of cheesecloth to remove sand.

Melt the butter in a sauté pan, and sauté the remaining 2 shallots until limp, 2–3 minutes. Add the remaining 2 tablespoons basil, ¼ teaspoon thyme, and ¼

cup parsley. Sprinkle the flour over the shallots and stir. Add 1 cup of the mussel broth a little at a time, stirring constantly to prevent lumps. Season with lemon juice and salt and pepper to taste. Pour this mixture into a heated dish and serve as a dipping sauce for the mussels.

Preparation Time: 25 minutes
Cooking Time: 10 minutes
Yield: 6 servings as an appetizer,
       4 servings as a main dish

Hungarian Goulash

When you cook onions for a long time, they become sweet and lose some of their "bite." That's why you can cook large quantities and not have the dish be overwhelmed by onions.

My grandmother says a good cook uses one onion in this dish for every year of her life. But when she was 85, she taught me how to make it with "only" 6 cups of onions.

2 tablespoons butter
2 tablespoons bacon fat
6 cups sliced onions
2 cups water
½ cup all-purpose unbleached flour
½ teaspoon dried thyme
¼ teaspoon dried marjoram
1½ pounds stew beef, cubed
2 tablespoons vegetable oil
½ cup dry white wine
1 bay leaf
1 tablespoon Hungarian paprika
½ cup sour cream
salt and pepper

In a large stew pot, heat the butter and bacon fat, and sauté the onions until they are golden brown, 10–15 minutes. Transfer to a bowl. Add ½ cup of the water to the pan and scrape up the brown bits clinging to the pan. Add the water to the onions.

Combine the flour, thyme, and marjoram in a bag. Add the stew beef a little at a time and toss to coat.

In the stew pot, heat the oil, and brown the beef, adding more oil if necessary. Save the extra flour mixture.

When the meat is browned, add the onions, the remaining 2 cups water, wine, bay leaf, and paprika. Cover the pot, and simmer until the beef is tender, 2–3 hours. Stir occasionally.

When the meat is done, remove the bay leaf. Remove 2 cups of sauce to a small saucepan. Pour a little warm water into the reserved flour mixture to make a paste the consistency of cream. Pour the flour paste into the 2 cups of sauce. Cook briefly, stirring until the sauce thickens, about 5 minutes. Add this mixture to the goulash and cook for 5 minutes more. Just before serving, stir in the sour cream. Season to taste with salt and pepper. Serve hot over noodles.

Preparation Time: 35 minutes
Cooking Time: 2–3 hours
Yield: 6 servings

BAKED GOODS

Scallion Crackers

Making crackers is almost a lost art. Yet you will see from this recipe that crackers are easy to make. If you like, make extra dough, roll it into a 1-inch log, wrap in waxed paper, and freeze. Slice off thin slices of dough and bake as needed.

1 tablespoon butter
1½ cups chopped scallions
2 cups all-purpose unbleached flour
½ cup wheat germ
½ teaspoon salt
1½ teaspoons baking powder
8 ounces cream cheese

Six cups of onions flavor this tasty Hungarian Goulash. I always serve it over noodles and with a green salad.

4 tablespoons water
1 egg, beaten
salt
sesame seeds, poppy seeds, or
    grated parmesan cheese

Melt the butter in a sauté pan, and sauté the scallions until limp, 3–5 minutes. Set aside to cool.

Combine the flour, wheat germ, salt, and baking powder. Mix well. Cut in the cream cheese to make a mixture that resembles gravel and sand. Mix in the scallions. Add the water and stir well until the dough forms a ball.

(If you have a food processor, combine the dry ingredients and add the cream cheese while the motor is running. Add the water and use the pulsing action until the dough forms a ball.)

Chill the dough for 1–2 hours.

Preheat the oven to 400° F. On a floured board, roll the dough to a thickness of 1/8 inch. Cut into circles with a 1–2-inch cookie cutter. Prick each cracker several times with a fork.

Transfer the crackers to a greased cookie sheet. Brush with the beaten egg and sprinkle with salt and sesame seeds.

Bake for 20–30 minutes, until golden brown. Transfer to a cooling rack and allow to cool. The crackers will crisp while cooling.

Preparation Time: 20 minutes
Chilling Time: 1–2 hours
Baking Time: 20–30 minutes
Yield: 3 dozen

Onion Spiral Bread

This recipe makes two large loaves. I like to freeze the second loaf. To serve a frozen loaf, defrost it first, then wrap it in foil, and heat it for 20 minutes in a 350° F. oven.

2 tablespoons dried baker's yeast
3 tablespoons plus 1 teaspoon sugar
2¼ cups warm water
1 tablespoon salt
3 eggs, slightly beaten
¼ cup vegetable oil
8½–9 cups all-purpose unbleached
    flour
¼ cup butter
4 cups diced onions
2 garlic cloves, minced
½ teaspoon dried thyme
½ teaspoon dried basil
½ teaspoon dried oregano
2 cups grated Swiss cheese
1 cup grated parmesan cheese
½ cup minced fresh parsley
salt and pepper
1 egg
2 tablespoons sesame seeds

In a small bowl, combine the yeast, 1 teaspoon of the sugar, and ¼ cup of the water. Set aside until the mixture becomes foamy, about 5 minutes.

In the meantime, combine the remaining 2 cups water, 1 tablespoon salt, the 3 beaten eggs, oil, and the remaining 3 tablespoons sugar in a large bowl. Mix well.

Stir in the yeast mixture. Beat in the flour, 1 cup at a time, to form a stiff dough. Turn the dough onto a floured board and knead for 10 minutes. Grease the bowl and return the dough to the bowl. Cover and let rise for 1½ hours, or until double in bulk.

While the dough rises, make the filling. Melt the butter in a sauté pan, and sauté the onions, garlic, and herbs until the onions are limp, 3–5 minutes. Transfer to a bowl and cool to room temperature. Add the cheeses and parsley. Season to taste with salt and pepper.

When the bread dough has doubled, punch it down and divide it into 2 pieces. Roll out each piece to form a rectangle 9 inches by 12 inches. Spread half the onion-cheese mixture on each rectangle, and roll the rectangle jelly-roll fashion to make a 12-inch loaf. Transfer the loaves to a greased baking sheet and cover loosely with a towel. Let rise until double in bulk, about 45 minutes. Preheat the oven to 350° F.

Beat the remaining egg and brush on the loaves. Sprinkle with sesame seeds. Bake for 45 minutes. Cool slightly before slicing.

Preparation Time: 2½ hours
Baking Time: 45 minutes
Yield: 16–20 servings

Parsnips

Patience and Cold Weather Make the Parsnip Sweet

What do you do with parsnips anyway? Just about anything you'd do with a carrot. Parsnips are a very versatile root vegetable, delicious in salads, pot roasts, soups, stews, or served as a vegetable. The important thing to remember when cooking with parsnips is to complement the sweet flavor.

Supermarket parsnips don't taste like homegrown parsnips. In fact, they don't taste like much of anything at all. When people tell me that they don't like parsnips, I ask them if they have ever eaten parsnips just harvested from the garden after a cold spell. If they say no, I tell them that they don't know what parsnips *really* taste like.

Parsnips are slow growers. The seeds take forever to germinate, and the roots grow very slowly—over 100 days to maturity. I keep my parsnip row thinned and weeded, but I don't bother to harvest until the first frost. The cold temperatures sweeten parsnips and bring out their "nutty" flavor.

You Won't Believe How Sweet Parsnips Are!

Many of my parsnips are left in the ground under mulch for the winter. During the winter and in the spring before the tops begin to grow again, I harvest the tender, sweet parsnips as I need them. (Carrots are the same way; they become sweeter if left in the ground over the winter. But young carrots are much more flavorful than young parsnips.)

You can substitute parsnips for carrots in many recipes, but you have to apply a little common sense. Parsnips cook a little faster than carrots. Overwintered parsnips may be *very* sweet. Also, remember that carrots are often used in recipes to add a little color, which parsnips won't do.

No part of the parsnip need be wasted. The strongly flavored greens and peels can enrich soup stocks. When you harvest parsnips in the spring, slice off the top to leave about ½ inch of root. Set the root in a shallow dish with water and the parsnips will send up green shoots which will grow for a month or more. You can do the same with radishes and carrots. I always keep a few parsnip roots growing in my kitchen. It reminds me of the good things to come when the garden is freed of its snow cover.

Although I leave most of my parsnips to overwinter in the ground, I do harvest and store some in my root cellar to have all winter when the snow makes it impossible to get to the garden.

Best Way to Keep Parsnips? Store Them in the Ground

Parsnips can be left in the garden under a heavy layer of mulch all winter. Dig them up before the tops begin to grow.

Parsnips may also be stored in a root cellar. Harvest after several hard frosts, and trim the tops but don't wash the roots. Store in perforated food-safe plastic bags or pack in boxes of moist sawdust or peat moss.

Parsnips will keep in the refrigerator for 2–3 months, but you may notice a slight loss of flavor.

Restore wilted, limp parsnips by soaking in ice water for up to 30 minutes.

Yields

1 pound fresh parsnips equals
    4 cups grated
or
    3 cups sliced or diced
or
    1½–2 cups cooked and pureed

Remove the woody core, if necessary

PARSNIPS AT A GLANCE

A Parade of Parsnip Serving Ideas

First wash and peel your parsnips. Then chop or slice according to the recipe directions. Usually parsnips are sliced into rounds, julienned, or diced. You can also slice parsnips into chunks or grate them.

Parsnips cook very quickly. Here is a timetable.

Blanch (for purees): 5 minutes
Steam: 5–8 minutes
Sauté: 5–8 minutes
Stir Fry: 3–4 minutes
Parboil (for salads): 2 minutes

Don't overcook parsnips! They become mushy.

"Steam sauté" is the best way to prepare tender parsnips.

To bring out the full flavor of parsnips, I steam them to tenderize, and then sauté to seal in the flavor. Here's how.

Pour ½ cup water in the bottom of a sauté pan. Add about 6 cups of diced parsnips. Cook, uncovered, until the water evaporates. Add about 2 tablespoons butter and about 2 tablespoons brown sugar, pure maple syrup, or honey to glaze the parsnips. If your parsnips are naturally sweet, add a little parsley, chives, or your favorite herbs instead of sweetener.

Parsnip tops

Mature Parsnips Make Perfect Purees

Even when parsnips are overgrown, the flesh remains tender and sweet. To make a puree, slice the parsnips and blanch in water to cover for about 5 minutes, until just tender. Then puree in a food processor or blender until smooth. Add water if necessary. Purees can be frozen or used immediately.

Flavored parsnip purees make tasty side dishes. Puree with orange juice, apple cider or juice, or milk or cream, instead of water. Season to taste with butter and salt and pepper. If you like, season with herbs, too. Rosemary and thyme are particularly nice with parsnips.

Oriental Flavored Parsnips Perk Up Any Meal

Here are two dishes that are simple and quick to prepare. They are too delicious to limit to Oriental-style meals.

Quick Parsnip Stir Fry

Grated parsnips cook so quickly that I recommend them for "hurry-up" dinners.

In a wok or large sauté pan, heat 1 tablespoon of sesame oil and 1 tablespoon vegetable oil. Add 8 cups grated parsnips and ¾ cup scallions sliced with their green tops. Stir fry for about 2 minutes. Add ½ teaspoon five spice powder and 2 tablespoons tamari or soy sauce. Continue to stir fry until the parsnips are just tender, about 2 minutes more. Serve immediately. This recipe serves 6.

Sweet and Sour Parsnips

Parboil 4 cups of sliced parsnips in water to cover for 2 minutes. Drain.

Mix 1 tablespoon sesame oil, 1 tablespoon vegetable oil, 1 tablespoon tamari or soy sauce, 2 tablespoons lemon juice, 2 teaspoons wine vinegar, 1 tablespoon brown sugar, 1 teaspoon grated orange rind, 1 teaspoon grated fresh ginger root, ½ teaspoon salt, and pepper to taste.

Pour this mixture into a sauté pan. Add the parsnips and cook until the parsnips are tender, 5–8 minutes. Serve hot. This recipe serves 4–6.

Two tasty side dishes: Orange Spiced Parsnips and Confetti Parsnips.

You can combine parsnips with strong flavors— The parsnips remain distinctive and nutty

Orange-Spiced Parsnips

You choose the spices for this recipe. The sweet Indian spices are a perfect match for the weather-sweetened parsnips in this "steam sauté" dish. Don't overcook the parsnips.

In a large sauté pan, heat ½ cup water and add 6 cups diced parsnips. Simmer until the water has disappeared. Add 2 tablespoons butter, ½ cup orange juice, and 1 teaspoon of spice. Choose from minced fresh ginger root, curry powder, ground fennel, cardamom, or ground coriander. Continue cooking, stirring occasionally, until the parsnips are tender, 3–5 minutes. Serve hot. This recipe serves 6–8.

Confetti Parsnips

Wait until the first frosts before you harvest parsnips for this fall dish. Your onions and carrots should be as fresh as ever in your root cellar.

Steam 6 cups of diced parsnips over boiling water for 5–8 minutes, or until just tender. Remove from the heat.

Melt 3 tablespoons butter in a large sauté pan, and sauté ½ cup finely diced onion, ½ cup finely diced celery, and ½ cup finely diced carrot until just tender, 3–5 minutes. Add the parsnips to the pan and stir to mix. Reheat. Season to taste with salt and pepper. Serve hot. This recipe serves 6–8.

Marinated Parsnips are great on relish trays, too!

Parsnip Cheese Nuggets

Keep your hands wet, and the nuggets will be easy to form.

6 cups diced parsnips
1 tablespoon vegetable oil
2 cups diced onions
2½ cups bread crumbs
2 teaspoons chili powder
½ teaspoon ground cumin
salt and pepper
½ pound sharp cheddar or mozzarella cheese
oil for deep frying

Steam the parsnips until tender, 5–8 minutes.

In a sauté pan, heat the oil, and sauté the onions until limp, 3–5 minutes.

Combine the parsnips, onions, 1 cup of the bread crumbs, chili powder, and cumin in a food processor and process until smooth. Add salt and pepper to taste.

Slice the cheese into ½-inch cubes.

Preheat the oil for deep frying to 375° F.

Wet your hands and form a small amount of the parsnip mixture around each piece of cheese to make walnut-sized balls. Roll each ball in the remaining bread crumbs.

Deep fry the balls until golden. Test one ball to see if the cheese

Wrap mixture around the cheese.

has melted and adjust frying time or oil temperature if necessary. Serve hot.

Preparation Time: 15 minutes
Cooking Time: 20 minutes
Yield: 6 servings

Parsnip Celery Seed Marinade

4 cups sliced parsnips
½ cup vegetable oil
2 tablespoons lemon juice
½ teaspoon white pepper
1 teaspoon celery seeds
1 teaspoon crumbled dried rosemary
1 teaspoon salt
2 tablespoons minced onion
¼ cup diced sweet red pepper

Parboil the parsnips for 2 minutes only. Plunge into cold water, and drain.

Combine the oil, lemon juice, white pepper, celery seeds, rosemary, and salt in a blender or food processor. Blend until well mixed. Toss the onion, red pepper, and parsnips together and pour the marinade over them. Allow the vegetables to sit for at least 1 hour. Serve cold.

Preparation Time: 15 minutes
Marinating Time: 1 hour
Yield: 6 servings

In some of these dishes, I treat parsnips as a potato substitute. The calories are about the same, and the variety is always welcome in my family.

Parsnip and Sausage Tart

2 cups all-purpose unbleached flour
1 teaspoon salt
⅔ cup butter or vegetable shortening
4 tablespoons water
3 cups sliced parsnips
1 pound bulk sausage
¾ cup sliced onion
2 cups peeled, cored, and sliced apples
2 tablespoons lemon juice
½ teaspoon ground rosemary
¼ teaspoon ground coriander
½ teaspoon salt
1½ cups grated Swiss cheese
2 tablespoons pure maple syrup

Preheat the oven to 350° F.

In a large bowl, combine the flour and salt. Using a pastry cutter or knife, cut in the butter or vegetable shortening until the mixture resembles gravel and sand. Add the water and mix just enough to form a ball. Roll the dough out to form a 12-inch circle. Fit the dough into a 9-inch springform pan, making sides that are 2-inches high. Chill the crust while you prepare the filling.

Parboil the parsnips for 2 minutes. Drain and set aside.

In a large frying pan, brown the sausage, breaking it up with a spoon. Reserve 2 tablespoons of fat and drain the sausage.

In the 2 tablespoons sausage fat, sauté the onion with the apples, lemon juice, rosemary, and coriander until the onion is limp, 3–5 minutes. Mix in the sausage, parsnips, and salt.

Sprinkle half the cheese on the bottom of the tart shell. Spoon in the filling. Sprinkle the remaining cheese on top of the filling. Drizzle the maple syrup on top. Bake for 50–60 minutes or until browned. Serve hot.

Preparation Time: 40 minutes
Baking Time: 50–60 minutes
Yield: 8 servings

Whole Stuffed Chicken With Parsnip Apple Dressing

I like to wait until a few frosts have sweetened the parsnips before I harvest and combine them with apples and cider for this sweet fall dressing.

4 tablespoons butter
1 cup finely diced celery
1 cup diced onion
¼ teaspoon ground sage
¼ teaspoon dried thyme
4 cups grated parsnips
1 cup peeled chopped apples
2 cups fresh bread cubes
⅓ cup apple cider
salt and pepper
1 whole 5–6 pound roasting chicken

Preheat the oven to 350° F.

Melt 2 tablespoons of the butter in a large sauté pan, and sauté the celery, onion, and herbs, until the onion is limp, 3–5 minutes. Add the parsnips and apples, and sauté until the parsnips are tender, about 3 minutes. Mix in the bread cubes and apple cider. Season to taste with salt and pepper.

Stuff the dressing into the chicken. Melt the remaining 2 tablespoons of butter and brush over the chicken. Cover the chicken loosely with foil. Bake, covered, for 45 minutes. Uncover and bake for 30 minutes more.

Preparation Time: 25 minutes
Baking Time: 1¼ hours
Yield: 4–6 servings

Corned Beef Parsnip Hash may become a family breakfast favorite in your house, too. The taste is a little sweet and pleasantly rich.

Corned Beef Parsnip Hash

I replaced the potatoes with parsnips in this old family favorite.

5 cups finely diced or shredded cooked corned beef
6–7 cups diced or grated parsnips
2 cups diced onions
½ cup cream or milk
salt and pepper
1–2 tablespoons vegetable oil

Combine the corned beef, parsnips, onions, and cream. Season to taste with salt and pepper.

Cover the bottom of a large frying pan with oil, and fry the hash until it is browned on one side. Turn the hash over and fry on the other side. Serve hot.

Preparation Time: 15 minutes
Cooking Time: 20 minutes
Yield: 8 servings

Peas

Time-Saving Sugar Snaps Should Be Standard For Working Gardeners

I like everything about peas. I like the fact that they can be planted early in the spring to get the garden going. I like the fact that grown in wide rows, they are a no-fuss crop, requiring nothing in the way of weeding, side-dressing, or spraying. I like the abundant harvest. In good years, I can raise both a spring and a fall crop. I love the taste of fresh peas—right out of the garden, if you please. I even like shelling peas.

In fact, I think shelling peas, sitting on a porch alone with my thoughts or sharing the task with a friend, is one of the simple pleasures of summer.

Sometimes there are a lot of peas to shell. Even though the pea harvest does stretch over a few weeks, it seems fast and furious.

That's why Sugar Snap peas have become so popular in the short time they have been available to gardeners. Have you tried them yet? Sugar Snaps are an edible pod variety. The pods are sweet and fairly tender, and the peas are sweet and full-size. Personally, I find the pods a little tougher than most snow pea varieties, and the peas a little on the bland side, but certainly the convenience of not having to shell the peas is a boon to working people. You use Sugar Snaps in recipes that call for either shelled peas *or* Snow Peas.

I Still Prefer Progress 9 for Freezing

I'll never give up on shelled peas—like Progress 9—for freezing. Although you can freeze both Sugar Snaps and snow pea varieties by blanching, tray freezing, then bagging, I think the result is inferior to the fresh pod. On the other hand, I like to have frozen shelled peas in the freezer and don't mind cooking with them. I usually blanch and freeze shelled peas in large quantities.

One thing I don't like: overripe peas. At the peak of ripeness, peas are loaded with sugar. Once picked, the sugar rapidly converts to starch. Or if left on the vine too long, the same chemical change occurs. You can tell a pea is slightly overripe when the pod becomes dry and the peas within the shell become visible. You can disguise overripe peas by adding a pinch of sugar to your blanching water (a trick my mother taught me), but I prefer to keep up with the harvest and enjoy peas at their peak.

This patch is solid peas! I can barely keep up with the harvest—even with the help of the neighborhood.

Yields

1 pound fresh pea pods equals about
   1¼ cups shelled peas

1 pound fresh pea pods equals
   4–5 cups

Storage

If the pea harvest gets ahead of you, you can store unshelled peas in perforated plastic bags in the refrigerator for 3–4 days. But peas are like strawberries, they lose flavor the minute they are picked.

Freezing is best for long-term storage.

Shelling and Stringing

Regular peas require shelling. Snap off the stem end and pull down on the thread, pushing open the seam as you pull. Pop out the peas.

Snap off the stem end and pull the thread from both seams of Sugar Snaps. Serve whole or sliced into thirds.

Pull the stem and blossom tassle of snow pea varieties. No stringing is necessary. Serve whole or cut in thirds.

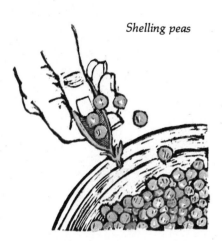

Shelling peas

PEAS AT A GLANCE

I'm Not Fussy About How Peas Are Cooked — As Long As They Aren't Overcooked

Peas can be blanched, steamed, sautéed, or stir fried. Here are some guidelines.

Cooking Timetable

Steam (shelled peas and Sugar
   Snaps): 3–4 minutes
   (snow pea varieties): 2–3
   minutes

Blanch (shelled peas): 2–4 minutes
   (Sugar Snaps and snow pea
   varieties): 1 minute

Stir Fry or Sauté (shelled, Sugar
   Snaps, and snow pea varieties):
   2–3 minutes

Tired of Just Plain Peas?

Toss blanched peas with an herb butter (pages 160 and 304). Herbs that go especially well with peas are tarragon, mint, chives, basil, and thyme.

Or toss blanched peas with sautéed walnuts, slivered almonds, sesame seeds, or sunflower seeds; or sautéed onions or mushrooms; or crumbled bacon or diced ham.

Add peas to stir fries, stews, other vegetable sautés, and casseroles.

Pleasing Pea Appetizers

Blanch snow peas for 1 minute. Split open along the seam. With a piping bag filled with homemade Boursin Cheese (page 158), fill the pods. It's a time-consuming process, but well worth it for special parties.

Or serve raw or parboiled Sugar Snaps or snow peas on vegetable platters with dips.

Parboil snow peas and wrap the pods around cooked marinated shrimp. Secure with toothpicks.

Stuffed snow peas

Snow peas and shrimp

Peas in Salads

Peas are enjoyable in all kinds of salads. Blanch shelled peas, Sugar Snaps, or snow peas for 1–2 minutes. Plunge into cold water, then drain. Toss into your favorite salad.

Fast, easy, delicious—all describe Hay and Straw made with garden-fresh peas.

Hay and Straw is a Summertime Favorite

Hay and straw is a classic pasta dish—usually made with white and green noodles. I make it with white noodles so the fresh green peas stand out—tasting wonderfully fresh.

The trick with this dish is to have all your ingredients prepared and hot at the same time, so you can toss it all together without having to reheat. And it helps to serve immediately after you have finished mixing it together.

So start by julienne-slicing 2 cups of ham and shelling 2–3 cups of peas (the more, the better). Grate and measure out 1½ cups parmesan cheese (you'll taste the difference when you use freshly grated cheese).

In plenty of boiling salted water, cook 1 pound of fettucine noodles until just tender. Drain and keep warm.

While the noodles cook, briefly sauté the ham in a tablespoon of butter until slightly browned and heated through. Keep warm.

Blanch 2–3 cups shelled peas until bright green and tender crisp, 2–3 minutes. Drain.

In a large serving bowl, toss together the hot noodles, the peas, and the ham. Add the cheese and ⅓ cup heavy cream. Season to taste with salt and pepper. Serve immediately.

This recipe serves 4–6. I prefer to keep the serving size small with such a rich dish.

A pinch of sugar added to the cooking water helps to disguise that these peas are slightly gone-by.

SOUPS

Provolone Pea Soup

A food processor won't make a smooth pea puree like a blender will, but some people don't object to the slight texture of processor-pureed peas. For a really smooth soup, strain the mixture through a fine metal sieve.

4 tablespoons butter
1½ cups diced onion
1½ tablespoons fresh tarragon or 2 teaspoons dried
¼ cup all-purpose unbleached flour
2 cups milk
5 cups raw peas
2 cups chicken broth
2 cups grated provolone cheese
salt and pepper

In a large soup pot, melt the butter, and sauté the onion and tarragon until the onion is limp, 3–5 minutes. Sprinkle the flour over the onion and stir to blend. Add the milk, a little at a time, stirring well after each addition to prevent lumps. Add the peas and chicken broth. Simmer for 15–20 minutes.

Cool the soup slightly. Process in a blender until smooth. Return the soup to the pot and add the cheese. Reheat, stirring constantly, until the cheese is melted. Season to taste with salt and pepper. Serve hot.

Preparation Time: 25 minutes
Cooking Time: 25 minutes
Yield: 6 servings

Pull both seams from sugar snaps.

SALADS

I often toss a handful of frozen peas into green salads, potato salads, tuna salads, pasta salads, and coleslaws.

Rice, Pea, and Tuna Salad

6 cups cooked brown rice
2½ cups blanched fresh or frozen peas
2 cups flaked tuna (one 13-ounce can)
⅓ cup minced fresh parsley
⅔ cup finely diced carrots
1 cup diced radishes
⅓ cup chopped scallion
¼ cup olive oil
1 teaspoon grated lemon rind
5 tablespoons lemon juice
1½ teaspoons Dijon-style mustard
salt and pepper

In a large bowl, combine the rice, peas, tuna, parsley, carrots, radishes, and scallion.

Whisk together the remaining ingredients and pour over the salad. Toss to coat. Chill the salad for at least 1 hour before serving.

Preparation Time: 20 minutes
Chilling Time: 1 hour
Yield: 8–10 servings

Shrimp, Pea, and Mint Salad

Don't be intimidated by cooking fresh shrimp. Drop the fresh shrimp into boiling water (seasoned with lemon juice, a bay leaf, or a few peppercorns). Reduce the heat and simmer for 3–4 minutes. Drain and cool under cold running water. Peeling and deveining can be done before or after cooking.

1 cup cooked shrimp, peeled and deveined
3 cups blanched fresh or frozen peas
1 tablespoon minced fresh chives
2 tablespoons minced fresh mint
½ cup sour cream
1 tablespoon lemon juice
½ teaspoon Worcestershire sauce
dash hot sauce
salt and pepper

Combine the shrimp, peas, chives, and mint in a bowl.

Whisk together the sour cream, lemon juice, Worcestershire sauce, and hot sauce. Pour over the salad and toss to coat. Season to taste with salt and pepper. Chill the salad for at least 1 hour before serving.

Preparation Time: 20 minutes
Chilling Time: 1 hour
Yield: 4 servings

Lemon juice seasons the water and whitens the color of the shrimp.

SIDE DISHES
AND MAIN DISHES

*Peas are so good plain that
you may never get around to
trying all these recipes. But I
assure you, you'll enjoy them if
you do.*

Fish Sauté With Tofu
And Pea Pods

*If you have a family that is
reluctant to try tofu, change their
minds with this recipe. The tofu
absorbs the marinade and is very
flavorful. I like to cook with tofu; it
stretches my meat and fish budgets
nicely.*

1½ pounds firm-fleshed fish fillets
1 cup diced tofu
2 tablespoons minced fresh ginger
　root
1 garlic clove, minced
⅓ cup sliced scallions
2 tablespoons tamari or soy sauce
2 tablespoons rice vinegar
1 tablespoon dry sherry
½ teaspoon sugar
1 teaspoon sesame oil
½ cup water
5 tablespoons peanut oil
1 cup sliced mushrooms
2 cups sliced pea pods

Slice the fish into strips ½ inch
by 2 inches. Place the fish and
tofu in a ceramic or glass bowl.

Whisk together the ginger,
garlic, scallions, tamari, vinegar,
sherry, sugar, sesame oil, water,
and 2 tablespoons of the peanut
oil. Pour over the fish and set
aside for 30 minutes.

Heat 1 tablespoon of the oil in
a large sauté pan, and sauté the
mushrooms and pea pods until
the peas are tender crisp, 3–4
minutes. Remove the vegetables
from the pan and set aside.

Heat the remaining 2
tablespoons peanut oil in the
sauté pan, and add the fish, tofu,
and marinade. Sauté, turning
gently, until the fish is cooked,
about 5 minutes. Add the peas
and mushrooms and reheat.
Serve immediately.

Preparation Time: 20 minutes
Marinating Time: 30 minutes
Cooking Time: 10 minutes
Yield: 4–6 servings

*Snow peas have long been a favorite in
stir fries. It is very important not to
overcook so the peas retain their bright
color and crisp texture.*

Much of my pea harvest
ends up in the freezer. Frozen
peas should be cooked a
minute longer than their fresh
counterparts. Added to a
salad, frozen peas will defrost
in about 15 minutes.

Chicken Potpie With Sugar Snaps

Sugar Snap peas won't get lost in the sauce like shelled peas do.

1 stewing hen (7–8 pounds)
water
1 celery rib, sliced in 2-inch pieces
1 carrot, cubed
1 medium-size onion, quartered
1 bay leaf
2 tablespoons butter
1 cup diced onion
1½ teaspoons fresh thyme or ½ teaspoon dried
1½ cups light cream
2¾ cups all-purpose unbleached flour
2 cups sliced Sugar Snap peas
salt and pepper
1 teaspoon salt
1 tablespoon baking powder
1 teaspoon baking soda
2 tablespoons minced fresh parsley
2 teaspoons crumbled sage
6 tablespoons vegetable shortening
¾ cup buttermilk

Place the chicken in a large stock pot and cover with water. Add the celery, carrot, onion, and bay leaf. Bring the water to a boil. Skim off any foam, reduce the heat, and simmer gently for 1 hour.

Remove the chicken from the pot. Strain the broth and save. Reserve 3 cups broth for this recipe. Let the chicken cool enough to handle, and remove the meat from the bones. Dice the meat into 1-inch pieces. Measure out 2 cups chicken meat for this recipe. Reserve the extra meat for another meal.

In a large sauté pan, melt the butter and sauté the diced onion and thyme until the onion is limp, 3–5 minutes. Add 3 cups of the chicken broth and 1½ cups light cream. Simmer until the sauce is reduced by half, 15–20 minutes. Sprinkle 3–4 tablespoons flour over the liquid and blend. Add the chicken.

Parboil the peas until they turn bright green, about 1 minute. Add the peas to the chicken and season to taste with salt and pepper.

Preheat the oven to 400° F.

Place the chicken mixture in a greased 2-quart casserole dish.

Sift together the remaining 2½ cups flour, 1 teaspoon salt, baking powder, and baking soda. Add the parsley and sage. Cut in the shortening until the mixture resembles gravel and sand. Stir in the buttermilk, just enough to moisten. Spoon the dough topping onto the chicken. Bake for 20 minutes or until the top is golden brown. Serve hot.

Preparation Time: 1½ hours
Baking Time: 20 minutes
Yield: 6 servings

I adapted an old family recipe for Chicken Potpie to make use of my Sugar Snap peas. The original recipe called for shelled peas. Most recipes that call for shelled peas can be adapted for Sugar Snaps.

Pea and Chicken Pasta

4 quarts salted water
½ pound fettucine noodles
2 tablespoons olive oil
¼ cup sliced scallion
½ cup thinly sliced sweet red pepper
2 cups sliced snow or Sugar Snap pea pods
2 cups shredded cooked chicken
3 tablespoons Pesto (page 161)
2 tablespoons lemon juice
2 tablespoons minced fresh basil

Bring the water to a boil and add the fettucine noodles. Cook until just tender. Drain.

While the pasta cooks, heat the olive oil, and sauté the scallion and red pepper for 3 minutes in a large sauté pan. Add the pea pods and continue to sauté until the pea pods turn bright green and tender crisp, about 1 minute. Add the chicken to the vegetables and heat.

In a small bowl, whisk together the Pesto, lemon juice, and basil.

When the pasta is drained, toss with the vegetables, chicken, and Pesto. Serve immediately. Pass grated parmesan cheese if desired.

Preparation Time: 20 minutes
Cooking Time: 8–10 minutes
Yield: 4 servings

German Meat Balls With Peas

¾ cup bread crumbs
¾ cup milk
2 pounds ground beef
1 cup minced shallots
2 tablespoons capers
2 eggs, beaten
¼ cup minced fresh parsley
1 tablespoon grated lemon rind
2 tablespoons plus 2 teaspoons lemon juice
¼ teaspoon salt
⅛ teaspoon pepper
4 tablespoons butter
¼ cup all-purpose unbleached flour
¼ cup light cream
¼ cup dry white wine
2 cups beef broth
1 teaspoon caper juice
salt and pepper
2 cups fresh or frozen peas

Preheat the oven to 350° F.

In a large bowl, combine the bread crumbs and milk. Let sit for 5 minutes until the milk is absorbed. Add the ground beef, ⅔ cup of the shallots, 1 tablespoon of the capers, the eggs, parsley, lemon rind, 2 tablespoons of the lemon juice, salt, and pepper. Mix all of these ingredients together and form into walnut-size balls. Place the balls on a greased cookie sheet and bake for 20 minutes or until browned.

Melt the butter in a sauté pan, and sauté the remaining ⅓ cup shallots until limp, about 3 minutes. Sprinkle the flour over the shallots and stir to blend. Add the cream and wine. Stir well to prevent lumps. Add the beef broth a little at a time, stirring well after each addition. Season with caper juice, the remaining 2 teaspoons lemon juice, and salt and pepper.

When the meat balls are browned, add them to the sauce with the peas. Simmer the meat balls until the peas are bright green, about 5 minutes. Serve over buttered egg noodles or rice.

Preparation Time: 30 minutes
Cooking Time: 25 minutes
Yield: 6–8 servings

Fried Rice

Fried rice is one of my favorite garden catch-all dishes. I vary the vegetables, depending on what's in season. Best of all, I can keep fried rice warm in the oven while I prepare another dish.

3 tablespoons vegetable oil
2 eggs, beaten
1 teaspoon sesame oil
⅓ cup chopped scallions
1 cup julienne-sliced Jerusalem artichokes
1½ cups baby shrimp, peeled and deveined
1½ cups diced snow peas, Sugar Snaps, or fresh shelled peas
2½ cups cooked rice
2 tablespoons tamari or light soy sauce
2 tablespoons oyster sauce (optional)

Heat 1 tablespoon of the oil in a wok or large frying pan. Pour in the eggs. Tip the pan to form a thin sheet of egg, similar to a pancake. Fry the egg lightly on 1 side, and then flip it over and cook the other side for 1 minute. Remove the egg from the wok, cool slightly, and julienne-slice.

Heat the remaining 2 tablespoons vegetable oil and the sesame oil. Stir fry the scallions and Jerusalem artichokes for 1 minute. Add the shrimp and snow peas, and continue to stir fry for 2–3 minutes, or until the snow peas are tender crisp and bright green. Add the remaining ingredients, including the egg, and stir fry until hot. Serve immediately.

Preparation Time: 20 minutes
Cooking Time: 10–15 minutes
Yield: 6 servings

Peppers

A Little Hot Pepper Goes a Long Way— So I Mainly Grow the Sweet Ones

The hottest year of my life was the year I swapped pepper plants with a group of friends. We each started seeds of a different variety of pepper plant, and before transplanting to the garden, we exchanged varieties so we would each have a few bell-type peppers, a few Jalapeños, Cubanelle Hots, Anaheim Hots, Hungarian Wax, and Sweet Bananas.

That was the year I discovered that a little hot pepper goes a long way. In fact, that summer left me enough hot peppers for years!

These days, I consider green and red bell peppers my "old reliables" and concentrate on growing and cooking them.

I'm more inclined to think of peppers as a flavoring than a vegetable that is served as a side dish, but that doesn't mean I don't have plenty of uses for an abundant harvest.

I Prefer to Dry Extras

I like to put aside some of my sweet pepper harvest for dehydrating or freezing. Peppers dry very easily. All you do is wash them well, slice or dice them (I like mine diced), and spread them out on dehydrator trays. The peppers will dry in 8–12 hours at 120° F. I use the peppers for flavoring in soups, stews, casseroles, and meat loaves. I just toss the pepper pieces in by the handful.

Before I started drying foods, I used to freeze extra peppers. This is an easy job, too. All you do is wash the peppers, dry well, dice, and freeze in a single layer on trays. When the peppers are frozen, transfer them to freezer bags. Again, just toss the frozen peppers into soups, stews, and the like, for flavoring. I think green peppers hold up better in the freezer than red peppers.

Pickling is another great way to preserve extra peppers. I love to have pepper relish on hand for hamburgers and sandwiches. Peppers can be preserved in any vinegar brine that is used for cucumber, cauliflower, and bean pickles.

Then again, you may not have to worry about preserving peppers because they keep so well. You can begin harvesting green peppers as soon as they have reached a decent size. Then keep harvesting green ones and red ones for use in salads, vegetable stir fries, and sautés all summer long.

Look at these beautiful peppers that came out of the garden. The sweet bell peppers—green, red, and yellow—are my favorites. It's fun to experiment with the different tastes of peppers.

Pepper Varieties: Sweet or Hot

Sweet varieties to grow include bell types (Gedeon Sweet, Golden Bell, Pepper Oritani), Hungarian Wax, Italian Sweet, Sweet Banana, and Gypsy Hybrid Sweet.

Hot types include Red Cherry, Cubanelle Hot, Cayenne Hot, Santa Fe Grande, Anaheim Hot, Tabasco Hot, Chili Ta Tong, and Jalapeno.

Immature peppers are usually green. They can be harvested at the green stage or allowed to ripen to a red or yellow color. Red bell peppers are sweeter than green ones.

Yields

1 pound fresh peppers equals
    4 cups cubed or julienne-sliced
or
    3½ cups diced
or
    5½ cups sliced in circles

Handle Hot Peppers Carefully!

Juices from hot peppers can be very irritating. You may want to wear gloves while working with them, and *never* rub your mouth or eyes with pepper-contaminated hands.

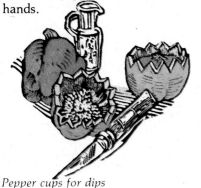

Pepper cups for dips

PEPPERS AT A GLANCE

Peppers Take No Time To Prepare

Just wash carefully, split open, remove the seeds and white membrane, and slice or chop.

Cooking Times
Sauté: 3–5 minutes
Stir fry: 3–5 minutes
Blanch (for stuffing): 2–3 minutes
Roast: 8–10 minutes

I Use Peppers to Spice Up My Cooking

Here are a few ideas for cooking with peppers.

Add green or red sweet peppers to all your salads: green, tuna, chicken, seafood, marinated vegetable, potato, pasta, and grain salads.

Serve sweet pepper strips with dips as "finger food."

Serve dips, pickles, and olives in pepper cups made with hollowed-out sweet bell peppers.

Toss diced peppers in the pan when you make liver and onions.

Sautéed peppers go well with onions, carrots, tomatoes, corn, eggplant, okra, celery, and summer squash. Create a sauté medley with any of these vegetables. Add fresh herbs and season to taste with salt and pepper.

Storage

Harvest peppers as you need them. If necessary, store peppers in the refrigerator for 3–5 days.

To dry whole hot peppers, string the whole peppers on a thread and hang. Dry diced or sliced peppers in a dehydrator for 8–10 hours at 120° F.

Roasted peppers can be stored in olive oil to cover in the refrigerator for an extended amount of time.

Hot Peppers Give Mexican Foods a Pleasant Bite

When I have fresh hot peppers, I always think of making some Mexican dishes. Most often, I roast and peel the hot peppers and use them as flavor accents for nachos, tacos, quesadillas, enchiladas, and the like. Roasted hot peppers can be stored in olive oil in the refrigerator just as roasted sweet peppers can.

Pepper rings for garnishes

1. *Remove seeds and membranes.*

2. *Blanch in boiling water for 2–3 minutes to tenderize.*

These peppers are stuffed with Spanish Rice, Green Rice, and sautéed vegetables seasoned with salt, pepper and thyme.

A peck of peppers packed with good garden eating

I think stuffed peppers are a great idea. They look so pretty sitting on a plate stuffed with fresh garden vegetables or even leftovers.

You can stuff whole peppers or half peppers. To prepare a whole pepper for stuffing, slice off the cap or top of the pepper. Scoop out the seeds and bitter white membrane. To prepare pepper halves, slice the pepper in half vertically and remove the seeds and white membranes.

Blanch the peppers in boiling water for 2–3 minutes until bright green, bright yellow, or bright red and slightly tender. Drain well. Then stuff with your favorite filling.

Place the peppers in a baking dish and cover the bottom of the dish with about ¼ inch of water. Cover the dish lightly with foil and bake at 350° F. for 30–45 minutes, depending on the filling. Brown the topping under the broiler just before serving if you have cheese on it.

Stuffings for "Cook's Night Out"

Stuffed Peppers can be a quickly prepared dinner made by a busy cook. I stuff peppers with whatever I have on hand — leftover filling from other stuffed vegetable recipes (see Cabbages, pages 72–81; Winter Squash, pages 262–271; Summer Squash,

pages 250–261), leftover chili, macaroni and cheese, stews, creamed chicken, tuna noodle casserole, poultry stuffing, or leftover chicken. I sometimes combine leftover meats and vegetables, with or without rice, in a cheese sauce and stuff into peppers. Candied carrots, lima beans in tomato sauce topped with cheese, creamed spinach, or Spanish rice, all get a new lease on life stuffed in a pepper.

Whatever the stuffing, I usually top the peppers with grated parmesan, mozzarella, cheddar, Swiss, or Monterey jack cheese. The cheese browns nicely under the broiler and "finishes" the dish.

These dips and spreads taste best with fresh peppers, but you could use frozen peppers instead.

Green Pepper Butter

Cream ¼ cup butter by adding the butter to a running food processor 1 tablespoon at a time. Add ½ cup diced green pepper and process until the butter is light green and the pepper is finely ground. Scrape the sides of the bowl down several times. Add 2 teaspoons Dijon-style mustard and process to mix. Season to taste with salt and pepper. Serve at room temperature.

Variation

Sweet Red Pepper Butter. Substitute ½ cup diced sweet red peppers for the green peppers. Omit the mustard and season with ½ teaspoon cardamom, ½ teaspoon lemon juice, and salt and pepper.

Red Pepper Cream Cheese Dip

In a food processor, combine 8 ounces cream cheese at room temperature, 1 cup diced sweet red pepper, 2 teaspoons lemon juice, 2 tablespoons minced onion, and ¼ teaspoon ground rosemary.

Process until smooth. Season to taste with salt and pepper. Serve at room temperature with raw vegetable sticks.

This Pepper Rice Salad can be served as a salad or a side dish.

SALADS

The red peppers add a lot of color to salads; but green or yellow peppers can be substituted.

Pepper Rice Salad

4 cups cooked rice, cooled to room temperature
1 cup finely diced green pepper
1 cup finely diced sweet red pepper
⅓ cup finely diced scallions
2 tablespoons currants
½ cup coarsely chopped walnuts
⅓ cup vegetable oil
3 tablespoons wine vinegar
½ teaspoon curry powder
¼ teaspoon turmeric
2 tablespoons orange juice
salt and pepper

In a large bowl, combine the rice, peppers, scallions, currants, and nuts. Whisk together the oil, vinegar, spices, and orange juice. Pour over the salad and toss to coat. Season to taste with salt and pepper. Chill for 1–2 hours before serving.

Preparation Time: 20 minutes
Chilling Time: 1–2 hours
Yield: 6 servings

Chicken Pesto Salad

1½ cups julienne-sliced green peppers
1 cup julienne-sliced sweet red peppers
1 cup diced scallions
3 cups shredded cooked chicken
¼ cup olive oil
3 tablespoons lemon juice
4 tablespoons Pesto (page 161)
salt and pepper

Place the peppers in a bowl and pour boiling water over them. Let them wilt for 10 minutes, drain, plunge into cold water to cool, and drain again. Combine the peppers, scallions, and chicken in a bowl.

Whisk together the remaining ingredients and pour over the salad. Toss to coat. Marinate for 30 minutes.

Preparation Time: 20 minutes
Marinating Time: 30 minutes
Yield: 6 servings

Seafood Pepper Pasta Salad

4 quarts salted water
½ pound uncooked pasta
1 cup water
1 tablespoon plus ⅓ cup lemon juice
2 cups raw shrimp and/or scallops
¾ cup julienne-sliced sweet red pepper
1 tablespoon minced red onion
2 tablespoons minced fresh parsley
¼ cup crumbled feta cheese
½ cup olive oil
1 garlic clove, minced
2 teaspoons minced fresh oregano or ½ teaspoon dried
¼ teaspoon white pepper
½ teaspoon salt

Bring the water to a rolling boil and cook the pasta until just done. Plunge into cold water, drain, and set aside.

In a large saucepan, bring 1 cup water and 1 tablespoon lemon juice to a boil. Simmer the seafood in the water until barely cooked, 3–5 minutes. Drain.

Combine the pasta, seafood, pepper, onion, parsley, and cheese.

Combine the remaining ingredients and whisk to blend. Pour over the salad and toss to coat. Chill before serving.

Preparation Time: 25 minutes
Cooking Time: 10–15 minutes
Chilling Time: 1 hour
Yield: 4–6 servings

SIDE DISHES AND MAIN DISHES

I've concentrated on creating recipes with sweet peppers. Hot pepper dishes are for the adventurous only!

Chiles Rellenos

I make the Chiles Rellenos when I have leftover refried beans.

1½ cups Refried Beans (page 36)
6 green peppers
8 ounces cream cheese
1 cup grated Monterey jack cheese
3 eggs, separated
1 tablespoon water
3 tablespoons all-purpose unbleached flour
½ teaspoon salt
vegetable oil for frying

Prepare the Refried Beans according to the recipe directions on page 36.

Broil the peppers until blistered and charred all over, 2–3 minutes per side. Place in a paper bag to steam for 10 minutes. When the peppers are cool enough to handle, remove the stem, peel off the skin, and clean out the seeds.

Combine the Refried Beans, cream cheese, and Monterey jack cheese.

Stuff the bean and cheese mixture into the peppers, allowing ¼–½ cup of filling per pepper.

Whisk together the egg yolks, water, flour, and salt. Beat the egg whites until stiff. Fold the

1. Spoon in the filling.

2. Dip into the batter.

3. Fry until golden on each side.

egg whites into the egg yolk mixture.

Heat ½ inch oil in a heavy frying pan.

Dip each pepper in the batter to coat and then fry in oil until golden brown on one side, about 3 minutes. Turn over and brown on the other side. Serve hot.

Preparation Time: 45 minutes
Cooking Time: 15 minutes
Yield: 6 servings

Pepper Cheese Bread

This bread tastes best toasted.

2 tablespoons dried baker's yeast
1 teaspoon sugar or honey
½ cup warm water
3 tablespoons olive oil
1 cup finely diced green pepper
1 cup milk
2 tablespoons honey
1½ teaspoons salt
1½ cups grated cheddar cheese
2 eggs, beaten
4–4½ cups all-purpose unbleached
    flour
½ cup wheat germ
beaten egg

Combine the yeast, sugar, and water in a small bowl and set aside until the yeast foams, about 5 minutes.

Meanwhile, in a sauté pan, heat 1 tablespoon of the oil, and sauté the pepper until limp, 3–5 minutes. Set aside.

Combine the milk, the remaining 2 tablespoons oil, 2 tablespoons honey, salt, and cheese in a saucepan and heat to lukewarm. Combine the peppers, eggs, and yeast mixture with the milk in a large bowl. Stir in 2 cups of the flour. Stir in the wheat germ and enough flour so the dough pulls away from the sides of the bowl, 2–2½ more cups. Cover the bowl and let the dough rise for 30 minutes. Stir the dough and divide into 2 parts.

Grease two 9-inch loaf pans. Turn the dough out of the bowl and shape to fit the pans. Let the bread rise for 30 minutes more in the pans.

Preheat the oven to 375° F.

Brush the top of the loaves with a beaten egg. Bake for 25 minutes. Cool before slicing.

Preparation Time: 1 hour, 20
    minutes (includes rising time)
Baking Time: 25 minutes
Yield: 2 loaves

Baked Fish With Three Pepper Sauce

2 tablespoons olive oil
1 large garlic clove, minced
1 cup thinly sliced onion
⅔ cup julienne-sliced green peppers
⅔ cup julienne-sliced yellow
    peppers
⅔ cup julienne-sliced sweet red
    peppers
1 teaspoon salt
2 tablespoons lemon juice
2 tablespoons dry white wine
½ teaspoon turmeric
1½ pounds of firm white fish

Preheat the oven to 350° F.

In a large sauté pan, heat the olive oil, and sauté the garlic, onion, green pepper, and yellow pepper for 2 minutes. Add the red pepper and sauté until the vegetables are limp, but not browned, about 3 minutes. Add the salt, lemon juice, wine, and turmeric. Sauté for 2 minutes more. Remove the vegetables from the pan.

Arrange the fish in a single layer in a greased baking dish. Cover with the peppers. Bake for 10–12 minutes or until the fish is flaky. Serve at once.

Preparation Time: 10 minutes
Baking Time: 10–12 minutes
Yield: 6 servings

Pepper Calzone

1 tablespoon dried baker's yeast
1⅓ cups warm water
2 tablespoons vegetable oil
pinch of sugar
1 teaspoon salt
4 cups all-purpose unbleached flour
6 Italian sausages (3 sweet and 3 hot)
1 cup diced onion
1 garlic clove, minced
1 tablespoon minced fresh basil or
    1 teaspoon dried
1½ teaspoons fresh thyme or ½
    teaspoon dried
1½ cups julienne-sliced sweet red
    peppers
1½ cups julienne-sliced green
    peppers
1 tablespoon olive oil
2 cups roughly chopped mushrooms
1½ cups grated mozzarella
½ cup grated parmesan cheese
beaten egg

Combine the yeast, water, vegetable oil, and sugar in a bowl and set aside until the yeast foams, about 5 minutes. Add the salt and 2 cups of the flour. Beat the dough until it is elastic and smooth. Then stir in the remaining 2 cups flour. Knead the dough for 10 minutes. Cover and let the dough double in bulk, about 45 minutes.

Remove the casings from the sausage, and brown it in a large frying pan, breaking up the meat with a spoon. Remove the meat from the pan and drain off all but 2 tablespoons of the fat. Sauté the onion, garlic, herbs, and peppers for 3–5 minutes, or until the onion is limp. Add the vegetables to the sausage. Heat the olive oil in the pan and sauté the mushrooms until limp, about

5 minutes. Add the mushrooms to the other vegetables. Stir in the cheeses.

When the dough has risen, punch it down and divide into 8 balls. Roll each ball out to an 8-inch circle. Spoon an eighth of the filling onto each circle. Brush the edges of the dough with water. Fold the dough in half and crimp the edges. Place the calzones on a greased cookie sheet and let rise, covered, for 20 minutes. Meanwhile, preheat the oven to 375° F.

Just before baking, brush the calzones with a beaten egg. Bake for 35 minutes. Serve hot.

Preparation Time: 35 minutes
Rising Time: 1 hour
Baking Time: 35 minutes
Yield: 8 servings

Roasted Peppers

I never realized how simple it is to make roasted red peppers until I made my first batch. What delicious eating they make! And roasted peppers are so easy to prepare.

Simply place the peppers under a broiler (or over hot coals for extra flavor) and broil until the skin is blistered and charred all over. Keep turning the peppers so they char evenly. This will take 2–3 minutes per side. Then place in a paper bag and let the peppers steam in the bag for about 10 minutes. This loosens the skins. Remove the peppers from the bag and peel away the skins. Slice into strips.

Roasted peppers can be stored in olive oil to cover in the refrigerator — or try this tasty marinade.

Variation
Marinated Red Peppers.

Roast and peel 5–6 medium-sized sweet peppers. Slice into strips.

Whisk together 3 tablespoons olive oil, 3 tablespoons lemon juice, ½ teaspoon turmeric, ½ teaspoon coriander, ½ teaspoon ground cumin, and ¼ teaspoon salt.

Pour the marinade over the peppers. Marinate for 20–30 minutes before serving at room temperature. These peppers will keep in the refrigerator for about 5 days.

I like to serve Roasted Marinated Red Peppers as an appetizer.

Some very tasty fillet of sole is smothered under julienne-sliced red, green, and yellow peppers. Isn't it a dramatic dish? Yet this Baked Fish With Three Pepper Sauce takes only 30 minutes to prepare. If you didn't grow yellow peppers, substitute equal amounts of red and green ones.

Potatoes

Homegrown Is Truly a Taste Treat, So Save Some Garden Space!

I've heard folks say that because potatoes are so inexpensive, they don't waste the space in their garden to grow them. What a shame! They are missing one of the best treats of summer—new, new potatoes, no bigger than a ping pong ball and wonderfully tender and tasty.

Sure, you can buy "new" potatoes in the stores, but they never taste as fresh as the immature ones you rob from your own potato patch in early July. And don't worry about harvesting those tiny potatoes. The plants don't mind being disturbed, and by removing some of the little potatoes, you enable the plant to concentrate on making the ones that are left larger.

Varieties Are Important to the Cook

For the most part, garden centers offer just two culinary choices in potatoes: all-purpose and russets (or baking) potatoes. I'd like to see them specialize more and offer potatoes that are especially developed for the cook. That way we could have extra waxy, low-starch potato varieties that are perfect for boiling and salads and dishes where you want the potatoes to hold their shape. And we would have more choices for mealy, starchy potatoes that are good for baking and mashing.

Of the potatoes grown at Garden Way Gardens, I have found the red-colored Norlands, which are low in starch, to be the best for boiling and for salads. It holds its shape well and is a tasty, early variety. I especially like to use Norlands in my New Potato Salad (page 213). Green Mountain and Fingerlings—so named because the tubers are small and shaped like fingers—are also good for boiling and salads.

The potatoes labeled "all-purpose" in the seed catalogs are usually medium-starch varieties. At Garden Way we have grown Kennebec and Katahdin, and these potatoes are indeed good for boiling or baking, although russets and Idaho potatoes have my vote for baking potatoes. Kennebecs often grow to be as large as one pound, which is nice for the show-off gardener, but not necessary—even hard to handle—for the cook. Whatever the size, I like to store my potatoes sorted by size; it's more convenient that way.

Isn't this root cellar a beauty? The potatoes will keep all winter in this well-insulated storage space. But a simpler root cellar in your basement will work just as well.

POTATOES AT A GLANCE

Harvest as soon as there is something big enough to eat.

Make it a point to harvest some new potatoes—of all varieties—all summer long.

Potatoes harvested for storage should have a chance to develop a thick, tough skin. Storage potatoes are harvested in the early fall. The tops of the plants die, sending the last of the plant's energy down to the potatoes. A week or so later, the potatoes are ready for harvest. If you can't rub the skin off easily, the potato is mature enough for storage.

Store potatoes in the coldest part of your root cellar for 4–7 months. Keep them out of the light.

Yields

1 pound fresh potatoes equals
  4 cups grated, diced, or sliced in sticks
or
  3 cups sliced or chopped
or
  2 cups cooked and mashed

To Peel or Not to Peel

This is the choice of the cook. With new potatoes, I don't bother. I simply scrub the skins well. With older potatoes, I prefer to peel, and I use my wide vegetable peeler to get the job done quickly. Since most of the vitamins are concentrated just under the skin, I try to peel away as little of the flesh as possible.

Don't peel your potatoes until just before you are going to cook them, or they will turn brown. You can peel and hold potatoes in ice water for up to 30 minutes. Be forewarned: there is some vitamin loss with this method.

An Accumulation of Potato Cooking Lore

Potatoes are such a common food—most of us have been cooking them for years. Here are a few tips I have picked up through experience:
• It saves time to dice and slice potatoes for salads before cooking. Your boiling and cooling time will be less.
• Don't mash or puree potatoes in a food processor. The consistency becomes too gooey.
• The food processor saves time for grating potatoes.
• Grated potatoes get rusty quickly, so they should be cooked as soon as possible.
• Potatoes don't freeze well.
• Starchy, old potatoes are especially good for potato pancakes and mashed potatoes.

Cooking Timetable

Boil (whole): 20 minutes
  (diced): 10 minutes
  (sliced): 10 minutes
  (cubed): 10–15 minutes
Sauté (sliced): 10 minutes
  (diced): 10 minutes
Bake (whole): 40–60 minutes at
  400° F.

If you want to get fancy, add sautéed peppers, bacon, caraway seeds, or minced chives to your Home Fries. I prefer mine plain.

In search of the perfect home fries

My search for the perfect home fries has led me to many enjoyable breakfasts at diners throughout the country. Most people rate a diner by the coffee. For me, it's the home fries.

There are many styles of home fries. The potatoes can be preboiled, or not. They can be sliced, diced, cubed, or grated. The fries can be cooked in butter, oil, or bacon grease. In some diners, paprika is added to the frying oil to give the potatoes that funny orange color. The potatoes can be cooked almost as a cake and flipped once. Or they can be stirred frequently. Then there are onions or no onions. The possibilities are great.

Here's my formula for the perfect home fries—crispy on the outside, soft on the inside, flavored with sweet, nearly burnt onions.

Parboil 6 cups cubed (1-inch pieces) potatoes for 5 minutes, until just barely tender. Drain.

Heat 2 tablespoons vegetable oil in a heavy frying pan and sauté 2 cups diced onions until limp, 3–5 minutes. Add the potatoes and continue cooking. Rather than stir, flip frequently with a spatula so potatoes brown evenly. The onions will get quite browned, which makes the flavor sweeter. Season to taste with salt and pepper. Serves 6–8.

Nothing Beats a Baked Potato

Baked potatoes are everyone's favorite—but they should be baked, not steamed! Never wrap a potato in foil, that's how you end up with soggy, steamed potatoes. I like to scrub my potatoes well, pierce with a fork in several places to allow steam to escape, and bake at 400° F. for 40–60 minutes. Pierce with a fork to test for doneness. Serve topped with butter, grated cheese, yogurt, or sour cream. Minced fresh herbs on top are also terrific.

French Fries Are an American Tradition, But Oven Fries Require Less Oil

I like to find substitutes for deep fried foods when I can. These oven fries are a great substitute for French fries—less oil, and less expensive to make.

Slice the potatoes into ³⁄₈-inch sticks. Dip each piece into vegetable oil and arrange in a single layer on a flat baking sheet. Bake for 30 minutes at 450° F.

Hash Browns: A Sunday Favorite

Hash browns make good use of leftover potatoes. Finely dice cooked potatoes. In a large frying pan, heat oil to cover the bottom of the pan. Drop the potatoes by the half cup into the oil. Press down with your spatula. Turn to brown both sides. Serve hot.

SOUPS

Potato Leek Soup, also known as vichyssoise, is as much a summer tradition as potato salad. It can be served hot, too, so consider it an almost year-round soup.

Potato Leek Soup

In a large soup pot, melt 2 tablespoons butter, and sauté 2 cups sliced leeks until limp, 3–5 minutes. Add 5 cups peeled and diced potatoes and 4 cups chicken broth. Simmer until the potatoes are tender, about 15 minutes. Cool the soup slightly. Puree in a blender or food processor until smooth. Stir in 1 cup heavy cream. Season to taste with salt and white pepper. Chill the soup well. Garnish with minced chives. Serves 6–8.

I like to put plenty of fresh herbs in my potato salads. It gives the salads a fresh, summery flavor.

Potato Cheese Soup

In a large soup pot, melt 2 tablespoons butter, and sauté 2 cups diced onions until limp, 3–5 minutes. Add 5 cups peeled and diced potatoes and 4 cups chicken broth. Simmer until the potatoes are tender, about 15 minutes. Cool the soup slightly. Puree in a blender or food processor until smooth. Return to the pot. Stir in 1 cup heavy cream, 2 cups grated cheese, and 2 teaspoons Dijon-style mustard. Reheat until the cheese is melted. Serve warm. Serves 6–8.

SALADS

Here are 6 different potato salads for fresh summer eating.

Oil-Free Potato Salad

6 cups diced potatoes
3 tablespoons lemon juice
2 scallions including some green tops, minced
2 teaspoons capers
¼ cup water
1 teaspoon Dijon-style mustard
¼ cup minced fresh dill (or other herb)
salt and pepper

Boil the potatoes until just tender, about 10 minutes. Drain and set aside.

In a blender or food processor, combine ⅓ cup potatoes with the lemon juice, scallions, capers, water, and mustard. Blend until smooth. Pour the dressing over the remaining potatoes and toss to coat. Add the dill and mix. Season to taste with salt and pepper. Chill for 1–2 hours before serving.

Preparation Time: 20 minutes
Chilling Time: 1–2 hours
Yield: 6 servings

New Potato Salad

6 cups diced new potatoes
2 teaspoons anchovy paste
¼ cup sliced scallion
¼ cup olive oil
1 tablespoon lemon juice
⅛ teaspoon ground rosemary
¼ cup crumbled feta cheese
½ cup sour cream
¼ cup minced fresh parsley
salt and pepper

Boil the potatoes until just tender, 10 minutes.

In the meantime, whisk together the anchovy paste, scallion, olive oil, lemon juice, and rosemary.

Drain the cooked potatoes and place in a bowl. Pour the marinade over the potatoes and cover. Let the potatoes cool to room temperature in the marinade, about 1 hour. Then stir in the feta cheese, sour cream, and parsley. Season to taste with salt and pepper. Chill for 2 hours before serving.

Preparation Time: 20 minutes
Marinating and Chilling Time: 3 hours
Yield: 6 servings

Pesto Potato Salad

8 cups sliced potatoes
4 tablespoons Pesto (page 161)
5 tablespoons wine vinegar
1 tablespoon capers
⅓ cup olive oil
⅔ cup sliced pitted Greek olives
1 cup diced sweet red pepper
½ cup minced fresh parsley
salt and pepper

Boil the potatoes until just tender, about 10 minutes. Drain and place in a large bowl to cool slightly.

Whisk together the Pesto, vinegar, capers, and olive oil. Pour the dressing over the potatoes and toss to coat. Add the olives, pepper, and parsley. Season to taste with salt and pepper. Toss the salad gently to mix. Chill for 1–2 hours before serving.

Preparation Time: 20 minutes
Chilling Time: 1–2 hours
Yield: 6–8 servings

Hot German Potato Salad

6 cups diced potatoes
¼ pound bacon, diced
¾ cup diced scallions
½ cup diced dill pickle
¼ cup wine vinegar
½ teaspoon celery seeds
1 teaspoon caraway seeds
¼ cup pickle juice
1 teaspoon sugar
salt and pepper

Boil the potatoes until tender, about 10 minutes.

In the meantime, brown the bacon and remove it from the pan. Drain off the bacon fat, reserving ¼ cup. Combine the bacon fat, scallions, pickle, vinegar, celery and caraway seeds, pickle juice, and sugar in the pan. Simmer for 3 minutes.

When the potatoes are cooked, drain and place in a large bowl. Pour the dressing over the potatoes and toss to coat. Add the bacon. Season to taste with salt and pepper. Serve immediately.

Preparation Time: 20 minutes
Yield: 6–8 servings

Traditional Potato Salad

8 cups diced potatoes
6 tablespoons white vinegar
1 cup vegetable oil
¼ cup diced onion
1 teaspoon ground rosemary
½ teaspoon dried savory
¼ teaspoon celery seeds
¼ teaspoon dried thyme
salt and pepper
½ cup mayonnaise
½ cup sour cream
½ teaspoon Dijon-style mustard
4 hard-boiled eggs, quartered and sliced
¼ cup minced fresh parsley

Boil the potatoes until tender, 10 minutes.

In the meantime, whisk together the vinegar, oil, onion, and herbs. Season to taste with salt and pepper.

Drain the cooked potatoes. Pour the marinade over the hot potatoes. Cover the bowl and marinate the potatoes for 20–30 minutes. Stir in the remaining ingredients. Chill the salad for 2 hours before serving.

Preparation Time: 20 minutes
Marinating and Chilling Time: 2½ hours
Yield: 6–8 servings

The sharp end on my peeler can remove eyes and bad spots.

Caesar Potato Salad

Keep this salad refrigerated! The raw egg makes it prone to spoiling in hot weather.

8 cups diced potatoes
1 egg
2 anchovies
2 garlic cloves, minced
¼ cup lemon juice
½ cup grated parmesan cheese
½ cup olive oil
salt and pepper
⅓ cup sliced scallions
¼ cup minced fresh parsley

Boil the potatoes until just tender, about 10 minutes. Drain and place in a large bowl to cool slightly.

In a food processor or blender, combine the egg, anchovies, garlic, lemon juice, and cheese. Process until smooth. With the processor running, slowly pour in the oil in a thin stream. The dressing will thicken slightly. Season to taste with salt and pepper. Pour the dressing over the potatoes, and add the scallions and parsley. Toss to mix and coat. Chill the salad for at least 2 hours before serving.

Preparation Time: 20 minutes
Chilling Time: 2 hours
Yield: 6–8 servings

SIDE DISHES AND MAIN DISHES

Potatoes are a good source of vitamin C and many important minerals. So think of them as a deserving vegetable, not "just a starch."

Minted Potatoes

Boil 6 cups quartered and sliced new potatoes until tender, about 10 minutes. Drain.

In a large sauté pan, melt 3 tablespoons butter and add ½ cup minced fresh mint and 1 tablespoon lemon juice. Sauté for 1 minute. Add the potatoes and toss to coat. Reheat and serve immediately. Serves 4–6.

Mashed Potato Patties

This is a great dish to make when you are faced with leftover mashed potatoes.

Mix 3 cups mashed potatoes and 1–1½ cups grated cheese (Swiss, cheddar, or Monterey jack). Season to taste with salt and pepper. Form the mixture into patties and brown in butter on both sides.

To vary the recipe, coat the patties with bread crumbs or wheat germ before frying or add minced herbs to the patties. Or shape the potato mixture into logs about 3 inches long and ½ inch in diameter. Roll the logs in ground nuts instead of bread crumbs.

Cheesy Potato Cups

Here's another recipe that uses leftover mashed potatoes.

5 tablespoons butter
1 cup diced onion
3 cups mashed potatoes
2 eggs, beaten
⅔ cup grated parmesan cheese
salt and pepper

Preheat the oven to 400° F.

Melt 1 tablespoon of the butter in a small sauté pan, and sauté the onion until limp, 3–5 minutes. In a bowl, combine the onion, mashed potatoes, eggs, and cheese. Season to taste with salt and pepper.

Melt the remaining 4 tablespoons butter. Brush 1 dozen nonstick muffin cups with butter. Press the mashed potatoes into the cups, making the sides and bottom ¼ inch thick. Brush the potato cups with melted butter. Bake the potato cups for 20–30 minutes or until golden brown. The potato cups will slip out of the muffin tin easily. Fill the cups with hot vegetables and serve immediately.

Preparation Time: 20 minutes
Baking Time: 20–30 minutes
Yield: 6 servings (2 per person)

Press into a cup shape.

Rich and Creamy Potatoes

This isn't a dish for dieters—but it's perfect for hard-working gardeners!

3 tablespoons butter
1 small garlic clove, minced
6 cups grated raw potatoes
1¼–1½ cups light cream
salt and pepper
1 cup grated Gruyère or Swiss cheese

Preheat the oven to 325° F.
Melt the butter in a large sauté pan, and sauté the garlic until golden. Add the potatoes and cream, and sauté for 2–3 minutes. Transfer the mixture to a greased 9-inch by 13-inch baking dish and sprinkle with salt and pepper. Sprinkle the cheese on top. Bake the potatoes for 30 minutes or until golden brown on top. Cut into squares and serve.

Preparation Time: 20 minutes
Baking Time: 30 minutes
Yield: 6–8 servings

Mustard Lemon Potatoes

Boil 4 cups of sliced or diced potatoes until just tender, about 10 minutes. Drain.
In a large sauté pan, melt 3 tablespoons butter, and add 2 tablespoons lemon juice, 2 teaspoons grated lemon rind, and 1½ teaspoons Dijon-style mustard. Add the potatoes and stir to mix and heat. Season to taste with salt and pepper. Serves 4–6.

Potato Pancakes

Potato Pancakes can be served as a side dish or main dish along with apple sauce, sour cream, or yogurt.

4 cups grated raw potatoes
1 cup grated raw onion
⅓ cup minced fresh parsley (optional)
3 eggs, beaten
⅓ cup all-purpose unbleached flour
1½ teaspoons salt
¼ teaspoon pepper
oil for frying

Mix the potatoes, onion, parsley, eggs, flour, salt, and pepper.
Heat a small amount of oil in a frying pan and spoon in ¼ cup potato mixture for each pancake. Gently flatten the pancakes with a spatula. Fry over medium heat until golden brown on both sides. Keep the pancakes warm in the oven.

Preparation Time: 10 minutes
Cooking Time: 20 minutes
Yield: 6 servings

Variations

German-Style Potato Pancakes. Add 1 cup grated carrots and 1 tablespoon caraway seeds to the batter.

Herbed Potato Pancakes. Add ½ cup fresh dill or 2 tablespoons minced fresh basil to the batter.

Indian-Style Potato Pancakes. Season the batter with ¼ teaspoon each of turmeric, curry powder, ground cumin, and coriander.

If you like your potatoes to retain some texture, try ricing them instead of mashing.

Potato Triangles

3 cups cold mashed potatoes
1 egg, beaten
2 teaspoons Dijon-style mustard
¼ cup minced fresh chives
salt and pepper
1 cup bread crumbs
4 tablespoons butter

Mix the potatoes, egg, mustard, and chives. Season to taste with salt and pepper. Shape the potato mixture into triangles 1½ inches long and ¾ inch thick. (This will be easier to do if you keep your hands wet.) Or press the mixture flat and then cut into triangles.
Dip the triangles into bread crumbs to coat. Fry in butter until golden brown. Serve hot.

Preparation Time: 20 minutes
Cooking Time: 15–20 minutes
Yield: 6–8 servings

Creamed Dill Potatoes

4 cups diced or sliced potatoes
2 tablespoons butter
¼ cup minced fresh dill
¼ cup minced fresh chives
1 teaspoon all-purpose unbleached flour
½ cup light cream
⅛ teaspoon white pepper
salt
½ cup sour cream

Boil the potatoes until just tender, about 10 minutes. In the meantime, melt the butter in a small saucepan. Sauté the dill and chives for 1 minute. Sprinkle the flour over the herbs and add the cream, pepper, and salt to taste. Whisk in the sour cream and keep the sauce warm. Do not boil. Drain the potatoes and combine with the sauce. Serve hot.

Preparation Time: 10 minutes
Cooking Time: 10 minutes
Yield: 6–8 servings

Breaded Potato Sticks

½ cup bread crumbs
2 tablespoons grated parmesan cheese
¼ teaspoon dried basil
¼ teaspoon dried thyme
¼ teaspoon dried oregano
¼ teaspoon salt
⅛ teaspoon pepper
3–4 cups ½-inch raw potato sticks
2 tablespoons vegetable oil

Preheat the oven to 400° F.
Mix the bread crumbs, parmesan cheese, herbs, salt, and pepper. Dip each potato stick into the oil, scraping off the excess oil on the side of the dish.

Coat the sticks with the bread crumb mixture and place on a greased or nonstick baking sheet Bake for 20–30 minutes or until potatoes are tender. Serve hot.

Preparation Time: 20 minutes
Baking Time: 20–30 minutes
Yield: 6–8 servings

Scalloped Potatoes

These scalloped potatoes become au gratin with the addition of 2 cups of grated cheese layered with the potatoes. Adding bacon, diced ham, sausage, or sliced hot dogs makes a complete casserole meal. Vegetables, such as radishes, carrots, turnips, rutabagas, green tomatoes, or cauliflower can be added to make a hearty "garden casserole."

4–6 cups thinly sliced potatoes
⅓ cup all-purpose unbleached flour
salt and pepper
1 cup diced onion
6 tablespoons butter
1½ cups milk
paprika

Preheat the oven to 350° F.
Grease a 2-quart baking dish. Cover the bottom of the dish with a layer of potatoes. Sprinkle with flour, salt and pepper, and onion. Dot with butter. Continue to layer the potatoes and flour, salt, pepper, onion, and butter in the dish until used. Pour the milk over the potatoes. Sprinkle with paprika. Bake covered for 1 hour, or until the potatoes are tender.

Preparation Time: 20 minutes
Baking Time: 1 hour
Yield: 6 servings

Smoked Pork Chops on a Potato Apple Bed

Most supermarkets carry smoked pork chops. You can substitute regular chops, but the flavor will be different.

6 cups peeled sliced potatoes
1 cup peeled sliced apples
1 tablespoon diced onion
1 cup grated Swiss cheese
6 smoked pork chops
1½ cups Hot Horseradish Cream Sauce (page 305)

Preheat the oven to 350° F.
Boil the potatoes until just tender, about 10 minutes.
Grease a 9-inch by 13-inch baking dish. Combine the potatoes, apples, and onion, and spoon into the baking dish. Sprinkle the cheese on top.
Sear the pork chops by rubbing the fatty ends of the chops around a hot frying pan, then laying the chops in the frying pan, and browning quickly on both sides over high heat. Place the pork chops on the potatoes. Cover the dish lightly with foil and bake for 30 minutes.
Prepare the Horseradish Sauce. Pour the sauce over the chops and potatoes and bake for 30 minutes more.

Preparation Time: 25 minutes
Baking Time: 1 hour
Yield: 4 servings

It's the combination—smoky pork, tart apples, and potatoes—that makes this a perfect one-dish meal.

Salmon Potato Pie

The potato crust that forms the base of this dish can be used for any quiche. It's delicious.

4 cups grated raw potatoes
1¼ cups minced onion
4 eggs
¼ cup all-purpose unbleached flour
½ teaspoon salt
⅛ teaspoon pepper
¼ cup vegetable oil
2 cups canned or fresh cooked salmon
1 cup heavy or light cream
3 tablespoons minced fresh dill
1½ cups grated cheddar cheese
paprika

Preheat the oven to 400° F.

Mix the potatoes, ½ cup of the onion, 1 of the eggs, the flour, salt, and pepper. Grease a 10-inch pie pan and press the potato mixture into the pan to make a crust. Brush the crust with oil and bake for 20 minutes.

In a sauté pan, heat 1 tablespoon of the vegetable oil and sauté the remaining ¾ cup onion until translucent, 3–5 minutes.

Remove the skin and bones from the salmon and break it up.

Beat together the remaining 3 eggs, cream, and dill.

When the crust is done, remove from the oven and reduce the heat to 350° F.

Sprinkle the sautéed onion over the bottom of the pie. Arrange the salmon over the onion. Pour the egg mixture over the salmon. Cover with cheese and sprinkle with paprika. Brush the edge of the crust with oil, and bake the pie for 30–40 minutes or until it is set. Allow the pie to sit for 10 minutes before serving.

Preparation Time: 25 minutes
Baking Time: 1 hour
Yield: 8 servings

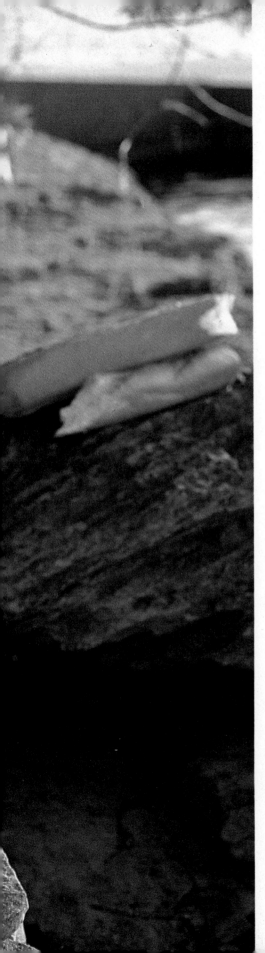

Sweet
Potatoes

The Vegetable That's So Sweet It's Like Having Dessert With Dinner!

Somehow I always feel like I'm cheating when I eat sweet potatoes for dinner. How can something this sweet be a vegetable?

I often serve sweet potatoes as a snack. I wrap a couple of sweet potatoes in aluminum foil and throw them into the woodstove after dinner. In an hour or so, I have a late-night snack, as sweet as cake, but loaded in vitamin A. If the potatoes aren't overbaked (which does happen occasionally in a blazing fire), they don't even need butter, they're so tasty. And without the butter, sweet potatoes are a very nutritious, low-calorie (161 calories) snack.

Those midwinter baked sweet potatoes are, I confess, store-bought. We can grow sweet potatoes up here in the North, but they are mostly for eating fresh. Our root cellars get too cold for storing sweet potatoes. The next best way to preserve extra is to steam and freeze it, but with freezer space at a premium, I don't often bother.

Sweet Potatoes Aren't True Potatoes

Sweet potatoes are so similar in appearance and cooking possibilities to Irish potatoes that it came as a surprise to me to learn that sweet potatoes aren't true potatoes. I should have known by their growth habits.

My mother often let me grow sweet potato vines in the kitchen. She'd give me a section of sweet potato to place in a jar of water. In a few weeks, we'd have a lovely vine climbing up the curtains. The vines look like morning glories—a close relative of sweet potatoes—and not like Irish potato plants at all.

Sweet potatoes are actually a perennial plant (although grown like an annual). Once they have set tubers, the plants don't die as Irish potatoes do. That's why you have to dig up a sweet potato to determine if it is large enough for harvest. You can harvest small potatoes early in the season, larger ones as the season progresses.

You have to harvest and handle sweet potatoes carefully. They bruise very, very easily. I prefer to harvest and cook my small crop of sweet potatoes as I need them, and not worry about providing perfect storage conditions. For me, the sweet potato season may be brief, but it is always enjoyed.

Sweet potato kabobs made with chicken and green peppers make a great barbecue dish—a nice change from hamburgers and steak. Add a green salad and you'll have a great meal!

SWEET POTATOES AT A GLANCE

Yields

1 pound fresh sweet potatoes equals
   approximately 3 potatoes
or
   4 cups sliced, grated, or french-fry
   cut
or
   3 cups julienne-sliced or diced
or
   3½ cups cubed
or
   1–1¼ cups cooked and pureed

Storage Can Be a Problem

Sweet potato plants will grow as
long as the weather stays
warm—they must be harvested
before the frost.

Sweet potatoes are fussy about
storage conditions. For long-term
storage, cure sweet potatoes for
10–14 days in a warm, dark place.
The temperature should be 70–80°
F. with high humidity. Then store in
a drier, well-ventilated area at
55–60° F. with a humidity of 75–80
percent.

If you can't provide those storage
conditions, you can freeze extra
sweet potatoes. Peel, parboil for 2–3
minutes, then freeze.

Sweet potatoes should not be
stored for any length of time in the
refrigerator because they will
develop soft spots.

Sweet Potatoes Brown Easily

When exposed to air, sweet
potato flesh turns brown. To
prevent this, as you peel and slice
sweet potatoes, drop the slices into
cold water.

Sweet potato vines

And They Cook Quickly

Sweet potatoes cook somewhat
faster than Irish potatoes. Watch
your times carefully. Cook sweet
potatoes until just tender. They
should not be mushy.

The times vary depending on the
size of the pieces.

Cooking Times

Parboil (for salads): 3–5 minutes
Boil: 5–10 minutes
Steam: 10–12 minutes
Sauté or stir fry (grated): 2–3
   minutes
   (slices or sticks): 5–8 minutes
Bake (sticks): 20–30 minutes
Bake (whole): 45–60 minutes

Sweet Potatoes and Rosemary—An Excellent Combination

There are lots of traditional sweet
potato combinations—like pineapple
and sweet potatoes. Many people
like sweet potatoes with Mustard
Butter (page 304). For others,
nothing beats "candied" sweet
potatoes made with butter and
maple syrup, honey, or brown
sugar.

Another excellent combination is
sweet potatoes sautéed for 5–8
minutes in Herb Butter (page 160)
made with rosemary.

Other herbs and spices that go
well with sweet potatoes are chives,
tarragon, parsley, thyme, nutmeg,
and cinnamon.

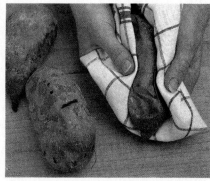

Before serving, roll the baked sweet potato between your hands to loosen the flesh from the skin. You'll get every bit of sweet potato goodness this way.

Garnish your baked sweet potatoes with bacon bits, chopped parsley or chives, grated cheese, chopped nuts—you name it!

Bake' em in the woodstove or in the oven — Nothing beats a roasted sweet potato

Sure, you can do all sorts of things to a sweet potato. You can even make it into cakes, and no one will be able to guess that a potato passed through the bowl. I love the flavor of sweet potatoes so much, I like best to serve them plain. The perfect baked sweet potato is one that is scrubbed well and placed in a preheated 400° F. oven to bake for 45 minutes. The potato is done when it is easily pierced by a fork.

Baked in a woodstove, the potato should be wrapped in foil to keep it clean and to prevent it from drying out in the intense heat.

Before serving, roll the potato between your hands (wear oven mitts) to loosen the flesh from the skin. That's where the sweetest flesh is, a secret I learned from a Southern friend.

Stuffed Baked Sweet Potatoes Are Tops

Slice a baked sweet potato in half and scoop out the flesh, saving the shell. Mash the flesh with a little milk, cream, orange juice, or apple cider, and butter. Season to taste with salt and pepper. Spoon back into the shells, reheat for 10–20 minutes at 350° F., and serve.

You can garnish baked sweet potatoes with bacon bits, sautéed mushrooms, parsley, chives, sesame seeds, chopped nuts, grated parmesan cheese, grated orange rind, sautéed apples, or cranberry relish.

This soup can be made with carrots, pumpkins, or winter squash, instead of sweet potatoes.

Sweet Potato Curry Soup

Here's a lightly curried soup with a fruity flavor. I like to garnish it with chopped chives, raw peas, finely diced red peppers, or an orange nasturtium blossom.

3 tablespoons vegetable oil or butter
1 cup chopped onion
8 cups cubed sweet potatoes
1 cup water
1 teaspoon curry powder
½ cup cider
4 cups milk
salt and white pepper

In a large soup pot, heat the oil, and sauté the onion until limp, 3–5 minutes. Add the sweet potatoes, water, and curry. Simmer until the potatoes are very tender, about 15 minutes.

Cool the soup slightly. Puree in a blender or food processor, adding the cider and milk. Add more milk if you prefer a thinner soup. Season to taste with salt and white pepper.

Reheat and serve.

Preparation Time: 15 minutes
Cooking Time: 20 minutes
Yield: 6–8 servings

The sweet potatoes are delicious in this Waldorf Salad. It's a crunchy, refreshing dish for an Indian summer day.

SALADS

Sweet potatoes cook faster than white potatoes, so I try to be careful with timing. A mushy potato salad is always disappointing.

Mixed Potato Salad

4 cups cubed sweet potatoes
4 cups cubed white potatoes
½ cup vegetable oil
3 tablespoons lemon juice
1 tablespoon white vinegar
3 tablespoons honey
1 teaspoon curry powder
1 teaspoon cardamom
½ teaspoon white pepper
½ teaspoon salt
2 tablespoons minced fresh chives

Parboil the sweet potatoes for 3–5 minutes, until just tender. Plunge into cold water. Drain and set aside.

Parboil the white potatoes for 5–8 minutes, until just tender. Plunge into cold water. Drain. Combine with the sweet potatoes.

Mix the remaining ingredients and pour over the potatoes. Toss gently to coat. Marinate for at least 1 hour to let the flavors mingle. Serve cold, garnished with alfalfa sprouts and halved cherry tomatoes.

Preparation Time: 20 minutes
Marinating Time: 1 hour
Yield: 8 servings

Sweet Potato Waldorf Salad

8 cups diced sweet potatoes
2 cups diced celery
4 cups unpeeled diced red or
  green apples (about 3 apples)
½ cup raisins or currants
¾ cup chopped walnuts
1½ cups mayonnaise
¼ teaspoon nutmeg (optional)

Parboil the potatoes until just tender, 3–5 minutes. Plunge into cold water. Drain.

In a large salad bowl, combine the remaining ingredients. Add the potatoes and toss to coat. Chill and serve cold.

Preparation Time: 25 minutes
Chilling Time: at least 1 hour
Yield: 8–10 servings

Sweet Potato Tarragon Salad

If it's cold and potato, it must be a salad, right?

4 cups julienne-sliced sweet potatoes
⅓ cup vegetable oil
5 tablespoons lemon juice
1 tablespoon minced fresh tarragon
salt and pepper

Parboil the potatoes for 3–5 minutes, until just tender. Plunge into cold water and drain immediately.

Mix the remaining ingredients and pour over the potatoes. Toss to coat. Marinate for at least 2 hours to allow the flavors to mingle. Serve cold.

Preparation Time: 20 minutes
Marinating Time: 2 hours
Yield: 4–6 servings

SIDE DISHES AND MAIN DISHES

A main dish made primarily of sweet potatoes is too rich for my blood! That's why most of the recipes here are for side dishes.

Baked Sweet Potato Sticks

5 cups sweet potato sticks (large french-fry size)
4 tablespoons butter
2½ teaspoons Dijon-style mustard
1 teaspoon brown sugar

Preheat the oven to 400° F.

As you slice the potatoes, drop the slices into cold water to prevent browning.

Melt the butter. Stir in the mustard and sugar until the mixture is smooth.

Pat the potatoes dry. Lay the potato sticks out on a baking sheet. Using a pastry brush, coat the sticks with the mustard butter mixture. Be sure to cover all surfaces or the potatoes will discolor.

Bake for 20–30 minutes, or until the potatoes are tender.

Preparation Time: 20 minutes
Baking Time: 20–30 minutes
Yield: 6 servings

Sesame Sweet Potatoes

I have found that julienne-sliced sweet potatoes always cook faster than I expect, so I am careful to cook this dish at the last minute.

1 tablespoon sesame oil
1 tablespoon vegetable oil
4 cups julienne-sliced sweet potatoes
1 tablespoon sesame seeds
1 tablespoon tamari or soy sauce

In a wok or large frying pan, heat the oils and stir fry the sweet potatoes until just tender, about 5 minutes. Add the sesame seeds and tamari; toss to coat. Serve immediately.

Preparation Time: 20 minutes
Cooking Time: 5 minutes
Yield: 4–6 servings

Sweet Potatoes in Ginger Honey Sauce

2 tablespoons minced fresh ginger root
1 teaspoon ground cardamom
2 tablespoons lemon juice
3 tablespoons honey
2 tablespoons butter
salt
1½ cups water
6 cups cubed sweet potatoes

In a large sauté pan, simmer the ginger, cardamom, lemon juice, honey, butter, salt, and water for 2 minutes.

Add the cubed sweet potatoes and simmer gently until the potatoes are just tender, 6–8 minutes. Serve immediately.

Preparation Time: 10 minutes
Cooking Time: 10 minutes
Yield: 6 servings

Sweet Potato and Chicken Kabobs

Kabobs are wonderful picnic food served with a salad and fresh, crusty French bread. When I make this dish indoors under a broiler, I substitute cooked rice for the bread.

2 medium-size sweet potatoes, cubed
1 teaspoon fresh minced ginger root
2 tablespoons honey
1 tablespoon tamari or soy sauce
1 teaspoon grated orange rind
¼ cup orange juice
2 tablespoons vegetable oil
2 boneless chicken breasts, cut in cubes
2 small oranges, cut in wedges and halved
2 medium-size green peppers, cut in cubes

Parboil the potato pieces for 5 minutes. Plunge into cold water. Drain.

In a small bowl, combine the ginger, honey, tamari, orange rind, orange juice, and vegetable oil. Add the chicken and sweet potatoes and toss to coat. Marinate for at least 30 minutes.

Alternate the chicken, sweet potato, orange, and pepper pieces on skewers. Brush with marinade. Grill or broil until the chicken and potatoes are done, about 5 minutes. Baste frequently. Serve hot.

Preparation Time: 40 minutes
Cooking Time: 5 minutes
Yield: 4–6 servings

Hold peeled sweet potatoes in ice water to prevent browning.

Sweet Potato Fries

Slice sweet potatoes into sticks. Soak in ice water for 30 minutes. Dry well. Heat oil for deep frying to 375° F. Deep fry the potatoes until golden brown. Sprinkle with salt and serve hot.

Sweet Potato Slices

Thinly slice sweet potatoes. Soak in ice water for 30 minutes to prevent browning. Dry well. Brush with melted butter and broil on one side until browned. Turn over and brush with butter again. Sprinkle with grated parmesan cheese, curry powder, or ground rosemary, and salt and pepper to taste. Broil until browned. Serve hot.

Sweet Potatoes With Cardamom

Mash 4 cups cooked sweet potatoes with ½ cup apple cider, 1½ teaspoons ground cardamom, and ¼ cup butter. Season to taste with salt and pepper. Reheat. Serves 4–6.

Sweet Potato Frittata

Sweet and smoky describes this mouth-watering frittata. It's perfect for dinner or brunch.

½ pound smoked ham or Canadian bacon
2 tablespoons butter
2 cups sliced quartered sweet potatoes
½ cup sliced scallions
2 cups peeled sliced apples
1¾ cups grated Swiss cheese
salt and pepper
6 eggs
dash nutmeg

Preheat the oven to 350° F. Julienne-slice the bacon or ham.

In a large frying pan, melt the butter. Sauté the sweet potatoes, bacon, and scallions for 2–3 minutes, turning gently. Add the apples and continue to sauté until the potatoes are almost tender, adding a few teaspoons of water if the pan gets too dry.

Butter a 10-inch pie pan and layer in half the sweet potato mixture and half of the cheese. Layer the remaining sweet potatoes and cheese on top. Sprinkle with salt and pepper to taste.

Beat the eggs and pour over the frittata. Sprinkle nutmeg on top. Bake for 40 minutes or until golden brown. Serve hot.

Preparation Time: 25 minutes
Baking Time: 40 minutes
Yield: 8 servings

Sweet Potato Apple Cups

I like to make this side dish with leftover baked sweet potatoes.

3 cups mashed sweet potatoes
2 eggs, separated
½ teaspoon salt
¼ teaspoon ground cloves
1 tablespoon honey
2 tablespoons butter, melted
2 apples, peeled, cored, and sliced into circles
2 tablespoons melted butter

Preheat the oven to 350° F.

Mix the sweet potatoes, egg yolks, salt, cloves, honey, and melted butter in a food processor or mixing bowl until well blended.

Beat the egg whites until stiff. Fold the egg whites into the sweet potatoes.

Butter 6 custard cups. Place one apple circle in the bottom of each cup. Divide the potato mixture among the cups. Top each cup with another slice of apple. Brush the tops with butter.

Place the custard cups in a baking dish and pour boiling water into the dish until it reaches halfway up the sides of the cups. Bake for 30 minutes.

Remove from the oven and let sit for 10 minutes. Run a knife around the sides of each cup. Invert onto a serving plate or individual plates and remove the cups. Serve hot.

Preparation Time: 30 minutes
Baking Time: 30 minutes
Yield: 6 servings

1. *Spoon the puree on the apple.*

2. *Top with an apple slice.*

3. *Loosen the baked custard with a knife.*

4. *Unmold just before serving onto a serving plate.*

BAKED GOODS

True, this is a recipe for sweet potato muffins. But just incidentally, it's also another great recipe for zucchini.

Sweet Potato Muffins

1½ cups all-purpose unbleached flour
½ cup sugar
½ teaspoon baking powder
2 teaspoons baking soda
½ teaspoon salt
1 teaspoon cinnamon
1 teaspoon nutmeg
½ cup vegetable oil
½ cup pure maple syrup
2 eggs, beaten
1 teaspoon vanilla extract
1½ cups cooked mashed sweet potatoes
1½ cups well-packed grated raw zucchini
¾ cup chopped walnuts

Preheat the oven to 375° F.

Sift together the dry ingredients. Beat together the oil, maple syrup, eggs, and vanilla. Stir the sweet potatoes and zucchini into the oil mixture. Add the dry ingredients and walnuts, mixing just until blended.

Grease or line with papers 2 muffin tins. Fill the muffin cups two-thirds full. Bake on the top rack of the oven for 20–25 minutes, until brown.

Preparation Time: 25 minutes
Baking Time: 20–25 minutes
Yield: 2 dozen muffins

Pumpkins

I Could Cook Pumpkin Every Day And No One Would Ever Be Bored

Until you start thinking of pumpkins as vegetables, you'll never explore all the wonderful things you can do with this vitamin-rich vine crop.

The cook and the gardener may disagree about a few pumpkin matters, however. As a cook, it is my opinion that there is no such thing as an "all-purpose pumpkin," despite the sales pitches of the seed catalogs. All-purpose pumpkins are not as sweet as pie pumpkins, nor do they have as much flavor after storage.

Grow Pie Pumpkin Varieties for Best Eating

The flesh of the best pumpkins is bright orange and firm. If your pumpkin is pale and soft, you can puree it and use it in pies and breads (with plenty of sweetener). My recommendation is to grow field pumpkins for jack o'lanterns, hull-less seed pumpkins for seeds (and compost the flesh), and pie pumpkins for all your baking and cooking needs. If the seed catalog doesn't mention that a pumpkin variety is suitable for pies and canning, look for a description of the flesh as "fine-grained." This, too, will make a good eating pumpkin.

Pumpkins are ready for harvest when they are full-sized and orange-colored. But you can enjoy the *flowers* of the pumpkin plant early in the summer. After the plant blossoms, it is a good idea to let it set three small pumpkins and to remove any additional flowers. This allows the plant to concentrate all its energy on the original pumpkins. The flowers are delicious sautéed in butter or coated with a tempura batter and deep-fried (page 309).

When you harvest your pumpkins, be sure to leave the stem on; otherwise, the pumpkin will not keep. Plan to store your best pumpkins—the ones that are firm, uncracked, and have no soft spots. The rest should be cooked immediately, or pureed or grated and frozen.

Pumpkins keep in a root cellar or attic at 50–55° F. for 2–3 months. You'll be able to tell right away if your pumpkins are reaching the limit of their storage capacity. The flesh becomes soft and watery, and the flavor deteriorates. When that happens, I usually make a puree with the remaining pumpkins and freeze it in 1-cup and 2-cup batches to use in breads, pies, and gravies.

Pumpkin pie and Halloween seem to go hand in hand. But there are dozens more ways to prepare pumpkin than just pie!

PUMPKINS AT A GLANCE

Yields

7 pounds whole pumpkin equals
3½ pounds flesh
1 pound fresh raw pumpkin equals
4 cups thinly sliced, diced,
or grated
or
2 cups thickened puree

Cold Storage Is Easiest But Freezing Extends Your Storage Time

Pumpkins will keep for 2–3 months in a root cellar or attic at 50–55° F.

Or you can make pumpkin purees to freeze and use year-round. To make a puree, slice the pumpkin in half and scoop out the seeds. Put a little water in the bottom of a baking dish and set the pumpkin in the dish, flesh side down. Bake for about 1½ hours at 350° F., or until the pumpkin flesh is tender. Scoop out the flesh and process it in a food processor, blender, or food mill. The puree should be thick enough to hold a spoon. If the puree is watery, cook before freezing in 1-cup and 2-cup batches.

Frozen Diced Pumpkin: Handy to Have on Hand

Using a chef's knife, peel the pumpkin. Cut it into wedges, remove the seeds, and dice into 1-inch cubes. Freeze in 1-cup and 2-cup batches. The pumpkin gets a little mushy, but it makes a nice addition to soups and stews.

Peeling pumpkin

Preparing Pumpkin For the Table

Sliced, Chopped, or Grated Pumpkin. Slice off the top and bottom of the pumpkin so it stands flat. Using a chef's knife, peel the skin from the pumpkin, following the contour of the flesh. Slice the pumpkin in half, scoop out the seeds, and slice, chop, or grate the flesh. Cook or bake.

Cooking Times

Steam (½-inch cubes): 5–10 minutes
Blanch (½-inch cubes): 5–10 minutes
Sauté (½-inch cubes): 6–10 minutes
   (grated): 4–6 minutes
Stir fry (½-inch cubes): 5–10 minutes
   (grated): 4–6 minutes
Bake (whole): 1½ hours at 350° F.
   (½-inch cubes): 20–30 minutes at 350° F.

Pumpkin Puree. To make a puree, follow the instructions given for a frozen puree. Use frozen and fresh pumpkin purees interchangeably.

Baked Stuffed Pumpkins. Slice off the top of the pumpkin and put it aside. Scoop out the seeds. Place the pumpkin in a large kettle and cover with boiling water. Simmer for about 30 minutes, or until it is tender. Drain well and fill with your stuffing mixture. Bake with the lid on.

Taking Care of Leftovers

Leftover raw pumpkin can be wrapped in plastic film wrap and stored in the refrigerator for up to 5 days.

Leftover purees may be added to gravies, soups, and stews.

Add grated raw pumpkin to turkey and chicken stuffings.

Sauté pumpkin slices with sausage patties and apple slices for lunch.

Roll up ham slices with sweetened pumpkin puree inside, drizzle with pure maple syrup, and serve for brunch.

Make a shepherd's pie using pureed pumpkin in place of mashed potatoes.

Steam or stir fry pumpkin and toss in sesame seeds, pumpkin seeds, peanuts, orange juice, maple syrup, prunes, raisins, apples, lemon juice and honey, cheese, or sour cream.

One all-purpose pumpkin made these Pumpkin Chips and Roasted Seeds. The seeds have hulls, which some people mind and some people don't. Both the chips and the seeds have more flavor when sprinkled lightly with salt.

You'll never want potato chips again After you've tried these tasty snacks

I've enjoyed many cozy winter evenings serving these delicious pumpkin snacks to friends. Hot mulled cider is the perfect thirst-quencher with the chips and seeds.

Rich In Vitamin A

The only trick with these snacks is to be sure to slice the pumpkin *very thin*. I recommend using a food processor for the task. Also, be sure your oil temperature is 375° F. I always use a frying thermometer to guarantee that the oil is hot enough. Oil that is not hot enough will make the chips greasy.

So, peel a whole sweet pie pumpkin and remove the seeds.

Slice the pumpkin into wedges and *very thinly* slice the pumpkin.

Heat the oil to 375° F. for deep fat frying. Fry a few pumpkin chips at a time until golden brown. Drain the chips well.

Toasted Pumpkin Seeds: Two Schools of Thought

There are some people who enjoy munching on pumpkin seeds and don't mind the labor of removing the hulls. I prefer the hull-less variety so much that I often throw pumpkin seeds with hulls right into the compost.

You can raise hull-less seeded pumpkins. Lady Godiva is a variety especially developed for its "naked" or hull-less seeds.

Pumpkin seeds, without the hulls, can be used as you use sunflower seeds: in trail food mixes, sprinkled on salads, tossed into stir fries, or toasted in butter and sautéed with vegetables such as snap beans or carrots. This recipe for preparing pumpkin seeds works for seeds with and without hulls.

Preheat the oven to 250° F.

Clean the seeds by rubbing off any fibers. Do not wash. Measure the seeds. Combine every cup of seeds with 1 tablespoon of vegetable oil or melted butter. Spread the seeds on a baking sheet or on the bottom of a baking dish. Sprinkle with 1 teaspoon of salt, if desired. Sprinkle 1 teaspoon curry powder along with the salt, if desired. Roast, stirring or shaking the pan frequently, for 30–40 minutes or until the seeds are crisp and evenly browned.

Cool, and store the seeds in an airtight container.

SOUP

If the Pumpkin Red Peppery Soup doesn't fit the bill, look at the soups in the Winter Squash and Sweet Potato chapters. All of those soups can be made with pumpkin instead.

Pumpkin Red Peppery Soup

2 tablespoons vegetable oil
1½ cups diced onion
1½ cups diced sweet red peppers
2 cups pumpkin puree
2½ cups milk
2 teaspoons chili powder
¼ teaspoon ground cumin
⅛ teaspoon cayenne
salt and pepper
½ cup minced sweet red peppers

In a large soup pot, heat the oil and sauté the onion and 1½ cups red peppers until limp, 3–5 minutes. Add the pumpkin puree and milk. Heat thoroughly.

Cool the soup slightly and puree the mixture in a blender or food processor until smooth. Add the spices and salt and pepper to taste. Continue cooking over low heat for 15 minutes. Serve hot and garnish with the ½ cup minced red peppers.

Preparation Time: 30 minutes
Yield: 6 servings

SIDE DISHES AND MAIN DISHES

This collection of recipes— from fritters to stews—makes one thing clear: pumpkins belong in all sorts of dishes.

Pumpkin Corn Fritters

These fritters can be served as a side dish or a Sunday brunch entrée. Either way, they are delicious with maple syrup drizzled on top.

oil for deep frying
2½ cups all-purpose unbleached flour
1 tablespoon baking powder
2 teaspoons salt
½ teaspoon nutmeg
2 eggs, beaten
1 cup milk
3 cups grated pumpkin, packed firm
1 cup corn kernels

In a large, heavy-bottomed pan for deep frying, preheat the oil to 375° F.

Beat together the flour, baking powder, salt, nutmeg, eggs, and milk. Stir in the pumpkin and corn.

When the oil is hot enough, drop the batter by the tablespoon into the pan. Fry 3–4 minutes, turning once. Drain on paper towels and serve warm with pure maple syrup.

Preparation Time: 25 minutes
Cooking Time: 15–20 minutes
Yield: 6 servings (12 fritters)

Pumpkin and Baked Beans

I think of baked beans as Sunday night cooking at its best. Of course, Boston Baked Beans is a grand New England tradition, and this recipe is quite similar to that classic dish.

There are many different recipes for baked beans. Maine cooks prefer soldier beans, and Vermonters usually bake navy beans. The soldier beans get mushier, which I happen to like. The navy beans hold their shape better, so they look nicer.

1½ cups dried navy or soldier beans
water
½ cup diced onion
¼ cup pure maple syrup or brown sugar
¼ cup dark molasses
1 teaspoon salt
2 cups diced pumpkin
1 teaspoon grated orange rind
juice of 1 orange (½ cup)
1 tablespoon brown sugar

Cover the beans with water. Bring to a boil and simmer gently for 30 minutes to tenderize.

Preheat the oven to 350° F.

Combine the remaining ingredients, except 1 tablespoon of the brown sugar, with the beans in a greased covered baking dish. Add water to cover and sprinkle 1 tablespoon brown sugar over the top. Bake uncovered for 4 hours, adding water if the beans become dry.

Preparation Time: 50 minutes
Baking Time: 4 hours
Yield: 4–6 servings

Pumpkin Tourtière

Vermont culinary traditions are partially based on the wonderful food of the French Canadians. Tourtière a la viande, *a savory spiced meat pie usually made with pork, is traditionally served after midnight mass on Christmas eve. Most families have their own special recipe for tourtière, but it is almost always a double-crusted pie. This recipe makes a real break with tradition.*

Bring the baked pumpkin to the table whole, and slice wedges for each serving.

3 tablespoons oil
3 cups diced onions
3 garlic cloves, minced
2½ pounds ground pork
3 cups water
¼ cup currants
6 slices dense bread, diced
½ teaspoon pepper
¼ teaspoon ground cloves
1 teaspoon cinnamon
2½ teaspoons salt
½–⅔ cup bread crumbs
1 whole 10-inch pie pumpkin

In a large saucepan, heat the oil, and sauté the onions and garlic until limp, 3–5 minutes. Set aside. Brown the pork, and drain off the fat. Return the onions and garlic to the pan, along with the water, currants, bread cubes, pepper, cloves, cinnamon, and 2 teaspoons of salt. Simmer until the liquid has disappeared and the mixture has thickened, about 45 minutes.

Meanwhile, using a sharp knife, cut a circular lid off the top of the pumpkin. Save the lid. With a sharp-edged spoon, scrape out the seeds and the fiber.

Place the pumpkin in a large kettle and cover with boiling water. Simmer until the pumpkin is almost tender, about 30 minutes. The shell should still hold its shape well. Carefully remove the pumpkin from the water and drain.

Preheat the oven to 350° F.

Sprinkle the interior of the pumpkin with the remaining ½ teaspoon salt. Skim the fat off the cooled pork and spoon into the pumpkin. Place the filled pumpkin in a greased baking dish. Top with the lid. Bake for 1 hour. Allow the pumpkin to cool for 15 minutes before serving.

Preparation Time: 1¾ hours
Baking Time: 1 hour
Yield: 6–8 servings

This Pumpkin Tourtiere was so named because it is filled with the spicy pork filling of the traditional tourtière. Other fillings can be baked inside a pumpkin, including bread pudding.

Pumpkin Beef Stifado

Like most stews, this Greek-inspired dish improves with age.

½ cup pitted prunes, halved
½ cup dry red wine
4 tablespoons butter
3 tablespoons olive oil
1 medium-size onion, diced
2 garlic cloves, minced
2 tablespoons all-purpose
   unbleached flour
1 teaspoon salt
1 teaspoon pepper
¼ teaspoon cinnamon
¼ teaspoon ground cumin
⅛ teaspoon ground cloves
1½ pounds stew beef, cubed
1 cup carrots, diagonally sliced in
   ½-inch pieces
1½ cups thick tomato puree
1½ cups diced pumpkin
½ cup diced sweet red pepper
½ cup diced green pepper
1 bay leaf, crumbled
¼ cup pure maple syrup
½ cup water

Preheat the oven to 350° F.

Combine the prunes and wine and set aside.

Heat 1 tablespoon of the butter and 1 tablespoon of the oil in a sauté pan, and sauté the onion and garlic until limp, 3–5 minutes. Spread the onion and garlic over the bottom of a casserole dish.

Combine the flour, salt, pepper, cinnamon, cumin, and cloves in a bag. Add the beef to the bag a little at a time, and shake.

Add 1 tablespoon butter and 2 tablespoons oil to the sauté pan and sauté the beef until browned. Add the beef to the onions.

Melt the remaining 2 tablespoons butter, and briefly sauté the carrots. Add the carrots to the beef.

Add ¾ cup of the tomato puree to the sauté pan and heat gently, stirring and combining with all the meat juices. Pour over the beef.

Add to the casserole the pumpkin, red and green peppers, bay leaf, maple syrup, prunes and wine, the water, and the remaining ¾ cup tomato puree. Mix all the ingredients.

Bake, covered, for 1 hour and 20 minutes or until the meat is fork tender.

Preparation Time: 45 minutes
Baking Time: 1 hour, 20 minutes
Yield: 6–8 servings

Piquant Pumpkin Sauce

This sauce is wonderful on fish and chicken. Pour it over any firm white fish, such as haddock.

2 tablespoons vegetable oil
1½ cups diced onion
1 cup thick tomato puree
1 cup pumpkin puree
¼ cup sour cream or yogurt
2 tablespoons lime juice
1 teaspoon dried cilantro or 1
   tablespoon fresh
salt and pepper

In a medium-size saucepan, heat the oil and sauté the onion until limp, 3–5 minutes. Add the remaining ingredients and cook until the mixture is heated through. Add water if the sauce is too thick.

Preparation Time: 20 minutes
Yield: 6 servings (3 cups)

BAKED GOODS

No, I haven't included a recipe for pumpkin pie. You can find good ones in dozens of other cookbooks, including my Desserts from the Garden. But do try the bread, cheesecake, and apple crisp. They are delicious!

Pumpkin Apple Crisp

This dessert is best served warm — with whipped cream or ice cream, as a special treat.

4 cups diced pumpkin
4 cups peeled and diced apples
½ cup pure maple syrup
1 cup all-purpose unbleached flour
1 cup brown sugar
½ teaspoon cinnamon
¼ teaspoon nutmeg
½ teaspoon salt
½ cup butter

Preheat the oven to 350° F.

Butter a 9-inch by 13-inch baking dish and fill it with the pumpkin and apples. Pour the maple syrup over the top.

Combine the flour, sugar, spices, and salt.

Cut the butter into the flour mixture with a pastry cutter or food processor. Sprinkle over the pumpkin. Bake for 40 minutes or until the pumpkin tests tender with a fork. Serve warm.

Preparation Time: 30 minutes
Baking Time: 40 minutes
Yield: 6–8 servings

Pumpkin Cornmeal Yeasted Bread

½ cup warm water

2 tablespoons dried baker's yeast

½ cup plus 1 tablespoon honey

¾ cup milk

6–8 cups all-purpose unbleached flour or 3–4 cups all-purpose unbleached flour and 3–4 cups whole wheat flour

½ cup melted butter

1½ teaspoons salt

1 teaspoon cinnamon

½ teaspoon ground cloves

½ teaspoon ground ginger

1 cup currants

1 cup pumpkin puree

½ cup cornmeal

beaten egg, milk, or butter

In a small bowl, combine the water, yeast, and 1 tablespoon of the honey, and set aside until the yeast foams, about 5 minutes.

Then combine the milk, the remaining ½ cup honey, 1 cup of the flour, the melted butter, salt, spices, currants, pumpkin, and the yeast mixture. Stir well until the batter is smooth. Stir in the cornmeal and add the remaining flour, 1 cup at a time, stirring after each addition. When the dough is stiff, turn it out onto a floured board and knead it for 10 minutes. Place the dough in a greased bowl. Roll the dough in the bowl to cover the top with oil. Cover and set in a warm, draft-free spot to rise for 1½ hours, or until the dough has doubled.

Punch down the dough and divide it into 2 pieces. Shape the loaves and place them in greased 9-inch bread pans. Let the loaves rise until they are double in bulk,

about 45 minutes. Meanwhile, preheat the oven to 350° F. Bake for 45 minutes.

To get a shiny top on your bread, brush the loaf with a beaten egg or milk as it goes into the oven, or brush with butter as it comes out of the oven. Cool the loaves for 10 minutes in the pan; then tip out and cool.

Preparation Time: 35 minutes plus 2¼ hours rising time
Baking Time: 45 minutes
Yield: 2 large loaves

Pumpkin Orange Cheesecake

You may have seen pumpkin cheesecakes, but have you ever seen the pumpkin in the crust? Try this.

¾ cup crumbled sliced almonds

¾ cup grated carrot

5 eggs

3 cups grated pumpkin

6 tablespoons all-purpose unbleached flour

1 teaspoon grated orange rind

½ teaspoon minced fresh ginger root

1¼ cups sugar

8 ounces cream cheese at room temperature

1 cup sour cream

½ teaspoon grated orange or lemon rind

¼ teaspoon salt

Preheat the oven to 350° F.

Set aside some almonds or grated carrot for the top of the cheesecake. Beat 3 of the eggs with ¾ cup of the sugar, and fold in the pumpkin, carrot, flour, orange rind, ginger root, almonds. With a fork, spread this mixture in a greased 9-inch

Orange and pumpkin make a great flavor combination. Try it with this two-layer cheesecake.

springform pan. Bake on a cookie sheet for 40 minutes. The center will have a custard-like consistency.

Beat the cream cheese in a food processor or mixing bowl until smooth. Add the remaining ½ cup sugar, the remaining 2 eggs, and the rest of the ingredients.

Pour the cream cheese mixture into the baked pumpkin shell. Sprinkle additional sliced almonds or grated carrots on top. Bake for 45 minutes or until firm. Chill.

Preparation Time: 30 minutes
Baking Time: 1 hour, 25 minutes
Chilling Time: 2 hours
Yield: 6–8 servings

Radishes

Salads are Just for Starters With This Surprisingly Versatile Root Crop

Radishes are great in green salads, and they make lovely garnishes, right? Wrong, if that's all you think radishes are good for!

A few years ago, I learned to plant radishes as a companion crop for just about everything in my garden—carrots, melons, onions, lettuce, parsnips—you name it. The radishes come up quickly and mark the rows; they break up the soil, acting like natural cultivators; and they distract bugs.

One day I asked a gardening friend who also plants radishes throughout his garden, "What do you *do* with all your radishes?"

He smiled and said, "I eat some. Compost some."

I'm happy to compost the tops of my radishes (they are prickly and bitter), but when I look at something edible, I want to *cook* it, not throw it out.

I Began My Quest For The Ultimate Radish Recipe

In other cultures, radishes are prepared in many different ways. The French make a Radish Butter (see page 238) that is just delicious served on dark bread. The Japanese and Chinese grow a white radish that is called "daikon" and is often available in American supermarkets. I like to add daikon to stir fries with other vegetables, which is how they are traditionally served. I use daikon and my own homegrown white icicle radishes interchangeably.

In addition to the familiar red and white radishes, there is a black fall radish which is supposed to store well in root cellars. I've never grown those. I think I get enough radishes during the summer, which is when I especially appreciate the crisp "hot" flavor radishes add to a dish. I like to make successive plantings of radishes, so I have them all summer long.

Radishes do vary in taste. Sometimes the same variety of radish, planted on the same day, in the same garden, will vary in flavor. Some radishes will be sharp and hot, others bland or sweet. Radishes become bitter when they overmature, and often the centers become pithy. Then I don't hesitate to compost them. With radishes growing in such abundance, and there being no satisfactory way to preserve the red and white radishes for winter eating, I choose only the best to eat and cook fresh.

I interplant radishes with other vegetables throughout my garden. They are great for marking the rows. And once I harvest these radishes, the carrots will have plenty of room to grow.

Harvesting and Storage Tips

Harvest spring (red and white) radishes as needed for best flavor. But don't let the radishes go to seed in the garden, or become overgrown and pithy. If necessary, refrigerate whole radishes, with greens removed, in a perforated plastic bag for 1–3 weeks.

Winter (black) radishes can be stored in a root cellar packed in wet sand.

Radish purees, for making soups and dips can be stored for up to a month in the freezer. To make a radish puree, parboil or steam whole or halved radishes for 5 minutes. Process in a blender or food processor fitted with a steel blade until smooth. Add water if necessary.

Black radish

Red radish

Daikon

Icicle radish

RADISHES AT A GLANCE

Yields

1 pound fresh radishes equals
   3 cups whole
or
   3½ cups sliced
or
   4 cups grated
or
   2 cups pureed

Preparation Tips

If you want to intensify the red color of the radishes in your dish, add a little lemon juice just before the cooking is completed.

A food processor takes the labor out of slicing and grating radishes.

Red radishes keep their color better when steamed than boiled.

Black radishes require a longer cooking time than other radishes, so adjust cooking times accordingly.

When radishes begin to go by, they develop black spots. It is okay to trim away the bad spots. I prefer to compost them and harvest new ones.

When planning meals with radishes, think of them as just another root vegetable.

Young tender radishes are best in salads or sliced into sandwiches. A favorite combination is cream cheese, sprouts, scallions, and radishes on pumpernickel.

But don't forget to try cooked radishes.

Steamed Radishes. Steam whole radishes for 8 minutes over boiling water. Top with a cream or cheese sauce (pages 305–306).

Radishes and Peas. Steam sliced radishes with baby peas for 2–4 minutes and top with an Herb Butter (page 160). Herbs that go especially well with radishes are mint, parsley, dill, marjoram, and summer savory.

Stir Fried Radishes. Radishes make a great homegrown substitute for water chestnuts. Use them in any recipe calling for water chestnuts. Or add them to your favorite stir fry. Or stir fry radishes as a side dish. Flavor the stir fry with garlic, scallions, or coriander. Season to taste with tamari or soy sauce.

Radishes and Scalloped Potatoes. Add sliced red radishes to your favorite scalloped potato recipe. The sauce will take on a subtle pink color.

Red radish garnishes: A gardener's signature

Wash the radishes. Trim off the tops (leaving a few small leaves if desired) and the tips of the roots. Scrape off any root hairs with the edge of your paring knife.

Radish Roses. Starting at the top of the radish, use the sharp tip of your paring knife to carve out 5–6 thin petals, leaving the petals attached about ¼ inch from the tip of the radish. Do not detach the petals. If you like, carve out a second petal layer inside the first petal layer, staggering the edges of the second layer with the first petals. Chill the radishes in ice water for a few hours so the petals will open.

Radish Fans. Using a sharp paring knife, cut most of the way through the radish with a series of slices as close together as possible. Chill the radishes in ice water for a few hours so the fans will open.

Radish Peonies. Make a radish fan. Then turn the radish 90 degrees and make a second series of cuts perpendicular to the first. Chill in ice water for several hours.

Radish Stars. Thinly slice a radish. Notch each slice, cutting to the center of the slice. Slide two slices together at the notch to form a star.

From left to right: radish stars, roses, fans, and peonies.

1. Make a radish fan.

Four or five sets of rose petals can be carved around an average-sized radish.

2. Turn 90 degrees and slice again for radish peonies.

APPETIZERS

My favorite appetizer of all is fresh radishes and salt—very refreshing after some hot work in the garden.

Radish Butter

Radishes can be transformed into this delicious spread in less time than it takes to harvest them.

Serve Radish Butter on pumpernickel or a similar dark bread, and it is sure to become a classic in your home, too.

½ cup butter at room temperature
½ cup sliced radishes
1 teaspoon lemon juice

In a food processor, cream the butter, and add the radishes and lemon juice. Using the pulsing action, process just enough to finely chop the radishes. Transfer the mixture to a bowl and serve.

Preparation Time: 5 minutes
Yield: ¾ cup

This Radish Butter makes a nice light appetizer after a hot day. Serve it with white wine or chilled tomato juice. The Radish Butter should be served at room temperature. If you made it up in advance, be sure to give it a good stir before setting it out; water tends to separate out of the mixture.

Pink Radish Spread

This is a mild spread, delicious on crackers or served as a dip for raw vegetables.

1 tablespoon butter
1½ cups diced onion
4 cups sliced red radishes
½ cup mayonnaise
½ cup yogurt
1 tablespoon lemon juice

Melt the butter in a sauté pan, and sauté the onion and radishes until both are translucent and wilted, 4–6 minutes. Transfer the vegetables to a food processor or blender and blend until smooth. Cool to room temperature and add the remaining ingredients. Allow the spread to sit for 30 minutes before serving.

Preparation Time: 20 minutes
Cooking Time: 8–10 minutes
Chilling Time: 30 minutes
Yield: 2 cups

Chili Tomato Radishes

I serve these radishes as a relish.

1½ cups tomato puree or crushed whole tomatoes
1 cup diced onion
2 garlic cloves, minced
1 tablespoon minced fresh basil or 1 teaspoon dried
1 tablespoon fresh crumbled oregano or 1 teaspoon dried
2 teaspoons ground cumin
1 teaspoon chili powder
2 teaspoons lemon juice
2 tablespoons sesame oil
¼ cup white vinegar
2 cups sliced radishes

Gently simmer all the ingredients except the radishes for 20 minutes. Pour the hot sauce over the sliced radishes, chill and serve.

Preparation Time: 20 minutes
Cooking Time: 20 minutes
Chilling Time: 2 hours
Yield: 6 servings

Cream of Radish Soup

This soup has my vote as the dish that uses the most radishes all at once — 8 cups of sliced radishes. It is so good, I can't imagine a gardening season without it.

5 tablespoons butter
1 cup diced onion
8 cups sliced red radishes
3 tablespoons all-purpose
**   unbleached flour**
3 cups milk
2 teaspoons ground anise
salt and pepper

Eight cups of radishes go into this delicate anise-flavored Cream of Radish Soup!

Melt 2 tablespoons of the butter in a large soup pot, and sauté the onion and radishes until both are translucent and limp, 3–5 minutes.

In a separate saucepan, melt the remaining 3 tablespoons butter, and stir in the flour to make a smooth paste. Add the milk a little at a time, stirring well after each addition to prevent lumps.

Put the vegetables into a food processor or blender and blend until smooth.

Combine the vegetables and white sauce in the soup pot and add the anise. Season to taste with salt and pepper. Reheat and serve.

Preparation Time: 25 minutes
Cooking Time: 15 minutes
Yield: 6 servings

During the summer, I automatically toss sliced or grated radishes into salads. They taste wonderful in every kind of salad.

Radishes and Fennel Au Grecque

¼ cup olive oil
¼ cup lemon juice
2 tablespoons tarragon vinegar
¼ cup water
½ teaspoon ground coriander
1 garlic clove, minced
¼ teaspoon salt
⅛ teaspoon pepper
3 cups sliced red radishes
1½ cups diced fresh fennel bulb
2 tablespoons minced fresh parsley
lettuce

In a small saucepan, combine the olive oil, lemon juice, vinegar, water, coriander, garlic, salt, and pepper. Heat until boiling.

Combine the radishes, fennel, and parsley in a bowl and pour the hot sauce over this mixture. Set aside to marinate for at least 1 hour, tossing occasionally to coat. Serve on a bed of lettuce.

Preparation Time: 20 minutes
Marinating Time: 1 hour
Yield: 6 servings

Spinach and Radish Salad

I call this my "early season salad." The spinach and radishes are ready for harvest at the same time. It's a terrific combination.

¼ cup olive oil
2 teaspoons anchovy paste
3 tablespoons wine vinegar
1 teaspoon dried oregano
1 teaspoon dried basil
½ teaspoon salt
pepper
½ cup sliced red onion
1½ cups sliced white or red radishes
10 cups torn spinach (bite-size pieces)
½ cup sliced black olives

Combine the olive oil, anchovy paste, vinegar, oregano, basil, salt, and pepper. Add the onion and radishes and marinate for at least 1 hour, or overnight.

Just before you are ready to serve the salad, combine the spinach and olives. Pour the radish mixture and marinade over the spinach and toss to coat. Serve immediately.

Preparation Time: 20 minutes
Marinating Time: at least 1 hour
Yield: 6–8 servings

Radishes do lose some of their sharp, biting flavor, and red radishes lose color, when cooked. For this reason, many people prefer raw radishes. Go slow when introducing cooked radishes to the uninitiated.

Oriental Radish And Chicken Salad

This dish could also be served hot as a main course with rice. Chili paste with garlic is a sauce available at most Oriental food stores.

4 tablespoons tamari or soy sauce
2 tablespoons white vinegar
6 tablespoons water
4 teaspoons honey
2 boneless chicken breasts, diced
2 tablespoons peanut oil
2 cups diced white or red radishes
1 pound sugar snap peas or edible pea pods, trimmed
½ teaspoon chili paste with garlic

In a small bowl, combine 2 tablespoons of the tamari, 1 tablespoon of the vinegar, 3 tablespoons of the water, and 2 teaspoons of the honey. Marinate the chicken in this mixture while you prepare the vegetables.

Heat the oil in a wok or large frying pan and stir fry the chicken until it is almost cooked, 3–5 minutes. Add the radishes and pea pods, and continue to stir fry until the pea pods are bright green, 2–3 minutes.

Remove the mixture to a bowl to cool. Mix the remaining tamari, vinegar, water, honey, and the chili paste and pour over the salad. Chill and serve cold.

Preparation Time: 25 minutes
Cooking Time: 8–10 minutes
Chilling Time: at least 1 hour
Yield: 6 servings

SIDE DISHES AND MAIN DISHES

Think of radishes as an ordinary root crop, not a salad vegetable, and you'll be amazed at all the ways there are to prepare them.

Radish Stir Fry

1 tablespoon vegetable oil
1 large garlic clove, minced
½ cup sliced scallions, including green tops
4 cups grated radishes
2 tablespoons tamari or soy sauce

Heat the oil in a wok or a large frying pan and stir fry the garlic, scallions, and radishes for 3–5 minutes, or until the radishes are tender crisp. Add the tamari and stir fry to coat. Serve immediately.

Preparation Time: 10 minutes
Cooking Time: 3–5 minutes
Yield: 4–6 servings

Radishes and Potatoes In Parsley Butter

Peel and cube 4 cups potatoes and chop 2 cups white radishes. Boil in water to cover for 15–20 minutes or until the potatoes are just tender; drain. Melt 3 tablespoons of butter in a sauté pan and sauté 1 tablespoon minced fresh parsley or 1 tablespoon minced fresh chives. Toss with the warm radishes and potatoes and serve. Serves 4–6.

Beef Stew With Radishes

2 pounds beef stew meat
½ cup all-purpose unbleached flour
½ teaspoon dried basil
½ teaspoon dried thyme
½ teaspoon ground rosemary
1 crumbled bay leaf
½ teaspoon pepper
1 teaspoon salt
2½ cups thick tomato puree
½ cup beef broth
½ cup medium dry red wine
  (Burgundy is recommended)
1 cup diced onion
1–1½ cups quartered mushrooms
1½ cups sliced or quartered baby
  carrots
1½ cups small radishes

Preheat the oven to 325° F.
Slice the beef into 1-inch cubes. Combine the flour, basil, thyme, rosemary, bay leaf, pepper, and salt in a bag. Add the beef cubes and shake until the meat is well coated.

In a large casserole with a tight-fitting lid, heat the tomato puree, beef broth, and wine on top of the stove. Add the seasoned beef mixture, including the flour. Add the onion and mushrooms. Bake, covered, for 1½ hours. Add the carrots and radishes and bake for 30 minutes more.

Preparation Time: 25 minutes
Baking Time: 2 hours
Yield: 6–8 servings

Radish Stuffing for Whole Fish

Red radishes look best in this recipe, but white or peeled black radishes can be used.

You can use this stuffing for pork chops, or double the recipe and use it to stuff a roasting chicken.

2 tablespoons butter
½ cup diced onion
1½ cups chopped radishes
1 tablespoon minced fresh basil or
  1 teaspoon dried
¾ teaspoon ground rosemary
1½ cups ½-inch bread cubes
½ cup minced fresh parsley
salt and pepper
1 whole 3–4 pound fish or several
  smaller fish

Preheat the oven to 325° F.
Melt the butter in a sauté pan, and sauté the onion, radishes, basil, and rosemary until the vegetables are limp, 3–5 minutes. Remove the mixture from the heat and add the bread cubes and parsley. Season to taste with salt and pepper. Pack the stuffing into the fish. Place the fish on a greased baking sheet and loosely cover with aluminum foil. Bake for 20–40 minutes.

Preparation Time: 25 minutes
Baking Time: 20–40 minutes
Yield: 6–8 servings

Mashed Potatoes And Radishes

Boil equal amounts of potatoes and radishes together until soft. Mash together and season with butter, salt, and pepper.

Don't be intimidated by a whole fish! It is as easy to stuff as a chicken, and even easier to serve. Just carve into wide slices and serve with a spatula.

Potato Pancakes With Radishes

Grate together 4 large potatoes, 1 medium-size onion, and 2 cups whole radishes. Add 3 beaten eggs, ½ cup all-purpose unbleached flour, ½ teaspoon salt, and ¼ teaspoon pepper. Mix well and fry in small amounts in oil or butter over medium heat until browned on both sides. Serve hot. Serves 4–6.

Spinach

Plant Wide Rows Both Spring and Fall — You'll Finally Have Enough!

Spinach is my favorite vegetable, and I have plenty of reasons for making this statement. Above all, I love the flavor of spinach: cooked or raw. I enjoy preparing it in both fancy dishes and simple ones. Finally, spinach is low in calories and high in vitamins and minerals.

So I look forward each spring to those first tender, young spinach leaves that make their way from the garden to the table, even before the soil has warmed up. Those first spinach leaves make the best salads.

The spinach season is all too short for me. Spinach has an unfortunate tendency to bolt and flower during hot weather. Once it has flowered, the leaves become bitter and the spinach is not worth eating.

New Zealand Spinach Is No Substitute

When I first heard about New Zealand spinach, I was delighted. I read that New Zealand spinach would keep producing all summer long, even in the heat, and that it tastes and cooks just like regular spinach. Well, I've grown New Zealand spinach, and I think it compares to spinach as well as carob compares to chocolate. Nothing substitutes for the real thing!

New Zealand spinach has an acceptable flavor in cooked dishes, but I think the texture is rather fuzzy and unpleasant. I prefer to savor fresh spinach all the more for its short growing season, and freeze extra for year-round eating.

Spinach is available in the supermarket all year, but the quality tends to be poor — the leaves are often slimey and attached to huge, tough stems. I prefer to rely on my frozen spinach for most cooked dishes, in the winter.

Having extra to freeze is no problem when you plant in wide rows. Because spinach is mostly water, a bushel of harvested spinach cooks down to just a few quarts. So you have to harvest many bushels if you want to have enough frozen spinach to get you through the winter. I like to plant a spring and a fall crop — to have plenty for eating fresh and freezing at the beginning and end of the gardening season.

I usually plant a fall crop of spinach, as well as a spring crop, so I can harvest as much spinach as possible. The fall crop is every bit as tender as the spring one.

Harvesting Tips

Begin to harvest spinach as soon as there are leaves large enough to eat.

Harvest by cutting the whole plant back to an inch of height while the leaves are still small and tender. More will grow back.

Stop harvesting when the plant begins to set seeds.

Plant a second crop when the weather is cooler.

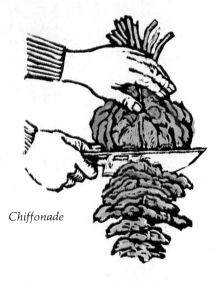

Chiffonade

Yields

1 pound fresh spinach equals
  24 cups loosely packed, washed, and trimmed leaves
or
  16 cups washed, trimmed, and finely chopped leaves
or
  3 cups trimmed and steamed (fresh or frozen) leaves

SPINACH AT A GLANCE

Never Overcook Spinach!

I briefly steam or sauté spinach just to wilt it and reduce its volume. **Spinach can be steamed with just the water that clings to the leaves after washing.** Or you can add spinach to a little butter, sesame oil, or olive oil in a large pan and toss to coat. Cover and steam briefly to wilt the spinach.

Cooking Times
  Steam: 3–5 minutes
  Blanch: 2–4 minutes
  Sauté or stir fry: 3–5 minutes
  For a variation, sauté the spinach with garlic, chives, onion, fresh basil, marjoram, thyme, oregano, tarragon, curry, or ginger.

Or toss steamed or sautéed spinach with grated cheese, lemon juice, ham or bacon bits, or tamari or soy sauce.

I don't like to put heavy sauces on spinach, but occasionally, I simmer about a pound of spinach in ¼ cup heavy cream until the spinach is wilted. Then I season with salt and pepper.

Raw spinach can be finely sliced (chiffonade) and added to soup at the last minute.

There's no secret to washing spinach. It just requires patience.

I fill my sink with lukewarm water (it's easier on the hands), and swish the spinach around. Then I lift the spinach out of the water and into a colander. If the spinach is particularly dirty, I fill the sink with clean water and repeat the process.

To trim large spinach leaves, I cut off the stems and peel the leaf from the center vein, which tends to be tough.

Spinach Salad Ideas

Here are a few combination ideas and a word of advice: Spinach salads wilt very quickly. Add the salad dressing JUST before serving.

Spinach Orange Salad. Combine chopped spinach, orange segments, sliced radishes or water chestnuts, sliced almonds, and apples. Toss with a Yogurt Cardamom Salad Dressing (page 303).

Spinach Caesar Salad Dressing. Combine spinach, cherry tomatoes, sliced red onions, and croutons. Toss with a Caesar Salad Dressing (page 303).

Spinach Celery Salad. Combine spinach, sliced celery, and sliced apples. Toss with a Blue Cheese Dressing (page 306).

1. *Squeeze out excess moisture.*

2. *The dough forms a ball.*

3. *Roll to ⅛ inch thick.*

4. *Cut noodles the desired width.*

A hand-cranked pasta roller takes the effort out of rolling.

Making pasta is easy with a food processor: The machine does the kneading for you

Spinach pasta only takes an hour to make, and that includes a half hour to rest the dough. This recipe serves 4–6.

Squeeze all the water out of ½ cup steamed spinach, condensing it to ⅓ cup. In a food processor, combine the spinach, 2 eggs, 1 tablespoon olive oil, and ½ teaspoon salt. Process to blend. Add 2 cups all-purpose unbleached flour and process to blend. Using the pulsing action, process just enough to form a ball. Allow the dough to rest for 30 minutes before rolling it out.

On a well-floured board, roll out the dough to a thickness of no more than ⅛ inch. Slice to make lasagna, fettucine, or linguine.

Lasagna noodles are cut into strips 3 inches by 9 inches. Fettucine are long noodles cut ¼-inch wide. Linguine noodles are cut ⅛-inch wide.

Machine powered or hand cranked pasta machines are necessary to make round shapes.

To cook immediately, boil the pasta in plenty of boiling salted water for 2 minutes, until the pasta is just tender.

To store, hang the pasta on a drying rack for 3–4 hours. Store in a moisture-proof jar in the refrigerator for 2–3 days or in the freezer for longer storage. To cook dried pasta, boil for 3–5 minutes in plenty of boiling salted water.

Spinach Onion Soup

The success of this vegetarian soup is all in browning the onions well to develop the fullest possible flavor.

2 tablespoons vegetable oil
2 tablespoons butter
1 tablespoon fresh thyme or
   1 teaspoon dried
7 cups sliced onions
¼ cup all-purpose unbleached flour
6 cups water
2 bay leaves
1¼ cups thick tomato puree
½ cup dry white wine
5 tablespoons tamari or soy sauce
10 cups finely chopped spinach
grated parmesan cheese

In a large soup pot, heat the oil and butter, and sauté the thyme and onion until the onions are golden brown and very soft, about 15 minutes. Sprinkle the flour over the onions and stir to blend. Add the water, bay leaves, tomato puree, wine, and tamari. Simmer the soup for 30 minutes. Remove the bay leaves. Add the spinach during the last 5–7 minutes of cooking time. Cook just long enough to wilt. Sprinkle parmesan cheese on each serving.

Preparation Time: 20 minutes
Cooking Time: 45 minutes
Yield: 6–8 servings

APPETIZER

Spinach Boursin

12 cups spinach
½ cup sliced scallions
1 large garlic clove, minced
1 pound cream cheese at room
   temperature
2 teaspoons minced fresh basil
1 teaspoon fresh marjoram or
   ¼ teaspoon dried
1 teaspoon fresh thyme or
   ¼ teaspoon dried
1 teaspoon fresh oregano or
   ¼ teaspoon dried
½ teaspoon Worcestershire sauce
1 teaspoon lemon juice

Steam the spinach over boiling water until wilted, 3–5 minutes.

Combine the scallions and the garlic in a food processor and process until finely chopped. Cut the cream cheese into cubes and add to the processor. Add the herbs, Worcestershire sauce, and lemon juice. Process until well blended.

Squeeze the spinach between your hands to remove as much liquid as possible. This should condense the spinach to about ¾ cup. Add the spinach to the cream cheese mixture in the processor and process until completely mixed. Spoon the cheese into a bowl lined with spinach leaves. Serve at room temperature.

Preparation Time: 10 minutes
Yield: 6–8 servings

SOUPS

Spinach is the ideal summer soup ingredient because it needs to be cooked only briefly.

Garden Green Soup

I cook this soup for less than 10 minutes, so the vegetables retain their "garden green" flavors and colors.

2 tablespoons butter
¾ cup chopped scallions
1 garlic clove, minced
4 cups peas
4 tablespoons fresh basil or
   4 teaspoons dried
½ cup minced fresh parsley
16 cups spinach
6 cups chicken broth
1 tablespoon lemon juice
¼ teaspoon white pepper

In a large soup pot, melt the butter, and sauté the scallions and garlic until limp, but not browned. Add the remaining ingredients and cook until the spinach is limp. Cool the soup slightly. Process in a blender or food processor until smooth. Reheat and serve.

Preparation Time: 20 minutes
Cooking Time: 5–8 minutes
Yield: 6–8 servings

SALADS

Don't forget to add spinach to your regular green salads.

Spinach Sugar Snap Salad

Take the bean sprouts from an "indoor kitchen garden," add baby spinach and young pea pods, and serve with a gardener's pride. Radishes or 1½ cups cooked chicken can be added if desired.

1 cup pea pods (Sugar Snap or Snow Pea), cut diagonally in halves or thirds
4 cups chopped spinach
½–¾ cup mung bean sprouts
½ cup vegetable oil
3 tablespoons lemon juice
2 tablespoons honey
2 teaspoons minced fresh ginger root
1 teaspoon curry powder
½ teaspoon white or black pepper
½ teaspoon salt

Steam the pea pods for 1 minute. Plunge into cold water to stop the cooking. Drain.
Combine the spinach, pea pods, and bean sprouts in a salad bowl. Combine the remaining ingredients in a blender or food processor, and process until mixed. Pour the dressing over the salad, toss, and serve immediately.

Preparation Time: 15 minutes
Yield: 4–6 servings

Hold the leaf in one hand and strip away the tough stem with the other.

SIDE DISHES AND MAIN DISHES

Tarragon Carrots and Spinach

Baby carrots and spinach cook quickly in this tender vegetable dish. Don't overcook!

1 tablespoon butter
2 cups baby carrots, cut in sticks
¼ cup light cream
1 tablespoon minced fresh tarragon or 1½ teaspoons dried
½ teaspoon ground rosemary
20 cups spinach
salt and pepper

In a large sauté pan, melt the butter and add the carrots, cream, tarragon, and rosemary. Cover the pan and simmer for 2 minutes. Stir in the spinach and cover again for 2–3 minutes, or until the spinach is wilted, stir occasionally. Season to taste with salt and pepper. Serve hot.

Preparation Time: 15 minutes
Cooking Time: 5–7 minutes
Yield: 4–6 servings

Spinach Stir Fry

In a wok or large sauté pan, heat 2 teaspoons of sesame oil and 2 teaspoons of vegetable oil. Stir fry 1 large minced garlic clove and ½ cup of diced onion until the onion is limp, 3–5 minutes. Add 24 cups spinach and stir fry until the spinach is limp, about 5 minutes. Add 1 tablespoon tamari or soy sauce and toss to coat. Serve immediately. This recipe serves 4–6.

Creamed Spinach With Garlic

24 cups spinach
2 tablespoons butter
2 large garlic cloves, minced
2 tablespoons all-purpose unbleached flour
1 cup milk
2 tablespoons heavy cream
¼ teaspoon dried marjoram or thyme
salt and pepper

Steam the spinach until limp, 3–5 minutes.
In a small saucepan, melt the butter and sauté the garlic. Stir in the flour to make a thick paste. Add the milk a little at a time, stirring well after each addition to prevent lumps. Transfer the sauce and the spinach to a food processor or blender and process until well blended. Reheat the spinach. Add the cream and marjoram, and season to taste with salt and pepper. Serve hot.

Preparation Time: 10 minutes
Cooking Time: 10 minutes
Yield: 4 servings

Chicken and Spinach Pastry

I usually put a piece of foil on the shelf below this tart as it bakes. Springform pans have a tendency to leak.

3 tablespoons vegetable oil
2½ cups diced onions
1½ cups grated carrots
1 tablespoon minced fresh dill
4 cups diced cooked chicken
½ cup sour cream
1 tablespoon lemon juice
1 teaspoon Dijon-style mustard
salt and pepper
30 cups spinach
2 garlic cloves, minced
1 tablespoon minced fresh basil
2 cups grated Swiss cheese
1 egg, beaten
½ cup butter, melted
1 pound filo dough

Preheat the oven to 350° F.

Heat 2 tablespoons of the vegetable oil in a sauté pan and sauté 1½ cups of the onions, the carrots, and dill until the onions are limp, 3–5 minutes.

Combine the vegetables, chicken, sour cream, lemon juice, and mustard in a bowl. Season to taste with salt and pepper.

Steam the spinach until limp, 3–5 minutes. Drain well.

Heat the remaining tablespoon of oil, and sauté the remaining 1 cup of onion with the garlic and basil. Mix the spinach, the onion and garlic, the cheese, and the egg. Set aside.

Brush a 9-inch springform pan with butter and line it with 1 sheet of filo dough. Brush the dough with butter. Continue to layer 8–10 sheets of filo dough in the pan with butter. Spoon in the chicken, then the spinach. Fold the corners of the dough over the spinach. Top with 3–4 more sheets of dough, cut or folded to fit the round pan.

Bake for 1 hour or until golden brown. Invert the pastry onto a serving platter. Allow to sit for 10 minutes. Cut into wedges and serve.

Preparation Time: 45 minutes
Baking Time: 1 hour
Yield: 8 servings

Greek Spinach Casserole

1 tablespoon vegetable oil
1 cup diced onion
2 pounds ground beef or lamb
¾ cup tomato puree
½ cup dry red wine
¾ teaspoon cinnamon
1 tablespoon minced fresh dill
4 cups cooked rice
1 egg, beaten
salt and pepper
30 cups spinach
3 tablespoons butter
1 tablespoon minced fresh chives
3 tablespoons all-purpose
   unbleached flour
1⅔ cups milk
1 cup crumbled feta cheese
¼ cup grated parmesan cheese

Preheat the oven to 400° F.

Heat the oil in a large sauté pan, and sauté the onion until translucent, about 3 minutes. Add the beef and brown it, breaking it up with a spoon. Add the tomato puree, wine, cinnamon, and dill. Cook for about 15 minutes to blend the flavors. Mix in the rice and the eggs, and add salt and pepper to taste. Spoon this mixture into a greased 9-inch by 13-inch baking dish.

Steam the spinach until wilted, 3–5 minutes. Drain. Cover the meat and rice mixture with the spinach.

Melt the butter in a saucepan. Sauté the chives briefly. Sprinkle on the flour and stir to make a thick paste. Add the milk a little at a time, stirring well after each addition to prevent lumps. Add the feta cheese and cook just enough to melt the cheese. Pour the sauce evenly over the casserole to cover. Sprinkle parmesan cheese over the top of the casserole. Bake for 30–40 minutes or until golden brown. Let the casserole rest for 10 minutes, then cut into squares, and serve.

Preparation Time: 35 minutes
Baking Time: 30–40 minutes
Yield: 8 servings

Spinach Pizza

By the time tomatoes are ripe, spinach is usually out of season.

1 tablespoon yeast
1⅓ cups warm water
4 cups sifted all-purpose
   unbleached flour
5 tablespoons olive oil
1 teaspoon salt
2 cups Italian sausage (hot), casing
   removed
1¼ cups chopped onion
2 garlic cloves, minced
¾ cup chopped green pepper
1½ cups sliced mushrooms
½ teaspoon dried oregano
½ teaspoon dried thyme
8 cups spinach
salt and pepper
3 cups grated mozzarella
½ cup grated parmesan cheese

Would you believe there are no tomatoes in this Spinach Pizza? It's an "early season" pizza—before the tomatoes are ripe.

Creamed Spinach With Celery and Mushrooms

This dish travels well and reheats easily—a great dish to bring to a potluck supper.

3 tablespoons butter
2 tablespoons vegetable oil
1½ cups chopped onion
2 cups chopped celery, including
   some leaves
2 cups sliced mushrooms
2 tablespoons all-purpose
   unbleached flour
¾ cup light cream
¾ cup milk
salt and pepper
12–14 cups spinach
¼ cup bread crumbs

Preheat the oven to 350° F.

In a large saucepan, heat 2 tablespoons of the butter and 2 tablespoons oil, and sauté the onion, celery, and mushrooms until limp, 3–5 minutes.

Sprinkle the flour over the sautéed vegetables. Stir and add the cream and milk a little at a time, stirring well after each addition to prevent lumps. Season to taste with salt and pepper. Add the spinach and continue cooking, stirring occasionally, until the spinach has wilted, about 5 minutes.

Transfer the mixture to a buttered, 2-quart casserole dish. Melt the remaining 1 tablespoon butter, and combine with the bread crumbs. Sprinkle the crumbs over the casserole. Bake uncovered for 20 minutes. Serve hot.

Preparation Time: 30 minutes
Baking Time: 20 minutes
Yield: 4–6 servings

Sprinkle the yeast over the warm water and set aside until the yeast foams. Add the flour, 2 tablespoons of the olive oil, and the salt. Mix to form a ball. Knead for 5–10 minutes on a floured board. Cover and let rise for 30 minutes while you prepare the filling.

Brown the sausage, drain, and set aside. Heat 2 more tablespoons of olive oil and sauté the onion, garlic, green pepper, mushrooms, oregano, and thyme, until the onion is limp and the green pepper is tender crisp, 3–5 minutes. Add the spinach, and sauté until it is wilted, about 2 minutes. Remove from the heat. Season to taste with salt and pepper.

Preheat the oven to 475° F.

Roll the dough out to fit a large cookie sheet or roasting pan, forming a ¾-inch edge. Sprinkle half the mozzarella cheese over the dough. Spread the spinach mixture over the mozzarella. Sprinkle the remaining mozzarella and the parmesan cheese on top. Grind fresh pepper and crumble a pinch of oregano on top. Drizzle 1 tablespoon oil over the top of the pizza. Bake for 30 minutes.

Preparation Time: 45 minutes
Baking Time: 30 minutes
Yield: 6–8 servings

Summer Squash

A Never Ending Search for New Recipes Means You **Can** Keep Up With the Harvest

Zucchini recipes! Can anyone ever have enough? Not only is zucchini a marvelously prolific vegetable, it is also a vegetable that, well, one can grow tired of, if served the same way day after day.

I'm quite sure that I could never tire of fresh asparagus, or freshly shelled peas, or spinach sautéed with a little garlic and tamari. But zucchini? I could get tired of zucchini before I run out of it—if I didn't invent new recipes every year.

Actually, it's *easy* to invent zucchini and summer squash recipes. The vegetables themselves are rather bland, which means you can use your entire repertoire of herbs and spices to accent a dish. Summer squashes require very short cooking times, so you don't want to try anything too complicated. Still, you can make everything from soups to breads with summer squash and zucchini.

Two Rules for Cooking Summer Squash

The first rule is one I *try* very hard to follow: never cook an overgrown summer squash or zucchini. Compost it! The ideal size for summer squash and zucchini is 3–6 inches. Anything larger than 12 inches will have huge seeds and watery flesh and just isn't worth cooking. (If I break this rule, it is usually when I am preparing a dish that calls for grated squash like the Zucchini Chocolate Cake on page 261. Then I'll seed the squash before grating.) The ideal size for patty pan squash is about 4 inches in diameter.

The second rule should never be broken: Don't overcook summer squash. Nothing is worse than mushy vegetables, and these vegetables get mushy fast.

I use "summer squash" to include zucchini, yellow squash, crookneck, and patty pan. These squashes can be used interchangeably in recipes. I sometimes indicate a preference for a specific variety, but that is usually because of its color. In addition to the common summer squash types, there are several varieties of winter squash, Jersey Golden Acorn among them, that can be harvested immature and cooked as summer squash. I haven't tried those squash yet. I have my hands full with zucchini.

Pick those summer squash when they are still young and tender. This may mean harvesting every day. But it is worth it. Young squash are more tender and have more flavor than overgrown squash.

SUMMER SQUASH AT A GLANCE

Yields

1 pound summer squash equals
  4 cups sliced, diced, or
  julienne-sliced
or
  3½ cups grated (after salting,
  this becomes 1¾ cups)

One day's extra growth can turn a baby squash into a monster.

Don't leave summer squash on the vine. Summer squash grows very rapidly and must be harvested while small for the best flavor and texture. Harvest by slicing through the stem when the squash is between 3 and 6 inches long.

Summer squash can be stored in the refrigerator for 3–5 days.

Some Folks Freeze Extra Squash

You can blanch and freeze sliced squash, but I really don't like the result — it's mushy.

I do freeze grated squash to use up leftovers and to have some on hand for baking throughout the year. When using frozen grated squash, defrost and squeeze out excess moisture before using in a recipe.

Baby Squash Make Delicious Eating

Tender young squash can be steamed and served with an herb butter (pages 160 and 304), or sautéed with butter and herbs such as dill, thyme, basil, mint, fennel, chives, parsley, oregano, marjoram, chervil, or tarragon.

The Tomato Fennel Sauce (page 306) and the Tomato Paprika Sauce (page 306) are excellent with steamed squash.

Or deep fry breaded squash fingers and serve as an appetizer or side dish.

Cooking Times

Steam (whole, diced, or sliced):
  2–5 minutes
Blanch (whole, diced, or sliced):
  2–5 minutes
Sauté or stir fry (diced or sliced):
  3–5 minutes
Sauté or stir fry (grated):
  2–4 minutes
Deep fry: 3–4 minutes (at 375° F.)
Parboil (for salads): 1 minute

Overgrown Squash Requires Special Attention

Older squash may have skin tough enough to require peeling. (Normally, I do not peel because the peels contain all the color.) Large squash should be seeded as cucumbers are.

Salting Takes Care of Excess Moisture

Grate summer squash and place about 1 inch of squash in a colander. Sprinkle with salt. Add another layer of squash and sprinkle with more salt. Use about 1 teaspoon of salt for every 6 cups of squash. Lay a heavy plate and weight on top of the squash and allow to drain for 30 minutes. Then rinse to get rid of the salt and squeeze out excess liquid. The volume of squash should be reduced by half.

I sometimes salt sliced or julienne-sliced squash before sautéeing, using this method.

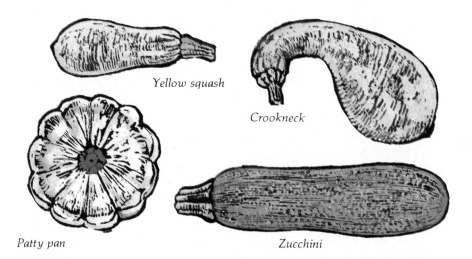

Yellow squash

Crookneck

Patty pan

Zucchini

1. Stuff with onions and tomatoes.

2. Sprinkle with minced fresh basil, then bake.

Those patty pan squash are a perfect size for stuffing—or for any dish. Giant zucchini are good stuffed, if you seed them first.

There's more than one way to stuff a squash

The usual way to stuff a squash is to scoop out the center and fill with a mixture of finely chopped vegetables. But that isn't the *only* way.

Squash Caterpillars

Preheat the oven to 350° F.

Select 1 small (4–6-inch) summer squash for each serving. Trim off the ends. Every ¼ inch, slice three-quarters of the way through the width of the squash so the slices are all still connected. Alternate slices of tomato and slices of onion between the slices of squash.

Place each squash on a separate piece of foil and sprinkle with minced fresh basil. Dot with butter and sprinkle with salt and pepper. Enclose the squash in the foil. Bake for 20–30 minutes.

The Giant Zucchini Solution

Preheat the oven to 350° F.

Slice a large zucchini in half lengthwise, remove the seeds, and scoop out the inside flesh. Reserve the flesh for later. Place the shell hollowed-out side down in a baking dish. Pour ¼ inch of water into the dish. Bake for 15 minutes while you prepare the filling.

Place ½ cup uncooked bulgur in a bowl and pour over it 1 cup boiling water. Cover the bowl and set aside. Grate or chop the reserved zucchini.

Heat 1 tablespoon butter and 2 tablespoons vegetable oil in a sauté pan, and sauté 1 cup chopped onion and 1 minced garlic clove for 2 minutes. Add the grated zucchini and continue to sauté for about 5 minutes. Remove from the heat and add ¼ cup diced sweet red pepper, ¼ cup or more minced parsley, ¼ cup minced fresh basil, 1½ teaspoons fresh oregano or ½ teaspoon dried, and plenty of salt and freshly ground pepper to taste. Mix in ¾ cup crumbled feta cheese (or grated Swiss or cheddar cheese) and the bulgur.

Spoon the filling into the zucchini shells and top with more cheese (about ¼ cup). Bake uncovered for 20–30 minutes or until tender. Serves 6–8.

APPETIZERS

I'm willing to bet Zucchini Egg Rolls have never been served in China. . . .

Zucchini Egg Rolls

6-8 cups grated zucchini
1 teaspoon salt
4-6 tablespoons peanut oil
2 cups sliced celery
1 cup chopped scallions
1 cup minced green pepper
1 cup chopped water chestnuts
1 garlic clove, minced
1 tablespoon minced fresh ginger
   root
2 cups sliced mushrooms
3 cups mung bean sprouts
tamari or soy sauce
pepper
oil for deep frying
flour or cornstarch
16-18 egg roll wrappers
1 egg white

Place the grated zucchini in a colander and sprinkle with salt. Toss to coat. Weight the squash with a heavy plate, and let drain for 30 minutes. Squeeze out any remaining excess moisture.

Heat 2 tablespoons of the oil in a wok or large frying pan and stir fry the zucchini for 2-3 minutes or until barely cooked. Remove from the wok. Heat the remaining oil and stir fry the celery, scallions, peppers, water chestnuts, garlic, and ginger for 2-3 minutes. Add the mushrooms and continue to stir fry 1 minute

more. Return the zucchini to the wok and stir in the mung beans. Season to taste with tamari and pepper.

The mixture should be moist, but not wet. If necessary, drain off extra liquid.

Preheat the frying oil to 375° F.

On a lightly floured board, lay down one egg roll wrapper with a corner toward you. Into the center of the wrapper, spoon about ½ cup of filling. Grasp the 2 side corners and fold over the filling. Bring up the corner nearest you and compress the filling into a log. Begin rolling the egg roll. Keep tucking in the extra dough along the sides as you roll. You are aiming for a tight roll, not a loose envelope.

Moisten the flap with a little egg white spread with a pastry brush or your finger. Seal. Set the rolled egg roll on a heavily floured baking sheet. Continue making rolls until all the filling is used. Do not allow the egg rolls to touch each other on the baking sheet. If you have drained the filling sufficiently, and if there is enough flour on the baking sheet, the egg rolls can be held for up to an hour before frying.

If you prefer, you can lightly fry the egg rolls once, drain, and refrigerate. Just before you are ready to serve, refry the egg rolls until golden brown. Fry a few at a time. Drain and serve with a mustard sauce or a sweet and sour sauce.

Preparation Time: 45-50 minutes
Cooking Time: 20 minutes
Yield: 16-18 egg rolls

SOUPS

Summer squash are light and low-calorie. For the most part, so are these soups—cooked briefly, satisfying to the palate, and pleasing on a hot summer day.

Summer Squash and Chervil Soup

Chervil is a licorice-flavored perennial herb that should have a place in every herb garden. Dried chervil just isn't as flavorful as fresh.

1½ cups diced onion
2 tablespoons fresh chervil or
   2 teaspoons dried
1 tablespoon minced fresh basil or
   1 teaspoon dried
6 cups grated summer squash
1 cup finely diced carrots
4 cups rich chicken broth
salt and pepper

In a large soup pot, melt the butter, and sauté the onion, chervil, and basil until the onion is limp, 3-5 minutes. Add the remaining ingredients and simmer for 10 minutes, until the vegetables are just tender. Serve hot.

Preparation Time: 15 minutes
Cooking Time: 15 minutes
Yield: 6 servings

Chilled Zucchini Mint Soup

The color of this soup is bright green. But it must be eaten the day it is prepared, or the color will be lost.

1 tablespoon butter
1 cup diced onion
8 cups sliced zucchini
1 cup water or chicken broth
1½ cups buttermilk
1 cup yogurt
½ cup roughly chopped fresh mint leaves
½ teaspoon salt

In a medium-size saucepan, melt the butter, and sauté the onion until limp, 3–5 minutes. Add the zucchini and water. Simmer, covered, for 10–15 minutes, or until the zucchini is very soft. Remove from the heat and cool slightly. Process in a food processor or blender until smooth. Add the remaining ingredients to the processor and mix. Chill the soup. Serve garnished with a sprig of mint.

Preparation Time: 15 minutes
Cooking Time: 15 minutes
Chilling Time: 2 hours
Yield: 6–8 servings

There's not a hint of chili in this mouth-cooling, refreshing Mexican Zucchini Shrimp Salad. It's the lime juice and the herb cilantro that gives this salad its characteristic Mexican flavor. Try it on a hot summer night!

SALADS

While I do add raw zucchini and summer squash to green salads, I prefer to parboil the squash in most other salads. Parboiling enhances the flavor and brightens the color.

Mexican Zucchini Shrimp Salad

4 cups sliced or diced zucchini or summer squash
¼ cup minced sweet red pepper
2 cups chopped cooked shrimp
¼ cup lime juice
⅓ cup olive oil or vegetable oil
2 tablespoons minced fresh cilantro or 1 tablespoon dried
1 teaspoon minced fresh dill or ¼ teaspoon dried
1 tablespoon minced fresh parsley
2 tablespoons minced scallion
1 teaspoon Dijon-style mustard
salt and pepper

Parboil the zucchini for 1 minute. Plunge into cold water, drain, and pat dry. Combine the zucchini, red pepper, and shrimp in a salad bowl.

Whisk together the remaining ingredients and pour over the salad. Toss to coat. Season to taste with salt and pepper. Serve cold.

Preparation Time: 20 minutes
Chilling Time: 1 hour
Yield: 6–8 servings

Summer squash pickles are rarely as crisp as cucumber pickles, but well worth making if you enjoy pickles. Slice the squash as thinly as possible and soak in salted ice water for at least 3 hours. Then raw pack in jars with your favorite pickling brine and process as you would cucumbers.

Zucchini Caesar Salad

4 cups sliced zucchini or summer squash
1 cup sliced carrots
1 cup sliced mushrooms
1 cup croutons
1 tablespoon minced fresh parsley
1 tablespoon minced scallion
¼ cup olive oil
3 tablespoons lemon juice
2 large garlic cloves, minced
1 egg yolk
1 teaspoon anchovy paste
¼ cup grated parmesan cheese
salt and pepper

Parboil the zucchini for 1 minute, drain, and plunge into cold water to stop the cooking. Drain well and pat dry.

Parboil the carrots for 2 minutes, drain, and plunge into cold water to stop the cooking. Drain well and pat dry.

Combine the squash, carrots, mushrooms, croutons, parsley, and scallion in a salad bowl.

Combine the remaining ingredients in a food processor or blender and mix. Pour over the salad and toss to coat. Season to taste with salt and pepper. Serve on a bed of lettuce, if desired.

Preparation Time: 20 minutes
Yield: 6 servings

Zucchini Raita

Raitas are yogurt-based salads that are meant to be mouth-coolers when served with hot curry dishes. I find raitas refreshing on hot summer nights with any sort of meal. Substitute cucumbers for the zucchini if you like.

2 cups grated zucchini or summer squash
¾ cup yogurt
1 tablespoon minced fresh mint
1 tablespoon lime juice
salt and pepper

Combine all ingredients and stir. Serve chilled with curry or lamb or as a side salad or relish.

Preparation Time: 5 minutes
Chilling Time: 1 hour
Yield: 6 servings

Mexican Rice, Zucchini, And Chicken Salad

3 cups diced zucchini or summer squash
1½ cups cold cooked brown rice
1½ cups diced or shredded cooked chicken
½ cup chopped scallions
2 tablespoons minced fresh parsley
⅓ cup vegetable oil
3 tablespoons olive oil
¼ cup lemon juice
½ teaspoon chili powder
½ teaspoon salt
pepper
½ cup crumbled farmer cheese

Parboil the zucchini for 1 minute. Plunge into cold water, and pat dry.

In a large bowl, combine the zucchini, rice, chicken, scallions, and parsley.

Whisk together the oils, lemon juice, chili powder, salt, and pepper to taste. Pour over the salad and toss to coat. Sprinkle the cheese on top just before serving.

Preparation Time: 20 minutes
Yield: 4 servings

Zucchini Marinade

This zucchini salad keeps well for 2 or 3 days, although the zucchini will turn olive color. If you like, you can save the marinade to use on more squash or other garden vegetables.

¼ cup lemon juice
¼ cup dry white wine
15 peppercorns
¾ teaspoon fresh thyme or ¼ teaspoon dried
¼ cup water
¼ cup wine vinegar
1 bay leaf
2 tablespoons olive oil
¼ teaspoon salt
¼ teaspoon fresh crumbled rosemary
4 cups thinly sliced zucchini or summer squash

In a medium-size saucepan, combine all the ingredients, except the zucchini, and simmer gently for 5 minutes. Add the zucchini and simmer for 2 minutes. Remove from heat and chill. The squash will absorb the flavors from the marinade in about 2 hours.

Preparation Time: 15 minutes
Marinating Time: 2 hours
Yield: 6 servings

Zucchini Tuna Salad

4 cups julienne-sliced zucchini or summer squash
1 six-ounce can tuna
1½ cups cooked white beans
1 tablespoon capers
¼ cup sliced black olives
2 tablespoons minced green olives
2 tablespoons minced fresh parsley
3 tablespoons minced scallions
3 tablespoons lemon juice
¼ cup olive oil
1 tablespoon minced fresh basil or 1 teaspoon dried
1 tablespoon minced fresh tarragon or 1 teaspoon dried
2 garlic cloves, minced
salt and pepper

Parboil the zucchini for 1 minute. Plunge into cold water, drain well, and pat dry. Drain the tuna.

In a large bowl, combine the zucchini, tuna, beans, capers, olives, parsley, and scallions.

Whisk together the lemon juice, olive oil, herbs, and garlic. Pour over the salad and toss to coat. Season to taste with salt and pepper. Chill at least 1 hour before serving on a bed of lettuce.

Preparation Time: 20 minutes
Chilling Time: 1 hour
Yield: 6 servings

SIDE DISHES AND MAIN DISHES

Because the flavor of summer squash runs from delicate to bland, I like to cook it in combination with other vegetables and plenty of fresh herbs.

Breaded Squash Fans

6–8 small (4–6-inch) summer squash
½ cup all-purpose unbleached flour
¼ teaspoon salt
⅛ teaspoon pepper
2 eggs, beaten
⅔ cup bread crumbs
¼ cup grated parmesan cheese
½ teaspoon dried basil
¼ teaspoon dried thyme
¼ teaspoon dried oregano
¼ cup olive oil

Slice each squash lengthwise every ¼ inch, leaving all the slices connected at the "neck" of the squash. Parboil the squash for 3 minutes and drain well. Spread out each squash in a fan pattern.

Place the flour, salt, and pepper in one bowl; the eggs in another bowl; and the bread crumbs, cheese, and herbs in a third bowl. Heat the olive oil in a frying pan. Dip the squash in the flour, then in the eggs, and then coat with the bread crumbs. Brown the squash on both sides. Serve hot.

Preparation Time: 15 minutes
Cooking Time: 10 minutes
Yield: 6–8 servings

1. Dip the squash in flour.

2. Then dip in the egg wash.

3. Fry until golden.

Squash blossoms are great to use for garnishes of special dishes.

Kirk's Zucchini Pancakes

These pancakes can become an appetizer, side dish, or main dish.

4 cups grated zucchini or summer
  squash
1 teaspoon salt
1 tablespoon butter
½ cup diced leeks
4 eggs, separated
1 cup ricotta cheese
⅔ cup all-purpose unbleached flour
½ teaspoon grated lemon rind
3 tablespoons grated parmesan
  cheese
2 tablespoons minced fresh parsley
salt and pepper
oil for frying

Place the zucchini in a colander and sprinkle with the salt. Toss to coat. Weight the squash with a heavy plate and drain for 30 minutes. When the squash has drained, rinse with water. Drain and squeeze out any excess water.

In a sauté pan, melt the butter and sauté the leeks until limp, 3–5 minutes.

In a large bowl, combine the zucchini, leeks, egg yolks, ricotta, flour, lemon rind, parmesan, and parsley. Season to taste with salt and pepper.

Beat the egg whites until stiff. Fold them into the zucchini mixture.

Pour enough oil into a large frying pan to cover the bottom of the pan. Heat the oil. Spoon about ¼ cup batter into the pan for each pancake and brown on both sides. Serve hot.

Preparation Time: 40 minutes
Cooking Time: 20 minutes
Yield: 4–6 servings

Chili peppers give Summer Squash Enchiladas the right zing!

Summer Squash Enchiladas

4 tablespoons butter
4 tablespoons all-purpose
  unbleached flour
2 teaspoons chili powder
2 cups milk
2 cups grated cheddar or Monterey
  jack cheese
salt and pepper
6 cups diced summer squash
2 tablespoons vegetable oil
1½ cups diced onion
3 garlic cloves, minced
1½ teaspoons minced fresh hot
  peppers or to taste
16 tortillas
3 cups diced tomatoes

In a small saucepan, melt the butter and stir in the flour and chili powder to make a thick paste. Add the milk a little at a time, stirring well after each addition to prevent lumps. Add the cheese and heat gently until the cheese is melted. Season to taste with salt and pepper.

Preheat the oven to 400° F.

Steam the squash until just tender, about 5 minutes.

In a sauté pan, heat the oil and sauté the onion, garlic, and hot peppers until limp, 3–5 minutes. Add the squash and two-thirds of the sauce. Toss to coat.

Grease a 9-inch by 13-inch baking dish. Spoon some filling onto each tortilla and roll like a crêpe. Place seam side down in the baking dish. Spoon the extra sauce on top and sprinkle with the tomatoes. Bake the enchiladas for 30 minutes, or until hot. Serve immediately.

Preparation Time: 25 minutes
Baking Time: 30 minutes
Yield: 8 servings

Summer Squash Sauté

¼ pound bacon, diced
1 cup diced onion
3 garlic cloves, minced
½ cup minced fresh parsley
6 cups diced summer squash
1½ cups diced tomatoes
¼ cup dry white wine
¼ cup water
2 tablespoons minced fresh basil or
   2 teaspoons dried
salt and pepper

In a large sauté pan, sauté the bacon until almost browned. Drain off all but 2 tablespoons of the bacon fat. Add the onion, garlic, and parsley to the bacon fat. Sauté for 3–5 minutes. Add the squash, tomato, wine, water, and basil. Simmer until the squash is tender, 5–10 minutes. Season to taste with salt and pepper.

Preparation Time: 15 minutes
Cooking Time: 10–15 minutes
Yield: 8 servings

Summer Squash Curry

2 cups julienne-sliced carrots
¼ cup water
2 tablespoons butter
6 cups julienne-sliced summer
   squash
¼ cup thick tomato puree
1 tablespoon lime juice
¼ teaspoon cinnamon
¼ teaspoon paprika
¼ teaspoon ground cumin
1 teaspoon curry powder or to taste
½ cup orange juice
salt and pepper

In a large sauté pan, combine the carrots and water and simmer uncovered until the water

evaporates, about 2 minutes. Melt the butter in the pan and add the remaining ingredients. Simmer, stirring often, until the squash is just tender, 5–10 minutes. Serve hot.

Preparation Time: 15 minutes
Cooking Time: 10–15 minutes
Yield: 6 servings

Joe Goodman's Squash

I've never met Joe Goodman, but the friend who shared this recipe with me said it came from Joe. I'd like to thank him. It's great!

2 tablespoons butter
1 cup diced onion
1½ teaspoons paprika
1 teaspoon sugar
1 teaspoon poppy seeds
4 cups diced summer squash
½ teaspoon salt
⅓ cup water
2 tablespoons all-purpose
   unbleached flour
¾ cup sour cream
1 teaspoon lemon juice

In a large sauté pan, melt the butter, and sauté the onion until limp, 3–5 minutes. Sprinkle with paprika, sugar, and poppy seeds. Add the squash, salt, and water. Cook uncovered until the water evaporates and the squash is softened, 3–5 minutes. Sprinkle the flour over the squash and stir to mix. Add the sour cream and lemon juice. Cook for 1 or 2 minutes more, until the sauce thickens. Serve immediately.

Preparation Time: 10 minutes
Cooking Time: 10–15 minutes
Yield: 4–6 servings

Zucchini Feta Squares

6 cups grated zucchini
½ teaspoon salt
1 tablespoon olive oil
⅔ cup diced onion
2 garlic cloves, minced
1 cup crumbled feta cheese
½ cup cottage cheese
1 tablespoon minced fresh dill
salt and pepper
½ cup butter, melted
10 sheets filo dough

Place the zucchini in a colander, sprinkle with salt, and toss to coat. Weight the squash with a heavy plate, and drain for 30 minutes. When the squash has drained, rinse and squeeze out the excess water.

Preheat the oven to 400° F.

Heat the olive oil in a sauté pan, and sauté the onion and garlic until limp, 3–5 minutes.

Combine the squash, onion, feta cheese, cottage cheese, and dill in a bowl. Season to taste with salt and pepper.

Brush an 8-inch by 12-inch baking dish with melted butter and place a folded sheet of filo dough into the dish to cover the bottom. Brush the dough with butter. Repeat 4 more dough and butter layers. Spread the zucchini mixture evenly over the dough. Layer the remaining folded filo sheets and butter on top. Bake for 30 minutes or until the crust is browned. Remove the pan from the oven and let the pastry sit for 10 minutes before cutting into squares.

Preparation Time: 45 minutes
Baking Time: 30 minutes
Yield: 4–6 main dish servings

Summer squash blossoms are tasty. I like to dip them in a Tempura Batter (p. 309) and deep fry them. So that I don't interfere with my harvest, I only pick the male blossoms. How do you tell the difference? The top photo shows a male blossom. It has a long stem. The bottom photo shows a female blossom. It has a small fruiting body at the base of the stem that will develop into a squash.

Harvest and enjoy winter squash and pumpkin blossoms in the same fashion.

Zucchini, Chicken, and Rice Casserole

This casserole is quick to prepare and can be made up in advance and held until you are ready to pop it in the oven to bake.

4 tablespoons vegetable oil
2 cups chopped onions
1 garlic clove, minced
3 cups diced zucchini
2 cups sliced mushrooms
3 cups diced cooked chicken
1 cup uncooked brown rice
2½ cups chicken broth or water
1½ teaspoons fresh thyme or
½ teaspoon dried
½ teaspoon ground rosemary
½ cup grated parmesan cheese
salt and pepper
2 cups chopped tomatoes
¼ teaspoon chili powder

Preheat the oven to 350° F.

Heat 3 tablespoons of the oil in a large sauté pan, and sauté 1 cup of the onions with the garlic for 2 minutes. Add the zucchini and mushrooms, and sauté for 3 minutes more. Combine the vegetables with the chicken, rice, broth, thyme, rosemary, and cheese. Season to taste with salt and pepper. Place this mixture in a greased 9-inch by 13-inch baking dish.

Heat the remaining 1 tablespoon oil, and sauté the remaining cup of onion for 3 minutes. Add the tomatoes and chili powder. Season to taste with salt and pepper. Spoon the topping over the rice and chicken mixture. Bake for 1 hour. Serve hot.

Preparation Time: 25 minutes
Baking Time: 1 hour
Yield: 6 servings

Carrot-Stuffed Patty Pan Squash

6 small (3–4-inch) patty pan squash
2 tablespoons butter
1 cup diced onion
½ cup minced fresh parsley
3 cups grated carrots
2 garlic cloves, minced
½ cup water
¾ teaspoon fresh thyme or
¼ teaspoon dried
¼ teaspoon ground rosemary
4 ounces cream cheese, cubed
1 teaspoon lemon juice
salt and pepper

Preheat the oven to 350° F.

Blanch the squash whole in boiling water for 5–8 minutes, or until just tender. Drain and plunge into cold water to stop the cooking. Drain again. Cut off the stem end of the squash, scoop out a small amount of the pulp, and discard.

Melt the butter in a large sauté pan, and sauté the onion for 2 minutes. Add the parsley, carrots, garlic, and water. Cook, stirring constantly, until the water evaporates. Add the herbs, cream cheese, and lemon juice. Heat until the cheese melts. Season to taste with salt and pepper. Spoon the filling into the squash. Place the squash on a baking sheet and bake for 15–20 minutes or until heated through.

Preparation Time: 20 minutes
Baking Time: 15–20 minutes
Yield: 6 servings

BAKED GOODS

Desserts and breads use up quantities of summer squash.

Zucchini Herb Cornbread

6 cups grated zucchini
2 teaspoons salt
2 cups cornmeal
1 cup all-purpose unbleached flour
3 tablespoons sugar
1 tablespoon baking powder
3 eggs, beaten
1½ cups milk
2 tablespoons fresh basil or
   2 teaspoons dried

Preheat the oven to 350° F.

Place the zucchini in a colander and sprinkle with 1 teaspoon of the salt. Toss to coat. Weight with a heavy plate, and drain for 30 minutes.

Sift together the cornmeal, flour, sugar, baking powder, and remaining 1 teaspoon salt.

Mix the eggs, milk, and basil. Combine the dry and wet ingredients and stir to mix.

Rinse the zucchini and squeeze out the liquid. You should have 3 cups of zucchini. Stir the zucchini into the batter.

Grease a 9-inch springform pan and pour in the batter. Bake for 40 minutes. Cool for 10 minutes before serving. Cut into wedges to serve.

Preparation Time: 20 minutes
Baking Time: 40 minutes
Yield: 8 servings

Zucchini Chocolate Cake

Zucchini Chocolate Cake — my favorite zucchini disguise! Cream cheese frosting is particularly nice on this cake. You'll find a recipe for it with Roger's Carrot Cake on page 89.

4 ounces unsweetened chocolate
½ cup vegetable oil
½ cup butter, at room temperature
2 cups sugar
3 eggs, beaten
1 tablespoon vanilla extract
2 cups sifted all-purpose unbleached
   flour
⅓ cup cocoa
2 teaspoons baking soda
2 teaspoons baking powder
1 teaspoon salt
⅓ cup buttermilk or sour cream
3 cups coarsely grated zucchini or
   summer squash
½ cup chopped nuts

Preheat the oven to 350° F.

Melt the chocolate and oil in a small saucepan over very low heat.

Cream the butter until light; add the sugar, eggs, and vanilla. Beat well. Add the melted chocolate and mix well.

Sift together the dry ingredients and stir them into the batter with the buttermilk. Mix the zucchini and nuts into the batter.

Grease and flour two 9-inch cake pans. Divide the batter between the pans. Bake on the middle shelf of the oven for 40 minutes, or until a toothpick inserted into the center of the cake comes out clean. Cool the cake completely before frosting with whipped cream or your favorite frosting.

Preparation Time: 25 minutes
Baking Time: 40 minutes
Yield: 8 servings

Late-night snackers really enjoy Zucchini Chocolate Cake!

Winter *Squash*

Here's Why I Consider This Vegetable Near Perfect . . .

Winter squash is so easy to grow, and so high in nutrition! It is a very good source of Vitamin A, and the vitamins don't deteriorate in storage. Any cool, dry place will do for no-fuss storage—an unheated bedroom, a cool pantry or attic. If these reasons aren't enough to recommend this vegetable, consider the wide range of dishes you can prepare with winter squash—from soups to desserts. You can bake it, stuff it, puree it, grate it, sauté it, and simmer it in soups and stews. Why you can serve winter squash for days on end—as the early settlers in this country did—and never become tired of it, especially if you prepare different varieties of winter squash, each with its own distinctive flavor.

Winter squash should be harvested and cured before the first fall frost. You can tell a squash is mature when you can't break the skin easily by pressing the rind with your thumbnail. If you break the skin with this test, use the squash soon; it won't keep. Don't try the test until the squash is the proper color for its variety.

To harvest winter squash, choose a dry, sunny day and cut the squash from the vine, leaving 2–3 inches of stem. Roll the squash over and leave them outside overnight if there is no chance of frost. Before storing, cure your squash by keeping them in a warm, well-ventilated place for 1–2 weeks. Then move the squash into cool storage (about 50–55° F.). Check the stored squash frequently and use up any that are softening before they deteriorate further.

Stored Squash Will Lose Flavor

I notice a flavor difference in squash that is beginning to soften. It loses sweetness, and the taste differences between varieties becomes less distinctive. When I think my squash is beginning to deteriorate, I make it into purees for breads, cakes, and pies, in which the sweetener is going to mask some of the flavor anyway. Or I make the squash into marmalade or mincemeat, as you'll see on page 265.

Winter squash are similar to pumpkins in the garden and in the kitchen although the flavor of winter squash is more delicate. Any recipes that you enjoy in the pumpkin chapter can be adapted for winter squash.

Winter squash is a Thanksgiving tradition that dates back to the colonists. A stuffed hubbard squash is a wonderful dish to make to celebrate the harvest.

WINTER SQUASH AT A GLANCE

Favorite Varieties

Butternut and Sweet Mama have buttery, moist flesh, good for cooking and baking. Good keepers. Butternut's thin skin makes it the most easily peeled to use in dishes calling for peeled, cubed squash.

Hubbards have a dry flesh that makes them good for baking, especially breads. Their large size (averaging 10–15 pounds) means that they usually produce leftovers, which can be frozen.

Bush varieties, such as Gold Nugget, are ideal for gardeners with little space. Gold Nugget is good for stuffing because it holds its shape well.

Vegetable Spaghetti Squash have slightly sweet, stringy flesh that makes an excellent pasta substitute.

Acorn squash has moist, firm flesh. The size makes it good for stuffing.

Golden Jersey Acorn can be cooked immature as a summer squash, or it can be left to harden on the vine as a winter squash.

Buttercup has fairly dry flesh that is good for baking and steaming.

Yields

1 pound fresh winter squash equals
   4 cups cubed
or
   3 cups diced
or
   6 cups grated
or
   2 cups cooked and pureed

Food Processors Make The Smoothest Purees

For a really smooth texture, puree cooked squash in a food processor or Squeezo® Strainer to break down the fibers. If the puree is watery, cook it slowly in an open pot, stirring frequently to prevent scorching. The puree should be thick enough to hold a spoon.

I Prefer to Bake Hard-Skinned Squash

Halve the squash, remove the seeds, and place flesh side down in a baking dish that holds ¼ inch water. Bake at 350° F. for 1–1½ hours, until the skin is easily pierced.

Bake Spaghetti Squash whole. Pierce the skin in several places and bake for about 1½ hours at 350° F., until the skin yields to pushing with your thumb. Or boil a Spaghetti Squash whole (pierced in several places) for about 1 hour.

Then slice in half, and use a spoon or butter curler to remove the seeds. Then with a fork, rake out the long spaghettilike strands.

Prebake squash for stuffing. Otherwise you will overcook the filling while the squash tenderizes.

Cooking Times

Steam (½–1-inch cubes): 5–10 minutes
Blanch (½–1-inch cubes): 5–10 minutes
Sauté (½–1-inch cubes): 6–10 minutes
(grated): 4–6 minutes
Stir fry (½–1-inch cubes): 5–10 minutes
(grated): 4–6 minutes
Bake (whole): 1½ hours at 350° F. (½-inch cubes): 20–30 minutes at 350° F.

Butternut

Sweet Mama

Hubbard

Golden Nugget

Acorn

Golden Acorn

Buttercup

Spaghetti Squash

Winter Squash Marmalade is a treat on toast. If you don't want to bother bringing the canner out of storage, seal with paraffin.

When winter squash softens, make *Marmalade*

This marmalade is tasty on toast and makes an excellent glaze for meat. Sometimes I add a few tablespoons of this marmalade to steamed cubed squash or sliced carrots to make a "candied" vegetable.

Use a vegetable peeler to peel 2 oranges and 2 lemons. Sliver the rinds very thin and place them in a heavy-bottomed pan with enough water to cover. Simmer the rinds for 5 minutes. Drain and repeat the process.

Cut the tops and bottoms off the oranges and, following the contours of the oranges, cut away the pith and skin with a knife. Divide the oranges into sections, seed, and chop. Add the oranges to the drained rind slivers. Add 16 cups grated raw winter squash, juice from the lemons, 1 cup orange juice, 2 tablespoons minced fresh ginger root, and a pinch of salt. Bring to a boil.

Add 4 cups white sugar. Return the marmalade to a boil, and remove it from the heat. It will be quite runny at this stage. If you cook the marmalade too long, it will become hard and rubbery.

Skim off the foam from the top of the marmalade and immediately ladle the hot marmalade into 4 hot, sterilized jelly jars, leaving ½ inch headspace if you are sealing with paraffin, or ¼ inch if you are using Mason jars. Seal, or cover with ⅛ inch of paraffin. Store in a cool dark place.

Winter Squash Mincemeat Makes Another Tasty Preserve

You can double or triple this recipe and freeze extra to use as a conserve or in pie fillings. In my *Red and Green Tomato Cookbook* and *Desserts from the Garden*, I developed several recipes for green tomato mincemeat: coffee cakes, cheesecakes, custard pies, muffins, and upside-down cakes. Squash mincemeat will work with any of those recipes with delicious results.

Steam 4 cups of peeled and cubed winter squash until tender, 5–10 minutes.

In a heavy-bottomed saucepan, combine the squash and 3 cups of peeled and chopped apples.

Place 2 tablespoons crystallized ginger in a food processor and process until finely minced. Add 1 cup raisins, and chop using the pulsing action. Add the ginger, raisins, 2 cups brown sugar, 1 tablespoon grated lemon rind, and 2 tablespoons lemon juice to the squash and apples. Simmer, stirring often, until the mixture is thick. Continue cooking for about 45 minutes. Be careful not to scorch the bottom of the pot.

The mincemeat can be used immediately or frozen. This recipe makes 5 cups.

Spaghetti Squash Pancakes

The squash for this dish can be prepared well in advance. Then it should only take you about 30 minutes to mix the batter and cook up the pancakes.

1 medium-size Spaghetti Squash
4 eggs, slightly beaten
¼ cup minced onion
1 cup grated parmesan cheese
½ cup all-purpose unbleached flour
½ teaspoon salt
⅛ teaspoon pepper
¼ cup olive oil

Preheat the oven to 350° F.

Pierce the squash with a fork in several places and bake for 1½ hours. Allow it to cool slightly so you can handle it. Then split it in half, remove the seeds, and rake out the flesh with a fork.

Measure 4 cups of Spaghetti Squash. If you have less than 4 cups, adjust your recipe accordingly.

Mix the squash, eggs, onion, cheese, flour, salt, and pepper. Heat a little oil in a frying pan, spoon 1 tablespoon of the squash mixture into the pan, and flatten to form a small patty. Spoon in more pancakes and fry until golden brown on one side. Then flip over to brown on the other side. Transfer the pancakes to a heated platter. Serve hot.

Preparation Time: 15 minutes
Baking and Cooking Time: 1¾ hours
Yield: 6 servings as a side dish, 8–12 servings as an appetizer

APPETIZER

Spaghetti Squash Pancakes are a treat whether you serve them as a side dish or as an appetizer. If you're feeling extravagant, serve the pancakes as an appetizer with sour cream and caviar.

I use a butter curler or a large spoon to rake out the flesh of the spaghetti squash. Pull your utensil in long strokes so you don't break up the long spaghetti-like strands.

SOUPS

The simplest winter squash soup can be made by thinning a winter squash puree with milk and seasoning with herbs and spices, such as curry powder. So easy, you don't even need a recipe!

Butternut Peanut Soup

3 tablespoons vegetable oil
1 cup diced onion
1 cup diced celery
4 cups diced raw butternut squash
1 cup roasted peanuts
2 cups chicken broth
¾ cup apple cider
1½ cups milk
2 teaspoons frozen orange juice concentrate
½ teaspoon grated lemon rind
½ teaspoon salt

In a large soup pot, heat the oil, and sauté the onion and celery until the onion is limp, 3–5 minutes. Add the squash, peanuts, chicken broth, and cider. Cover the pot and simmer until the squash is tender, about 30 minutes. Cool the soup slightly, and puree in a blender or food processor with the milk. Return the soup to the pot and add the remaining ingredients. Heat and serve.

Preparation Time: 20 minutes
Cooking Time: 40 minutes
Yield: 6–8 servings

Winter Squash Chowder

This soup can be made with leftover squash, which I often have after I bake a large hubbard.

2 tablespoons vegetable oil
1½ cups diced onion
7–8 cups cubed squash
¾ pound ham hocks (1 large ham hock)
4 cups water or chicken broth
2 bay leaves
½ cup water
1 cup diced carrots
1 cup diced celery
1 cup lima beans or diced green beans
1 cup grated sharp cheddar cheese
½ cup heavy cream
salt and pepper

In a medium-size soup pot, heat the oil and sauté the onion until limp. Add the squash, ham hocks, 4 cups water or broth, and bay leaves. Simmer until the squash is tender, 15–20 minutes. Remove the bay leaves and ham hocks and cool the soup slightly. Process in a food processor or blender until smooth.

In a separate pot, simmer the carrots, celery, and beans in the remaining ½ cup of water until tender. Add these vegetables, the cheese, and cream to the squash and heat gently. Remove the meat from the ham hocks and add it to the soup. Season to taste with salt and pepper and serve.

Preparation Time: 30 minutes
Cooking Time: 30 minutes
Yield: 6–8 servings

Winter Squash Chowder lends itself to hundreds of variations; it's one of those "kitchen sink" soups. Toss in whatever you have on hand—except the kitchen sink—and you'll have a delicious, always-different soup.

SIDE DISHES AND MAIN DISHES

Most of my squash dishes are pretty hearty, well-suited for the winter season. But I like to serve a green salad along with squash to lighten the meal and add some greenery.

Curried Squash Compote

This compote is best served warm. It is wonderful as a side dish with meat or chicken.

2 cups cider
1 tablespoon minced fresh ginger root
2 teaspoons curry powder
½ teaspoon salt
6 cups cubed winter squash
3 cups peeled and diced firm apples
½ cup slivered almonds

Simmer the cider, ginger, curry, and salt in a medium-size saucepan over high heat. Add the winter squash to the cider, and continue cooking until the squash is almost tender, 10–15 minutes. Add the apples and almonds, and simmer, stirring occasionally, until the apples are just barely tender. Stir gently from the bottom with a fork to retain whole apple pieces. Serve warm.

Preparation Time: 20 minutes
Cooking Time: 15–20 minutes
Yield: 4–6 servings

Winter squash makes a hearty addition to any stew. Butternut is my favorite squash for using in this Winter's Day Stew.

A Winter's Day Stew

I call this A Winter's Day Stew because it is such a hearty, satisfying dish to eat after an invigorating day outside in the cold.

1½ pounds pork roast
2 tablespoons vegetable oil
2 tablespoons butter
2 cups diced onions
2 garlic cloves, minced
2 tablespoons all-purpose unbleached flour
1 teaspoon cinnamon
1 teaspoon ground cumin
¾ cup cider
¾ cup dark beer
4 cups finely diced winter squash
salt and pepper
1 cup finely diced green peppers
2 cups peeled and finely diced apples

Preheat the oven to 350° F. Slice the pork into 1-inch cubes. Heat the oil and butter, and sauté the pork until lightly browned on all sides. Transfer to a 2-quart casserole dish. Sauté the onions and garlic in the same pan until softened. Add more oil if necessary. Add the flour, cinnamon, and cumin. Cook briefly. Stir in the cider, beer, squash, and salt and pepper to taste. Transfer the mixture to the casserole dish and mix. Cover and bake for 1 hour. Then stir in the green peppers and apples. Cover and continue to bake for 10 minutes. Serve hot.

Preparation Time: 30 minutes
Baking Time: 1 hour, 10 minutes
Yield: 6 servings

Winter Squash Noodle Pudding

Brunch is my favorite time to serve this particularly rich dish. I serve it as a side dish, but some people think it is sweet enough to be a dessert.

12 ounces egg noodles
3 cups grated raw winter squash
3 eggs, beaten
1½ cups cottage cheese
1 cup sour cream
⅓ cup honey
1 cup raisins
1 teaspoon vanilla extract
¼ teaspoon salt
1 teaspoon cinnamon
½ cup wheat germ
2 tablespoons brown sugar (optional)
2 tablespoons melted butter

Preheat the oven to 350° F.

Cook the noodles in rapidly boiling salted water just until tender. Do not overcook, because the noodles will finish cooking in the pudding. Drain well.

Mix the noodles, squash, eggs, cottage cheese, sour cream, honey, raisins, vanilla, salt, and ½ teaspoon of the cinnamon. Spread this mixture in a greased 9-inch by 13-inch baking dish or 2-quart casserole dish.

Mix the wheat germ, brown sugar, and remaining ½ teaspoon cinnamon. Sprinkle over the pudding. Drizzle the melted butter evenly over the top. Bake for 30 minutes. Serve warm.

Preparation Time: 20 minutes
Baking Time: 30 minutes
Yield: 6–8 servings

Squash and Orange Sauté

When the apple harvest is in, I sometimes make this dish with apples instead of oranges. Apple juice or cider replaces the orange juice in the ingredients list.

½ pound bacon
4–6 cups grated raw winter squash
¼ cup orange juice (juice of 1 orange)
salt and pepper
1–1½ cups peeled, seeded, and halved orange segments
1 tablespoon pure maple syrup

Slice the bacon into 1½-inch pieces, and sauté until lightly browned. Pour off half of the bacon fat. Add the squash to the remaining bacon fat, and sauté for 2–3 minutes. Add the orange juice and salt and pepper to taste. Cover and cook over low heat for 2 minutes or until the squash is almost tender. Uncover. Add the orange segments and maple syrup, and continue to cook until the squash is tender, about 2 minutes more.

Preparation Time: 20 minutes
Cooking Time: 20 minutes
Yield: 6–8 servings

When cooked and pureed, hubbard squash has the smoothest texture of all the winter squash. For this reason, it makes excellent baby food. Hubbard squash puree freezes well. So don't be intimidated by its large size. Cook up a hubbard squash and plan to freeze all the extras.

Chicken and Squash

The spices here are Indian, but I season this dish pretty mildly. It's great served with rice, a green vegetable, and a tossed salad.

2 tablespoons vegetable oil
1 cup diced onion
2 garlic cloves, minced
3 cups shredded cooked chicken or turkey
4 cups thick tomato puree
1 teaspoon curry powder
1 teaspoon ground cumin
½ teaspoon turmeric
4 cups grated raw winter squash
½ cup currants or raisins
½ cup dry red wine
salt and pepper

Heat the oil, and sauté the onion and garlic until limp, 3–5 minutes. Add the chicken, tomato puree, spices, squash, currants or raisins, and wine. Simmer uncovered, until the squash is tender and the sauce has thickened a bit, 25–30 minutes. Adjust the salt and pepper to taste and serve.

Preparation Time: 20 minutes
Cooking Time: 30 minutes
Yield: 6 servings

Thanksgiving Stuffed Squash

Leftovers are an inevitable, and usually welcome, part of Thanksgiving. This dish keeps the spirit of Thanksgiving and combines the usual leftover ingredients in an interesting way. Thanksgiving Stuffed Squash has been a family favorite for years.

1 whole squash (a small Blue
   Hubbard is recommended)
¼ cup water
2 tablespoons vegetable oil
1½ cups diced onion
1½ cups minced celery
½ teaspoon dried marjoram
1 orange
2 cups roughly chopped raw
   cranberries
4 cups cubed or shredded cooked
   turkey or chicken
¼ cup pure maple syrup
3 tablespoons butter
1 cup bread crumbs
salt and pepper

Preheat the oven to 375° F.

Cut the squash in half and scoop out the seeds. Place the squash flesh side down in a baking dish and pour in ¼ cup water to cover the bottom of the pan. Bake the squash for 30 minutes while you prepare the filling.

Heat the oil, and sauté the onion and celery until limp, 3–5 minutes. Add the marjoram.

Peel the orange with a vegetable peeler and sliver 1 tablespoon of the rind. Squeeze the juice out of the orange. Add the orange rind, juice, and the cranberries to the onion and celery, and sauté briefly. Add the turkey and maple syrup and remove from the heat.

In a separate pan, melt the butter and stir in the bread crumbs. Add 3 tablespoons of the bread crumb mixture to the turkey and toss. Season to taste with salt and pepper.

Remove the squash from the oven and divide the stuffing between the halves. Sprinkle the stuffing with the remaining bread crumbs and bake for 1 hour.

Preparation Time: 30 minutes
Baking Time: 1 hour, 30 minutes
Yield: 6–8 servings

Mexican-Style Stuffed Squash

I have never seen a recipe for stuffed squash in a Mexican cookbook, but most winter squash did originate in Mexico and Central America, so the idea seems like a natural. I took some Mexican ingredients, added fresh vegetables from the garden, and created this Mexican-Style Stuffed Squash. When I want to make a vegetarian stuffed squash, I substitute 1½–2 cups of brown rice for the sausage.

1 large winter squash, such as
   Blue Hubbard
1 pound bulk sausage (1 cup cooked
   and drained)
1½ cups diced onion
1½ cups diced celery
2 cups diced zucchini
1 cup quartered cherry tomatoes
1½ cups cooked kidney beans
1½ teaspoons chili powder
½ teaspoon ground cumin
¼ teaspoon dried thyme
1 cup grated cheese (cheddar,
   Monterey jack, or mozzarella)

Preheat the oven to 375° F.

Cut the squash in half and scoop out the seeds. Place the

Place the squash flesh side down to steam bake.

squash flesh side down in a large baking dish with ¼ cup water in the bottom, and bake the squash for about 30 minutes, while you prepare the filling.

Sauté the sausage in a sauté pan until browned, breaking it up with a spoon. Remove the meat from the pan. Drain off all but 2 tablespoons of fat. Sauté the onion and celery in the fat until the onion is limp. If the bottom of the pan is crusty from the sausage, add 2 tablespoons of water and mix all the brown scrapings with the onion and celery. Add the zucchini, tomatoes, beans, and seasonings.

Remove the squash from the oven and stuff each half with half the filling. Sprinkle the cheese on top. Return it to the baking dish. Make sure there is still water in the baking dish. Cover the dish with foil. Return it to the oven and continue baking for 1 hour, or until the squash is tender. Just before serving, broil the squash to brown the cheese on top.

Preparation Time: 35 minutes
Baking Time: 1 hour
Yield: 6–8 servings

DESERTS AND BREADS

Here's where the frozen pureed squash is particularly convenient.

Squash and Cream Cheese Roll

3 large eggs, separated
½ cup brown sugar
½ cup white sugar
1 cup squash puree
¾ cup all-purpose unbleached flour
1 teaspoon baking powder
2½ teaspoons cinnamon
1 teaspoon ground ginger
¼ teaspoon mace
½ teaspoon salt
1 cup finely chopped walnuts
¾–1 cup confectioners' sugar
12 ounces cream cheese

Preheat the oven to 375° F.

Grease a 15-inch by 9-inch jelly roll pan and line with waxed paper. Grease and flour the paper.

Cream together the egg yolks, brown sugar, white sugar, and ⅔ cup of the squash puree.

Sift together the flour, baking powder, 2 teaspoons of the cinnamon, the ginger, mace, and salt.

Beat the egg whites until stiff and set them aside.

Mix the dry ingredients in with the sugar mixture. Fold in the egg whites and the nuts. Pour the batter into the prepared cake pan and spread evenly. Bake for 12–15 minutes, or until the top springs back to the touch.

Sprinkle a tea towel with a little confectioners' sugar. As soon as it is baked, turn the hot cake out onto the towel and peel off the paper. Roll the cake in the towel and set aside until it has cooled.

In a food processor or mixing bowl, beat until smooth the cream cheese, the remaining ⅓ cup squash, ¾ cup confectioners' sugar, and the remaining ½ teaspoon cinnamon.

Unroll the cake roll and spread the filling over the cake. Roll the cake up again and chill for at least 30 minutes. Dust with additional confectioners' sugar.

Preparation Time: 30 minutes
Baking Time: 15 minutes
Chilling Time: 30 minutes
Yield: 6–8 servings

1. Prepare for steaming.

2. Cook the puree until a spoon will stand up in it.

Squash Apple Nut Bread

Frozen or fresh puree can be used in this delicious quick bread.

1¼ cups vegetable oil
1 cup brown sugar
¾ cup white sugar
4 eggs
1¾ cups winter squash puree
1 cup all-purpose unbleached flour
1 cup whole wheat flour
2 teaspoons baking soda
1 teaspoon cinnamon
½ teaspoon ground cloves
½ teaspoon nutmeg
½ teaspoon salt
1¾ cups peeled and diced apples
¾ cup chopped walnuts
½ cup raisins

Preheat the oven to 350° F.

Cream together the vegetable oil, sugars, and eggs. Add the squash puree and mix until smooth.

Sift together the flours, baking soda, spices, and salt. Add the dry ingredients to the wet ingredients and mix until smooth. Mix in the apples, walnuts, and raisins.

Grease and flour two 9-inch loaf pans.

Divide the batter between the pans. Bake for 50 minutes. Cool the loaves for 10 minutes in the pans. Then turn out on cooling racks and cool completely before slicing.

Preparation Time: 20 minutes
Baking Time: 50 minutes
Cooling Time: 1½ hours
Yield: 2 loaves

Tomatoes

A Bumper Crop Launched My First Cookbook — I'm Still Inventing Recipes!

A few years ago, I was working at Garden Way's Test Kitchen and preparing meals for some of the Garden Way staff. We had a surplus of early tomatoes *and* a bumper crop of green tomatoes once the cold weather set in (early as usual). I was constantly challenged to find new tomato recipes. Word reached the publisher at Garden Way Publishing that some fancy green tomato cookery was going on in the Kitchens, and the next thing I knew, I was writing my first cookbook, *Garden Way's Red and Green Tomato Cookbook*. It took me a year to do all the final recipe testing and writing for that cookbook. During that year, I ate tomatoes day in and day out.

With the exception of my old favorite Green Tomato Chocolate Cake recipe, all the recipes in this chapter are new. With bumper crop after bumper crop of tomatoes at my disposal, I am constantly challenged to find new tomato recipes.

There's a Tomato Variety for Every Cooking Occasion

What have I learned with all my tomato experience? First, I have some definite variety preferences. I much prefer to can paste-type tomatoes than any other variety, because the puree is so much richer and heartier in flavor. I grow one or two early-ripening Pixies, a couple of cherry tomatoes for salads, a couple of big slicing tomatoes (usually Big Girl) for salads, sandwiches, and stuffing, and then at least a dozen paste tomatoes for canning and for making hearty Italian tomato sauces.

Fresh tomato purees are a little on the thin side. With the home-canned product, the thickness varies depending on the ripeness of the tomatoes. If I have the time, I cook the puree for several hours to thicken it before canning. Otherwise, I cook down the canned puree before using it in a recipe. Most of the recipes in this book specify "thin" or "thick" puree. Thin puree has the consistency of tomato juice, while thick puree should be thick — about as thick as commercial tomato sauce.

As for green tomatoes, you can make wonderful dishes with them by disguising them in combinations with other flavorful ingredients. You can pickle them, or you can let them ripen in a warm, dark, place. But if you are lucky, all your tomatoes will turn red.

I can some of my tomatoes in a flavored Italian sauce. The rest is put up as unflavored puree. Sometimes I can whole peeled tomatoes, but I find it more work than putting up puree.

TOMATOES AT A GLANCE

Yields

1 pound fresh tomatoes equals
   3 cups sliced ½ inch thick
or
   2 cups quartered or cubed
or
   1¾ cups diced
or
   1½ cups pureed

Turn Green Tomatoes Red

Most gardeners have had the experience of harvesting green tomatoes before frost destroys them. If you don't want to cook the tomatoes green, ripen them in a warm dark place. I put green tomatoes on a shelf in the root cellar and cover with a layer of newspaper. I check just about every day to "harvest" the ripe ones and remove any that are starting to rot.

Green tomatoes do not ripen well on a windowsill. The sun will redden the tomatoes without allowing them to ripen from the inside out.

Ripening from the inside out

Peeling Tomatoes

I prefer to peel tomatoes for most cooked dishes. It takes very little effort. In a deep saucepan, bring water to a boil. Add a few tomatoes at a time to blanch for 15–30 seconds. Remove to a bowl of ice water. When cool enough to handle, peel away the skin with a paring knife.

Seeding Tomatoes

Sometimes a recipe will require you to seed tomatoes for a very smooth texture. To seed, cut in half and gently squeeze and shake out the seeds.

I Rely on Tomato Purees

With a Squeezo Strainer making tomato purees is so easy that I inevitably can large quantities of tomato puree and find uses for it all year long.

With a Squeezo[R], you simply run quartered or halved raw tomatoes through the hand-cranked strainer. In minutes you have quarts of smooth, seed-free puree.

For small quantities, you can make a smooth puree in a blender or food processor by peeling and seeding the tomatoes first. It's more work.

Fresh tomato purees are rather thin. I like to cook mine down to concentrate the flavor. I look for the consistency of commercial tomato sauce.

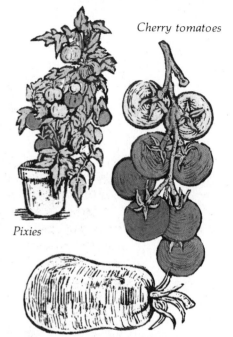

Cherry tomatoes

Pixies

Plum tomato

Beefsteak tomato

Frozen vs. Canned Tomato Puree

Many gardeners prefer to freeze their extra tomatoes and tomato puree. They claim there is less work involved.

Personally, I'd rather set aside time to can quarts of tomatoes and have them recipe-ready when I am rustling up dinner, than to have to remember to defrost the tomatoes before I can cook them.

Nothing beats pizza Made from the Garden

I love to make pizza! I know a lot of people shy away from making pizza for themselves, but the yeast dough crust is simple. While the dough rises, you can prepare the filling and still have time to relax.

This recipe is for my "basic" pizza. I have several others in this chapter. I even have a recipe for a no-tomato pizza in the Spinach chapter (page 248).

This recipe uses garden fresh vegetables—tomatoes, onions, green peppers, zucchini, and fresh herbs. The flavor is unlike any you might find in a frozen pizza—well worth the 45 minutes you will spend in preparation.

You can add your own toppings to the pizza. Hamburger, sausage, black olives, parboiled broccoli, fried eggplant, and hot peppers are all terrific on pizza.

I prefer to make a fresh tomato puree for this pizza by peeling, seeding, and chopping 6 cups of tomatoes. In a large sauté pan, I cook the tomatoes until the volume is reduced to about 3½ cups. The fresh tomatoes have more taste and texture than canned.

To make the pizza, prepare pizza dough according to the directions on page 309. While the dough rises, prepare the filling and preheat the oven to 475° F.

In a saucepan, combine 3½

Pizza made from fresh garden vegetables is tops!

cups thick tomato puree, 2 minced garlic cloves, 1½ cups finely diced onion, 2 tablespoons minced fresh basil, 1 teaspoon fresh oregano, 1 teaspoon fresh thyme, and ½ teaspoon salt. Simmer for 20 minutes, then cool slightly while the dough rises.

When the dough has doubled in bulk, roll it out to fit a 9-inch by 15-inch cooking sheet. With your fingertips, press up the edges of the dough to form a ¾-inch rim around the edges.

Spread the tomato sauce over the dough to cover it completely. Sprinkle 1 cup diced green peppers and ½ cup julienne-sliced zucchini over the sauce. Sprinkle 1½ cups grated mozzarella cheese and ¼ cup grated parmesan cheese over the pizza. Drizzle with olive oil. Bake for 30 minutes. Serve hot.

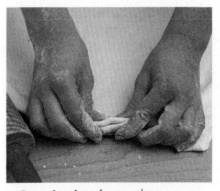

1. Press dough to form a rim.

2. Spread the tomato sauce from edge to edge.

An Herbed Tomato Sorbet is so refreshing on a hot summer day that I don't wait for a fancy dinner party to serve it. You can make it up hours in advance so you don't have to be in the kitchen in the heat of the day.

APPETIZER

Sorbets can be served as a first course in place of soup on a hot day, or after an appetizer and before the main course during a multicourse meal.

Herbed Tomato Sorbet

¼-ounce package gelatin
½ cup cold water
3 cups tomato juice or thin tomato
   puree
1½ cups clam juice
1 rib celery, including leaves
slice of onion
¾ teaspoon salt
3 tablespoons lemon juice
5–6 drops hot pepper sauce
2 tablespoons minced fresh basil,
   savory, parsley, or chives

Sprinkle the gelatin over the water and set aside until the gelatin is absorbed, about 5 minutes.

In the meantime, combine the remaining ingredients, except the herbs, in a saucepan and simmer for 5–10 minutes. Remove the mixture from the heat and remove the celery and onion. Add the gelatin and blend well. Pour into ice cube trays or shallow loaf pans and place in a freezer for 1–3 hours or until nearly frozen.

Place the sorbet and herbs in a food processor fitted with a steel blade. Using the pulsing action, pulse 3–4 times to partially break up the sorbet and mix in the herbs. Refreeze the sorbet for 2–3 hours. Serve with an ice cream scoop.

Preparation Time: 15 minutes
Freezing Time: 5 hours
Yield: 4–6 servings

SOUPS

Hot or cold, tomato soups are hard to beat.

Fresh Cream of Tomato Soup

Tomato soup may be a standard, but it should never be boring. I like to spoon interesting toppings into individual soup bowls for variety. Some I've enjoyed are a handful of croutons; a sprinkling of nutmeg; a dollop of sour cream; a pat of cream cheese; minced fresh chives, parsley, basil, or oregano; crumbled feta or blue cheese; and grated parmesan cheese.

4 cups thin tomato puree
4 tablespoons butter
1½ cups diced onion
2 garlic cloves, minced
3 tablespoons all-purpose
   unbleached flour
½ cup milk
¼ cup heavy cream
½ teaspoon sugar
salt and pepper

If the tomato puree is freshly made, simmer for 10 minutes. Otherwise, use it straight from the jar. Melt 1 tablespoon of the butter in a soup pot, and sauté the onion and garlic until the onion is limp, 3–5 minutes. Remove from the pot and set aside.

Melt the remaining 3 tablespoons butter in the soup pot and blend in the flour to make a smooth paste. Add the milk a little at a time, stirring well after each addition to prevent lumps. Slowly add the heavy cream and the tomato puree.

Place 1½ cups of the soup and the sautéed onion and garlic in a blender or food processor. Process until smooth. Return to the pot. Season with sugar, and salt and pepper to taste. Simmer for 10 minutes. Serve hot or cold.

Preparation Time: 30 minutes
Cooking Time: 30 minutes
Yield: 6 servings

Variations

Cream of Tomato Soup Mexican-Style. Sauté 2 teaspoons chili powder and 1 teaspoon ground cumin with the onion.

Herbed Cream of Tomato Soup. Sauté 1 teaspoon ground rosemary or 1 tablespoon minced fresh basil with the onion.

Cheesy Cream of Tomato Soup. After you add the cream and tomato puree to the soup, add 2 cups grated Swiss or cheddar cheese and an extra ½ cup milk.

Cream of Tomato Vegetable Soup. Add 2 cups of blanched corn or zucchini or sautéed peppers after you have returned the pureed soup to the pot.

Cream of Tomato and Shrimp Soup. Add 2 cups of cooked, peeled and deveined shrimp after you have returned the pureed soup to the pot.

I have so many variations for my fresh Cream of Tomato Soup, I rarely get a chance to serve them all in one season.

Cold Tomato Yogurt Soup

5 cups peeled, seeded, chopped tomatoes
¼ cup sliced scallion
2 tablespoons minced fresh parsley
¼ cup minced fresh fennel leaves
½ teaspoon ground fennel
¾ teaspoon salt
1 teaspoon lemon juice
2 teaspoons wine vinegar
1 cup yogurt
2 cups buttermilk
salt and cayenne

Combine all the ingredients in a food processor or blender and process until smooth. Season to taste with salt and cayenne. Chill the soup well before serving, at least 1 hour.

Preparation Time: 25 minutes
Chilling Time: at least 1 hour
Yield: 6 servings

Variation

Cold Tomato Cilantro Soup. Omit the fennel and flavor the soup with 2 tablespoons minced fresh cilantro.

Tomato Lime Soup

1 tablespoon vegetable oil
1 cup finely diced onion
1 garlic clove, minced
¼ cup minced fresh cilantro
6 cups thin tomato puree
4 tablespoons lime juice
¾ teaspoon hot sauce
1½ teaspoons Worcestershire sauce
½ teaspoon ground cumin
1 cup minced cooked shrimp
salt

In a large soup pot, heat the vegetable oil, and sauté the onion, garlic, and cilantro until the onion is limp, 3–5 minutes. Add the tomato puree, lime juice, hot sauce, Worcestershire sauce, and cumin. Simmer for 10 minutes. Add the shrimp and season to taste with salt. Serve hot or chill and serve cold.

Preparation Time: 35 minutes
Cooking Time: 15 minutes
Yield: 6 servings

SALAD

I didn't provide a recipe for my favorite tomato salad: freshly picked Big Girl tomatoes, sliced and sprinkled with minced fresh basil, salt, freshly ground pepper, and a light drizzle of olive oil.

Tomato Mushroom Salad

5 cups chopped tomatoes
4 cups sliced mushrooms
½ cup sliced scallions
1 tablespoon minced fresh cilantro (optional)
⅓ cup minced fresh parsley
⅓ cup peanut oil
2 garlic cloves, minced
2 tablespoons tamari or soy sauce
2 tablespoons rice vinegar
2 teaspoons minced fresh ginger root
½ teaspoon sugar

Combine the tomatoes, mushrooms, scallions, cilantro and parsley in a salad bowl. Whisk together the remaining ingredients and pour over the salad. Toss gently. Serve at room temperature or chill for 1 hour and serve.

Preparation Time: 20 minutes
Chilling Time: 1 hour (optional)
Yield: 6–8 servings

SAUCES

Italian Meat Sauce

1 tablespoon olive oil
4 hot Italian sausages, casings removed
2 cups diced onions
3 garlic cloves, minced
1 pound ground beef
8 large ripe tomatoes, peeled and cubed (approximately 8 cups)
⅔ cup tomato paste
1½ cups sliced mushrooms
2 cups water
2 tablespoons chopped fresh oregano or 2 teaspoons dried
2 tablespoons chopped fresh basil or 2 teaspoons dried
1 teaspoon minced fresh thyme or ¼ teaspoon dried
1 bay leaf
3–4 tablespoons dry red wine
salt and pepper

In a large soup pot or Dutch oven, heat the olive oil and brown the sausage meat, breaking it up with a spoon. Remove the meat from the pot and drain off all but 2 tablespoons fat. In the remaining fat, sauté the onions and garlic until limp, 3–5 minutes. Add the ground beef and brown it, breaking it up with a spoon if necessary. If the meat is fatty, drain it. Then add the remaining ingredients and the sausage meat. Simmer the sauce for at least 1½ hours. Serve hot over pasta.

Preparation Time: 30 minutes
Cooking Time: at least 1½ hours
Yield: 8 servings (2 quarts)

Dip the raw tomato in boiling water for 30 seconds, then in ice water until cool enough to handle. Then peel.

This Hearty Italian Meat Sauce can be made year-round with fresh, canned, or frozen tomatoes.

You'll find tomatoes are used for their flavor in many recipes in other chapters. But I think these recipes particularly show off the fine fresh flavor of homegrown tomatoes.

Fried Green Tomatoes

An interesting variation for this popular dish is to place a slice of provolone cheese between slices of tomatoes and bake at 350° F. until the cheese is melted, about 10 minutes.

5–6 medium-size green tomatoes
3 tablespoons butter or vegetable oil
2 eggs
¼ cup milk
1 cup bread crumbs
½ teaspoon dried oregano
½ teaspoon dried thyme

Slice the green tomatoes into ¼-inch slices.

Beat together the eggs and milk in one bowl. Mix the bread crumbs and herbs in a second bowl.

Dip the tomato slices in the egg wash, then in the bread crumbs.

Melt the butter in a frying pan and fry the tomato slices for 3–5 minutes, until the breading is golden and the tomatoes are softened. Serve warm.

Preparation Time: 10 minutes
Cooking Time: 15 minutes
Yield: 6 servings

Fresh Tomato Sauce

This sauce is fresh! You don't even cook it. So start with sun-warmed (or room temperature) tomatoes and make sure you pour the sauce over piping hot pasta. It's such a light sauce that it is perfect on a side dish of spaghetti served with chicken or fish.

3 cups peeled, seeded, and finely diced tomatoes
¼ cup finely minced shallots
1 tablespoon olive oil
2 tablespoons minced fresh basil
¾ teaspoon fresh thyme or ¼ teaspoon dried
1 tablespoon minced fresh parsley (optional)
salt and pepper

Combine the tomatoes, shallots, olive oil, and herbs. Season to taste with salt and pepper. Pour over hot pasta. Pass grated parmesan cheese with the pasta.

Preparation Time: 15 minutes
Yield: 4 servings

Stewed Tomatoes

2 tablespoons vegetable or olive oil
1 cup diced onion
1 garlic clove, minced
1 tablespoon minced fresh parsley,
    basil, tarragon, oregano, or
    marjoram, or 1 teaspoon dried
6 cups peeled and cubed tomatoes
salt and pepper
1 teaspoon sugar or honey
    (optional)

Heat the oil in a large sauté pan, and sauté the onion, garlic, and parsley until the onion is limp, 3–5 minutes. Add the tomatoes and cook for 10 minutes more, or until the tomato mixture has thickened slightly. Season to taste with salt and pepper, and sugar. Serve hot.

Preparation Time: 15 minutes
Cooking Time: 15 minutes
Yield: 6 servings

Herbed Cherry Tomatoes

2–3 tablespoons butter
1 tablespoon minced fresh basil
1 teaspoon fresh thyme
1 garlic clove, minced
4 cups cherry tomatoes
salt and pepper

In a large sauté pan, melt the butter and sauté the herbs, garlic, and tomatoes for 2–3 minutes, or until hot. Season to taste with salt and pepper. Serve immediately.

Preparation Time: 5 minutes
Cooking Time: 2–3 minutes
Yield: 6 servings

English Fish Pie

This is an adaptation of a dish I enjoyed in England.

1 double pastry crust (page 308)
1½ pounds cod or haddock
½ cup water
salt and pepper
4 tablespoons butter
1½ cups diced onion
¼ cup minced fresh basil or
    4 teaspoons dried
3 tablespoons all-purpose
    unbleached flour
1 cup milk
4 tomatoes, peeled, seeded, and
    sliced
3 hard-boiled eggs, sliced
1 egg, beaten

Preheat the oven to 350° F. Prepare the dough according to the recipe directions and refrigerate while you prepare the filling.

Place the fish in a baking dish in a single layer. Pour the water over the fish. Sprinkle with salt and pepper. Bake for 10 minutes, or until the fish flakes easily with a fork. Remove from the oven, drain off the liquid, and reserve. Remove any bones or skin from the fish.

Melt the butter in a medium-size saucepan, and sauté the onion and basil until the onion is limp, 3–5 minutes. Sprinkle the flour over the butter and onion. Blend to make a smooth paste. Add the milk a little at a time, stirring well after each addition to prevent lumps. Add the liquid from the fish and blend well.

Tomatoes are a go-with-anything vegetable. These Herbed Cherry Tomatoes, Fried Green Tomatoes, and Stewed Tomatoes are side dishes that can be served to accompany just about any meal.

Season to taste with salt and pepper. Set aside.

Roll out the bottom crust on a lightly floured surface and fit it into a 10-inch pie pan. Spoon a third of the sauce into the bottom crust. Layer in half the fish and half the sliced tomatoes. Spoon in a third more sauce, the sliced eggs, and the remaining fish and tomatoes. Top with the remaining sauce.

Roll out the top crust and fit it over the pie. Crimp the edges. Brush the crust with the beaten egg and pierce in several places to allow steam to escape.

Bake for 50 minutes. Allow to set for 10 minutes before serving.

Preparation Time: 40 minutes
Baking Time: 50 minutes
Yield: 8 servings

Pizza Rustica

This deep-dish pizza is made with a regular pie crust instead of a yeast dough.

1 double pastry crust (page 308)
6 cups peeled, seeded, diced tomatoes
1 tablespoon fresh thyme or 1 teaspoon dried
1½ teaspoons fresh oregano or ½ teaspoon dried
2 cups ricotta cheese
1 cup grated parmesan cheese
2 large garlic cloves, minced
½ cup minced fresh parsley
¼ cup minced fresh basil
2 tablespoons olive oil
1½ cups diced onion
1½ cups diced zucchini
1 cup diced green pepper
½ pound mozzarella cheese, sliced
1 egg, beaten

Prepare the pie dough according to the recipe directions and chill while you prepare the filling.

In a large sauté pan, combine the tomatoes, thyme, and oregano and simmer until the sauce is reduced to 3 cups, about 15 minutes.

In the meantime, combine the ricotta, parmesan, garlic, parsley, and basil in a food processor or mixing bowl. Process until well blended.

In another sauté pan, heat the olive oil, and sauté the onion, zucchini, and green pepper until the onion is limp, 3–5 minutes.

Preheat the oven to 400° F.

Roll out the bottom pie crust and fit it into a 10-inch pie pan. Spread half the ricotta cheese mixture onto the bottom crust. Spoon in half the tomato

mixture. Cover with the sautéed vegetables. Then spoon in the remaining ricotta mixture and tomato sauce. Top with the cheese.

Roll out the top crust and fit it over the pie. Crimp the edges and pierce the crust in several places to let steam escape. Brush the top of the pie with a beaten egg. Bake the pie for 10 minutes at 400° F. Reduce the oven temperature to 350° F. and continue baking for 35 minutes. Allow the pie to set for 10 minutes before serving.

Preparation Time: 45 minutes
Baking Time: 45 minutes
Yield: 8 servings

Broiled Tomatoes

Select 1 tomato per person. Slice the tomato in half and brush with melted butter. Top each tomato with a teaspoon of dried herbs, bread crumbs, grated or crumbled cheese, fried onion or scallions, crumbled bacon, sesame seeds, or anchovies. Broil the tomatoes on a low rack until the tops are browned, but not burned, and the tomatoes are heated all the way through.

Stuffed tomatoes are a great dish to prepare for a crowd; they are easy to make and can be prepared in advance.

For stuffing with sautéed vegetables, cheese, and bread crumbs, I like to use a medium-size slicing tomato. Stuffed cherry tomatoes make a great appetizer.

To seed a tomato, simply cut the tomato in half and squeeze out the seeds.

Greek-Style Lamb

2 tablespoons olive oil
6 shoulder round bone lamb chops
2 cups diced onions
3 garlic cloves, minced
⅔ cup minced fresh parsley
1 tablespoon fresh thyme or
   1 teaspoon dried
1½ teaspoons fresh oregano or
   ½ teaspoon dried
½ teaspoon ground rosemary
5 cups peeled diced tomatoes
½ cup sliced green olives
salt and pepper

In a large sauté pan, heat the olive oil and brown the lamb chops on both sides. Remove the lamb from the pan and drain off all but 2 tablespoons fat. In the reserved fat, sauté the onions, garlic, parsley, thyme, oregano, and rosemary, until the onions are limp, 3–5 minutes. Return the lamb to the pan. Add the tomatoes and olives. Loosely cover the pan and simmer for 1 hour or until the meat is very tender. Season to taste with salt and pepper. Serve over rice.

Preparation Time: 20 minutes
Cooking Time: 1 hour, 10 minutes
Yield: 6 servings

Tomato and Artichoke Bake

2 tablespoons olive oil
2 garlic cloves, minced
1 cup diced onion
¼ cup minced fresh cilantro
2 tablespoons minced fresh basil
5 cups peeled cubed tomatoes
14-ounce can artichoke hearts,
   drained and halved
2 eggs, beaten
½ teaspoon salt
⅓ cup sour cream
⅓ cup yogurt
1 cup grated Monterey jack cheese
2 tablespoons grated parmesan
   cheese

Preheat the oven to 350° F.
Heat the olive oil in a large sauté pan, and sauté the garlic, onion, cilantro, and basil for 3–5 minutes. Add the tomatoes and sauté for 2 minutes more.
Transfer the vegetables to a greased 9-inch by 13-inch baking dish. Spoon the artichokes on top.
Whisk together the eggs, salt, sour cream, yogurt, and Monterey jack. Pour this mixture over the vegetables. Sprinkle the parmesan cheese over the top. Bake for 30 minutes. Serve hot.

Preparation Time: 25 minutes
Baking Time: 30 minutes
Yield: 6–8 servings

Pasta Stuffed Tomatoes

6 medium-size tomatoes
2 tablespoons butter
2 cups finely diced zucchini
2 garlic cloves, minced
1½ cups cooked vermicelli, cut in
   1-inch pieces
¼ cup whipping cream
salt and pepper
¼ cup crumbled farmer cheese or
   feta cheese

Preheat the oven to 400° F.
Scoop out the insides of the tomatoes and reserve to use in a soup. Turn the tomatoes upside down on a paper towel to drain.
In a sauté pan, melt the butter and sauté the zucchini and garlic until the zucchini is tender crisp, 3–5 minutes. Combine the zucchini with the vermicelli and cream and toss. Season to taste with salt and pepper.
Spoon the filling into the tomatoes and sprinkle the tops with the cheese. Bake for 15 minutes, or until the tomatoes are soft but still hold their shape. Serve immediately.

Preparation Time: 30 minutes
Baking Time: 15 minutes
Yield: 6 servings

If the tomatoes are well-drained they will keep their shape.

Herbed Chicken With Tomatoes

Sometimes I sprinkle ¾ cup feta cheese on top of the chicken during the last 15 minutes of baking. The cheese adds a nice tang.

3 large boneless chicken breasts, halved
4 cups peeled, roughly chopped tomatoes
¼ cup chopped shallots
2 garlic cloves, minced
1 tablespoon minced fresh thyme
2 teaspoons fresh rosemary
1 bay leaf
1 cup chicken broth
1 cup dry white wine
¼ teaspoon salt
¼ teaspoon pepper

Place the chicken in a single layer in a baking dish. Combine the remaining ingredients and pour over the chicken. Cover and refrigerate the chicken to marinate for 2–3 hours.

Preheat the oven to 350° F. Pour off the marinade into a large sauté pan and bring to a boil. Reduce by half, which takes 10–15 minutes. Pour the sauce over the chicken and bake uncovered for 30 minutes.

Preparation Time: 40 minutes
Marinating Time: 2–3 hours
Baking Time: 30 minutes
Yield: 6 servings

Extra Cheesy No-Sauce Pizza

This pizza uses sliced tomatoes and no sauce—so it takes very little time to prepare. I serve it as a main dish or an appetizer.

pizza dough (page 309)
2 cups ricotta cheese
1 cup grated parmesan cheese
2 eggs, beaten
4 tablespoons minced fresh basil
3 garlic cloves, minced
4 medium-size tomatoes, peeled and sliced
salt and pepper
2 tablespoons olive oil

Make the pizza dough according to the directions on page 309.

Preheat the oven to 400° F.

While the pizza dough rises, combine the ricotta, parmesan, eggs, basil, and garlic in a food processor or mixing bowl. Process until well blended.

Roll out the pizza dough to fit in a cookie sheet or baking dish and make a ¾-inch edge. Spread the cheese mixture over the dough. Arrange the sliced tomatoes in a single layer over the cheese. Sprinkle with salt and pepper and drizzle with olive oil. Bake for 30 minutes. Serve hot.

Preparation Time: 45 minutes
  (including rising time)
Baking Time: 30 minutes
Yield: 6–8 servings

BAKED GOODS

Andrea's Green Tomato Chocolate Cake

⅔ cup butter
1¾ cups sugar
4 ounces unsweetened chocolate, melted
2 eggs
1 teaspoon vanilla extract
½ cup cocoa
2½ cups sifted all-purpose unbleached flour or 1½ cups sifted all-purpose unbleached flour and 1 cup sifted whole wheat flour
2 teaspoons baking powder
2 teaspoons baking soda
¼ teaspoon salt
1 cup beer
1 cup pureed green tomatoes
¼–½ cup water (optional)

Preheat the oven to 350° F.

Cream together the butter and sugar. Stir in the melted chocolate, then the eggs, one at a time. Add the vanilla.

In another bowl, sift together the cocoa, flour, baking powder, baking soda, and salt.

Add the flour mixture to the butter mixture alternately with the beer and green tomatoes. If the batter appears stiff, add the water. Turn the batter into a greased and floured 9-inch by 13-inch baking dish. Bake for 35 minutes. Ice when cooled.

Preparation Time: 25 minutes
Baking Time: 35 minutes
Yield: 12–15 servings

Turnips *and* Rutabagas

Savor These First Cousin Root Crops — Turnips in Summer, Rutabagas in Fall

Supermarket produce managers may not make a distinction between turnips and rutabagas, but I do. Turnips are delicate, crispy vegetables, eaten for both the greens and the white roots. Rutabagas are yellow-fleshed root vegetables, enjoyed for the slightly sweet, mild-tasting root.

There are more differences.

Turnips are fast growers. Most gardeners like to plant them early in the spring, especially to enjoy their mustardy greens. And they harvest them soon, too. Turnips become bitter, pithy, and woody if left unharvested. The greens also must be eaten young; older greens become bitter and prickly.

Rutabagas, on the other hand, are much slower to grow. They are harvested in the fall, before the first frost, and they keep well in a root cellar. The greens are not eaten.

Turnips have a sharp, crisp flavor; eaten raw, they are reminiscent of radishes. Rutabagas are milder, sweeter, and starchier. Interestingly, they can be used interchangeably in recipes, but the flavors of the final dishes will vary.

Not Just Mashed Like Potatoes!

Most people think of cooked dishes when they think of turnips and rutabagas, but the raw vegetables are delicious. Young turnips, in particular, are tasty sliced or grated into salads.

Towards the end of the gardening season, I often find occasion to serve a harvest platter of raw vegetable sticks with dips. Turnips and rutabagas are cut into finger-size sticks, along with carrots, beets, celery, snap beans, scallions, and broccoli and cauliflower florets.

For this special winter vegetable platter, I harvested the kale and brussels sprouts fresh from the garden. The other vegetables — beets, rutabagas, carrots, and turnips — all came from my root cellar. Serve with a Spinach Boursin (page 246) and you'll get rave reviews from your guests.

TURNIPS AND RUTABAGAS AT A GLANCE

Gardening and Harvesting Tips

Plant turnips early in the spring and late in the fall for tasty greens.

The greens should be harvested before the roots develop. Once the roots start developing, the greens get bitter.

Rutabaga greens do not make good eating.

Harvest turnips when they are small—from marble size to golf ball size. Small-sized rutabagas are tastiest, too.

Rutabagas take longer to mature than turnips. They can be left in the ground until just before the first frost.

Both turnips and rutabagas can be stored in a root cellar, but the rutabagas will store better longer.

To store in a root cellar, remove the green tops. Poke a few holes in a food-safe plastic bag and fill it with the turnips and rutabagas. Store in the coldest spot of your root cellar.

To store in the refrigerator, trim the tops and pack in perforated plastic bags.

To restore wilted turnips, peel and soak in ice water for about 30 minutes.

Cooked Turnips and Rutabagas Come in Many Different Shapes

First, trim off the long tap roots and tops. Peel rutabagas and older turnips. It isn't necessary to peel baby turnips; the skins are thin and tender. Then chop or slice according to recipe directions.

Yields

1 pound fresh turnips or rutabagas equals
   5 cups grated
or
   4 cups sliced or chopped
or
   3½ cups cubed
or
   2–3 cups finely diced
or
   2 cups cooked and pureed

There's More Than 1 Way To Cook a Turnip

Here are some time guidelines for cubed turnips.
Blanch: 4 minutes
Steam: 4 minutes
Sauté or stir fry: 2½ minutes
For rutabagas:
Blanch: 10 minutes
Steam: 12 minutes
Sauté or stir fry: 12 minutes

Steamed Baby Turnips Need Just a Little Butter for Delicate Flavor

The best way to prepare baby turnips is to steam them until tender, 12–15 minutes, then drizzle butter over them. Sometimes I sprinkle dill, parsley, basil, tarragon, rosemary, oregano, or caraway seeds on top.

Turnips and rutabagas are delicious with herb butters (page 160), mustard butters (page 304), cream sauces (pages 305–306), and Tomato Fennel Sauce (page 306).

Decorate With Rutabaga Lilies

Here's a special decoration I use on platters of meats or vegetables.

Thinly slice a rutabaga. Steam until the slices are pliable, 5–10 minutes. Then slice a carrot into tiny matchsticks, about 1 inch long.

Take a rutabaga slice and roll it to form a cone. Set a few carrot slivers into the point of the cone. Secure with a toothpick. You should have a "calla lily" with orange stamens.

Even in the dead of winter I enjoy crisp garden salads!

A salad doesn't have to be made with greens. When the frost puts an end to the growing season up north, I turn to my root cellar to make fresh vegetable salads.

Grated turnips, grated carrots, grated beets, and shredded cabbage form the base of many of my winter salads. To these basic ingredients I add diced apples, raisins, nuts, and sunflower seeds.

I like to use mild red onions for flavor and color in winter salads. Parsley and kale can be minced and added for that fresh "green" flavor. Both do well transplanted into garden pots and cared for on a kitchen windowsill.

Sometimes I add a handful of frozen peas to a salad, just before serving. By the time the salad is served onto a plate, the peas have mostly defrosted. They add a cool crunchiness to a salad.

Grated Turnip Salad

Here's a salad made with grated turnips and diced carrots. The basic vinaigrette dressing can be used with other vegetable combinations.

Toss 5 cups grated turnips with 2 cups finely diced carrots, ½ cup minced red onion, and ½ cup minced fresh parsley.

Whisk together a dressing made of ¼ cup olive oil, 3 tablespoons lemon juice, ½ teaspoon sugar, and salt and pepper to taste. Pour the dressing over the salad and toss to coat. Serve the salad on a bed of shredded red cabbage. It serves 4–6.

For small quantities of turnips, I use a hand grater. For larger quantities, I use my food processor. Tender young turnips, fresh out of the garden, do not need to be peeled. But I peel stored turnips because their skins get tough.

Grated turnips are surprisingly tasty in salads. They taste sweetly sharp and add just the right crunch.

SOUPS

Pureed turnips can be used to thicken vegetable soups. The puree tastes sweet and light.

Cream of Turnip Soup

This is one of my favorite hearty fall soups. For something a little less hearty (and high in calories), substitute milk for the cream.

2 tablespoons butter
2 cups diced onions
6 cups finely diced turnips
   or rutabagas
1 quart chicken broth
2 bay leaves
1 cup minced kale
1 cup heavy or light cream
salt and pepper

In a large soup pot, melt the butter, and sauté the onions until limp, 3–5 minutes. Add the turnips, chicken broth, and bay leaves. Simmer the soup until the turnips are tender, 15–20 minutes. Remove the bay leaves.

Cool the soup slightly and puree two-thirds of it in a blender or food processor. Return the soup to the pot and reheat.

Add the kale and cream. Simmer gently for 10 minutes or until the kale is limp. Season to taste with salt and pepper. Serve hot.

Preparation Time: 20 minutes
Cooking Time: 25–30 minutes
Yield: 6–8 servings

SIDE DISHES AND MAIN DISHES

The younger the turnip, the better it tastes prepared simply. *Stored turnips and rutabagas have a little less flavor than fresh ones. I like to combine them with other ingredients to make satisfying dishes for cold weather.*

Garlic Butter Turnips

1 tablespoon butter
1 tablespoon vegetable oil
1 garlic clove, minced
5 cups thin, bite-size pieces turnips
   or rutabagas
2 tablespoons minced fresh parsley
1/8 teaspoon ground rosemary
salt and pepper

Heat the butter and oil in a sauté pan, and sauté the garlic until golden brown. Add the turnips and sauté until tender and golden brown. Add a tablespoon of water if the turnips are browning too quickly.

Season with parsley, rosemary, and salt and pepper.

Preparation Time: 10 minutes
Cooking Time: 15–20 minutes
Yield: 6–8 servings

Potato Rutabaga Cake

This dish comes straight out of the root cellar.

4 cups grated rutabagas or turnips
2 cups grated potatoes
1/2 cup minced onion
2 tablespoons butter
2 tablespoons vegetable oil
salt and pepper

Mix the rutabagas, potatoes, and onion. Melt 1 tablespoon butter and 1 tablespoon oil in a large cast iron or non-stick frying pan. Spoon in the vegetable mixture, flatten it evenly in the pan, and sprinkle with salt and pepper. Turn the heat to medium low, cover the pan, and fry the cake until it is golden brown on the bottom, 10–15 minutes. To turn the cake, slip it out of the pan onto a plate. Place another plate on top of the cake and invert it. Add the remaining 1 tablespoon butter and 1 tablespoon oil to the pan and heat. Slip the cake back into the pan to brown the second side. Fry uncovered until browned. Slice into wedges to serve.

Preparation Time: 10 minutes
Cooking Time: 20–25 minutes
Yield: 6 servings

The Potato Rutabaga Cake will be easier to flip using a plate.

This Apple Cheese Bake is a sweet, hearty dish to serve on a cold day.

Turnip Turnovers

4 cups diced turnips or rutabagas
¼ pound bacon, diced
2 cups diced onions
2 cups grated carrots
¼ teaspoon ground sage
1 teaspoon dried thyme
2½ cups grated sharp cheddar cheese
salt and pepper
3 cups all-purpose unbleached flour
3 teaspoons sesame seeds
½ teaspoon salt
1 cup vegetable shortening
½–⅔ cup cold water
1 egg, beaten

Preheat the oven to 350° F.

Parboil the turnips until tender crisp, 8–10 minutes.

In a sauté pan, sauté the bacon until almost browned. Drain off all but about 2 tablespoons bacon fat, and sauté the onions, carrots, and herbs with the bacon until the onions are limp, 3–5 minutes. Mix in the turnips and cheese. Season to taste with salt and pepper.

In a large bowl, combine the flour, sesame seeds, and ½ teaspoon salt. Cut in the shortening until the mixture resembles gravel and sand. Add enough water to form the dough into a ball. Divide the dough into 4 sections.

On a floured board, roll out each piece of dough to a rectangle ⅛–¼ inch thick. Trim the edges with a knife. Cut the dough into 5–6-inch squares. Spoon about ½ cup of filling onto each square of dough. Brush the edge of the dough with water. Fold over to make a triangle and press the edges with a fork to seal.

Transfer the turnovers to a greased cookie sheet and brush with the beaten egg. Bake the turnovers for 35–40 minutes or until golden.

Preparation Time: 45 minutes
Baking Time: 35–40 minutes
Yield: 6–8 servings (2 turnovers per person)

Apple Cheese Bake

If you didn't grow turnips and rutabagas, prepare 4 cups of whichever vegetable you have on hand.

1 tablespoon butter
2 tablespoons vegetable oil
¼ cup chopped onion
2 cups peeled sliced apples
2 cups cubed turnips
2 cups cubed rutabagas
¼ cup cider
1 cup grated Swiss or cheddar cheese

Preheat the oven to 350° F.

In a sauté pan, heat the butter and oil, and sauté the onion until it is limp, 3–5 minutes. Add the apples and sauté for 2 minutes more.

Parboil the turnips and rutabagas for 5–8 minutes or until tender crisp. Add the turnips, rutabagas, and cider to the onion and apples. Place the vegetables in a greased 2-quart baking dish. Sprinkle the top with cheese and bake for 30 minutes or until the top is golden brown.

Preparation Time: 20 minutes
Baking Time: 30 minutes
Yield: 6–8 servings

New Vegetables

Try These "Oddball" Vegetables — They're Easy to Grow and Fun to Eat!

I find it exciting to grow a "new" vegetable every year. As I sort through my seed catalogs each January, I am always on the lookout for something new to grow that will extend my repertoire as a cook.

Sometimes my choice is made when I taste a new vegetable at a restaurant or at a friend's. A friend introduced me to Jerusalem artichokes in salad one fall. Another friend served me my first celeriac—a funny-looking root which he scrubbed, peeled, and grated on top of the salad. I remember my first taste—so much like summer and celery.

Here Are My Favorites

In this chapter, I have presented recipes for my favorite "oddball" vegetables: Jerusalem artichokes, fennel, kohlrabi, and celeriac. These are vegetables I have been enjoying for several years, and they are becoming increasingly popular. Someday they won't even be unusual —just like spaghetti squash, which was unheard of a few years ago.

In fact, you don't have to grow these vegetables to try them. I can understand why you would want to taste an "oddball" before growing it. I have seen all of these vegetables in the supermarket or at specialty produce stands.

Look for fresh fennel in the fall. The leafy tops should be unblemished and not limp; there should be no brown spots or cracks on the bottom of the bulb. Fall is a good time to look for Jerusalem artichokes, too. They should be firm to the touch, not spongy. Chances are you can find a friend who will be glad to share some Jerusalem artichokes with you; they grow so abundantly. Celeriac can sometimes be found in specialty food markets in the fall. The root should be firm. Try to avoid roots with deep cracks or excessive gnarling, which will mean more waste when you peel. Look for the kohlrabi in the spring and fall, as it is a cool weather crop. The bulb should be about 2 inches in diameter and the leaves should not be limp.

If you can't buy these vegetables, don't be afraid to grow them; experimenting in the garden is fun!

Can you name these vegetables? Starting clockwise from the top, we have Celeriac and Grape Salad; Kohlrabi, Corn, and Tomato Sauté; Broccoli Fennel Sauté; and Jerusalem Artichokes and Carrots.

Jerusalem Artichokes Grow So Prolificaly Some People Call Them Weeds!

If you aren't sure you like Jerusalem artichokes, buy some at a supermarket or specialty produce stand, or ask a friend for a sample. Once you've planted them, you'll have enough for life; Jerusalem artichokes are a perennial, and they grow like weeds.

Jerusalem artichokes are related to sunflowers; they are sometimes called sunchokes. You plant and harvest the knobby tubers, which are starchy like potatoes, but sweeter. Above the ground, Jerusalem artichokes send up tall stems topped with sunflower-like blossoms. The best time to harvest is in the fall, after a few frosts have sweetened the tubers. Then continue to harvest as you need them, leaving the artichokes in the ground, where they keep best.

What do they taste like? Raw, they have the crunch and bland flavor of water chestnuts and are good in salads and stir fries. Cooked, they have a sweet, nutty flavor.

To Peel or Not to Peel

I don't think Jerusalem artichokes look very attractive, so I usually peel them, after I have scrubbed them well. They darken quickly, so as I peel, I drop them into cold water to which I have added a tablespoon of lemon juice.

An Easy Vegetable to Cook

Jerusalem artichokes are an easy vegetable to experiment with. The only trick is not to overcook. They turn mushy with an instant of overcooking, so watch your cooking times carefully.

Cooking Timetable
Parboil: 5–8 minutes
Stir fry: 5–10 minutes
Sauté: 8–12 minutes
Steam: 12–20 minutes
Blanch: 12–15 minutes
Bake (coated in butter, at 350° F.): 30 minutes

The simplest way to prepare Jerusalem artichokes is to sauté in butter with herbs, such as thyme, tarragon, rosemary, curry, caraway seeds, fennel, or sage.

Or you can sauté Jerusalem artichokes in butter, then add orange juice or cider and steam briefly.

I like to blanch Jerusalem artichokes, place them in a baking dish, sprinkle with grated cheese, and broil until the cheese melts.

Blanched Jerusalem artichokes are delicious topped with any cheese or cream sauce (pages 305–306), tomato sauce (page 306), or flavored butter (page 304).

Jerusalem Artichokes and Carrots

2 tablespoons olive oil
1 cup diced onion
1 large garlic clove, minced
1 tablespoon fresh thyme or
   1 teaspoon dried
4 cups sliced Jerusalem artichokes
2 cups julienne-sliced carrots
¼ cup minced fresh parsley
⅓ cup water
½ cup dry white wine
1 tablespoon lemon juice
salt and pepper

Heat the oil in a large sauté pan, and sauté the onion, garlic, and thyme for 2 minutes. Add the Jerusalem artichokes, carrots, parsley, water, and wine. Cover the pan and steam, stirring occasionally, until the artichokes are tender crisp, 10–15 minutes. Add the lemon juice and season to taste with salt and pepper. Serve hot.

Preparation Time: 25 minutes
Cooking Time: 10–15 minutes
Yield: 6 servings

Jerusalem Artichoke Waldorf Salad

The Jerusalem artichokes give this familiar salad more crunch than ever.

3 cups cubed Jerusalem artichokes
1 cup diced pears
1 cup diced apple
4 teaspoons lemon juice
1 cup diced celery
¼ cup raisins
¼ cup chopped walnuts
1 tablespoon minced fresh parsley
2 egg yolks
1 tablespoon orange juice
1 teaspoon lemon juice
½ teaspoon salt
½ teaspoon poppy seeds
½ cup vegetable oil

Blanch the Jerusalem artichokes until just tender, 5–10 minutes. Plunge into cold water to cool. Drain and set aside.

In a large salad bowl, toss the apple and pear with 3 teaspoons of the lemon juice. Add the Jerusalem artichokes, celery, raisins, walnuts, and parsley. Toss to mix.

In a blender or food processor, combine the egg yolks, orange juice, salt, poppy seeds, and remaining 1 teaspoon lemon juice. Blend until well mixed. With the blender going, pour in the oil in a thin stream. The dressing will thicken as you add the oil. Spoon the dressing over the salad and toss to coat. Chill for 1–2 hours and serve on a bed of lettuce.

Preparation Time: 30 minutes
Chilling Time: 1–2 hours
Yield: 4–6 servings

Jerusalem Artichoke Stew

1½ pounds pork
4 tablespoons vegetable oil or bacon fat
1½ cups diced onion
⅔ cup all-purpose unbleached flour
1 teaspoon ground rosemary
1 teaspoon salt
½ teaspoon pepper
5 cups cubed Jerusalem artichokes
2 cups sliced carrots
3 cups water
½ cup dry white wine
½ cup minced fresh parsley
1½ cups fresh or frozen peas

Slice the pork into ½-inch cubes. You should have about 4 cups.

Combine ⅓ cup of the flour with the rosemary, salt, and pepper in a bag. Toss the pork in the bag, and coat with the flour mixture.

Heat 2 tablespoons of the oil in a large soup pot, and sauté the onion until translucent, 2–3 minutes. Add the pork and sauté until browned. Add the Jerusalem artichokes, carrots, water, and wine. Simmer for 1 hour, until the meat is tender.

Remove 1½ cups cooking liquid from the pot. Whisk the remaining ⅓ cup flour into the cooking liquid to make a smooth paste. Stir the flour mixture into the stew. Add the parsley. Simmer for 15 minutes. Add the peas during the last 5 minutes of cooking.

Season to taste with salt and pepper. Serve hot over buttered noodles.

Preparation Time: 30 minutes
Cooking Time: 1½ hours
Yield: 6–8 servings

Fresh Celeriac for Salads All Winter Long

I remember clearly my first taste of celeriac. It was in March, in Vermont. The celeriac came from a friend's root cellar and was grated fresh into a salad. And how fresh it tasted!

If you have a root cellar, growing celeriac makes sense, since it will enable you to keep this fresh salad vegetable most of the winter.

I prefer raw celeriac, in salads, to cooked; although it does lend itself to use in soups, stews, and sautés.

Celeriac must be peeled before serving. Use a paring knife and slice off the top and bottom of the root. Then follow the contours of the root and cut away the peel. Be prepared for a significant amount of waste.

Celeriac darkens on exposure to air. So peel just before cooking or serving. Immediately drop the peeled celeriac into cold water or salad dressing.

You can cook celeriac as you do celery. Here are the cooking times.

Cooking Timetable
Blanch: 5–8 minutes
Steam: 5–8 minutes
Sauté or stir fry: 5 minutes

Put a little lemon juice in your blanching water to prevent darkening. Or cook the celeriac unpeeled.

I like to hose off most of my root crops before I bring them into the kitchen. Celeriac seems to pick up quite a bit of soil with its irregular, knobby skin. First I trim off the tops, leaving about 1 inch of stem. Then I hose the soil off.

Celeriac Grape Salad

1½ cups julienne-sliced carrots

1½ cups seedless red or
   green grapes

3 cups julienne-sliced celeriac

3 tablespoons wine vinegar

½ cup vegetable oil

1 tablespoon minced fresh mint or
   1 teaspoon dried

¼ cup minced scallions

1 teaspoon sugar

½ teaspoon salt

¼ teaspoon pepper

Toss together the carrots, grapes, and celeriac in a large bowl. Whisk together the remaining ingredients and pour over the salad. Toss to coat. Serve immediately.

Preparation Time: 20 minutes
Yield: 6 servings

Celeriac and Cabbage Slaw

2½ cups julienne-sliced celeriac

2 cups shredded cabbage

1 cup mayonnaise

¼ cup Dijon-style mustard

¼ cup grainy mustard

2 tablespoons wine vinegar

salt and pepper

Combine the celeriac and cabbage in a large salad bowl. Whisk together the mayonnaise, mustards, and vinegar. Pour over the salad. Season to taste with salt and pepper. Refrigerate for at least 2 hours before serving.

Preparation Time: 20 minutes
Chilling Time: at least 2 hours
Yield: 4–6 servings

Celeriac and Chicken Salad

1½ cups julienne-sliced celeriac

2 cups diced cooked chicken

¼ cup minced fresh parsley

1 egg yolk

3 tablespoons tarragon vinegar

1 tablespoon lemon juice

½ cup olive oil

1 garlic clove, minced

1 teaspoon Dijon-style mustard

¼ cup light cream

1 tablespoon fresh tarragon or
   1½ teaspoons dried

1 teaspoon salt

freshly ground pepper

Combine the celeriac, chicken, and parsley in a large salad bowl.
Combine the remaining ingredients in a blender or food processor and blend until smooth. Pour over the salad and toss to coat. Chill for at least 1 hour. Serve on a bed of lettuce.

Preparation Time: 20 minutes
Chilling Time: 1 hour
Yield: 4 servings

Fennel: The Flavorful Fall Crop With the Delicate Anise Taste

Fresh fennel is a fall crop you won't want to miss. As a vegetable, it most resembles celery, with a wonderful taste difference—like licorice.

Fennel, also known as Florence fennel and finocchio, has numerous stalks which arise from a fat "bulb" and is topped with feathery dill-like weeds.

Eat the Bulb; Save the Leaves for Garnishes

To prepare fennel, trim off the base of the root, then chop off the stalks at the top of the bulb. Save the stalks for your stock pot and the leaves for flavoring and garnishing. Older fennel may need stringing, just as older celery does. Then slice or dice the tender bulb.

Raw Fennel Is Delicious

Did you know that fresh fennel has very few calories—making it a perfect snacking vegetable. Fennel makes a welcome addition to any raw vegetable platter or salad.

Sautés Bring Out The Delicate Flavor

Sautéed fennel has so much flavor, it doesn't need any special recipe. Just sauté the fennel in butter until tender, 3–8 minutes.

This lovely Cream of Fennel Soup should be served right away.

Fennel Broccoli Sauté

Fennel is a popular flavoring in Italian cooking. Here's a classic example.

8 tablespoons water
3 cups julienne-sliced fresh fennel bulb
2 tablespoons olive oil
2 garlic cloves, minced
4 cups broccoli florets
3 tablespoon dry white wine
2 tablespoons lemon juice
salt and pepper

In a large sauté pan, heat the water and add the fennel. Steam sauté the fennel until the water disappears and the fennel is barely cooked, about 3 minutes. Add the oil, garlic, and broccoli and sauté for 1 minute. Add the wine and steam sauté the vegetables until the wine disappears and the broccoli is tender crisp, 3–5 minutes. Sprinkle the lemon juice over the vegetables. Season to taste with salt and pepper. Serve at once.

Preparation Time: 20 minutes
Cooking Time: 8–10 minutes
Yield: 6 servings

Cream of Fennel Soup

2 tablespoons butter
1½ cups diced onion
4½ cups chopped fresh fennel bulb
3 cups chicken broth
½ cup light cream
½ cup milk
salt and pepper

In a large soup pot, melt the butter, and sauté the onion until limp, 3–5 minutes. Add the fennel and the chicken broth. Simmer for 30 minutes or until the fennel is tender. Cool slightly.

In a blender or food processor, puree two-thirds of the soup, return to the pot, and add the cream and milk. Cook until heated through. Season to taste with salt and pepper. Serve hot.

Preparation Time: 25 minutes
Cooking Time: 35 minutes
Yield: 6 servings

Apple Fennel Sauté

2 tablespoons butter
2 tablespoons vegetable oil
4 cups sliced fresh fennel bulb
½ cup sliced scallions
4 cups peeled sliced apples
1–2 tablespoons water
½ teaspoon anise seed
¼ teaspoon ground coriander
salt

In a large sauté pan, heat the butter and oil, and sauté the fennel and scallions for 3–4 minutes, until limp. Add the apples, water, anise, and coriander. Sauté until the apples and fennel are tender, 3–5 minutes. Season to taste with salt. Serve at once.

Preparation Time: 20 minutes
Cooking Time: 6–10 minutes
Yield: 6–8 servings

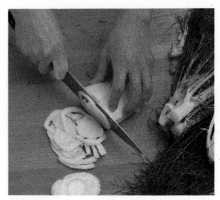

First, remove the leaves. Then slice with a chef's knife.

Fennel Pasta Sauce

This is a very richly flavored sauce. Italian sausage contains fennel seed, so the licorice flavor of fennel isn't overpowered by the tomatoes—a pasta sauce with a difference!

1¼ pounds hot Italian sausage
1½ cups diced onion
2 garlic cloves, minced
3 cups finely diced fresh fennel bulb
½ cup minced fresh parsley
6 cups thick tomato puree
½ cup dry red wine
1 tablespoon fresh basil or
    1 teaspoon dried
1 tablespoon fresh oregano or
    1 teaspoon dried
1 tablespoon fresh marjoram or
    1 teaspoon dried
salt and pepper

Remove the casings from the sausage and brown it in a large soup pot. When the meat is browned, remove it from the pan and drain off all but 2 tablespoons fat. Sauté the onion, garlic, fennel, and parsley until the onion is limp, 3–5 minutes. Add the tomato puree, wine, herbs, and meat. Simmer for 45 minutes to 2 hours on low heat. Season to taste with salt and pepper. Serve hot over pasta.

Preparation Time: 25 minutes
Cooking Time: 45 minutes–2 hours
Yield: 8–10 servings

Kohlrabi Tastes Exactly As It Looks

Kohlrabi is one of the oddest-looking vegetables in my garden. It looks like a cross between a turnip and a cabbage—and that's exactly what it tastes like!

Most people eat just the bulb of the kohlrabi, but the leaves are tasty, too. The bulbs can be prepared in any recipe calling for turnips. The dish will taste a little different, with a slight cabbage flavor.

Harvest When Young

The younger the kohlrabi, the better. The flavor will be sweeter, and the texture will be crisp, not pithy. I like to harvest it as I need it, when the kohlrabi is about 2 inches in diameter.

Preparation Means Peeling

Use a paring knife to peel kohlrabi. Peeling after you have cooked it enhances the flavor, but it is okay to peel first. To prepare the leaves, remove the tough center rib.

Delicious Raw or Cooked

Sliced raw kohlrabi can be added to any salad. Or serve it with dips.

I like to steam or blanch kohlrabi and top with a lemon or herb butter. Here are some cooking times for sliced kohlrabi.

Blanch: 7 minutes
Steam: 7 minutes
Sauté or stir fry: 5–10 minutes

Kohlrabi and Red Radish Salad

3 cups grated kohlrabies
1 cup sliced red radishes
⅓ cup olive oil
1 tablespoon lemon juice
2 tablespoons white vinegar
2 teaspoons sugar
¼ teaspoon salt
⅛ teaspoon pepper
1 tablespoon minced fresh mint
1 teaspoon minced fresh parsley

Combine the kohlrabies and radishes in a salad bowl. Whisk together the remaining ingredients and pour over the salad. Toss to coat. Serve.

Preparation Time: 20 minutes
Yield: 4–6 servings

Tarragon Kohlrabi Sauté

4 tablespoons butter
4 tablespoons minced shallots
3 teaspoons Dijon-style mustard
2 teaspoons minced fresh tarragon
    or ¾ teaspoon dried
2 teaspoons minced fresh parsley
2 tablespoons lemon juice
4 cups julienne-sliced kohlrabies
2 cups julienne-sliced carrots
salt and pepper

In a large sauté pan, melt the butter and add all the ingredients. Sauté until the kohlrabies are tender crisp, about 8–10 minutes. Season to taste with salt and pepper. Serve hot.

Preparation Time: 15 minutes
Cooking Time: 8–10 minutes
Yield: 6–8 servings

Kohlrabi Ham Soufflé

3 cups diced kohlrabies
2 cups diced potatoes
4 bacon slices, diced
1 cup finely diced ham
2 tablespoons minced scallion
1 tablespoon minced fresh parsley
¼ teaspoon paprika
⅛ teaspoon cayenne
½ teaspoon dried savory
pinch thyme
½ teaspoon Worcestershire sauce
6 eggs, separated
2 tablespoons flour
½ cup grated cheddar cheese
½ teaspoon salt
pepper

Preheat the oven to 325° F.

Parboil the potatoes until just tender, about 10 minutes.

Blanch or steam the kohlrabies until just tender, about 5 minutes.

In the meantime, sauté the bacon until browned and remove it from the pan. Pour off all but 2 tablespoons of bacon grease, and sauté the ham, scallion, parsley, and herbs for 2 minutes. Stir in the Worcestershire sauce.

In a large bowl, combine the kohlrabies, potatoes, bacon, and ham and vegetable mixture.

Whisk together the 6 egg yolks and the flour and mix with the kohlrabi mixture. Mix in the cheese, salt, and pepper to taste.

Beat the egg whites until stiff. Fold into the kohlrabi mixture.

Spoon into a greased, shallow 1½ quart baking dish. Bake for 40–50 minutes or until the top is golden. Serve hot.

Preparation Time: 35 minutes
Baking Time: 40–50 minutes
Yield: 6 servings

This Kohlrabi Soufflé is unusually hearty. It contains potatoes, ham, and kohlrabi—an excellent one-dish meal.

Kohlrabi Basil Sauté

2 tablespoons olive oil
3 garlic cloves, minced
2 tablespoons minced fresh basil or 2 teaspoons dried
1 tablespoon minced shallot
1 teaspoon minced fresh parsley
½ cup finely diced sweet red pepper
4 cups diced kohlrabies

Heat the oil in a large sauté pan and add all the ingredients. Sauté for 8–10 minutes, or until the kohlrabies are tender. Serve at once.

Preparation Time: 15 minutes
Cooking Time: 8–10 minutes
Yield: 4–6 servings

Kohlrabi, Corn, and Tomato Sauté

4 cups diced kohlrabies
2 tablespoons butter
1 cup corn kernels
1½ cups chopped tomatoes
1 garlic clove, minced
½ cup chopped scallions
1 tablespoon minced fresh parsley
½ teaspoon chili powder
salt and pepper

Blanch or steam the kohlrabies until tender crisp, about 5 minutes. Drain and set aside.

Melt the butter in a large sauté pan, and sauté the corn, tomatoes, scallions, garlic, parsley, and chili powder for 2 minutes. Add the kohlrabies and sauté for another 2 minutes. Season to taste with salt and pepper. Serve hot.

Preparation Time: 20 minutes
Cooking Time: 10 minutes
Yield: 6 servings

Basic Recipes

Dressings, Sauces, Batters, and Doughs: Add Variety to Your Vegetables

Cooking in restaurants, I learned that the most respected chef is the "saucier," the one who makes the sauces. And when people rave about fine foods they have eaten, particularly French foods, they will usually speak of the sauces in reverent tones.

Personally, I would rather be known as a cook who always serves the crispiest, tenderest, green beans or the sweetest tomatoes, than one who makes the best sauces. On the other hand, every once in a while, I like to dress up my freshly cooked vegetables with a perfectly flavored sauce.

Variety in cooking is awfully important. I love to eat with the seasons, eating the vegetables as they ripen. Sometimes this means eating one vegetable for days on end. Asparagus, peas, and beans often get singled out as big garden producers that I serve and serve—rather than let go by. No one gets tired of these cooked vegetables, as long as I serve them with different sauce or topping.

Sauces Should Be Light

My sauces do tend to be mild and light. I want the flavor of the vegetables to come through and not be overwhelmed by the sauce. The heavier sauces should be served with a light touch. For example, 1 cup of Hollandaise Sauce is ample for 4–6 servings.

If you don't find the sauce you are looking for here, look for vegetable-based sauces scattered throughout the book, particularly in the herb, tomato, and onion chapters.

I have included many salad dressings in this chapter. Many of the dressings do double duty as marinades *and* salad dressings.
You'll find more special salad dressings in the chapters on cucumbers, onions, and lettuce and salad greens.

Basic batters—tempura and crêpes—and doughs for pie and pizza comprise the rest of this chapter. These are recipes I have used over the years and found dependable.

It's often the so-called basic recipes that make a meal special. Try the Sweet Mustard Glaze (page 304) or a dab of Garlic Mayonnaise (page 301) on vegetables. Even the basic Double Pastry Pie Crust (page 308) can take on a new look with different edgings.

Vinaigrette;

It's a Fancy Way to Say Oil and Vinegar

Vinaigrette dressings are particularly tasty on salads made of mixed vegetables. If you heat your vinaigrette and combine it with your still-warm parboiled vegetables, the vegetables will absorb the flavors best. Of course, vinaigrettes are good on green salads, too. Add cheese to the Herb Vinaigrette for extra flavor.

Lemon Vinaigrette

This makes an excellent marinade for vegetables.

1 cup vegetable or olive oil
¼ cup lemon juice
1 teaspoon Dijon-style mustard
¼ teaspoon white pepper
salt

Whisk together the oil, lemon juice, mustard, and pepper.

Season to taste with salt. Pour over salads. To use as a marinade, pour over parboiled vegetables and marinate for 1–2 hours. Serve chilled.

Preparation Time: 5 minutes
Yield: 1¼ cups

Spicy Lemon Dressing

⅔ cup vegetable oil
¼ cup lemon juice
2 garlic cloves, minced
2 tablespoons grated lemon rind
½ teaspoon hot sauce
½ teaspoon ground coriander
¾ teaspoon ground cumin
½ teaspoon ground mustard
½ teaspoon paprika
½ teaspoon sugar
1 teaspoon salt
1 tablespoon minced fresh parsley

Combine all the ingredients and blend until well mixed.

Preparation Time: 10 minutes
Yield: 1¼ cups

Herb Vinaigrette

Whisk together 2 tablespoons red wine vinegar, 2 tablespoons lemon juice, ¾ cup oil, 1 teaspoon salt, and 3 tablespoons minced fresh herbs or 1 tablespoon dried. Add plenty of pepper.

Fresh garden vegetables are only the beginning of a great salad. A simple vinaigrette dressing is equally good on green and mixed vegetable salads.

You'll Never Buy Another Bottled Dressing Once You've Tasted These Homemade Classics

Green Goddess Dressing

⅓ cup mayonnaise
1 egg
⅓ cup vegetable oil
2 garlic cloves, minced
¼ cup chopped scallion greens
1 tablespoon minced fresh chives
¼ cup minced fresh parsley
1 tablespoon white vinegar
2 tablespoons lemon juice
salt and pepper

Combine all the ingredients in a food processor or blender and process until smooth. Season to taste with salt and pepper.

Preparation Time: 15 minutes
Yield: 1½ cups

French-Style Dressing

½ cup chopped tomatoes
2 tablespoons lemon juice
1 tablespoon red wine vinegar
⅓ cup vegetable or olive oil
1 tablespoon tomato paste
1 garlic clove, minced
salt and pepper

Combine all the ingredients in a blender or food processor and blend until smooth. Season to taste with salt and pepper.

Preparation Time: 10 minutes
Yield: 1 cup

Garlic Mayonnaise

2 egg yolks
3 tablespoons lemon juice
4–5 garlic cloves, minced
1 teaspoon minced fresh parsley
1 tablespoon minced shallots
2 teaspoons Dijon-style mustard
¾ teaspoon salt
pepper
½ cup olive oil

Combine all the ingredients, except the oil, in a blender or food processor. Blend until smooth. With the blender going, pour in the oil in a thin stream. The mayonnaise will thicken as the oil is poured in.

Preparation Time: 15 minutes
Yield: ¾ cup

Either a blender or a food processor can be used to make mayonnaise. Simply combine the egg yolks, lemon juice, and flavorings. With the motor running, pour in the oil in a thin steady stream. The mayonnaise will thicken as the oil is incorporated.

Bring a Touch of the Orient To Your Vegetables

Here are some out-of-the-ordinary dressings for vegetables and fruit.

Exotic-tasting dressings can be as simple to make as the old favorites. There's no reason not to try something new!

Oriental Salad Dressing #1

¼ cup orange juice
1 tablespoon tamari or soy sauce
2 tablespoons rice wine vinegar
2 tablespoons lemon juice
½ teaspoon sesame oil
1 teaspoon ground mustard
2 garlic cloves, minced
⅛ teaspoon minced fresh ginger root

Whisk together all the ingredients and serve.

Preparation Time: 10 minutes
Yield: about ¾ cup

Oriental Salad Dressing #2

Serve on salads or as a marinade.

½ cup vegetable oil
½ teaspoon sesame oil
1 tablespoon tamari or soy sauce
2 tablespoons lemon juice
2 tablespoons white vinegar
1 teaspoon ground mustard
⅛ teaspoon minced fresh ginger root
2 garlic cloves, minced

Whisk together all the ingredients and serve.

Preparation Time: 10 minutes
Yield: ¾ cup

Yogurt Curry Dressing

Whisk together ¾ cup yogurt, 1½ teaspoons curry powder, 1½ tablespoons lemon juice, 1 tablespoon minced fresh parsley, ½ teaspoon honey or sugar, ¼ cup buttermilk, and salt and pepper to taste. Serve with green and sliced vegetable salads.
Yield: 1 cup.

Tahini Dressing

Whisk together 1 cup tahini, 2 tablespoons tamari, 6 tablespoons water, and 4 minced garlic cloves. Pour over salads. Yield: 1½ cups.

Honey Curry Dressing

Whisk together ⅔ cup oil, 3 tablespoons lemon juice, 2 tablespoons white vinegar, ¼ cup honey, 1 teaspoon curry powder, ½ teaspoon salt, and ½ teaspoon pepper. Pour over salads. Yield: 1½ cups.

Oriental Marinade and Dipping Sauce

Whisk together 3 tablespoons tamari, 1 teaspoon sesame oil, ½ teaspoon chili paste with garlic, 1 minced garlic clove, 2 tablespoons water, and 2 teaspoons honey. Pour the sauce over vegetables and marinate for at least 2 hours. This recipe makes ⅓ cup, enough marinade for 1 pound of vegetables.

Yogurt Cardamom Dressing

Combine ¾ cup yogurt, ¼ cup apple cider, 2 teaspoons lemon juice, 1 tablespoon honey, and ½ teaspoon ground cardamom. Pour over parboiled vegetables or fresh fruit. Yield: 1 cup.

More Dressings to Liven Up Summer Salads

Caesar Salad Dressing

1 large garlic clove, minced
1½ teaspoons minced shallot
1½ teaspoons anchovy paste
1 teaspoon Dijon-style mustard
½ teaspoon Worcestershire sauce
6 tablespoons lemon juice
1 egg
½ cup grated parmesan cheese
¾ cup olive or vegetable oil
salt and pepper

Combine the garlic, shallot, anchovy paste, mustard, Worcestershire, lemon juice, egg, and cheese in a blender or food processor. With the motor running, slowly pour in the oil. Season to taste with salt and pepper.

Preparation Time: 5 minutes
Yield: 1½ cups (6–8 servings)

Hot Bacon Salad Dressing

Don't dress your salad until just before you serve. The hot dressing makes the salad go limp fast.

4 bacon slices, diced
2 tablespoons red wine vinegar
1–2 tablespoons lemon juice
1 garlic clove, minced
1 tablespoon sugar
½ teaspoon ground mustard
2 tablespoons minced fresh parsley
3 tablespoons vegetable oil

Brown the bacon, remove from the pan, and pour off all but 2 tablespoons bacon fat. Combine the remaining ingredients in the pan with the bacon fat, and heat until warm. Return the bacon to the dressing and serve.

Preparation Time: 10 minutes
Yield: 1 cup

Chive Salad Dressing

½ cup sour cream
½ cup buttermilk
3 tablespoons minced fresh chives
1 garlic clove, minced
½ teaspoon Worcestershire sauce
2 teaspoons tarragon vinegar
salt and pepper
hot sauce

Whisk together the sour cream, buttermilk, chives, garlic, Worcestershire, and vinegar. Season to taste with salt, pepper, and hot sauce. Serve with any green salad or parboiled and chilled vegetables.

Preparation Time: 5 minutes
Yield: 1½ cups

Cold Creamy Horseradish Dressing

Mix together ¾ cup sour cream or yogurt, 4 tablespoons cream, and 4 teaspoons prepared horseradish. Season to taste with salt. Serve with chilled vegetables or on top of a green salad. Yield: 1 cup.

Butter and Vegetables Were Meant for Each Other

Lemon Butter is one of those basic toppings that goes with almost any steamed vegetable—carrots, broccoli, cauliflower, snap beans, summer and winter squash, and spinach and other greens. It's easy to make. You just combine melted butter, lemon juice, and grated lemon rind. Pour the Lemon Butter over your vegetables just before serving.

These simple toppings are a treat on vegetables. Don't forget the Herb Butter on page 160.

Lemon Butter

Melt ¼ cup butter and add 2 tablespoons lemon juice and ½ teaspoon grated lemon rind. Toss with 4–6 cups cooked vegetables and serve. Serves 4–6.

Curry Butter Sauce

Brown ¼ cup butter over medium heat. Blend in 2 tablespoons lemon juice, ½ teaspoon curry powder, and salt and pepper to taste. Toss with 4–6 cups cooked vegetables and serve. Serves 4–6.

Sweet Mustard Glaze

Root vegetables, such as beets, carrots, and parsnips, are greatly enhanced by this spicy sweet glaze.

3 tablespoons butter
1 tablespoon Dijon-style mustard
1 tablespoon honey or maple syrup

Melt the butter in a small saucepan. Stir in the mustard and honey or syrup to make a smooth sauce. Add 4–6 cups of cooked vegetables to the pan and toss to coat. Serve immediately.

Preparation Time: 5 minutes
Yield: glaze for 4–6 cups vegetables

Special Sauces Make Vegetables Special

Dijon Sauce

In a small saucepan, melt 2 tablespoons butter and stir in 2 tablespoons all-purpose unbleached flour. Add 1 cup milk a little at a time, stirring well after each addition to prevent lumps. Add more milk if the sauce is too thick; continue cooking if the sauce is too thin. Add ¼ cup dry white wine, 2 teaspoons Dijon-style mustard, 2 teaspoons grainy mustard, and salt and pepper to taste. Pour the hot sauce over hot vegetables. Yield: 1½ cups (6 servings).

Caraway Mustard Sauce

In a small saucepan, melt 2 tablespoons butter and stir in 2 tablespoons all-purpose unbleached flour. Add 1 cup milk a little at a time, stirring well after each addition to prevent lumps. Add more milk if the sauce is too thick; continue cooking if the sauce is too thin. Add 1 teaspoon caraway seeds, ¼ cup sour cream, 1 tablespoon Dijon-style mustard, and salt and pepper to taste. Yield: 1¼ cups (6 servings).

Cheese Sauce

4 tablespoons butter
4 tablespoons all-purpose unbleached flour
1½ cups milk
1½ cups grated cheddar or Swiss cheese
dash hot sauce
dash Worcestershire sauce
½ teaspoon Dijon-style mustard
salt and pepper

In a saucepan, melt the butter and stir in the flour. Add the milk a little at a time, stirring well after each addition to prevent lumps. Add the remaining ingredients, and heat to melt the cheese. Season to taste with salt and pepper. Serve with 6–8 cups cooked vegetables.

Preparation Time: 10 minutes
Cooking Time: 10 minutes
Yield: 3 cups

Marjoram Nut Sauce

In a blender, combine ½ cup toasted almonds, ¾ cup milk, and ½ teaspoon marjoram. Process until smooth. Heat until warm. Season to taste with salt and pepper. Pour over hot vegetables. Yield: 1 cup (6 servings).

Caper Sauce

In a small saucepan, melt 2 tablespoons butter, and stir in 2 tablespoons all-purpose unbleached flour. Add 1 cup milk a little at a time, stirring well after each addition to prevent lumps. If the sauce is too thick, add more milk; if the sauce is too thin, continue cooking for a few minutes more, stirring constantly. Add 1 tablespoon minced capers, 1 teaspoon Pernod, 1 tablespoon caper liquid, and salt and pepper to taste. Pour the hot sauce over hot vegetables. Yield: 1 cup (6 servings).

Hot Horseradish Cream Sauce

In a small saucepan, melt 2 tablespoons butter, and stir in 2 tablespoons all-purpose unbleached flour. Add 1 cup milk a little at a time, stirring well after each addition to prevent lumps. Add more milk if the sauce is too thick; continue cooking if the sauce is too thin. Add 4 teaspoons prepared horseradish, 1 teaspoon Dijon-style mustard, and salt and pepper to taste. Pour the hot sauce over the hot vegetables. Yield: 1¼ cups (6 servings).

Fennel Cheese Sauce

Especially delicious with the Swiss Chard Cheese Balls (page 108), this sauce can be served on any vegetable.

¼ cup butter
⅓ cup all-purpose unbleached flour
2 cups milk
½ cup grated parmesan cheese
2 teaspoons Dijon-style mustard
¼ teaspoon ground fennel
salt and pepper

In a small saucepan, melt the butter and stir in the flour to make a thick paste. Add the milk a little at a time, stirring well after each addition to prevent lumps. Stir in the cheese, mustard, and fennel. Season to taste with salt and pepper. Keep warm.

Preparation Time: 10 minutes
Yield: 2 cups (6 servings)

Blue Cheese And Scallion Sauce

In a small saucepan, melt 2 tablespoons butter, and briefly sauté 2–3 minced scallions, including some green tops. Stir in 2 tablespoons all-purpose unbleached flour. Add 1 cup milk a little at a time, stirring well after each addition to prevent lumps. Add more milk if the sauce is too thick; continue cooking if the sauce is too thin. Add ¾ cup crumbled blue cheese and salt and pepper to taste. Pour the hot sauce over hot vegetables. Yield: 1½ cups (6 servings).

Don't Limit Tomato Sauce To Pasta . . .

Tomato sauces can be used to top cooked vegetables or pasta, or they can be used in casseroles. The Italian Tomato Sauce that follows is a good basic sauce I use in many recipes in this book. I like to make the sauce in quantities and freeze the extra.

Italian Tomato Sauce

2 tablespoons olive oil
1 cup diced onion
2 garlic cloves, minced
1½ teaspoons fresh thyme or
⅓ teaspoon dried
1½ teaspoons fresh oregano or
⅓ teaspoon dried
1½ teaspoons minced fresh basil or
⅓ teaspoon dried
1 bay leaf
¼ cup minced fresh parsley
¼ cup grated parmesan cheese
½ cup dry red wine
1 teaspoon sugar or honey
4 cups thick tomato puree
salt and pepper

In a medium-size saucepan, heat the olive oil and sauté the onion and garlic for about 5 minutes. Add the remaining ingredients and cook for 30 minutes or more.

Preparation Time: 10 minutes
Cooking Time: 35 minutes
Yield: 4–5 cups

Tomato Fennel Sauce

1 tablespoon olive oil
½ cup diced fresh fennel bulb
½ cup diced onion
2 cups thick tomato puree
salt and pepper

Heat the olive oil in a sauté pan, and sauté the fennel and onion until the vegetables are limp, 3–5 minutes. Add the tomato puree and simmer for 10 minutes. Season to taste with salt and pepper. Serve hot.

Preparation Time: 10 minutes
Cooking Time: 15 minutes
Yield: 2½ cups

Tomato Paprika Sauce

1 tablespoon vegetable oil
1 garlic clove, minced
½ cup minced onion
1 teaspoon paprika
2 teaspoons lemon juice
1½ teaspoons fresh basil or
⅓ teaspoon dried
¾ cup finely diced peeled tomatoes
or thick tomato puree
2 tablespoons sour cream
2 teaspoons sugar
salt and pepper

Heat the oil in a saucepan, and sauté the garlic, onion, and paprika until the onion is limp, 3–5 minutes. Add the lemon juice, basil, and tomatoes. Cook for 5 minutes, stirring occasionally. Remove from the heat and stir in the sour cream and sugar. Season to taste with salt and pepper.

Preparation Time: 5 minutes
Cooking Time: 10 minutes
Yield: 1 cup

Yes, Hollandaise Can Be Tricky . . .

Hollandaise splits, or curdles, easily. If you make it in the blender, as I describe below, your chances of having the sauce split are greatly reduced.

3 egg yolks
2 tablespoons lemon juice
¼ teaspoon salt
pinch white pepper
½ cup melted butter

Just before you are ready to serve, combine the egg yolks, lemon juice, salt, and pepper in a blender. Blend until smooth.

With the blender running, pour in the hot butter in a thin, steady stream. Serve at once.

If you must reheat the sauce (not advised), do so in a double boiler, gently. If the sauce begins to split, beat in 1 tablespoon of boiling water and whisk as rapidly as possible.

Preparation Time: 10 minutes
Yield: 1 cup (4–6 servings)

Variations

Orange Hollandaise Sauce. Add 1 teaspoon grated orange rind to the egg yolk mixture. Substitute 1 tablespoon orange juice for 1 tablespoon lemon juice.

Mustard Hollandaise Sauce. Add 1 teaspoon ground mustard and 2 teaspoons Dijon-style mustard to the egg yolk mixture.

Just before you are ready to serve, pour in the hot butter in a thin steady stream while the blender is running.

 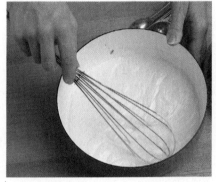

Hollandaise will split if reheated. To save a split sauce, beat in 1 tablespoon of boiling water as rapidly as possible.

Basic Batters and Doughs

1. Cut butter into flour.

Double Pastry Crust

2 cups all-purpose unbleached flour
1 teaspoon salt
⅔ cup butter, margarine,
**   shortening, or lard**
6–7 tablespoons cold water
1 egg, beaten

In a medium-size bowl, mix together the flour and salt. Cut the butter or shortening into the flour with a pastry blender, 2 knives, or your fingers (working quickly), until the mixture resembles peas and cornmeal. Sprinkle the water over the flour and blend lightly into the dough as it forms a ball. Cut the ball in half and wrap each piece in plastic film wrap. Refrigerate for at least 1 hour or until you are ready to use them.

On a lightly floured surface, roll out one dough ball, gently working from the center out in all directions until you have a 12-inch circle and the dough is ⅛ inch thick.

Fold the rolled dough in half and ease it carefully into a pie pan with the fold in the center. Unfold the dough and trim the crust to the edge of the pie pan.

Pour your filling into the crust and brush the edge of the crust with water.

Roll out the top crust in the same manner, but make a slightly larger circle. Trim the crust ½ inch beyond the edge of the pie plate. Fold the extra pastry under the bottom crust. Crimp the edges. Brush the crust with a beaten egg and pierce in several places to allow steam to escape.

Bake as directed according to the individual recipe.

Preparation Time: 15 minutes
Baking Time: according to specific
    recipe instructions
Yield: top and bottom pie crusts for
    a 9-inch or 10-inch pie

Single Crust Variation

Use only 1 cup all-purpose unbleached flour, ½ teaspoon salt, ⅓ cup butter or shortening, and 2–2½ tablespoons cold water. Fit the bottom crust into the pie pan as instructed above, and trim and crimp the edges. To bake unfilled, prick the dough with a fork, covering the surface of the pie shell with tiny holes that will allow steam to escape. Bake in a 450° F. oven for 10–15 minutes or until browned.

2. Roll out the dough.

3. Fold into pie pan.

4. Crimp edges.

Crêpes

1 cup all-purpose unbleached flour
4 eggs
¼ cup melted butter
½ teaspoon salt
1¾ cups milk
butter

Combine the flour, eggs, melted butter, salt, and milk in a food processor or blender and process until smooth. Add more milk if necessary; the batter should have the consistency of light cream. Chill for at least 30 minutes.

To cook the crêpes, heat a small, nonstick frying pan or omelet pan, and melt a teaspoon of butter in the pan. Spread the butter to cover the bottom and part of the sides of the pan. Pour a little less than ¼ cup of batter into the pan and quickly tip the pan, moving it in a circular fashion to evenly spread the batter over the bottom and sides. Cook over medium heat for about 2 minutes. Then flip the crêpe and continue cooking for 30 seconds. Remove the crêpe to a plate and fill.

Crêpes can be frozen, unfilled, and used later. Place waxed paper between layers of crêpes before freezing.

Preparation Time: 10 minutes
Chilling Time: 30 minutes
Cooking Time: 1 hour
Yield: 24–26 crêpes

Basic Pizza Dough

This recipe will make one large pizza the size of a cookie sheet (9 inches by 15 inches).

1 tablespoon dried baker's yeast
1⅓ cups warm water
2 tablespoons olive oil
1 teaspoon salt
4 cups all-purpose unbleached flour

Sprinkle the yeast over the warm water and set aside until the yeast foams, about 5 minutes. Add the olive oil and salt. Beat in the flour and form a ball.

On a lightly floured board, knead the dough for 5–10 minutes, until the dough is light and elastic. Cover and let rise in a warm, draft-free place for 30 minutes, while you prepare the filling.

When the filling is ready, roll out the dough to fit a 9-inch by 15-inch cookie sheet. You can try to pull and stretch the dough to fit into the pan. I find using a rolling pin faster and less likely to leave me with holes in the dough. With your fingertips, press up on the edges of the dough to form a ¾-inch rim all around.

Cover the dough with the sauce and filling of your choice and bake at 475° F. according to the individual recipe directions.

Preparation Time: 45 minutes
Baking Time: 30 minutes (or according to recipe directions)
Yield: 6–8 servings

Tempura Batter

2 cups all-purpose unbleached flour
3 egg yolks
1 cup flat beer
1 cup water
½ teaspoon salt

Combine all the ingredients and mix just enough to moisten the flour. Allow to sit for 20 minutes. Dip vegetables into batter and deep fry until golden brown.

Preparation Time: 5 minutes
Yield: 3 cups batter (6–8 servings)

The Joy of Gardening Cookbook Shopping List

Have you ever planned to prepare a certain dish, and then found that you didn't have all the ingredients on hand? It happens to all of us.

I've compiled a list of foods — common and uncommon — that I keep on hand for cooking. Of course, you must add to this list the vegetables that come from your garden. Then you truly will be ready to cook almost anything in this book.

Looking over my "shopping list," I see that the list makes a statement about my cooking style.

For one thing, I use flavoring ingredients from many different cuisines — particularly from the Far East, Middle East, and Mexico. I also use many ingredients that are most easily found in health food stores. Like many of today's cooks, I want my food to be varied, flavorful, *and* healthful.

Cooking With Fresh Ingredients Need Not Be Time-Consuming

The list is fairly short and contains little in the way of "prepared foods." Cooking exclusively with fresh ingredients is the tastiest (and most healthful) way to prepare foods, and it need not be time-consuming. Some staples, like chicken stock, can be cooked in advance and stored in the freezer. Many of my recipes take so little time to prepare, they can be made in the time it takes to heat a can of soup.

I know that many ingredients called for in this book can't be grown in the home garden and aren't mentioned in this shopping list, but many are. A cupboard and freezer stocked with the ingredients below will get you started on many pleasurable meals from your garden.

The local farmers' market supplies me what my garden doesn't. I combine a trip to the market with a trip to the supermarket and specialty food stores. It would be nice to grow all my own food — but I think the variety would be awfully limited.

Bacon

I love the taste of bacon, but I prefer to use it sparingly—as a flavoring. I keep a 1-pound package of bacon in my freezer. When I need some, I cut off the amount I need while the bacon is still frozen, and return the remainder to the freezer. This way, the bacon doesn't spoil, although I keep it for a long time.

Two slices of bacon equals ¼ cup, diced.

Cheeses

I keep a variety of cheeses in my refrigerator because I like to use cheese as a flavoring and as a protein source when I'm cooking meatless meals. The cheeses I commonly use are feta, cottage, Swiss, cheddar, Monterey jack, and parmesan.

I always use fresh parmesan cheese and grate my own. There is just no comparison in flavor to the packaged grated cheese.

Feta cheese is a soft, heavily salted goat cheese. Crumbled feta makes a delicious addition to a green salad. Feta cheese is becoming so popular it is now available in supermarkets, as well as in imported food stores.

Chili Paste With Garlic

Chili paste, made of chili peppers, vinegar, garlic, and spices, is a hot sauce, available where Oriental foods are sold. (Most large supermarkets have such a section these days.) Some chili paste comes without garlic, too. This sauce has a special hot flavor and is commonly called for in Szechuan-style dishes. I can't think of a substitute for it.

Cilantro

An herb common in Chinese and Mexican dishes, cilantro is sometimes called Chinese parsley. You can grow your own or buy fresh cilantro in Oriental food stores or where fresh herbs are sold. I prefer fresh cilantro, so I don't keep dried cilantro in my spice rack.

Filo (Phyllo) Dough

This paper-thin dough comes to us from Greece. It can be used to make all sorts of pastries, from turnovers to strudels.

In large cities, you can sometimes find fresh filo dough. I buy mine frozen at supermarkets. The dough comes in 1-pound packages, which usually contain 20–24 sheets of the dough.

Frozen dough should be defrosted in its wrapper. It will take 1½–2 hours to defrost at room temperature. Leftover dough may be refrozen, although refreezing does make the dough crumbly and hard to handle.

Once the dough is completely defrosted, unwrap and unroll the dough. Keep it covered with a damp towel when not in use. Rewrap in plastic as soon as possible.

Filo dough pastries freeze well. Do not defrost before baking. Place the frozen pastries in a preheated oven and bake for 45–60 minutes, until well-browned and heated all the way through. Serve immediately.

Fish

If you notice, some of my recipes do not actually specify a particular type of fish to use. That's because it is *always* best to buy whatever fresh fish is available, rather than buy frozen fish just to meet the requirements of a recipe. In fact, even when I do specify a type of fish — sole, for example — feel free to substitute any fresh white-fleshed fish.

Fish markets generally have fresher fish than supermarkets, and they often have limited quantities of a wide range of fish. That's how I discovered inexpensive shark, which is a tasty, firm-fleshed white fish. Be courageous and experiment.

Five Spice Powder

This sweet spice blend is made of star anise, fennel, cinnamon bark, cloves, and Szechuan peppercorns. It is available where Oriental foods are sold.

Herbs and Spices

I try to grow and dry most of the herbs I need, but I also buy many herbs and spices. Basil, parsley, and dill are so easy to grow that I always count on fresh supplies. Feel free to substitute dried herbs, even when the recipes call for fresh. In alphabetical order, here's what my spice rack contains:

Allspice
Anise
Basil
Bay leaves
Caraway seeds
Cardamom, ground
Cayenne
Celery seeds
Chili powder
Cinnamon, ground and sticks
Cloves, ground and whole
Coriander, ground
Cumin, seeds and ground
Curry powder
Dill, seeds and weed
Fennel, seeds and ground
Five spice powder
Ginger, ground
Mace
Marjoram
Mint
Mustard, ground and seeds
Nutmeg, ground
Oregano
Paprika
Rosemary
Pepper, black and white
Sage
Savory
Tarragon
Thyme
Turmeric

Flours

When I'm not using whole wheat flour, I inevitably use all-purpose unbleached flour, simply because this flour has more nutritional value than "white" flour, and gives the same results.

Whole wheat bread flour works best with yeast breads, but whole wheat pastry flour can be substituted.

Ginger Root

Fresh ginger root has a sharp, sweet ginger flavor that tastes fresher than ground ginger. It is available in most supermarkets now, in the produce section. It is also available at Oriental food stores.

Before mincing, peel the skin away from as much of the root as you will be using.

Ginger root will keep indefinitely in the refrigerator if stored in ginger ale or dry sherry to cover. You can keep ginger root for a few months in a perforated plastic bag. Or you can mince peeled ginger root and store in the freezer.

Hoisin Sauce

The Chinese equivalent of barbecue sauce, hoisin sauce is usually made from soybeans, vinegar, chili, garlic, sugar, and spices. It's available where Oriental foods are sold, and there's no substitute for it.

Horseradish

Horseradish makes me weep! So I prepare my horseradish in one large batch, rather than handle the powerful root frequently.

It is easy to make your own prepared horseradish. Wash and peel the root, then shred or chop into small pieces. In a blender or food processor, combine each cup of horseradish with 3–4 tablespoons water and 1–2 tablespoons vinegar. Process until it reaches the desired consistency. You can add a few slices of raw beet to the horseradish. The flavor difference won't be noticeable, but the color will change from white to pink.

Store the horseradish in sterilized jars in the refrigerator. It will keep for months, although it loses potency over time.

You can also buy prepared horseradish at the supermarket. It is usually kept in the dairy case.

Lemon Juice

Lemon juice brings out the flavor of fresh vegetables better than any other flavoring agent. Many people are finding that they can use lemon juice in place of salt in their diets.

I always use fresh lemon juice because it tastes better than bottled lemon juice. Figure that the juice from one medium-size lemon equals 4 tablespoons of bottled juice. To get the most juice from a lemon, drop the whole lemon in hot water, roll the lemon between your hands then slice and squeeze.

Lemon or Orange Rind

The outer rinds of these fruits are very flavorful, and not at all bitter, if you grate *only* the rind and avoid the white part of the peel. In some cookbooks, the rind is referred to as "zest," and the perfect tool for slicing off a thin sliver of rind is called a "zester." A zester is a handy tool to have. Otherwise, you can grate lemon or orange rind with a fine grater, but it's a difficult tool to clean. I use the grater on the end of my vegetable peeler.

Maple Syrup

You may have noticed that all of my recipes that call for maple syrup call for "pure" maple syrup. Pure maple syrup may be a luxury, but it's a Vermont tradition I grew up with. The commercial corn syrups that are flavored with maple just don't have the same flavor as the pure syrup. My feeling is if you can't get the real stuff, use brown sugar.

I always use Grade B or Grade C maple syrup. The grading system dates back to the time when New Englanders baked only with maple syrup. They preferred the Fancy and Grade A syrups because they sweetened without imparting a strong maple flavor. When I use maple syrup, I want the maple flavor.

Mustards

Prepared mustards are made from ground seeds that are mixed with a liquid. Wine and vinegar are commonly used. Then spices and herbs are added. Mustard flavors vary greatly, so I always specify what type of mustard works best in a recipe.

Dijon-style mustard is available wherever imported foods are sold and in some supermarkets. This mustard is made with white wine and spices.

Grainy mustard is made with whole or coarsely chopped mustard seeds. This type of mustard is available only where imported foods are sold. I use Pommery brand mustard when a grainy mustard is required.

Mustard sauce goes perfectly with egg rolls. It is made by mixing ground mustard with just enough water, vinegar, or white wine to make a smooth paste.

Oyster Sauce

Available where Oriental foods are sold, this is a dark soy sauce combined with an oyster extract. It is most commonly used with beef dishes. You can substitute tamari or a dark soy sauce for oyster sauce, but the flavor loss is noticeable.

Nuts

I use nuts for flavoring and protein-stretching in many of my recipes. Nuts can add a heartiness to meatless dishes. The nuts I most commonly use are cashews, pecans, walnuts, pine nuts (for pesto), and sunflower seeds.

I buy my nuts by the pound at my local food coop and store them in the freezer. Buying in bulk gives me an inexpensive source of raw, roasted, and unsalted nuts.

Roasting makes nuts crispier and enhances the flavor. To roast any nut, spread the nuts in a single layer and place in a 300° F. oven. Roast, turning or shaking frequently, until the nuts are slightly browned, 10–15 minutes.

To shell chestnuts, use a sharp knife to mark an X on the flat side of the nut. Spread the chestnuts in a single layer on a baking sheet. Then place in a 350° F. oven for 10–15 minutes. Cool enough to handle and remove both the inner and outer skins.

Oils

I am fairly fussy when it comes to oils, so I often specify the type of oil to use in a recipe. Here are some of my preferences.

Olive oil has a distinctive rich flavor, which is particularly nice in salad dressings and sautéed vegetables. Sometimes I sauté vegetables in half olive oil, half butter. This is mainly for flavor. Also, the olive oil reduces the tendency of the butter to burn.

Sesame oil is made from sesame seeds and has a rich, smoky flavor that is used to season a dish. It is too strongly flavored and heavy to use on its own as a frying oil, but in combination with peanut oil, it adds a lot of flavor to a stir fry.

When I specify "vegetable oil," any oil—soy, corn, peanut, safflower, olive—will do.

I often use peanut oil when stir frying vegetables. The oil is light and delicate and imparts a very subtle peanut flavor.

You can substitute any vegetable oil if you don't have a specific oil on hand—but the flavor will vary somewhat.

Pasta

America is in the midst of a pasta renaissance. Where once spaghetti was a favorite (especially for kids), today pasta refers to spaghetti plus a host of noodles in various shapes and sizes. Best of all, fresh pasta is easy to make with a food processor (see page 245), or it can be easily purchased in specialty food stores.

When a recipe refers to "pasta" or "pasta noodles," use whatever shape or size pasta is available to you.

To cook pasta, boil plenty of salted water: 4 quarts of water, 1 teaspoon salt, and 1 tablespoon olive oil (to prevent sticking) to 1 pound of pasta. Drop the pasta into the rapidly boiling water and cook until tender. The cooking times vary, depending on whether the pasta is fresh or dried, and the size of the noodles. Properly cooked pasta

is tender yet firm—what the Italians call *al dente*.

Drain the pasta in a colander; do not rinse. Add the sauce and serve.

Pesto

This is an Italian staple fast becoming popular in America. You make it yourself with fresh basil, olive oil, parmesan cheese, and pine nuts. See page 161 for instructions on how to prepare and store this flavoring ingredient.

Rice

I keep cooked brown rice in my freezer in 2-cup and 4-cup batches as a staple. Whenever a recipe calls for rice, I go to my freezer and use the rice undefrosted.

Why brown rice? It has a lot more flavor and more vitamins than white rice. You can substitute white rice for brown rice, but why settle for less flavor and less nutrition?

There's no trick to cooking rice. To make 3 cups of brown rice, bring 2½ cups water to a boil. Add ½ teaspoon salt. Slowly stir in 1 cup brown rice. Cover and cook over low heat for 40–50 minutes, until all the water is absorbed. Add more boiling water if necessary, and cook until the additional water is absorbed. Fluff with a fork and serve.

Soup Stock

Many of my soups are made with stock; I usually use chicken stock. Although you can buy quality, ready-to-use canned chicken broth to use in soups, I prefer to make my own.

During the summer, when I often make barbecued chicken, I stock up on soup stock. Before grilling the chicken, I parboil the chicken pieces in water to cover for 20 minutes. (This assures that the chicken will be cooked evenly, cuts down on barbecuing time, and gives me the basis of soup stock.)

After I remove the chicken from the cooking water, I add onions, celery, carrots, and a few bay leaves to the cooking liquid and cook to reduce the stock to a strongly flavored broth. Then I strain the stock, skim off the fat, and freeze in 2-cup and 3-cup batches for later use.

Salt

Most of my recipes that are seasoned with salt do not specify amounts. Excessive amounts of salt are not healthful, and many people are on low-salt diets. I have found that by using fresh herbs and lemon juice to enhance the flavor of vegetables, I am naturally using less salt in my cooking.

Tahini

Used frequently in Middle Eastern dishes, tahini is a spread made from ground sesame seeds, just as peanut butter is a spread made from ground peanuts.

The flavors of these two nut butters are fairly similar, and so are the nutritional values. You can find tahini at natural food stores and where imported foods are sold.

Tamari

A rich, concentrated soy sauce, tamari adds a hearty, almost nut-like taste to the dishes it flavors. It is very salty and is often used in place of salt. Tamari is sold at health food stores. If you can't find tamari, substitute any high-quality soy sauce.

Tofu

The Chinese gave us tofu, and it has been widely adopted as an inexpensive, versatile protein source. Basically, tofu is a "cheese" made from soy milk, which is extracted from soy beans.

You can buy tofu by the pound, or by the individual cake at health food stores and wherever Oriental foods are sold. Recently, tofu has become available in supermarkets, but I'd hate to have anyone make their first acquaintance with tofu from the supermarket variety. Fresh tofu is far superior in flavor to the supermarket tofu.

Try fresh tofu first. If you find you like tofu, then feel free to use supermarket tofu in highly seasoned dishes, where you won't notice the flavor difference.

Store tofu in the refrigerator in water to cover. Change the water daily. Depending on how fresh the tofu is when you buy it, the tofu will keep for 5–10 days.

Tofu that has gone bad will smell sour, become moldy, or turn brown. A slight pinkish color means the tofu is about to go bad, but can still be eaten.

Vinegar

When I refer to just "vinegar" in a recipe, I mean distilled or white vinegar, made from grains. "Wine vinegar" means red wine vinegar unless otherwise specified. I also use rice vinegar, which is made from rice wine and is available in supermarkets and where Oriental foods are sold.

Herb vinegars can be substituted whenever a recipe calls for wine vinegar. Instructions for making herb vinegars can be found on page 157.

Acknowledgments

Grateful acknowledgment is made to the following manufacturers for the use of their products:

Alper International: Old Fashioned Enamelware, Mahogany Utensils, Red Oak Serving Systems, Northern Hardwood bowls.

Anacapa Corp: Provence and Helarious® flatware, Picnique® tablecloths and napkins.

Arabia of Finland: Valencia tableware, Fuuga vases, Alli bird, Fasaani bird, red enamel bowls, brown enamel cookware.

Asta Designs: Dutch Floral bakeware.

Bennington Potters: Bennington Cook's Ware and Classic Dinnerware.

Corning Designs: Table Attire™ tabletop accessories, Culinaria™ bakeware.

Dansk International Designs, Ltd.: Christianshavn Blue, Maribo, and Bisserup Blue dinnerware; Elsinore flatware.

Hammarplast: tableware.

Hartstone: New Country Gear® dinnerware, All American Apple Pie stoneware server.

Himark Enterprises: Country Cuisine tableware and cannisters, marble salt & pepper shaker.

Progressive International Corporation: marble utensils.

Riekes®: champagne and wine glasses, vase.

Rowe Pottery Works®: Traditional American Salt Glaze stoneware crocks, bowls, honey jar.

Sanyei American Corporation: Country Field Stoneware, Artifex™ cookware.

Ted Scatchard: pottery.

Schiller & Asmus: Le Creuset Iron Cookware.

Wheaton Fine Glassware: Le Jardin Crystal Jars, Salad Set, Nouveau salt and pepper shaker, Champion steins, Monticello stemware, Cuisine tumblers.

Special thanks to Grace Bottamini of The Owl in the Attic Antiques, Vergennes, Vermont, for so generously loaning many beautiful things.

Thanks also to the following individuals for the loan of antiques:

Marjorie Graves, The White House Antiques, Burlington, Vermont.

Judy Pascal, The Chestnut Tree Antiques, Charlotte, Vermont.

Ty Anderson, Donna Stoddert, Nesting Box Antiques, North Ferrisburg, Vermont.

Bridget Meyers, Winooski, Vermont.

Pam Swatkins, Vergennes, Vermont.

Sandy Herman, Nostalgia Antiques, Shelburne, Vermont.

A very special thank you goes to my friend David Sokol for his support and encouragement throughout this project and all my other projects.

Index